Constitutions Compared
An Introduction to Comparative Constitutional Law

A.W. Heringa
Ph. Kiiver

Constitutions Compared
An Introduction to Comparative Constitutional Law

Third Edition

Ius Commune Europaeum

A.W. Heringa
Ph. Kiiver

Constitutions Compared
An Introduction to Comparative Constitutional Law

Third Edition

Intersentia Ltd
Trinity House | Cambridge Business Park | Cowley Road
Cambridge | CB4 0WZ | United Kingdom
Tel.: +44 1223 393 753 | Email: mail@intersentia.co.uk

ISBN 978-1-78068-078-1
NUR 823

© 2012 Intersentia
Cambridge – Antwerp – Portland
www.intersentia.com | www.intersentia.co.uk

Cover photograph © Zagorskid - dreamstime. com

British Library Cataloguing in Publication Data. A catalogue record for this book is available from the British Library.

No part of this book may be reproduced in any form, by print, photo copy, microfilm or any other means, without written permission from the authors.

PREFACE TO THE THIRD EDITION

The first two editions of *Constitutions Compared* have proven to be valuable teaching tools. Students of comparative constitutional law continue to appreciate the book's clarity and user-friendly structure: comparative overviews of certain aspects of constitutional law (like federalism, election systems or the role of judges) are followed by more detailed country chapters on that specific aspect. Country chapters cover the US, Germany, the UK, France and the Netherlands, which in their diversity help illustrate broader concepts of constitutional law.

In this third edition, we have expanded several paragraphs and chapters to provide for even more detail on national legal systems and constitutional comparison. In addition, we have updated the discussion wherever necessary. Thus, the third edition most notably takes account of the new election system in Germany adopted in 2011; the start of the operation of the constitutional review procedure in France; the coalition government, the 2011 electoral reform referendum and the adoption of the Fixed-Term Parliaments Act 2011 in the UK; the minority government and the reform of the Charter for the Kingdom in the Netherlands; the entry into force of Protocol 14 to the European Convention on Human Rights; and the entry into force of the European Union's Treaty of Lisbon. To the benefit of both students and teachers, we have included a catalogue of possible exam questions at the end of this book, to facilitate and encourage self-testing and to provide suggestions for possible exam question formats.

It has been pointed out that this book might cover more systems, including non-Western systems. However, we decided to keep the current selection of five constitutional systems in the third edition as well. These systems represent generic models of constitutional solutions across the world, and understanding these five systems in turn makes most other systems much easier to understand. The presidential systems of Brazil and the Philippines will be more accessible to readers who have already familiarized themselves with the US system; those who know the federal systems of Germany and the US, including their differences, will quickly gain a grasp of Australia, Nigeria or India; knowledge of the British and Dutch monarchies opens insight into the monarchies of Norway, Spain and Thailand; the French semi-presidential system offers a point of reference for the study of the systems in Romania and Russia; bicameral parliaments, election systems and constitutional courts around the world can be put into context based on the different models and blueprints that we discuss in this book.

Like we said in the preface to the first two editions, we believe that comparative law is an essential element in the curriculum of any law student. May this book continue to help promote the mainstreaming of comparative constitutional law in the main body of legal education.

Maastricht, March 2012

Prof. Aalt Willem Heringa   Dr. Philipp Kiiver

Note: Constitutional offices or functions, such as King, Prime-Minister, or candidate, shall be referred to in the masculine form. All offices and functions can of course be exercised by both men and women, unless indicated otherwise.

TABLE OF CONTENTS

PREFACE TO THE THIRD EDITION v

CHAPTER 1: INTRODUCTION TO COMPARATIVE CONSTITUTIONAL LAW 1

1. Introduction 1
2. The Meaning of a Constitution 2
3. The Flexibility of Constitutions 5
4. Terminology 9
4.1. State 9
4.2. Country 10
4.3. Nation 10
4.4. Government 10
4.5. Republic 11
5. Further Reading 13

CHAPTER 2: CONSTITUTIONS COMPARED: ORIGINS AND MAIN FEATURES 15

1. Overview 15
1.1. The Notion of Sovereignty 15
1.1.1. Popular versus Royal Sovereignty 16
1.1.2. Popular versus National Sovereignty 17
1.1.3. Popular versus State Sovereignty 17
1.1.4. Parliamentary Sovereignty 18
1.1.5. The Absence of Sovereignty 19
1.1.6. Sovereignty and European Integration 19
1.2. Parliamentary and Presidential Systems 20
1.3. Separation of Powers and Checks and Balances 22
1.4. The Role of Judges 24
1.5. State Structure: Unitarism and Federalism 25
1.6. Summary 26
1.7. Further Reading 26

2.	The United States	27
2.1.	Civil War and Reconstruction	27
2.2.	The US Constitution	28
3.	Germany	30
3.1.	National Unification	30
3.2.	Division and Reunification	32
3.3.	The Basic Law	33
4.	The United Kingdom	35
4.1.	Monarchy and Parliament	35
4.2.	The UK Constitution	37
4.3.	The UK and Europe	39
5.	France	40
5.1.	A Sequence of Constitutions	40
5.2.	The Constitution of the Fifth Republic	41
6.	The Netherlands	43
6.1.	Dutch Independence and the French Period	44
6.2.	The Kingdom of the United Netherlands	45
6.3.	The Dutch Constitution	45
6.4.	The Charter for the Kingdom	47

CHAPTER 3: FEDERALISM, UNITARISM AND DECENTRALIZATION ... 49

1.	Overview	49
1.1.	Degrees of Federalism and Devolution	51
1.2.	Types of Federalism and Devolution	52
1.3.	Federalism and the European Union	53
1.4.	Summary	54
1.5.	Further Reading	55
2.	The United States	55
2.1.	US Federalism: The Senate	56
2.2.	Federalism and the House of Representatives	56
2.3.	Vertical Separation of Powers	57
2.4.	Federalism at Presidential Elections	59
2.5.	Federalism and the Executive and Judicial System	59
3.	Germany	60
3.1.	German Federalism: The *Bundesrat*	61
3.2.	Federalism and the *Bundestag*	62
3.3.	The Competences of the Federal Lawmaker	62
3.4.	Federalism and the Election of the Federal President	63
3.5.	Federalism and the Executive and Judicial System	63
4.	The United Kingdom	64
5.	France	66

6.	The Netherlands	68
6.1.	Decentralization in the Netherlands	68
6.2.	The Overarching Kingdom	69

Chapter 4: Parliaments and Lawmaking 71

1.	Overview	71
1.1.	Principles of Elections	74
1.2.	Election Systems	76
1.3.	Bicameralism	78
1.4.	The Legislative Process	79
1.5.	Referendums	81
1.6.	The Government and the Head of State	83
1.7.	Summary	84
1.8.	Further Reading	84
2.	The United States	85
2.1.	The House of Representatives	85
2.2.	The Senate	86
2.3.	Federal Lawmaking	87
2.4.	The President	88
3.	Germany	89
3.1.	The Bundestag	89
3.2.	Election System	89
3.2.1.	Seat Distribution	90
3.2.2.	The Threshold	91
3.2.3.	Unconstitutionality	92
3.3.	The Bundesrat	93
3.4.	Federal Lawmaking	94
3.4.1.	The Legislative Process	95
3.4.2.	The Bundesrat	96
3.4.3.	The President	98
4.	The United Kingdom	98
4.1.	The Commons	99
4.2.	The Lords	100
4.3.	The Legislative Process	101
4.3.1.	Royal Assent	102
4.3.2.	The Lords	103
5.	France	104
5.1.	The National Assembly	104
5.2.	The Senate	105
5.3.	The Legislative Process	107
5.3.1.	The Senate	108
5.3.2.	Organic Statutes	109
5.3.3.	The President	109
5.3.4	The Constitutional Council	110

6.	The Netherlands	112
6.1.	The Second Chamber	112
6.2.	The First Chamber	114
6.3.	The Legislative Process	115
6.3.1.	Statutes for the Netherlands in Europe	115
6.3.2.	The King	116
6.3.3.	Statutes for the Overall Kingdom	116

CHAPTER 5: GOVERNMENTS, THEIR PARLIAMENTS AND THEIR HEADS OF STATE 119

1.	Overview	119
1.1.	Heads of State and Government	119
1.2.	The Rank of the Prime-Minister	122
1.3.	Parliamentary Investiture	123
1.4.	Ministerial Accountability	124
1.5.	National Parliaments and the European Union	128
1.6.	The Immunity of the Head of State	130
1.7.	Dissolution of Parliament	131
1.8.	Summary	133
1.9.	Further Reading	133
2.	The United States	134
2.1.	The President and Vice-President	134
2.2.	The President and Congress	136
3.	Germany	138
3.1.	The Federal President	138
3.2.	The Chancellor and his Government	139
3.3.	Ministerial Accountability	141
3.4.	Confidence Question	142
4.	The United Kingdom	143
4.1.	The King	143
4.2.	The Prime-Minister and his Cabinet	144
4.3.	Ministerial Accountability	146
5.	France	147
5.1.	The President	148
5.2.	The Prime-Minister and his Government	149
5.3.	Ministerial Accountability	150
6.	The Netherlands	151
6.1.	The King	151
6.2.	The Prime-Minister and his Cabinet	153
6.3.	Ministerial Accountability	153
6.4.	Motions of No-Confidence	155
6.5.	The Government of the Kingdom	156

Chapter 6: Judicial Review and Human Rights 159

1. Overview 159
1.1. Constitutional Review of Legislation 160
1.2. The Procedural Setting of Constitutional Review 161
1.3. Review of Treaty Law Compliance 163
1.4. European Union Law 165
1.5. Summary 167
1.6. Further Reading 168

2. The United States 168
2.1. The Court System 168
2.2. Constitutional Review 169
2.3. International Treaties 171

3. Germany 172
3.1. The Court System 172
3.2. Constitutional Review 172
3.3. International Treaties and the ECHR 174
3.4. European Union Law 175

4. The United Kingdom 176
4.1. The Court System 176
4.2. Constitutional Review 177
4.3. International Treaties and the ECHR 177
4.4. European Union Law 179

5. France 180
5.1. The Court System 180
5.2. Constitutional Review 180
5.3. International Treaties and the ECHR 181
5.4. European Union Law 181

6. The Netherlands 182
6.1. The Court System 182
6.2. Constitutional Review 183
6.3. International Treaties and the ECHR 183
6.4. European Union Law 184

7. European Human Rights 185

8. The ECHR, the European Union and the National Constitutions 187

Annex 1: Useful Links 189

Annex 2: Exercises and Model Exam Questions 191

Annex 3: Glossary 197

Annex 4: Overview of Constitutions Compared 202

Annex 5: The Constitution of the United States 205

Annex 6:	The French Constitution 219
Annex 7:	The French Declaration of the Rights of Man 241
Annex 8:	The German Basic Law 243
Annex 9:	The Charter for the Kingdom of the Netherlands 287
Annex 10:	The Dutch Constitution 299
Annex 11:	Selected Statutory Provisions from the United Kingdom 315
Annex 12:	The ECHR 331
Annex 13:	The Treaty on European Union 345

Chapter 1

INTRODUCTION TO COMPARATIVE CONSTITUTIONAL LAW

1. Introduction

Why comparative constitutional law? First, like any comparative study of law, the international comparison of constitutional systems helps us better appreciate and understand our own system and to broaden our world view. If we were only exposed to our own legal system, we would run the risk of taking features of that system for granted. We might see our own system's design as the only 'natural' state of affairs. Comparison allows us to critically assess a system, and to better see not only what a constitution says but, crucially, what it does *not* say on a particular subject. Thus, comparative constitutional law serves an educational aim in an academic curriculum.

Second, comparative law can provide helpful material for constitution-building and constitutional engineering. When a country considers a constitutional reform, when it must interpret the wording of its own constitution, or when a newly independent country needs a completely new constitutional setup, international comparison helps courts and constitution-drafters to learn from other systems' achievements. It also helps them to avoid repeating their mistakes.

Third, comparative constitutional law often proves crucial in the particular context of the creation and development of international organizations. The institutional design of the European Union, even though it is not a state, has much in common with domestic institutional setups. The Court of Justice of the EU, and the European Court of Human Rights, routinely rely on comparative constitutional law to develop their case-law. The Court of Justice of the EU refers to constitutional traditions common to the member states when establishing general principles of European law; the European Court of Human Rights seeks to identify common ground between the contracting states in interpreting the meaning of certain provisions of the European Convention on Human Rights. When a transnational entity must develop law 'from scratch', a comparative survey of the law of its member states is a sensible start.

This is not to say that engaging in comparative constitutional law is entirely uncontroversial. One argument against it is that international comparison in the area of constitutional law is futile, since countries differ too much in history, culture, self-perception, population structure, etc. Thus, the constitutional law of different systems is riddled with idiosyncrasies and is not readily comparable. For similar reasons, constitutional transplants or constitutional borrowing from one system to another can be unworkable at best, and dangerous at worst. As regards international organizations, in particular the European Union, comparison between states may yield unreasonable expectations when results are applied to an entity that is manifestly *not* a state.

Yet another argument is directed against the use of comparative methodology to constitutional interpretation by judges. The debate is most heated in the United States, where the Supreme Court at one point took international consensus into account when interpreting the meaning of the US Constitution. In *Roper* v. *Simmons* (543 U.S. 551), decided in 2005, the Supreme Court partly relied on international practice to establish that the death penalty for juvenile offenders is 'cruel and unusual punishment' in the sense of the 8th Amendment to the US Constitution. Opponents of this approach argued, among other things, that the American people should not be subjected to foreign law on which they have had no influence.

When and if we are using comparative constitutional law, we must therefore always be aware of *why* we are using it. Depending on the context, we must be aware of the limitations and sensitivity of the exercise. Comparative studies do not have to be uncritical; cross-border exchange of ideas does not have to mean to simply copy-and-paste provisions from one constitution to another. The controversy of using international comparison in domestic constitutional interpretation depends on the system at hand; in the US it is much related to the controversy surrounding the role of judges in general. In most European countries, such controversy simply does not exist.

This book is meant to serve the first purpose of comparative constitutional law: to allow us to better understand the constitutional system of our own country and that of other countries, to assess their advantages and disadvantages, and perhaps even to discover our own preferences.

2. The Meaning of a Constitution

What is a constitution? The term 'constitution' can have a narrow or formal meaning and a broad or substantive meaning. In its *narrow* or *formal* meaning, a constitution is a central written document that sets out the basic rules that apply to the government of socio-political entities, in particular states. Such a central constitutional document can be called appropriately 'constitution', but also, for example, 'basic law' or 'charter'. Thus, the American Constitution is a document, adopted in 1787 and taking effect in 1789, which, in short, establishes the United States of America, defines the powers of its President and Congress, outlines the federal court system, regulates the competences between the central authorities and the individual States, and guarantees the fundamental human rights of its people.

In its *broad* or *substantive* meaning, meanwhile, a constitution comprises the entire body of fundamental rules that govern that socio-political entity: be they contained in a central document or in many documents, be they written down or be they customary rules. Substantively, therefore, a constitution is a body of law that:

- attributes power to public authorities;
- regulates the fundamental relations between public authorities; and
- regulates the fundamental relations between the public authorities and the individual.

One might say that this is a technical and minimalist approach to the function of a constitution, and that in many countries constitutions also have a deeper societal significance. Thus, a constitution, notably a written constitution, can mark a break with the past, settle past conflicts in writing, codify a social contract between the citizens and their rulers so that they may rule to the benefit of the people, or strengthen national identity and people's feeling of belonging. But even in societies where a constitution neither marks a historical rupture nor means much for a nation's identity, it will nevertheless remain a body of law that, at the very least, does what all constitutions do: it attributes power and regulates its exercise.

Constitutional law in the broad sense is typically divided into two branches: institutional law and human rights. Institutional law governs the way how the state and its institutions function, for example the term and the powers of a parliament, the prerogatives of a government, as well as the system how voters elect their representatives. Human rights in the classical sense (like the prohibition of torture or the freedom of speech) protect the citizen against the state, and thus also regulate relations between public authority and the individual. The present volume is mainly devoted to the institutional aspect of constitutional law, including institutional and procedural rules regarding human rights enforcement in courts.

Even a state that formally does not have a central written constitutional document – a basic law or charter – can nevertheless substantively have a constitution. The best-known example here is the United Kingdom. There is no legal document that would have as its title 'The Constitution of the UK'. There is therefore no constitution in the narrow sense. However, like any state, the UK does have a constitution in the broad sense, namely a body of constitutional law. Some of these rules are laid down in judge-made case-law; some are laid down in statutes, laws made by Parliament; and some take the form of customs, conventions, or gentlemen's agreements. For example, nowhere is it written that the King appoints as his Prime-Minister the leader of the political party that has, alone or in coalition with other parties, a majority in the House of Commons – that is a convention, or customary rule. At times it is noted that the UK has an 'unwritten constitution', but that is not entirely correct, because some parts of it are indeed written. For example, the devolution of certain legislative competences to Scotland, which affects the distribution of power within the UK, and therefore its constitutional law, is laid down in a written statute adopted by the UK Parliament. Israel does not have a consolidated constitutional document either; Sweden has a collection of fundamental statutes of constitutional rank but no central charter.

Conversely, even states which do have a 'written' constitution in the formal sense can and do have unwritten rules that form part of their broader constitution. For example, judges in the United States have the right to declare legislation unconstitutional; the US Constitution itself does however not explicitly give judges this right. This right was established by case-law, that is by court decisions, and arguably these court decisions on the interpretation of the written Constitution also form part of the US 'constitution' in a broad sense. Some pieces of legislation might also be considered broadly constitutional rules even if they are not laid down in the central document. This typically includes the law on the election system, the statute of a constitutional court, the rules of procedure of parliament, etc. International law, and international treaties in particular, may also have a domestic constitutional effect. Furthermore, customary rules can form part of the constitution in a broader sense as well. The rules pertaining to the relations between the parliament and ministers in the Netherlands are, for instance, almost entirely customary. They are part of the Dutch constitution even though they are not spelt out in the document itself, or the constitution in the formal sense. For greater clarity, we shall use capitalization when referring to specific constitutional documents, such as the French Constitution, but use lower case when using constitution in a generic sense and in the broad sense of a body of constitutional rules.

> *Terminology*
>
> Some languages actually distinguish between the constitution in a narrow sense and the constitution in a broad sense. In German, *Verfassung* can be a generic term for a written constitution but it can also mean the broader constitutional system. The German written constitutional document in force is called *Grundgesetz*, or basic law. The Dutch language distinguishes between the *constitutie*, a body of constitutional rules, and *grondwet*, a basic law in which such rules may be written down. The Swedish *författning* in a broad sense comprises a collection of fundamental written statutes, or *grundlagar*.

A constitution in the narrow sense – a constitutional document – cannot in fact capture and exhaustively codify the entire body of the constitution in the broad sense. Case-law, customs, secondary legislation, learned writing, as well as concepts such as 'natural law' which transcend positive law, would also form part of the broader constitution. Another useful distinction can therefore be drawn between the *written* constitution and the *working* constitution. The former covers the black-letter law; the latter covers the entirety of rules and perceptions regarding this subject in society. Actors that take part in the working constitution include not only political institutions and courts, but also media, churches, trade unions, etc. One frequent criticism against comparative constitutional law is in fact that it only compares written constitutions and is unable to capture the entirety of working constitutions. An incumbent president may, for example, have the exact same legal powers as his predecessor, but still be less powerful, because he lacks political support, has a less persuasive authority, or operates under complicated social conditions. Like we said earlier on, this is exactly why legal studies in this area need to make clear what they are meant to analyze. If they limit themselves to legal analysis proper, such as a review of case-law on a constitutional rule, there is nothing objectionable about it. If they want to make broader claims about the effect that constitutional law has on society, legal scholars are indeed well-advised to take political practice and the findings of social sciences into account. At the same time, political practice can have an impact on the operation and even the scope of constitutional law itself. Sanctions against office-holders, for example, may well be real – loss of popularity, an embarrassing defeat in a parliamentary vote – but are not necessarily stipulated in constitutional texts; conversely, office-holders may, through their very actions, give rise to the emergence of customs or conventions, which may enter the body of constitutional rules.

Yet there are extreme cases where the working constitution deviates so much from the written constitution that it renders the written document almost meaningless. Communist regimes, dictatorships and other forms of authoritarian systems may well preserve a written constitution that regulates the state's institutional design and proclaims the state's attachment to the rule of law and human rights. What is seen in reality, then, are phony institutions, sham elections and human rights abuses. The Soviet Constitutions since 1922 for instance guaranteed the right for every constituent republic to freely leave the Soviet Union. In reality, these were just words on paper and had a purely propagandist value.

The idea of limited government, where the exercise of public power is governed and constrained by a constitution and the rule of law, is called 'constitutionalism'. Constitutionalism presupposes that political actors will obey legal norms in how and to what extent they govern. Historically, from the late 18th century onwards, the idea of absolutism, where the monarch was sovereign and not bound by law, ceded ground to the idea of constitutionalism in most of Europe. Thus, now even a monarch was bound by the constitution. Modern constitutional monarchies are the result of exactly that shift in thinking from absolutism towards constitutionalism.

> *What If?*
>
> In the course of a comparative constitutional survey, the question is sometimes raised what would happen if a certain office-holder were to ignore a certain constitutional rule. What is the punishment? In areas like private law or criminal law, law enforcement through the police and the courts is a relatively straightforward matter. The enforcement of constitutional law is not that simple, since it governs exactly those who themselves govern. The answer to what might happen in case of a violation of constitutional law therefore depends on the robustness of constitutionalism and the rule of law in a system. If the law is accepted as governing the state, including its rulers, then the rulers will obey the law. Complying with conventions may ideally become a matter of decency and common sense. Making different branches of government interdependent and allowing them to keep each other in check also helps ensure that power is not abused. Opposition parties as well as civil society, including the media and non-governmental organizations, also play a role in insisting that rulers comply with the law.

3. The Flexibility of Constitutions

A state that has adopted a single charter as its constitution in the narrow sense, codifying most of its broader constitution in that document, typically gives that document a special status. Among other things, that special status is reflected in the fact that in order to change that document, a special procedure has to be followed. Special procedures then differ from the normal legislative process by which statutes, or acts of parliament, are adopted. Sometimes certain important elements in the constitution cannot even be changed at all. Constitutions that are harder to change than ordinary legislation are called 'rigid constitutions' or 'entrenched constitutions'. There, it is made more difficult to change the rules of the game, as it were, than to play the game itself.

Typical amendment procedures for rigid or entrenched constitutions include the requirement for super-majorities in parliament (e.g. Germany, Portugal); two parliamentary readings of the amendment and new elections in between readings (e.g. the Netherlands, Sweden); ratification of the amendment in the state's component territorial sub-units (e.g. United States, India in certain cases) or a referendum (e.g. Australia, France usually).

Some constitutions are more rigid than others. The German Basic Law is harder to amend than ordinary statutes are, because both legislative chambers have to adopt an amendment with a higher-than-usual majority. Nevertheless, the text was amended that way about fifty times during its first fifty years of operation. The US Constitution, by contrast, has in its first two hundred years of existence seen only twenty-seven amendments, the first ten of which were included as a block right at the beginning. Yet then again, a constitutional amendment in the US requires, once the proposal is adopted, the approval of three-quarters of all the individual States. For fifty States that means thirty-eight approvals, something that is not necessary for amendments in Germany, and that may explain the endurance of the original text in the US.

At the same time, the German Basic Law excludes some of its fundamental features from future amendment: human-rights principles and its federal character, for example, may not be changed. The French Constitution does not allow any change to the republican character of its government. The US Constitution has no such 'forever clause', and is formally less rigid in that respect, although the deprivation of a State's equal representation in the Senate requires that State's consent. Rigidity may thus refer to both the *procedure* and the *scope* of a possible amendment: the former makes change relatively difficult to accomplish, the latter limits the subjects that can be changed in the first place. The most rigid constitutional arrangements are those that can only be amended by unanimity, i.e. with the consent of each and every constituent party. The founding treaties of the European Union, which is often compared to a constitutional system in its own right, can in principle be changed only if all member states have ratified an amendment treaty, which gives every single country a veto against all others. To introduce a measure of flexibility, the Treaty of Lisbon, which entered into force in 2009, provides for simplified amendment procedures (Art. 48 TEU), but even they are still governed by the principle of unanimity.

The opposite of hard-to-amend rigid constitutions are 'flexible constitutions'. The constitution of the United Kingdom, since it is not contained in a central document, does not prescribe any special amendment procedures. Therefore, it can be changed in the course of an ordinary legislative process, or as a result of the emergence of new customs or case-law in practice. For example, the statute that gave certain powers to Scotland is just an ordinary statute, adopted by simple parliamentary majority like any other statute. The rule that the UK Parliament will not interfere with Scottish powers unless the Scottish parliament has invited it to do so, is a relatively new custom. Thus, one piece of legislation and one unwritten understanding have already significantly changed the way the UK constitution functions. This flexibility should not be confused with arbitrariness, though. Customs may in fact be harder to change than texts are; and just because the UK Parliament *might* change the constitution easily does not mean it will do so, or do so light-heartedly.

It should be noted that a constitution's flexibility, in terms of scope and procedure, merely points to *formal* amendment requirements. Yet even if a constitution is rigid formally, which means that it provides for special procedures for the amendment of its text, this still says little about the rigidity of that constitution's substantive content. A constitution's *substantive* rigidity depends on whether the text is accepted as meaning what it says in a narrow sense, or whether it is perceived as a 'living document' that evolves together with the society it serves. Changing customs and conventions in political practice can give a different meaning to written constitutional provisions, occasionally undermining them or developing them further. The upper chamber of the Dutch parliament, for example, is formally not granted the right to propose amendments to legislative drafts, only the right to accept or reject them. It does, however, at times make known that it will only accept a bill if it is amended in a certain way. That, for all practical purposes, comes down to a 'hidden' and extra-constitutional right of amendment. It is an example of the substantive flexibility of the Dutch constitution, whereas the text of the Constitution itself has remained formally unchanged.

The powers of interpretation by judges, most notably constitutional courts, also play a crucial role in determining the substantive flexibility of a constitutional text. The German Federal Constitutional Court, for example, is prepared to interpret the Basic Law rather actively, in the light of new societal developments and on the basis of open-ended principles including human dignity and rule of law. The European Court of Human Rights also applies a 'dynamic' interpretation of the European Convention on Human Rights. Though the Convention is an international treaty, rather than a constitution, it is often considered to be a quasi-constitutional charter in the area of fundamental rights, not least because it has its own Court to uphold it. Thus, the term 'family life' as found in the Convention no longer exclusively means the life of married couples but, since societal norms have evolved across Europe, also includes the life of unmarried couples.

The United States, meanwhile, is struggling between a 'liberal' interpretative approach and a more 'conservative' or literalist approach. Supporters of the former approach would, for instance, bring the right to abortion of a pregnancy under constitutional protection, citing privacy principles, the spirit and the systemic logic of the Constitution. Literalists, by contrast, would seek to restrict constitutional interpretation only to the original intention of the 18th century drafters of the Constitution, who of course did not mention anything concerning abortion rights.

A distinction closely related to the substantive flexibility of a constitution concerns the nature of its development. Usually, the adoption of a new constitution marks a new beginning for a society. The constitution is then a *revolutionary* constitution, even if has not been preceded by any actual violent upheaval, because it marks a transformational event. What therefore distinguishes a revolutionary constitution is the fact that it has been adopted in what is often called a 'constitutional moment': a special event in time when an old order is replaced by a new one.

France cherishes the notion – one might say the tradition – of having revolutionary constitutions: counting from 1789, the year the absolute monarchy fell, the country is already into its fifth republic. Each new constitution replaces an old order with a new one. The constitutions of the US, Germany and the Netherlands, like most other constitutions in the world, also were to mark a new beginning – independence, regained statehood, republicanism following monarchy or vice versa, democracy following dictatorship – and are revolutionary in that sense.

The opposite of a revolutionary constitution is an evolutionary constitution, one that develops gradually over time. The classical example of an evolutionary model is the constitution of the United Kingdom. Over time, the UK has seen, among other things, the emergence of the office of the Prime-Minister as the leader of the cabinet; the consolidation of cabinet bureaucracy; a shift of power from the House of Lords to the House of Commons; devolution of power to Scotland and the other countries of the UK; and more generally the gradual limitation of royal prerogative by statute, for example through the Fixed-Term Parliaments Act 2011 which denied the traditional right for the crown to call early elections at discretion. Yet there has been no spontaneous constitutional rupture since the 'Glorious Revolution' of 1688 when Parliament asserted its supremacy over the crown. Instead, new features were embedded in the existing framework. The development of the Dutch constitution, since its entry into force in 1815 or at least since the large democratic reform of 1848, has also been distinctly evolutionary. Dutch statehood has been remarkably continuous for two centuries: neither the secession of Belgium from the Netherlands in 1830 nor the German occupation during World War II fundamentally changed the constitutional character of the Dutch state. The major constitutional transformation of the Kingdom in 1954 – from a European motherland with overseas colonies towards a quasi-federation between the Kingdom's European and overseas lands – barely affected the way the (European) Netherlands was governed. And also the development of the law of the European Union may be said to have an evolutionary nature. European law has long surpassed the realm of classical international treaty law, it is a quasi-constitutional system of its own kind. And it is evolutionary as new treaties and case-law keep developing this body of law. A genuine 'constitutional moment' has not been witnessed: the establishment of the European Coal and Steel Community, the Union's earliest predecessor organization, in 1951, was a starting point for incremental steps towards ever-closer European integration rather than a genuinely transformative event. A spontaneous unification of Europe in a giant nation-state, which would certainly mark a constitutional moment, is not likely either.

4. Terminology

Before we start our more detailed exploration of different constitutional systems, we need to make sure that we all speak the same language. That is, like for any comparative study, we need to agree on a set of terminology, a definition of technical terms and expressions, so that it is always clear what we mean when we refer to something from our field. This agreement comprises two overlapping elements. First, we must note that words in English can have different meanings depending on how or where we use them. Take the word 'convention', which can mean 'international treaty', or 'assembly of delegates', or 'customary rule', depending on the context. Second, we must be aware that words that can pass for translated equivalents in different languages, or that look similar or even identical, can mean different things across system borders. For example, 'secretary of state' in Dutch means a junior government minister; in the UK, however, it is a senior minister; and in the US it is the minister of foreign affairs. Let us address some key notions of constitutional law that can have multiple meanings in English, or that can easily become a translator's false friends. We already discussed the different meanings of the word 'constitution'. In the following paragraphs, we shall consider the terms 'state', 'country', 'nation', 'government' and 'republic', terms that point to fundamental concepts of constitutional law.

4.1. State

'State' can mean a number of things. One possibility is to use 'state' in the sense of 'public authority', as in 'wages are determined by the free market or by the state' or 'the state sometimes interferes with private life'. In that sense, 'state' is often used synonymously with 'the government' as opposed to the private realm. For practical purposes, two other usages will be particularly relevant for comparative constitutional law:

- State as in sovereign country. In that sense, a state is a socio-political entity with its own set of government institutions exercising control over its population and territory. This should correspond with the definition of a state under public international law. Thus, Germany, the UK, France, the Netherlands and the US, along with, e.g., Canada, Norway, Brazil, Kenya and Japan, are all states.

- State as in federal entity. In some countries that have a federal structure, the territory is made up of several sub-entities that are called States. Thus, the US comprises fifty States; India, Australia and Brazil also have States, and the federal components of Germany, called *Länder* in German, are usually translated as States as well. This means that Germany is a federal state, because it is a country that has a federal structure; and Bavaria is a federal State, because it is a State that together with fifteen other States forms part of the German federation. We shall use capitalization to describe States in the sense of entities that form part of a federation. In all other cases we shall use the lower case.

4.2. Country

In informal speech, 'country' is usually used synonymously with 'state', as in 'France is a sovereign country'. In the United Kingdom, the term country acquires a formal meaning, however. That is because the UK comprises England, Scotland, Wales and Northern Ireland, which are called 'countries of the UK'. The Kingdom of the Netherlands consists of the countries of the Netherlands proper as well as Aruba, Curacao and Saint Martin in the Caribbean. When referring to sovereign countries we shall use the formal term 'state', and only occasionally refer to 'country' in order to avoid ambiguities. We shall use 'country' in UK and Dutch context as appropriate.

4.3. Nation

Another term that is sometimes used interchangeably with 'state' is 'nation'. Strictly speaking, a nation refers to an ethnic-cultural category. The 'nation' can be a founding concept in a constitutional system, such as the source of all sovereign power. Equating 'state' with 'nation', however, is a habit deriving historically from nationalist thinking, holding that every nation deserves to have its own state. Hence the word 'inter-national' relations, even if they are in fact inter-state relations. Since virtually all states in the world are multi-ethnic, we shall avoid the term 'nation', and only occasionally use terms such as 'national capital' or 'nation-wide' in order to prevent ambiguities.

4.4. Government

The term 'government' is also a term that gives rise to ambiguities and translation problems in comparative constitutional discourse. The three most important meanings for our purposes are the following.

- Government as in state order. In that sense, government, or system of government, broadly refers to the entirety of the organs of public authority, including lawmakers, ministers, and judges. Thus, legislature, executive and judiciary are referred to as the three 'branches of government'. It is in particular an American habit to use 'government' broadly, for example to contrast the 'US government' against the fifty 'State governments'.

- Government as in executive. In that sense, the government comprises the head of government and a body of ministers, or 'secretaries', representing executive power as opposed to the parliament and the courts. 'Government' is then usually (but not always) synonymous with 'cabinet', which would roughly correspond to the presidential 'administration' in the United States.

- Government as in governing majority. In parliamentary democracies, the political party or parties that have a majority in parliament can form the government. This means that they are entitled to compose the cabinet, but they can also be referred to as actually *being* the government, as opposed to the minority or parliamentary opposition.

We shall use the term 'government' in the sense that is most appropriate for the context, but mostly in the sense of 'cabinet' or 'executive'.

4.5. Republic

The term 'republic' is usually meant to denote a particular system of government; the name of the state which has adopted such system; and the period of time when the state is or was governed by such system. Firstly, a state that has adopted a republican form of government is one whose head of state is not a monarch. Thus, for all practical purposes, republic is the opposite of monarchy. This is also the sense in which the constitutions of the US, France and Germany refer to 'republicanism': they safeguard this principle so as to bar the (re-)introduction of a monarchy.

Secondly, 'republic' can refer to the name of a state which has a republican order, such as French Republic, the Federal Republic of Germany, the Portuguese Republic or the Republic of Cyprus. Not all republics bear the republican character of their constitution in their official name, though. The United States, for example, does not. Conversely, Germany after 1919, even though it had become a republic, retained the imperial-sounding term *Reich* as its name and as the corresponding prefix for its institutions such as *Reichstag* (parliament) and *Reichspräsident* (head of state).

The term 'republic' derives from the Latin *res publica*, meaning common affairs or the common good. In the history of Rome itself, the Republic stands for the period when public power was normally shared between different institutions in a complex system including, among others, the senate, plebeian assemblies and two elected consuls as supreme executive officers. The Republic succeeded the Kingdom in 510 BC and it ended with the dictatorship of Julius Caesar and the rise of the Roman Empire under Augustus. Thus, thirdly, 'republic' can also refer to a period in a state's history when a republican order prevailed, especially after the deposition of a monarch or before the establishment of a monarchy in the same system. Some countries have had a number of different systems over time so that they keep count, as in First Republic, Second Republic, and so on. Such numbering applies, for example, to France, but also to Poland and Austria.

Sometimes a term in the local language is applied instead of the Latin term republic, but it is taken to mean the same thing. In the revolutionary period of 1918/1919, when the monarchs of the German principalities were forced to abdicate, several German States proclaimed a *Freistaat* or 'free state', which at the time was a German term for republic. Today's German States of Bavaria, Thuringia and Saxony label themselves as 'free states', not meaning that they are independent but that they are republics. The Estonian *Vabariik* also means free state in the sense of republic. 17th century England saw the establishment of a brief republican order under Oliver Cromwell which was named *Commonwealth*. 'Common wealth', or common good, is a more or less literal translation of the Latin *res publica*. The same holds true for the Polish term *Rzeczpospolita*, applied to the historic Polish-Lithuanian Commonwealth and the present-day republic.

Even where a state is a monarchy, it need not be governed by absolute one-man rule. Most European monarchies, such as the Netherlands, Luxembourg or Norway, are constitutional monarchies, whereby the power of the monarch, such as a king or grand-duke, actually derives from, and is limited by, a constitution. The same holds true for Thailand, Malaysia and Japan. In 2008, after the Luxembourgish grand-duke had refused to sign a bill regarding euthanasia into law, for example, the constitution was changed so that royal assent is in fact no longer required and the grand-duke is obliged to sign all bills passed by parliament. Monarchies can therefore in reality just as well live by 'republican' values in a broader sense: democratic representation, rule by many with the consent of the governed, separation of powers, limited government and rule of law. Absolute monarchies or near-absolute autocracies are rare in the contemporary world: the Vatican in Europe, Swaziland in Southern Africa, Brunei in East Asia, Saudi Arabia and a number of emirates along the Persian Gulf are the last of their kind; Bhutan abolished absolutism and adopted a constitutional monarchy in 2008.

Durable Democracy

One of the greatest advantages of a democracy governed by the rule of law, as opposed to dictatorships, is its systemic stability and long-term durability. That is because it allows for a peaceful and bloodless transition of power from one office-holder to another, one elite to another, under fixed rules that bind all governments. It also allows the population to air criticism of an incumbent by 'voting the rascals out', which in turn allows those ousted from power to correct their own mistakes and seek re-election at a later stage. Dictatorial regimes, by contrast, will have to crack down on dissent to preserve their power lest they lose it forever. Also, since usually there are no legally binding rules of succession, dictatorships often do not outlive their founding leader. A democracy's weakness lies in the short term: since it is a pluralist method of government, rather than an actual ideology, it is vulnerable to authoritarian movements which use democratic rights of participation in order to overturn democracy itself. Several democracies therefore include defensive mechanisms, such as the possibility to outlaw unconstitutional political parties.

Nor do monarchies need to be hereditary, they can also be elective. In that case, a new monarch, rather than ascending the throne by a fixed line of succession, gets chosen by a body of electors. The Holy Roman Empire, a patchwork of territories in Central Europe which lasted through the Middle Ages until 1806, was an elective monarchy where each new Emperor was chosen by prince-electors. The King of Malaysia gets elected from among the Malaysian sultans for a rotating five-year term. The Vatican State is an elective monarchy as well, where the Pope gets elected by a college of cardinals. Conversely, even republics can, if they are run like dictatorships, come to resemble a monarchical autocracy in the sense of absolute one-man rule and without any notion of limited government. A republic can even become de facto hereditary. A transition of power from father to son or to another relative has been observed in authoritarian republics, such as North Korea in 1994 and again in 2011, Syria in 2000 or Cuba in 2008. Already some early European republics quickly turned hereditary: in the brief republican Commonwealth period in 17th century England, Lord Protector Oliver Cromwell was succeeded in office by his son Richard; the key offices in the Republic of the United Netherlands became monopolized by the Province of Holland and turned hereditary in the 18th century. The last Emperors of the Holy Roman Empire, though notionally elected, all came from the House of Habsburg.

5. Further Reading

M. Claes, 'Constitutional Law', in J. Smits (ed.), *Elgar Encyclopedia of Comparative Law* (Cheltenham: Elgar 2006).
S.E. Finer, V. Bogdandor & B. Rudden, *Comparing Constitutions* (Oxford: OUP 1995).
T. Ginsburg & R. Dixon (eds.), *Comparative Constitutional Law*, (Cheltenham: Edward Elgar Publishing 2011).
R. Hague & M. Harrop, *Comparative Government and Politics*, 8th ed. (New York: Palgrave Macmillan 2010).
V. Jackson & M. Tushnet (eds.), *Comparative Constitutional Law*, 2nd ed. (New York: Foundation Press 2003).
V. Jackson & M. Tushnet (eds.), *Defining the Field of Comparative Constitutional Law* (Westport: Praeger 2002).
J. McHugh, *Comparative Constitutional Traditions* (New York: Peter Lang 2002).

Chapter 2

CONSTITUTIONS COMPARED: ORIGINS AND MAIN FEATURES

1. Overview

The current Constitutions of the United States, the Netherlands, France and Germany can be viewed as expressions of an effort to replace an old order with a new one. In the case of the US, the Constitution was to bring about a closer unification in the late 18th century of thirteen newly independent colonies. In the case of Germany, the Basic Law was adopted as a partial reestablishment in 1949 of republican democratic statehood. France's present-day Constitution was meant as a far-reaching institutional overhaul in the late 1950s of battered state structures. The Dutch Constitution of 1814/1815 meant the restoration of a monarchy and, at the same time, the creation of a unitary and independent state after two decades of French domination; in the 1950s, the Charter for the Kingdom was adopted so as to establish a quasi-federal rather than colonial relation between the Netherlands proper and its overseas territories. The constitution of the United Kingdom, meanwhile, is evolutionary in character. New features are added and powers shift within an extraordinarily stable institutional framework. The last truly revolutionary moment took place when, in 1688, Parliament deposed one King and installed another, establishing the lasting principle that Parliament is not subordinate to the crown. When Parliament and the King together make a statute, whereby the monarch gives assent to Acts of Parliament, the resulting law is the highest norm in the UK. This principle of legislative supremacy remains the cornerstone of the UK's modern constitution, even though, as shall be seen later, it sits uncomfortably with the country's membership of the European Union.

1.1. The Notion of Sovereignty

Who actually makes a constitution? The 'maker' of a constitution is not necessarily its physical author, but rather the entity from whose authority the constitution is derived. This authority resides with the *sovereign*: the original source of all public power from which all other power flows. Most constitutions derive their claim to authority from having been enacted by the people, a concept called popular sovereignty.

Sovereignty as such is the ultimate power to exercise authority over oneself. For states this contains an internal and an external dimension. External sovereignty means the possibility for a state to exercise control over its population and territory without interference from outside. This concept had its breakthrough in the 1648 Peace of Westphalia that ended the Thirty Years' War in Europe, and it is still a fundamental concept in public international law. It is the *internal* sovereign, meanwhile, who is the original source of public authority within the state itself. Usually, one can identify who is the sovereign on the basis of the preamble to the constitution, if it has one. If the preamble, the declaratory introduction to the constitution, starts with 'The people...' or 'We the People...', or variations of that phrase, then it is clear that the constitution claims to be derived from popular will. The model are the famous first words of the US Constitution: 'We the people of the United States, in order to form a more perfect union (...) do ordain and establish this Constitution for the United States of America'.

It should again be noted that sovereignty in this sense is a rather abstract notion. Even in those systems which claim that the people are the sovereign, it was not the people who actually wrote the constitutional document. Often the people did not even approve the document in a referendum. The German Basic Law for example came into force after having been ratified by the parliaments of the States, and yet it firmly points to the will of the people as its source in the preamble, provides that only the German people can again abolish it, and reiterates that all public power emanates from the people. The French Constitution, by contrast, actually *has* been adopted by referendum in 1958, in fact by an overwhelming majority.

1.1.1. Popular versus Royal Sovereignty

The notion of popular sovereignty, as endorsed by republican democracies, stands in marked contrast with the claim to sovereignty as expressed by monarchs. In absolutist systems, the original source of all public authority is, after all, the King. Often the monarch's sovereignty is coupled with a religious claim: he is then sovereign 'by the grace of God', or he exercises 'divine rights'. In such cases the monarch remains the sovereign even if he chooses to grant his people a constitution. Especially in the course of the 19th century, when the ideals of the French Revolution had spread across Europe, many monarchs decided to appease their people by enacting constitutions. A constitution was meant to limit and direct the use of power by public authority; yet these constitutions still derived their authority from the monarch himself, who could at any point change or repeal them. The documents thus became known as the *constitutions octroyées*, or 'imposed constitutions'. Historical examples include the charter offered (in vain) to the French Third Estate by King Louis XVI in 1789; the Prussian constitution unilaterally enacted by King Frederick William IV after having rejected the constitution offered to him by the revolutionary National Assembly in 1849; or the constitution enacted by Tsar Nicholas II of Russia in 1906. Revolutions that established republics would do away with royal sovereignty. As regards surviving monarchies, even as the personal powers of kings and grand-dukes have in reality faded and become purely ceremonial in many countries in modern times, these monarchs are still often referred to as 'the sovereign'.

1.1.2. Popular versus National Sovereignty

There is a further subtlety to the notion of sovereignty as residing with the people. A distinction can be made between *popular* sovereignty, or sovereignty of the people, and *national* sovereignty, or sovereignty of the nation. National sovereignty was prominently proclaimed by the French Declaration of the Rights of Man in 1789. For practical purposes, national and popular sovereignty are often used synonymously. The difference, however, is that the people are a concrete and real entity, namely the existing population at any point in time, while the nation is a somewhat more abstract philosophical notion that does not coincide with the current population. In a system of popular sovereignty, the sovereign population is able to exercise its will though, for example, a referendum to change the constitution. If the nation is the sovereign, then such possibility could be excluded, since the nation is an abstraction and is not able to act on its own. National sovereignty can only be exercised by the nation's representatives, in the manner laid down in the constitution. The representatives of the nation could be the people, but it does not necessarily have to be the people.

To name a practical example, in Belgium sovereignty lies not with the people but with the nation. The nation is defined as comprising all Belgians who have ever lived, who live, and who will live in the future. Thus, the current population is not the nation. Who exactly *represents* the nation is laid down in the Constitution, and according to the Constitution the nation is represented by parliament – the nation, not just the voters. One of the consequences of this doctrinal principle is that it is justified to exclude binding referendums. After all, the Belgian population is neither the sovereign itself (the nation is) nor does it represent the nation (parliament does).

France considered a choice between popular and national sovereignty when drafting the post-War constitutions of 1946 and 1958. The compromise was to claim that 'national sovereignty belongs to the people, who exercise it through their representatives and by means of referendum.' The effect is that the principle of the sovereignty of the nation is preserved, but that the living population is capable of exercising such sovereign powers. This would justify how President Charles de Gaulle and his successors called for referendums amending the Constitution without following the regular amendment procedure that would have involved parliament. Since the people exercise sovereign powers one way or another, the procedural basis was less relevant.

1.1.3. Popular versus State Sovereignty

A potential conflict as regards popular sovereignty claims in a federal system lies in the claim of the individual States to continued sovereignty (in the meaning of independence). In the US, for example, the States gave life to the new Union in the first place, and without them the Union would not exist. In that sense, the term sovereignty sometimes reappears as a nominal remnant of the original autonomy and independence of the individual States. Thus, powers that are not delegated to the federal level are said to be 'sovereign' powers of the individual States. In modern reality, Union-friendly case-law, and the practical consolidation of stable federal institutions supported by all-American national identity, as well as the Union's victory over the secessionist Confederates in the Civil War, have cemented the US order whereby the sovereign people have set up a permanent federal system of government for the entire country, defining its powers in the Constitution. The German Basic Law of 1949, incidentally, is clearer on the sovereignty point from the start. While ratified by the parliaments of the individual States, whose existence preceded the modern federation by two years, and while enshrining federal principles, the Basic Law is explicitly based on the sovereignty of the German people.

1.1.4. Parliamentary Sovereignty

The United Kingdom is famous for allocating sovereignty with Parliament. Parliament should be understood here as the King-in-Parliament, a construction whereby bills are adopted by Parliament and then receive royal assent from the monarch. Sovereignty of Parliament therefore, perhaps more accurately, means legislative supremacy. Acts of Parliament (statutes made by Parliament with royal assent) are the highest law of the land. Thus, there is no public authority, legislative or executive or judicial, national or regional or local, secular or ecclesiastical, that may invalidate Acts of Parliament. Only the King-in-Parliament himself may undo his previous legislation. The scholar Albert Dicey coined the term 'sovereignty of Parliament' in 1885 to describe a founding principle of the UK constitutional system. 'Parliament' is shorthand for the Commons, Lords and the King acting together, because Parliament is considered the politically dominant institution. Since the late 17th century the monarch may not legislate without parliamentary approval; statute overrides royal prerogative and conventionally the monarch never refuses royal assent to bills. The King is notionally still called 'the sovereign', but he is effectively bound by the will of Parliament. What is important here is that in any event UK constitutional law does not allocate sovereignty with the people. Of course, the electorate can determine the composition of the House of Commons and otherwise express its democratic will, but that is not the decisive point. As a matter of doctrine, sovereignty in the sense of supremacy is held by Parliament and the King acting together.

> *Parliamentary Sovereignty in the Age of Europeanization*
>
> The accession of the UK to the European Communities in 1973 required a number of compromises, rationalizations and doctrinal justifications regarding the status of European law in the UK. After all, it is difficult to maintain parliamentary sovereignty in the sense of legislative supremacy whereas European law can override domestic law and judges may set aside Acts of Parliament for violations of European law. Parliament is still considered sovereign because Parliament agreed to be bound by European law itself. The reasoning is awkward and sits uncomfortably with other constitutional notions, such as the rule that later statutes prevail over earlier statutes.

> Yet it serves as a pragmatic means to keep the fundamental principle of UK constitutional law intact in spite of EU membership.

1.1.5. The Absence of Sovereignty

The complications of determining what sovereignty means, and where it resides, can in some cases actually be avoided altogether. The constitutional law of the Netherlands does not occupy itself with the question of sovereignty. In order not to be drawn into sectarian conflicts between republicans (for whom sovereignty lies with the people), royalists (for whom sovereignty lies with the monarch), and clericals (for whom sovereignty lies with God), in their Constitution the Dutch have opted to simply leave the question open. Thus, the Dutch Constitution contains no preamble, where references to sovereignty would usually be found. The issue could have been clarified during the general constitutional overhaul of 1983, when the entire text was modernized, but it deliberately was not. The rules governing the relation between the monarch, the parliament and the government are still almost entirely defined by custom, not by the constitutional text. In effect, the Netherlands pragmatically functions as a democratic constitutional monarchy with a parliamentary system which is governed by the rule of law. Who is the Dutch sovereign is a question that is unresolved, but it is not perceived as one that needs urgent resolving.

1.1.6. Sovereignty and European Integration

To those states that have joined the European Union, the constitution is no longer limited to strictly national terms. In order to see the full picture, one cannot ignore the constitutional impact of a state's EU membership. European Union law is part of the member states' national law and deserves to be treated as such (see also Chapter 6).

Several approaches are possible with respect to the European Union. A very far-reaching approach would be to argue that the EU is, or has become, a state, and the member states form part of a larger federation. In that case, federal (i.e., European) law would override State (i.e., national) law as a matter of course. While intriguing, this approach goes too far: the EU comprises states, but it is not a state itself. Alternatively, one might argue that the EU is simply an international organization, based as it is on a set of international treaties, most notably the Treaty on European Union and the Treaty on the Functioning of the European Union. While such an approach would fit most easily with national constitutions, it would not be quite adequate as regards the effective pursuit of the organization's ambitious objectives. After all, as the European Court of Justice argued already in the early 1960s, if the European Union (then: Community) left it entirely up to the member states to decide how to embed European law in the national legal order, the uniform Union-wide application of European law could be frustrated. It would then depend on the member states whether or not to allow individuals to rely on European law in national courts, and whether or not to give European law precedence over national law. Yet the Union, especially its internal market but also other areas of integration, cannot function in the envisaged manner if it were governed by such a 'normal' treaty-law regime. We must assume, so the European Court of Justice held, that the member states wanted their Union to work, and thus a normal treaty approach would not suffice: a new legal order, one of its own kind, has been created instead. What is special about it is that EU law, according to the Court, is capable of generating direct effect in the member states, and supremacy over all conflicting national provisions, irrespective of how member states otherwise treat international treaty commitments. Combined with the possibility for the Council, the representation of the member state governments at European level, to act by (qualified) majority, overriding individual member states, the European Union possesses characteristics that stand out in the world.

Problems inevitably arise within the member states. How can a country still be sovereign if European law overrides it at every turn? How can the national constitution still be the supreme law if the European Court of Justice insists that European law overrides all national law, including constitutions? Is the national lawmaker not already a European lawmaker, transposing European law and acting domestically subject to European restraints? Is the national judge not already a European judge, applying European law on a day-to-day basis under the interpretative guidance of the Court of Justice? On a different note, how can democracy be ensured when the national government is hard to control while acting in Brussels, and if that government can even be outvoted in the Council, whereas the legal effects of European decisions are nevertheless so far-reaching?

What remains uncontested is that the European Union only possesses those powers that the member states have conferred upon it (Art. 5 (2) TEU), namely in a treaty that they have all voluntarily and unanimously ratified. Since in the European framework such treaties have domestic constitutional implications, unlike usual trade agreements, it might be appropriate to include a specific 'Europe clause' in the national constitution. Germany and France have such a clause; the Netherlands does not; the UK statute of accession to the (then) European Economic Community is an ordinary piece of legislation on the face of it, but has extraordinary constitutional consequences. Yet even if a Europe clause is in place, it does not mean that the last word about supremacy is already spoken. From a national perspective, even a Europe-friendly constitution can still be a supreme constitution. The art is then to reconcile European claims to supremacy with national claims to sovereignty. Irrespective of the outcome, a study of European systems that does not take full account of their EU membership would be incomplete.

1.2. *Parliamentary and Presidential Systems*

When comparing government-parliament relations in different systems, a very fundamental distinction can be drawn between *parliamentary* systems and *presidential* systems. In order to fall into either category, it is not enough that a state has a parliament or a president. Thus, Germany has a Federal President, but it is in fact a parliamentary system; the US does have a parliament, but is nevertheless presidential. The defining feature is whether the head of the executive is elected with a mandate of his own, or whether he owes the continuation of his office to parliament and is therefore accountable to parliament in the sense of a confidence rule (see also Chapter 5).

In the US, both parliament, i.e. Congress, and the head of the executive, i.e. the President, each have their own mandate. The President owes his authority to being elected, and he is therefore not accountable to Congress in the sense of a confidence rule. Whether Congress has confidence in him or not, the President stays in power. The same applies to other presidential systems such as Mexico, Brazil or the Philippines.

In parliamentary systems, by contrast, the head of the executive is not directly elected, but stays in office because he enjoys the confidence or tolerance of the parliament. This applies to the Prime-Minister of the Netherlands, the Prime-Minister of the UK, and the Chancellor of Germany: all three can be voted out of office via a parliamentary vote of no-confidence, albeit with different procedures. It should be noted that a vote of no-confidence, or motion of censure, is not the same thing as impeachment in the US. Impeachment is a criminal trial for very heavy criminal offences, whereby the Senate acts as a court of law. In order to oust a prime-minister or chancellor in a parliamentary system, the parliament does not need to prove that he has committed a crime, let alone a serious crime. In fact, parliament does not need to give any reasons for the censure at all. The principle of a parliamentary confidence rule applies to all other parliamentary systems in the world, for example Canada, Spain or Israel.

While the terminological labelling may imply that presidential systems have a particularly strong president, while parliamentary systems have a particularly strong parliament, in reality the opposite tends to be the case. True, while European prime-ministers can theoretically be ousted more easily compared to the US President, they in fact wield far greater political power, at least domestically. That is because they are typically the heads of a loyal parliamentary majority, often also chairmen of the main political party. Through their majority in parliament, prime-ministers can have desired legislation adopted, so that their parliamentary power-base for executive action is at the same time their lever for implementing legislative strategies. The US President, meanwhile, may be formally safer in his office compared to a European prime-minister, but his clout to push through legislation or secure a budget of his liking is limited. Elected independently from Congress, he does not need a loyal majority in Congress in order to stay in office, but the majority in Congress need not be loyal to the President either. It is Congress that adopts statutes and decides on the budget. Parliaments in presidential systems in fact tend to be more independent, and more assertive with regard to the executive, than parliaments where the executive is formed by the majority within.

A hybrid between parliamentarism and presidentialism is the so-called semi-presidential system. France represents such a blend. The defining feature is that France has both a directly elected President who exercises many executive functions, and who is accountable only to the people, and a Prime-Minister, who also holds executive power, and who is accountable to parliament (although he is appointed by the President). France therefore features a two-headed executive, with a President and a Prime-Minister side by side. Without the directly elected

President, or at least without the executive powers that he wields, France would be fully parliamentary like Germany; without the Prime-Minister, and with executive power concentrated with the President, it would be presidential like the US. With both offices in place, it is half-half. Which half dominates in practice much depends on the personality of the office-holders involved. Presidents may choose to adopt a restrained and representative figurehead role above politics – what is often referred to as a *presidential* attitude – and focus on foreign policy only; or they may exercise a hands-on *executive* presidency, steering policy on the domestic scene as well. The balance also depends on whether the President can count on a friendly parliamentary majority or not. If yes, he can become the most dominant figure in the French political landscape; if not, he might have to accept sharing much of his power with an assertive, parliament-backed Prime-Minister. Finland was considered a semi-presidential system until 2000, when presidential powers were shifted to the prime-minister and the cabinet. The Russian Constitution of 1993 created a semi-presidential setup as well.

There are also other hybrids between presidentialism and parliamentarism, apart from the French-style system. In South Africa, the President is both head of state and head of government, similar to his US counterpart, but unlike the US President he is elected, and can be dismissed, by the lower chamber of parliament like a prime-minister in a parliamentary system. In the 1990s, Israel experimented with yet another hybrid model, in that it allowed the prime-minister to be directly elected in an otherwise parliamentary system. The reform was to strengthen the role of the prime-minister, but the experiment was considered a failure and was reverted. The problem was that voters 'split their ticket', voting for a prime-minister of their choice but not for the corresponding political party for parliament, preferring a coalition setting instead. As a result, the prime-minister's position was even weaker than before as he had to build a multi-party coalition from a hyper-fragmented parliament.

1.3. Separation of Powers and Checks and Balances

We have come to use the terms 'legislative' or 'executive' rather naturally. In fact, they are rooted in a guiding principle of Western constitutional legal tradition that deserves a closer look, namely the principle of separation of powers. Originally defined by Montesquieu, a scholar of the Enlightenment, in his observations of the British constitutional system, separation of powers has had a heavy impact on the drafters of the US Constitution and constitution-making worldwide. Essentially, separation of powers holds that public authority can be dissected into three different functions: a legislative power, which makes laws; an executive power, which enforces them; and a judicial power, which interprets and applies them in cases of conflict. This describes a *functional* separation of powers. Coupled to this functional separation of powers can be the *institutional* separation of powers, which would mean that these three functions should be allocated with different organs. The final component is the *personal* separation of powers, which would mean that these different organs should be actually staffed by different people.

The degree to which separation of powers is implemented, the form that it is given, and the consequences that are attached to it, even the degree to which adherence to the principle is actually acknowledged, varies from one system to another. The system of the United States is one of the conceptually clearest in that respect. Federal legislative power is exercised by Congress, executive power by the President and his subordinates, judicial power by the courts, all neatly addressed in Articles I, II and III of the Constitution, respectively. In the US, separation of powers however does not mean that the three branches operate in total isolation from each other. Separation is complemented by a system of *checks and balances* between the branches. This is to ensure that no single branch accumulates too much power for itself. For example, Congress is the lawmaker, but the President can veto bills. The President is the head of the executive and is not accountable to Congress like a prime-minister in a parliamentary democracy is: he does not need the confidence of parliament to stay in office. However, Congress can impeach the President, and remove him from office, if he is found guilty of having committed a heavy criminal act, and Congress can exercise day-to-day parliamentary oversight.

Again, the implementation and doctrinal adherence to separation of powers varies. What is a fundamental consensus among Western democracies is that in any event the judiciary should be impartial and independent from, in particular, government interference. For the rest, opinions differ. In the US, for example, *separation of powers* is taken to mean that the three branches should control one another and that judges should check whether the legislature stays within the limits of power attributed to it by the Constitution. In France, meanwhile, *séparation des pouvoirs* means exactly the opposite, namely that judges must be kept separate from lawmaking and that they should apply the law and not question its constitutionality. In that light, the 2008 reform that allowed judges to refer questions regarding the constitutionality of statutes to the Constitutional Council is quite remarkable.

As regards legislative-executive relations, in Western parliamentary democracies the line can easily blur. Here it is somewhat more difficult to say that parliament is *the* legislature and the government is *the* executive. After all the government plays a leading role in the legislative process, drafting and introducing new bills with the help of its civil service. Parliament is usually to debate, approve and thereby legitimize legislation, so that in practice it does not actually make new laws itself (see for details Chapter 4). Some constitutional monarchies, where the King's government and the elected parliament operate side by side, use a different notion of 'legislature' altogether. In the Netherlands and Belgium, legislative power is exercised by the government and the parliament jointly: the King's government can propose new bills, and bills adopted by parliament need the King's signature (plus the countersignature of ministers). In the UK, it is also technically not Parliament but the King-in-Parliament who makes statutes: the monarch enacts laws with the consent of Parliament. Statutes in monarchies typically start out with a preamble along the following lines, illustrated here with the Dutch enactment formula under the reign of Queen Beatrix: 'We Beatrix, by the Grace of God Queen of the Netherlands (...), Thus it is that We, having heard the Council of State, and in consultation with the States-General, have approved and decreed, as We hereby approve and decree.' This formula is used even though statutes must always first be approved by parliament and the monarch does conventionally not withhold his own blessing. Indeed, no statute can enter into force without parliamentary approval, which makes it rather implausible to speak of a royal 'consultation' of parliament; the UK enactment formula at least uses the term 'with the advice and consent' of the Lords and Commons, which is a bit more accurate.

Also as regards personal separation of powers, the lines can blur. In France and the Netherlands, a member of the cabinet cannot at the same time be a member of the parliament. In Germany he can be, and usually is. In the United Kingdom, he actually *must* be: the monarch appoints cabinet members from the membership of the House of Commons (and exceptionally from the House of Lords).

In fact UK doctrine rather embraces a *fusion* of powers, rather than separation of powers. This ironically exposes Montesquieu's observations of 18th century Britain as misleading. How can there be separation of powers in a system where the government actually sits within Parliament? Or where, historically, the upper chamber of Parliament, the House of Lords, was also the highest court? Or where the Lord Chancellor has a seat in the government, and historically presided over the House of Lords, and exercised judicial power as supreme judge and head of the judiciary of England and Wales all at once? Functionally, however, these offices and bodies and their subdivisions still can be distinguished. Furthermore, 20th century practice and constitutional reform have consolidated a more explicit separation. Thus, conventionally the law lords who acted as supreme judges would not participate in the legislative process. In 2005 judicial functions have been extracted from the House of Lords to emphasize judicial independence even more, and a proper Supreme Court of the UK has been created. The Lord Chancellor has been stripped of his presidency of the Lords and of his judicial function under the same 2005 reform. The accountability of the government to Parliament, and the fact that UK statutes in principle have to pass through two chambers of Parliament, rather than one, are further signs that also checks and balances do exist in the UK system.

1.4. The Role of Judges

An independent judiciary is usually seen as essential to the protection of the rule of law. Rule of law means that all public authority derives its power from legal norms and is constrained by legal norms in exercising these powers. The state, just like the individual citizen, is placed under the law, not above the law. Judges are typically charged with upholding the law as against unlawful government action.

Yet the relations between the judiciary and the other branches of government, notably the legislature, can also give rise to debate. The most controversial institution in this context is *constitutional review of legislation*: the power of judges to check whether laws which are made by the central parliament comply with the constitution. The most pertinent question that arises is why an unelected judge should claim supremacy in correctly interpreting what the constitution means, and thereby overrule what the democratic representation of the people has determined. Many arguments exist that support judicial review; there are also many arguments against it (see for details Chapter 6).

For a quick comparative scan, it suffices to note that different constitutional systems have chosen different answers to the same questions. In the US, all judges have the power to review the constitutionality of legislation. This is essentially justified by the supremacy of the Constitution over ordinary laws, so that the latter may not violate the former, and it is embedded in more fundamental notions of checks and balances. Germany, along with many other systems around the world, allows judicial review but limits this function to a special constitutional court. The UK and the Netherlands are among the very few states that do not allow judges to invalidate legislation for alleged breaches of the constitution. These systems stress legislative supremacy instead. In the UK, the principle of parliamentary sovereignty would not tolerate if judges were to ignore or contradict the will of the lawmaker. Dutch doctrine insists that it is a responsibility of the lawmaker himself to obey the Constitution, subject to democratic control. Nevertheless, the UK has introduced a form of judicial review for the area of human rights protection under the Human Rights Act 1998 (although it still does not allow judges to actually invalidate statutes on such grounds); in the Netherlands, a constitutional amendment bill that would allow for constitutional review on human rights grounds has been introduced as well, and has been approved in first reading. France has for a long time allowed only constitutional review of bills *before* they entered into force, and even then not by a genuine court but by a special Constitutional Council. Laws in force were immune. Since 2008 France also allows legislation that is in force already to be submitted to constitutional review by that Constitutional Council, thus making the Council safely comparable to a constitutional court.

1.5. *State Structure: Unitarism and Federalism*

In our comparative observations of different systems, as far as state structure is concerned, we can distinguish between unitary states and federations. Virtually all states in the world have territorial subdivisions, of course, such as regions, provinces, departments, prefectures, oblasts, cantons, rayons, territories, districts or counties. The difference is that a federation is composed of territorial sub-units whose privileges are enshrined in the constitution itself. The sub-units in unitary states, by contrast, receive their power from the central authority (see for details Chapter 3).

France, the UK and the Netherlands are, for example, unitary states. The powers enjoyed by regions, departments or provinces are laid down in laws enacted in the national capital. Such powers can be taken back in the same manner. The same holds true for other unitary states such as Iceland, Portugal, Slovakia, Turkey or Japan. The privileges of US States and the States, or *Länder*, in Germany meanwhile flow immediately from the respective federal constitution. The most important such privileges are the protection of the States' autonomous legislative powers in the constitution; the participation of the States in federal decision-making; and the involvement of the States in the procedure by which the federal constitution is amended. Other federal systems include Austria, Switzerland, India, Australia and Brazil.

The picture is not entirely black-and-white, however. Unitary states can be heavily centralized, but some of them have devolved so much power to their regions that they have become quasi-federations. Belgium has become fully federal this way; Spain is arguably the unitary state with the most far-reaching regional devolution of power in Europe, followed by Italy. Conversely, not all federations protect their states' prerogatives to the same extent: Austria or Canada do so much less than Germany or Belgium, for example. It is therefore useful to see both federalism and unitarism as points on a scale rather than as mutually exclusive categories.

1.6. Summary

In the light of the above overview, the complexity of constitutional comparison becomes readily apparent. Depending on the feature studied, different systems can be placed into different categories.

For example, of the five systems under more detailed consideration, three are republican (the US, Germany and France) and two are constitutional monarchies (the UK and the Netherlands). Three of the systems embrace the notion of popular sovereignty in various forms (the US, Germany, France), one stresses the sovereignty of Parliament in the sense of legislative supremacy (the UK) and one avoids the question of sovereignty altogether (the Netherlands). One system of government is presidential (the US), one is semi-presidential (France) and three are parliamentary (Germany, the UK and the Netherlands). The state structure in two of the systems is federal (the US and Germany), in three of them it is unitary (France, the UK and the Netherlands). Constitutional review of legislation is present in three systems (the US, Germany and France) and it is absent in two of them (the UK and the Netherlands).

This complexity is of course exactly what makes the study of comparative constitutional law so rewarding. With this overview in mind, let us now discuss, for each system under consideration, the historical background of the current constitutional system and the main characteristics of the constitution, in particular the institutional setup, in somewhat greater detail.

1.7. Further Reading

B. Ackerman, *We the People: Foundations* (Cambridge: Harvard University Press 1991).
B. Ackerman, *We the People: Transformations* (Cambridge: Harvard University Press 1998).
L. Besselink, ed., *Constitutional Law of the Netherlands* (Nijmegen: Ars Aequi 2004).
A.W. Bradley & K.D. Ewing, *Constitutional & Administrative Law*, 15th ed. (Edinburgh: Pearson 2011).
S. Boyron, 'Constitutional Law', in J. Bell, S. Boyron & S. Whittaker (eds.), *Principles of French Law*, 2nd ed. (Oxford: OUP 2008).
Th. Dienes & J. Barron, *Barron and Dienes' Constitutional Law in a Nutshell*, 7th ed. (Eagan: West Law School 2010).

K. Haylbronner & M. Kau, 'Constitutional Law', in J. Zekoll & M. Reimann (eds.), *Introduction to German Law* (2nd edition, Alphen: Kluwer Law International 2005).
J. Jowell & D. Oliver (eds.), *The Changing Constitution*, 6th ed. (Oxford: OUP 2007).
C. Kortmann & P. Bovend'Eert, *Constitutional Law of the Netherlands – An Introduction* (Alphen: Kluwer Law International 2007).
N. Parpworth, *Constitutional and Administrative Law*, 7th ed. (Oxford: OUP 2012).
L. Prakke & C. Kortmann (eds.), *Constitutional Law of 15 EU Member States* (Deventer: Kluwer 2004).
A. Stevens, *Government and Politics of France*, 3rd ed. (Basingstoke: Palgrave-MacMillan 2003).
M. Troper, 'Constitutional Law', in G. Bermann & E. Picard (eds.), *Introduction to French Law* (Alphen: Kluwer Law International 2008).
C. Turpin & A. Tomkins, *British Government and the Constitution: Text and Materials*, 6th ed. (Cambridge: CUP 2007).

2. The United States

The United States of America is a federal republic and a presidential democracy. In 1776, thirteen colonies along the Atlantic coast of North America declared their independence from the British colonial empire. These thirteen States – New Hampshire, Massachusetts, Rhode Island, Connecticut, New York, New Jersey, Pennsylvania, Delaware, Maryland, Virginia, North Carolina, South Carolina and Georgia – in 1781 formed a confederation that was governed by 'Articles of Confederation'. The Articles provided for a unicameral legislature but no confederal executive and no confederal courts, and most powers remained with the individual States. As economic and military pressure on the confederation rose, a constitutional convention was assembled in 1787 to draft constitutional provisions for a more effective union. The document that was eventually drafted became the present US Constitution. It entered into force after its ratification by the ninth of the then thirteen constituent States and became effective for all States in 1789.

2.1. Civil War and Reconstruction

In spite of the entry into force of the new Constitution, at first it remained unclear how strong and active the federal government should be, and how much autonomy or sovereignty the individual States had retained within the overall Union. A strong American national identity did initially not exist, and attachment with one's own State remained strong. In the mid-19th century, political tensions split the US along a north-south divide. The mostly rural Southern States insisted on keeping the institution of slavery, and feared that the industrializing and economically mighty North would impose a ban on them. As points of constitutional law, the South insisted on the right for individual States to leave the Union if they so wished, and prominent Southern politicians argued that States could nullify federal law if it violated the Constitution. The eventual secession of eleven Southern States in 1861, which together formed the Confederate States of America, led to the American Civil War. The Union government, with its power-base in the North, held unilateral secession to be unlawful. Union armies eventually defeated and occupied the Confederacy in 1864.

The unionist victory over the secessionists cemented American statehood. It became clear that the US was indeed not merely a loose alliance of States but a nation, albeit a federal one, and that the Union enjoyed supremacy over State law under the terms of the federal Constitution. In fact, it was only after the Civil War that the United States came to be referred to in the singular (the United States *is*, rather than *are*). In the Reconstruction process which followed the Civil War, military administration of the secessionist territories was phased out and one by one the Southern States were re-admitted to the Union.

The emancipation of slaves was enshrined in the Constitution, although a racist backlash in the South undid many of the Reconstruction's achievements from the late 19th century onwards. Only in the 1950s and 1960s would federal case-law and civil rights legislation again seek to abolish discrimination, such as racial segregation of schools, in the South. Constitutionally, this development once again expanded the power of federal authority as against the States. Federal supremacy was famously asserted by force in 1957, when President Eisenhower sent in federal troops to escort black students to school after Arkansas had refused to comply with a desegregation order. The exact legal delimitation of federal and State competences still occupies lawmakers, judges, scholars and political commentators; the robustness of federal authority throughout the US as such is however uncontested.

2.2. The US Constitution

The US Constitution was drafted by a constitutional convention which met at Philadelphia in 1787. The convention comprised delegates from the individual States, and included George Washington, Benjamin Franklin, James Madison, Thomas Jefferson and Alexander Hamilton as prominent figures. The drafters are sometimes called the 'founding fathers' or the 'framers' of the Constitution.

The US Constitution distributes power between federal institutions and the by now fifty individual States (see Chapter 3). A central and recurring theme in the US constitutional system is the separation of powers: the distinction between legislative, executive and judicial functions and the assignment of each of these functions to different institutions. The President is both head of state and head of the federal executive; he is elected by indirect popular vote, as he is chosen by an electoral college whose members are in turn elected within the individual States (Art. II (1) and 12th Amendment US Constitution, see also Chapter 5). Federal legislative power is exercised by a bicameral Congress, a parliament comprising the House of Representatives and the Senate (Art. I (1) US Constitution); the House is popularly elected in districts within the States (Art. I (2) and 14th Amendment US Constitution, see also Chapter 4) while the Senate, reflecting the Union's federal character, is composed of two Senators from each State (Art. I (3) and 17th Amendment US Constitution, see also Chapters 3 and 4). Highest federal judicial authority is exercised by the US Supreme Court (Art. III US Constitution, see also Chapter 6).

Separation of powers does not mean isolation of powers, however. The three branches of government – the legislature, the executive and the judiciary – interact with each other in a system of checks and balances. They thereby keep each other at bay via mutual institutionalized interference. The system is to ensure that no single branch grows too powerful. Examples of such checks and balances between the branches are manifold. Congress, the federal lawmaker, exercises the sole power to adopt federal statutes; yet the President, the head of the federal executive, can counter-balance Congress through his veto in the legislative procedure. That veto, in turn, can be overridden by two-thirds majorities of members present in both chambers of Congress (Art. I (7) US Constitution, see also Chapter 4). The President is commander-in-chief of the armed forces (Art. II (2) US Constitution), but he needs Congress to approve a military budget (and, although this is somewhat obsolete, to declare war in the first place under Art. I (8) of the Constitution). The President has an independent electoral mandate and cannot be ousted by a simple no-confidence vote in Congress, but Congress can impeach and remove him from office if he is found guilty of having committed heavy crimes (Art. II (4) US Constitution, see also Chapter 5). As head of the executive, the President appoints his own ministers ('secretaries') and heads of executive agencies, but he needs the approval of the Senate for his nominees (Art. II (2) US Constitution). The same holds true for the President's nominations for federal judgeships, which is how the President and the Senate jointly exercise influence over the staffing of the federal judiciary. The judiciary, in turn, holds the power of constitutional review and can declare Congress's legislation as well as executive action unconstitutional (see for the constitutional basis of judicial review Chapter 6).

Even within Congress, the idea of checks and balances is implemented, here also with a vertical dimension. The individual States of the US are represented at the federal level through the Senate, which is, overall, co-equal to the House of Representatives at lawmaking. Bills must pass both chambers (Art. I (7) US Constitution). The Senate plays a prominent role in controlling presidential nominations, as well as in trying impeachments; however it is the House that has the sole power of legislative initiative as far as tax bills are concerned (Art. I (7) US Constitution), and it is the House that has to start the impeachment procedure in the first place (Art. I (2) US Constitution). The Vice-President of the US is the president of the Senate; he is replaced in that capacity, however, by the chief justice of the Supreme Court during impeachment procedures against his President (Art. I (3) US Constitution).

The US Constitution proper is partly complemented and partly superseded by subsequent amendments. Thus, the original text is not changed, but amendments are annexed thereto and form an integral part of the Constitution. For example, the Constitution proper still stipulates that Senators are elected by the parliaments of the States (Art. I (3) US Constitution), but the 17th Amendment supersedes this by stipulating direct elections of Senators. The first ten of the constitutional amendments, which all entered into force in 1791, include a Bill of Rights which is to limit the exercise of public power in the light of individual freedoms.

The US Constitution can be amended on the initiative of either two-thirds majorities of members present in both chambers of Congress, or based on the proposals drawn up by a convention that Congress convenes by application of two-thirds of State parliaments (34 out of 50). Whether proposed by a convention or by

Congress itself, proposed amendments have to be ratified within three-fourths of the States (38 out of 50), either by the State parliaments or by State-level conventions, depending on the choice of procedure as made by Congress (Art. V US Constitution). The Constitution does not provide for any nation-wide referendums, neither for the purpose of constitutional amendment nor otherwise. Important past amendments, apart from the Bill of Rights, include the reformed presidential election system of 1804; the introduction of direct elections for the US Senate in 1913; and the two-term limit on the presidency in 1951.

3.   Germany

The Federal Republic of Germany is a state in central Europe; its present-day constitution dates back to 1949. For most of its history, the area roughly corresponding to present-day Germany was not unified but a patchwork of separate principalities, city-states and other entities. The 19th century saw a sequence of alliances between German states in different configurations. The desire for national unification, which was inspired by the French Revolution, was hampered by the entrenched autocratic rule of the several princes as well as by the rivalry between Prussia and Austria for leadership in the region. In the event, Prussia asserted dominance in the northern part of the lands in question and forged a German nation-state to the exclusion of Austria.

3.1.   *National Unification*

Throughout the Middle Ages, the lands comprising present-day Germany were loosely held together by the Holy Roman Empire of the German Nation. The Empire's central institutions were relatively weak, and the influence of the Emperor, who was elected by a body of prince-electors, mostly depended on how much power he personally held as the monarch of his own principality. The Thirty Years' War tore the Empire apart, and the 1648 Peace of Westphalia, which recognized the sovereignty of the individual principalities, rendered the Empire largely meaningless. The last Emperors, who were all members of the House of Habsburg, concentrated on strengthening their Austrian power-base instead. The Empire collapsed when the lands were invaded by Napoleonic armies; the number of principalities was first drastically brought down as smaller statelets became part of larger states, and the Empire was formally dissolved in 1806 when Francis II abdicated as Emperor of the Holy Roman Empire and instead became Emperor Francis I of now-separate Austria. The powerful Kingdom of Prussia remained independent. Most other states of the former Holy Roman Empire united under French pressure to form the Confederation of the Rhine. The Confederation, which became a French vassal, collapsed in 1813 as Napoleon suffered military defeat.

In 1815 the Congress of Vienna created the German Confederation to replace the former Holy Roman Empire. The Confederation included most of present-day Germany and also comprised the western part of Prussia and the western part of Habsburg Austria. The Confederation featured a central assembly called *Bundestag* or Confederal Diet, but this body comprised representatives of the several states rather than parliamentarians representing the people as a whole. In 1848 a liberal revolutionary movement sought to establish a unified German nation-state, and in 1849 a National Assembly which had gathered at Frankfurt offered Frederick William IV of Prussia the German imperial crown, to be held under a constitutional monarchy. The King refused to be proclaimed Emperor by an act of the population, however, and the revolution was crushed. A longing for both liberalism and national unity remained.

The continued rivalry over dominance in the German lands finally led to the Austro-Prussian War of 1866. Prussia defeated Austria, left the German Confederation and together with its smaller allies in the northern half of present-day Germany formed the North German Confederation. Under its Constitution of 1867, this entity became a genuine state, rather than a mere alliance of states. The successful war of Prussia and its allies against France in 1870-1871 built momentum for complete national unification. The southern states – Bavaria, southern Hesse, Baden and Württemberg – joined the Prussian-dominated North to form the first modern German nation-state in history: the German Empire, founded in 1871. Prussian premier Otto von Bismarck is credited as having masterminded this Prussian-led national unification, including the wars in the run-up thereto; the 1871 Empire is therefore sometimes called the Bismarck Empire.

The German Empire was a federation between its constituent States. Effectively it was an expanded version of the North German Confederation: the pre-existing constitutional design was applied to the new Empire. The Empire was a hereditary monarchy tied in personal union to the dynasty of Prussia: the Prussian King would automatically be German Emperor. The imperial government was headed by a chancellor who was accountable to the Emperor. The *Reichstag*, or Imperial Diet, was a directly elected parliament which possessed, crucially, budgetary powers. The governments of the constituent States were represented at national level in the *Bundesrat*, or Federal Council, although dominant Prussia wielded enough votes to veto any proposal.

Following Germany's defeat in World War I and the fall of the imperial monarchy in 1918, Germany adopted a republican form of government. The Weimar Republic was established, named after the city where the new Constitution was drafted in 1919. Instead of an Emperor, the Republic had a directly elected President as its head of state. The government was headed by a chancellor and was this time accountable to the directly elected parliament. The representation of the constituent States at federal level was kept in place. Suffering from poor popular support for a republican form of government and a multi-party system, the Weimar Republic's institutional design proved too fragile to withstand political extremism at a time of economic crisis. What was particularly problematic was the fragmentation of the parliament into a plethora of small political parties; the instability of a succession of governments that were appointed by the President and were voted out of office by parliament; and the far-reaching emergency powers that the head of state used from the end of the 1920s onward to fill the political void. The Weimar Republic effectively ended with the appointment of Adolf Hitler as chancellor and the resulting takeover of the National Socialists in 1933, with Germany becoming a dictatorship that lasted until its defeat in World War II in 1945.

3.2. Division and Reunification

After Germany's surrender in 1945, its remaining territory, and, within that, its capital city of Berlin, was divided into four Allied occupation zones. Against the backdrop of the increasing antagonism between the Western powers of the US, the UK and France, on the one hand, and the Soviet Union, on the other hand, two German states emerged in 1949. The German Democratic Republic (GDR) in the Soviet-controlled Eastern zone, with the Eastern part of divided Berlin as its capital, became a Socialist state with its own constitution and government bodies. The Federal Republic of Germany was founded in the three merged Western zones, with West Berlin as an exclave and with its seat of government in Bonn.

The GDR became, after the re-constituted German States in the East had been replaced by administrative districts, a unitary state. Formally, legislative power was exercised by the unicameral People's Chamber, operating next to the GDR government as well as a President and later a Council of State, a collective presidential body whose chairman was effectively head of state. In practice, however, the GDR functioned as a Socialist one-party regime with the politburo of the Socialist Unity Party being the decisive decision-making body. Thus, only a single Socialist-controlled party list was admitted to parliamentary elections, and the government ministries were expected to implement the decisions taken by the Party.

While the GDR in the East saw itself as an independent sovereign state, and increasingly so over time, the Federal Republic in the West made a point of being the true successor of the whole of Germany. In that view, the constitutional order of the Federal Republic applied to some parts of the overall German territory, namely the West, but it temporarily could not apply to some other parts of Germany, even though it should. The GDR was not recognized as a sovereign state, although bilateral relations existed in practice. To express the temporary character of the West German construction, its federal Constitution was not actually called 'constitution' or *Verfassung* but a more artificial-sounding *Grundgesetz*, or 'Basic Law'. Two scenarios were envisaged to overcome the division of Germany. First, territories outside the area of application of the Basic Law might accede to the Federal Republic one by one, under the old Article 23 of the Basic Law; second, reunification might happen instantaneously, so that the united German people could, under Article 146, adopt a proper *Verfassung* instead of the placeholder Basic Law. In the event, after the fall of the Berlin Wall and the collapse of Socialism, the whole GDR in 1990 acceded to the area of application of the Basic Law under Article 23. Dogmatically speaking, the instantaneous unification might have called for a fresh start with a new constitution for now-unified Germany; pragmatically, however, it was far more feasible to follow the accession scenario. The post-unification workload and forty years' worth of good experience with the Basic Law in the West made a major constitutional overhaul seem superfluous. Article 146 was amended together with the Preamble to reflect the fact that the German people was now united. Article 23 was scratched, because there were no longer any German territories outside Basic Law application that might accede; the now vacant slot of Article 23 was used for a new provision concerning the European Union. The Basic Law, which began as a temporary charter for the Western part of a divided

Germany, today is the constitution for the whole of Germany. While retaining the name 'Basic Law', it is in effect the present-day German Constitution.

3.3. *The Basic Law*

The main elements of the Basic Law were drafted in 1948 by a conference of experts, who had been appointed by the premiers of the Western States, at Herrenchiemsee in southern Germany. The draft was revised and the final version adopted in 1949 by the so-called Parliamentary Council, an assembly which consisted of delegates elected by the Western State parliaments. The text was approved by the military governors of the Western Allied occupation forces and entered into force when the parliaments of two-thirds of the States where the Basic Law would apply ratified the text. Only Bavaria rejected the text, but it nevertheless accepted the Basic Law's binding character. Carlo Schmid is widely credited as one of the most influential 'founding fathers' of the Basic Law; Konrad Adenauer presided over the Parliamentary Council and went on to become the first Federal Chancellor under the Basic Law.

The institutional setup under the German Basic Law of 1949 follows the logic of a federal republic and a parliamentary democracy. The constituent States, suppressed under National Socialism and in the GDR, are given a representation at the federal level through the Bundesrat, or Federal Council. The Bundesrat comprises members of the governments of the States, which wield a fixed number of votes roughly reflecting their population size (Arts. 50 and 51 Basic Law, see also Chapters 3 and 4). There are sixteen States: eleven 'old' States of former West Germany including Berlin, and the five 'new' States of the former GDR. The Bundestag, or Federal Diet, is the directly elected federal parliament (Art. 38 Basic Law, see also Chapter 4). The federal government, headed by the Federal Chancellor, is elected by, and is accountable to, the Bundestag (Arts. 63, 67 and 68 Basic Law, see also Chapter 5). In many respects, the 1949 Basic Law draws lessons from the failure of the Weimar Republic, featuring stabilized democratic institutions and measures to prevent any future concentration of power and its abuse by anti-democratic radicals.

The Basic Law prominently starts out with a catalogue of human rights. Its first provision stipulates that human dignity is inviolable (Art. 1 (1) Basic Law). The principle enshrined in this provision is entrenched in the Basic Law forever, meaning that it cannot be changed. Nor can Germany's character as a federal, democratic and social state be changed via constitutional amendment (Arts. 20 and 79 (3) Basic Law).

To avoid a fragmentation of the parliament, and keep small radical parties out, the Bundestag features a five-percent electoral hurdle for proportional representation (see for details Chapter 4). The stability of the government is further enhanced by the introduction of a constructive vote of no-confidence. Under Weimar, the parliament could oust a sitting government by majority vote, possibly creating a power vacuum; under the present Basic Law, the Bundestag can only oust a Chancellor if it manages to (constructively) elect a new Chancellor at the same time (Art. 67 Basic Law, see also Chapter 5). The head of state is the Federal President who is no longer elected by popular vote; instead, he is elected by an electoral college comprising the Bundestag members and delegates from the States (Art. 54 Basic Law). While the President retains some important powers, especially as regards the promulgation of statutes and the dissolution of the Bundestag, his functions are largely ceremonial (see Chapter 5). Crucially, and in contrast to Weimar, the head of state is stripped of his emergency powers and the power to call a referendum. The Bundestag can only be dissolved, and early elections can only be called, in case the Bundestag fails to elect a Chancellor by absolute majority in the third round or if the sitting Chancellor fails to obtain an explicit vote of confidence and asks for early elections (Arts. 63 (4) and 68 Basic Law).

Bundestag and Bundesrat, the elected national parliament and the representation of the State governments, together carry out federal legislative tasks. The powers of the federal lawmaker are defined in competence catalogues, delineating them from the autonomous legislative powers of the individual States (Arts. 72, 73 and 74 Basic Law). Power of legislative initiative lies with the government, the Bundestag members and the Bundesrat (Art. 76 Basic Law). To pass federal statutes, the Bundestag must agree; the Bundesrat may object but the former can in such case overrule the latter's veto (Arts. 77 and 78 Basic Law) unless the Basic Law provides that the Bundesrat's active consent is required (see Chapter 4). Legislation, as well as other acts of public authority, are controlled for their compliance with the constitution by the judicial branch, most importantly the Federal Constitutional Court (Art. 92 Basic Law, see also Chapter 6).

(West) Germany is a founding member of the European Economic Community, the most important predecessor of what is now the European Union; transfer of sovereign competences to the European Union is authorized explicitly (Art. 23 (1) Basic Law) but requires the approval of both the Bundestag and the Bundesrat following the qualified procedure of constitutional amendment.

The Basic Law, in as far as it may be amended in the first place, can only be changed by a statute passed by a two-thirds majority of the members of the Bundestag and a two-thirds majority of total votes in the Bundesrat (Art. 79 Basic Law). The only instance where the Basic Law provides for a referendum as a matter of federal law is the procedure for redrawing the borders between States (Art. 29 Basic Law). The theoretical repeal of the Basic Law and the adoption of an entirely new constitution would require popular approval as well (Art. 146 Basic Law). Important past amendments to the Basic Law include the regulation of a state of emergency in 1968; the admission of individual constitutional complaints, even against legislative acts, before the Federal Constitutional Court in 1969; and the federalism reform of 2006 which sought to disentangle federal and State competences. The Basic Law is in fact amended relatively frequently, but these reforms are rarely momentous or headline-making: they usually concern technical provisions such as those on finances and the distribution of tax revenue between the federation and the States, about which the Basic law has an elaborate chapter, or the privatization of public services.

4. The United Kingdom

The United Kingdom comprises four 'countries': England, Scotland and Wales, which together form Great Britain, as well as Northern Ireland. Historically, England had conquered Wales already in the 13th century and had tied it to itself legally in the 16th century. England and Wales, on the one hand, and Scotland, on the other hand, united in 1707, as both their Parliaments passed Acts of Union, together forming the Kingdom of Great Britain with a single British Parliament. In 1800, Great Britain and Ireland united, again via Acts of Union, creating the United Kingdom of Great Britain and Ireland. Ireland, with the exception of its predominantly Protestant north-eastern counties, was granted autonomy again in 1922. As a result, the present-day state is appropriately called United Kingdom of Great Britain and Northern Ireland.

4.1. Monarchy and Parliament

Much of the constitutional history of England (and later Britain) was marked by a power struggle between the King, on the one hand, and Parliament, on the other hand. Already the Anglo-Saxon Kings of England, from the 9th century onwards, would convene advisory assemblies. After the Norman conquest in 1066, the King would convene noble landowners as well as senior clergy to form a King's Council. In the newly introduced feudal system, the King depended on the lords of the fiefdoms in the country for tax revenue and law enforcement, and thus sought consultation. The members of the convened assembly would increasingly use the opportunity of a dialogue with the King in order to present grievances from the population of their home region. Thus, the King's Council developed into what became known as Parliament: a chamber for debate and the airing of criticism. The term Parliament has been used from the 13th century onwards.

Throughout the period, the Kings of England reigned as sovereigns claiming divine rights for their self-rule. Nevertheless, Parliament gradually asserted itself. Already in 1215, the English nobility forced King John to accept the Magna Carta, a document which provided for a number of civil liberties and which later became a symbol showing that the monarch could be bound by law. In the 1260s, aristocrats led by Simon de Montford rebelled against King Henry III and in 1265 convened a Parliament which included not only feudal nobility and clergy but also representatives of counties, towns and boroughs: the so-called Commons. After the rebellion was quelled, Edward I, Henry's son, would continue to summon the Commons to Parliament, along with feudal nobility and clergy, so as to consolidate popular support for his rule. The Parliament he convened in such composition in 1295 would become the so-called Model Parliament, a blueprint for later Parliaments.

The 17th century saw an outbreak of open conflict between Parliament and the ruling House of Stuart. King Charles I was criticized for ruling arbitrarily; he dissolved Parliament in 1629 and re-convened it only years later, in 1640, when he needed additional tax revenue. Charles entered the House of Commons and unsuccessfully tried to arrest his main critics in 1642. Parliament raised an army of its own and fought the King's army in the English Civil War. Parliament's professional 'New Model Army' defeated the royalists; Charles was tried and executed in 1649. The parliamentarians' military commander Oliver Cromwell purged Parliament of his opponents and established a brief republican system; yet even then Parliament proved an independent critic of the head of state. After the restoration of the monarchy in 1660, relations between King and Parliament continued to be tense. King Charles II sought to restore royal prerogatives and, in addition, was inclined towards Catholicism; James II, his successor on the throne, openly supported Catholicism and started to prosecute Protestants. In 1688, Parliament forced James II to flee the country in an event commonly referred to as the Glorious Revolution. In the Bill of Rights, adopted in 1689, Parliament declared James II deposed and invited James's daughter Mary and her Protestant husband, William of Orange, to ascend the throne as co-regents. By replacing one monarch with another, Parliament had asserted supremacy over the crown. In the Bill of Rights it also enshrined other principles, declaring most notably that the King may not suspend or repeal laws, raise taxes, establish extraordinary tribunals or support a standing army in peacetime without the consent of Parliament, and that freedom of speech in Parliament and the citizens' right to submit petitions must be respected. In 1701, Parliament adopted the Act of Settlement, regulating the rules of royal succession to ensure that future monarchs be neither Catholic themselves nor be married to a Catholic. This definitively ended the Stuart dynasty and George I from the Protestant House of Hanover ascended the throne.

In spite of the assertion of parliamentary powers, the monarchy was preserved. Legislation is formally not made by Parliament alone, but by the King-in-Parliament: bills receive the approval of the Commons and, normally, the Lords, and enter into force with royal assent. In reality, however, the King is not free to withhold assent; a monarch has not refused to approve a bill since 1707. Parliamentary independence from the crown is also expressed in more ceremonial ways. The King addresses the Commons and the Lords in a joint gathering to open a new session of Parliament, but the address takes place in the House of Lords because the King (since the episode of Charles I trying to arrest his critics in the 17th century) may not enter the House of Commons. In a ritual repeated at each such opening, when the King's officer seeks entry to the House of Commons in order to instruct the members to follow him to the Lords, the door is slammed in his face. Only after the officer has knocked on the door thrice is he allowed in and do the members of the Commons proceed to the Lords, in a deliberately noisy manner. After the King has addressed his Parliament – a member of Parliament is symbolically held hostage at the royal palace the entire time to ensure the monarch's safe return from Parliament's premises – the Lords and the Commons enter a debate. Yet they do not immediately discuss the King's speech (the speech is actually written by the Prime-Minister); instead they insist that they themselves choose what to discuss and when. The Commons first discuss the Outlawries Bill; the Lords discuss the Select Vestries Bill. Both bills are centuries old, their actual content is meaningless, and neither is meant to make any progress. Yet their consideration is an important symbolic act emphasizing the control of Parliament over its own agenda. Only in second instance is the King's speech discussed.

4.2. The UK Constitution

From a purely functional point of view, the constitutional system of the United Kingdom of today can be briefly summarized in the following terms. The UK is a constitutional monarchy: the King is the head of state but his powers are limited by constitutional rules, especially the independent position of the Parliament and the convention that he must act upon the advice of his Prime-Minister (see Chapter 5). Parliament is composed of a directly elected House of Commons and an unelected House of Lords (see Chapter 4). The system of government is parliamentary, as the cabinet is appointed by the King but must be supported or tolerated in office by Parliament, specifically the House of Commons. The state structure is unitary, although some competences are passed down from the capital to regional authorities, notably for Wales, Scotland and Northern Ireland, in a process called 'devolution' (see Chapter 3). Power of legislative initiative lies with the government and individual members of the Commons and Lords. Both Commons and Lords have the power of amendment and rejection with respect to bills, but the Commons can in most cases ultimately insist on the adoption of legislation even against the will of the Lords (Parliament Acts 1911/1949). The court systems in the countries of the UK exercise judicial functions; Acts of Parliament enjoy supremacy and judges may not set them aside except for violations of European Union law (see Chapter 6).

The UK constitutional system stands out in several ways. First and foremost, its basic constitutional rules are not codified in a central constitutional document. Instead, rules that would in most other systems be found in a single written constitution are in the UK scattered across three main sources: statutes, meaning legislation made by the King-in-Parliament; case-law, meaning court decisions; and constitutional conventions, which are unwritten customs that are not judicially enforceable but that are still universally observed as being authoritative.

A number of specific statutes are usually cited as forming part of the UK constitution, because they enjoy significance for the organization of the state. They include, among others, the Magna Carta of 1215 which limited the discretion of the King; the Bill of Rights 1689 which cemented the Glorious Revolution and which binds the King to the will of Parliament; the Act of Settlement 1701 which regulates the order of royal succession; the Reform Acts between 1832 and 1928 which step by step democratized the election system; the Parliament Acts of 1911 and 1949 which practically abolished the veto power of the House of Lords; the European Communities Act 1972 by which the UK joined the European Economic Community, which in turn had constitutional consequences; the Scotland Act 1998 and the devolution statutes for Wales and Northern Ireland, which decentralized power in the UK; the Human Rights Act 1998 which transposed the European Convention on Human Rights into UK law; the Constitutional Reform Act 2005 which, among other things, set up a Supreme Court to replace the House of Lords as the highest court of appeal; and the Fixed-Term Parliaments Act 2011 which restricts the possibilities to declare a dissolution of Parliament, thereby abolishing the King's – effectively the Prime-Minister's – discretionary right to call early elections for the House of Commons.

Important conventions include the rule that the King gives his royal assent to all bills that have passed Parliament; that he convenes Parliament once a year, and not when he deems fit; and that he appoints as Prime-Minister whoever happens to be the majority leader in the House of Commons. The long-standing convention that the King does not dissolve the Commons unless the Prime-Minister has asked him to, and that he does not refuse if he does ask, has been rendered obsolete with the entry into force of the Fixed-Term Parliaments Act 2011.

The entirety of the UK constitutional system is underpinned by the notion of the sovereignty of Parliament. The term describes the supremacy of Acts of Parliament, which are adopted by Parliament and King acting together, over all other sources of law. Statutory law prevails over all other authorities, including the government, the monarch and his remaining royal prerogatives, regional and local authorities, the Church of England, and the courts and their judge-made law. The King-in-Parliament can pass any statute he desires within the scope of the physically possible; courts are not to question the validity of Acts of Parliament, but to apply them faithfully. Parliamentary sovereignty in the sense of legislative supremacy has been formulated by the 19th century scholar Albert Dicey. In his view, which remains authoritative, Parliament (as in King-in-Parliament) cannot be bound by anyone; it cannot bind its successors, which means that later Parliaments are not bound by earlier Parliaments; and only Parliament itself, no-one else, can repeal and undo an Act of Parliament. Legislative supremacy over the judiciary is actually upheld by the courts themselves, as in their case-law they give precedence to statute over their own precedent-based judge-made law, namely common law and equity.

It follows from the above that even though constitutional reality has moved on, certain dignified notions and traditions are nevertheless still upheld in the UK. This in particular concerns the ceremonial status of the monarchy. The King is not dethroned, but he exercises his notional royal prerogatives within the tight margin set by constitutional law and custom. Thus, it is the King who is kept in place as head of state. By consequence, it is the King's Parliament – even though he has no power over its composition, neither regarding the Lords and certainly not regarding the Commons. It is the King's statutes, as he gives royal assent to bills – even though he has no choice but to sign everything Parliament passes and can make no laws himself without parliamentary approval. It is the King's courts – even though the judiciary is independent and otherwise bound by statute like he himself is. It is the King's government – even though the government is formed by the popularly elected majority in the House of Commons. It is the King's Prime-Minister – even though the King has no choice but to appoint the Commons majority leader. It is the King's Speech by which the monarch opens parliamentary sessions and announces policy priorities – even though the speech is in fact written under the ministerial responsibility of the Prime-Minister and the King merely reads it out aloud. And it is even the King's opposition: the minority in the Commons criticizes the political decisions of the majority government, but does not challenge the authority of the King himself, which is why it is called His Majesty's Loyal Opposition.

Since there is no central constitutional document that might be hard to amend, a change to the UK constitution does not require the completion of any special procedures. In as far as a constitutional rule is laid down in a normal statute, it can be changed by a normal statute. For example, the rule that the Commons can pass statutes even against the will of the Lords is based on the Parliament Act 1911; it has been adopted by Parliament and it can also be changed or revoked by Parliament at any time. A statute may provide for a referendum, too. Two nation-wide referendums have been held in the UK: a consultative referendum on whether or not to remain as a member state in what was then the European Economic Community, the European Union's predecessor, in 1975; and a binding referendum on whether or not to introduce the alternative vote system for elections of the House of Commons (see Chapter 4) in 2011. Referendums do not override statute, however. The statute calling for the binding 2011 referendum provided for automatic consequences depending on the referendum outcome, in that the new system had to be either enacted or repealed. The proposed new election system was eventually rejected, but legally this does not preclude Parliament from adopting a new statute at a later stage to change the election system nonetheless.

In as far as a constitutional rule is based on convention, the emergence of new customs in practice lead to constitutional change. The rule that Lords will not even try to oppose bills that implement the government party's manifesto, and that are therefore close to the heart of the democratic majority in the Commons, is nothing but a convention; the Lords may theoretically decide to adopt a more hostile stance. Indeed, the custom is coming under pressure as voter turnout and therefore the legitimacy of the party manifesto decreases.

In as far as a constitutional rule is laid down in case-law, a change in case-law, for example on the interpretation of statutes by the courts, will have constitutional consequences. Since there is no special qualified procedure for constitutional amendment, the UK constitution is called 'flexible'; it is seen as a dynamic process that keeps settling questions regarding the exercise of power. Constitutional law acknowledges developments in practice.

4.3. *The UK and Europe*

It was notably European developments that posed dilemmas within the framework of constitutional legal thinking in the UK. The first dilemma is how to give effect to human rights, primarily the ones enshrined in the European Convention on Human Rights, in the UK legal order. The second is how to accommodate the supremacy of European Union law over national law. In both cases, giving judges the power to set aside legislation in case of conflict with a higher norm would mean to undermine the sovereignty of Parliament, or legislative supremacy.

The solution under the Human Rights Act 1998, which transposes the applicable individual rights from the European Convention on Human Rights into UK law, is a compromise between judicial review and legislative supremacy. Judges may declare a human-rights violation – in a so-called declaration of incompatibility – but must nevertheless apply the statute in question, and it is ultimately up to Parliament whether or not to change its statutory law. As regards the supremacy of European Union law over national law, judges indeed may, and even must, set aside conflicting national statutes. This unique rule is justified as it was Parliament itself that voluntarily decided to join the European Economic Community by virtue of the European Communities Act 1972, and the doctrines of direct effect and supremacy had by then been long established as part of European law (see Chapter 6). If Parliament is no longer satisfied with these European doctrines, it may, according to UK thinking, repeal the Act and unilaterally withdraw from the Union. In actual fact, EU law allows for a member state's withdrawal only since 2009, when the Treaty of Lisbon entered into force, and even then such withdrawal must be negotiated (Art. 50 TEU). In the meantime, the European Communities Act 1972 and the Human Rights Act 1998 may be seen as yet another part of the UK constitution.

5. France

France is a country in Western Europe. France became recognizable as a separate Kingdom when the larger Carolingian Empire was split up. Under the terms of the Treaty of Verdun of 843, Charles the Bald inherited the Western part of the Empire, which would become known as the Western Frankish Realm and, later, the Kingdom of France. Absolutist royal rule consolidated in early modern France. This absolutism, where the King would rule without constraint, which is referred to as the *ancien régime* or 'old order', ended with the French Revolution of 1789. The Revolution was inspired by ideals of the Enlightenment, and led to a breakthrough for notions that are still important today, including national sovereignty, constitutionalism rather than personal rule, the idea of the nation-state and the codification of law. Still, it must be noted that since the Revolution France has experienced a baffling number of coups, revolutions, different systems of government and a sequence of different constitutions. The exact number of constitutions depends on the definition used, but post-1789 France has in any event seen about a dozen different constitutional documents, ranging between liberal republican ones and imperial and dictatorial ones.

5.1. A Sequence of Constitutions

In the course of the 18th century, the absolutist monarchy proved unable to reform itself and to respond to popular demands for greater freedoms, social justice and democratic participation. In 1789 the Third Estate, the representation of the citizenry as opposed to the clergy and nobility, proclaimed itself a single National Assembly. France adopted a constitutional monarchy: the King would reign together with the National Assembly. In 1791 France's first written constitution was adopted, which enshrined the constitutional monarchy and a unicameral parliament. This period however swiftly ended in 1792, when the powers of King Louis XVI were suspended and a newly elected National Convention proclaimed a Republic, later to be known as the First Republic. The King was decapitated the following year. The Republic was to be governed by the Constitution of 1793, but the document's entry into force was suspended. The government of the National Convention was overshadowed by the internal Terror regime against suspected opponents of the Revolution as well as by the external wars against coalitions of restoration-minded

European monarchies. The Terror ended in 1794 and power reverted to a more moderate National Convention. What then followed was a quick succession of increasingly dictatorial constitutions named after the respective year in the French revolutionary calendar.

The constitution of 1795, or Constitution of Year III, established a Directory. The Directory was an executive committee of five next to a bicameral parliament. In 1799, after a coup led by the young general Napoleon Bonaparte, a new constitution, the Constitution of Year VIII, established a Consulate, which was an executive committee of three next to a tricameral parliament. In 1802 Napoleon emerged from the Consulate as First Consul for life, his powers laid down in the Constitution of Year X. In 1804 Napoleon crowned himself Emperor, thus ending the First Republic and raising the First Empire under the Constitution of Year XII.

After France's defeat in the Napoleonic Wars, the European monarchies in 1814 restored the old Bourbon monarchy. This monarchy was succeeded in 1830 by the so-called July Monarchy, as King Charles X was overthrown and Louis Philippe, from the Orleanist branch of the House of Bourbon, ascended the throne to establish a liberal constitutional monarchy. Louis Philippe abdicated after the revolution of 1848, and the Second Republic was established. Louis Napoleon Bonaparte, Napoleon Bonaparte's nephew, was elected President; he staged a coup in 1851 to become President for life and in 1852 styled himself Emperor Napoleon III, ending the Second Republic and establishing the Second Empire. The Second Empire collapsed during the Franco-Prussian War in 1870 and it was replaced by the so-called Third Republic.

The Third Republic lasted effectively until the German invasion of France in 1940, when an authoritarian and collaborationist regime with its seat in Vichy in central France was set up. As France was liberated by the Western Allies, a provisional government under the anti-Vichy general Charles de Gaulle took over, and eventually handed over power to the government of the Fourth Republic in 1946. The Fourth Republic, a parliamentary democracy, in many ways represented a restoration of the pre-war order of the Third Republic. It also suffered from the same structural weaknesses, in particular a feeble executive that had no grip on parliament. The Fourth Republic became politically unstable as France went through de-colonization: the Algerian struggle for independence from France escalated, and parts of the French military threatened a coup unless Charles de Gaulle were returned to power to restore order. De Gaulle agreed under the condition that he could draft an entirely new constitution. Thus, de Gaulle became the last prime-minister of the Fourth Republic. His Constitution was approved in a referendum in 1958 and he became the first President of what was now called the Fifth Republic.

5.2. *The Constitution of the Fifth Republic*

The Constitution of the Fifth Republic has been tailored to the ambitions of Charles de Gaulle. Michel Debré is widely credited as the main drafter of the Constitution's text, and he also became President de Gaulle's first Prime-Minister in 1959.

France under the Fifth Republic is a unitary state with limited decentralization (Art. 1 and Title XII French Constitution, see also Chapter 3). The parliament is bicameral and comprises the National Assembly, the directly elected lower chamber, and the Senate, an upper chamber elected by a body of electors (Art. 24 French Constitution, see also Chapter 4). As far as the executive is concerned, the Fifth Republic is a semi-presidential democracy. The President is the head of state, but he also exercises leading executive functions; the President appoints a Prime-Minister as head of the government in a stricter sense (Titles II and III French Constitution, see also Chapter 5). The presidential aspect of this two-headed executive lies in the fact that the powerful President of the Republic is (since 1962) directly elected (Art. 7 French Constitution) and not accountable to parliament in the sense of a confidence rule; the parliamentary aspect of this semi-presidentialism lies in the fact that the Prime-Minister is accountable to parliament and can be removed from office by a vote of censure in the National Assembly (Arts. 20, 49 and 50 French Constitution). President and Prime-Minister operate side by side.

In contrast to its predecessors, the Fifth Republic enhances the power and stability of the government as regards the parliament. Parliament is 'rationalized', its powers of legislative initiative, amendment, deliberation and censure are restrained and made subject to conditions. The government can in effect take charge of the legislative process (see Chapter 4). Parliamentary legislative competences are enumerated (Art. 34 French Constitution), with residual legislative power in matters not reserved for parliament belonging to the government (Art. 37 French Constitution). Initiative lies with the government, and the members of the National Assembly and the Senate (Art. 39 French Constitution). The government also has the power to propose amendments, while the power of amendment and even rejection of parliamentarians is or can be restricted. Statutes within the parliament's competence must pass both chambers; the government may in most cases ask the National Assembly to override the Senate to resolve a deadlock, however (Art. 45 French Constitution). In the large-scale reform of 2008, which was designed to 'modernize' the French Constitution, the constraints on parliament have been loosened somewhat. For example, parliament can now actually set its own agenda half the time (Art. 48 French Constitution); before, government initiatives had always to be debated by priority, and only during one meeting per month could parliamentarians set the agenda. Furthermore, the possibility for the government to push bills through the National Assembly without its explicit approval (the bill is then considered adopted unless the National Assembly brings down the government) has been limited (Art. 49 French Constitution, see also Chapters 4 and 5). Nevertheless, overall parliament remains rationalized. The constitutionality of bills adopted in parliament is monitored by a Constitutional Council via mandatory review and review upon request from enumerated state officials (Art. 61 French Constitution). The President can call referendums sidelining parliament altogether (Art. 11 French Constitution), both to seek the adoption of legislation and to seek approval for a constitutional reform.

Originally, statutes in force were immune from judicial review of their constitutionality. Popular sovereignty and separation of powers were seen to be incompatible with judicial constitutional review of statutes. Since the constitutional reform of 2008, however, the constitutionality of statutes contested before a lower court may be reviewed by the Constitutional Council, upon a preliminary reference from the Court of Cassation, the supreme court of general jurisdiction, or the Council of State, the supreme administrative court (Art. 61-1 French Constitution, see also Chapter 6). International treaty provisions can be directly applied by the courts as before, and they continue to override conflicting national legislation (Art. 55 French Constitution).

France is a founding member of the European Economic Community. Transfer of competences to the European Union is authorized specifically (Art. 88-1 French Constitution), but treaties may not deviate from the French Constitution and thus may necessitate prior constitutional amendment (Art. 54 French Constitution).

The Constitution, according to the explicitly prescribed procedure of Article 89, is amended in two stages. First, both chambers of parliament must pass a proposal in identical terms by a simple vote. Then the proposal is submitted to a referendum; alternatively, if the proposal comes from the government and the President so orders, instead of a referendum it may be referred for discussion to a joint session of both parliamentary chambers, which may pass the amendment by a three-fifths majority of votes cast. France's republican form of government may not be changed, however, nor can constitutional amendment be pursued while France's territorial integrity is being jeopardized. In historical practice it proved difficult to get the two chambers of parliament to agree on proposed amendments. Thus, several constitutional amendments have been adopted by popular vote as the President bypassed parliament and called for a referendum directly under Article 11 of the Constitution. Though this might arguably violate the procedure as prescribed by the Constitution, the Constitutional Council accepts the results since a referendum is, in one way or another, an expression of national sovereignty through popular vote and as such is beyond contestation. Important past amendments to the 1958 Constitution include the 1962 reform which introduced direct elections of the President; the 1974 reform allowing sixty parliamentarians of either chamber to submit a bill for constitutional review before it entered into force; the synchronization of the terms of office for the President and the National Assembly in 2000; and the reform of 2008 which, among other things, imposed a two-term limit on the presidency, gave slightly more powers to the parliament and allowed for constitutional review of statutes after their entry into force.

6. The Netherlands

A discussion of the constitutional system of the Netherlands requires a preliminary definition of what exactly is meant by 'the Netherlands'. In its popular use, the Netherlands is a state in Western Europe, north of Belgium, west of Germany, along the coast of the North Sea. Its present-day Constitution dates back to 1814/1815, when after the defeat of France in the Napoleonic Wars an independent state in the lowlands was re-established. Strictly speaking, however, the Kingdom of the Netherlands of today is in fact a quasi-federal construct between these Netherlands proper, i.e. the country in Europe, and three other constituent countries, namely Aruba, Curacao and Saint Martin in the Caribbean. The Kingdom as an overarching federal entity was created by the Charter for the Kingdom of the Netherlands, the so-called *Statuut*, an instrument adopted and ratified by the constituent countries in 1954. It redefined the Kingdom as having several component parts – originally three, since 2010 four – the Netherlands no longer being the colonial motherland but being notionally co-equal to its former dependencies. Only the islands of Bonaire, Saint Eustatius and Saba, the so-called BES islands, which used to belong to the Netherlands Antilles, were converted into decentralized public entities of the Netherlands proper in 2010. Thus, the constitution of the Kingdom of the Netherlands is the Charter for the Kingdom; the Dutch Constitution of 1815, called *Grondwet*, today is 'merely' the constitution of the Netherlands proper: the Kingdom's European part including the BES islands.

6.1. Dutch Independence and the French Period

The first modern political entity that emerged in the territory roughly corresponding to the present-day Netherlands was the United Provinces created by the Union of Utrecht in 1579. Via the Union, which was a treaty primarily on military cooperation, the seven northerly provinces of the lowlands – Friesland, Groningen, Holland, Utrecht, Overijssel, Zeeland and the northern parts of Guelders – formed a confederation in their rebellion against Spain and the Habsburg monarchy. The United Provinces are also known as the Republic of the Seven United Netherlands. The southern provinces, which remained under Spanish rule, became known as the Southern Netherlands or the Spanish Netherlands. That area roughly corresponds with present-day Belgium.

In 1581, the United Provinces declared themselves independent from Habsburg. They were recognized as such in the 1648 Peace of Westphalia, which ended not only the larger Thirty Years' War in Europe but also the Eighty Years' War between the Dutch Provinces and Spain. The United Provinces functioned on confederal principles. Each province kept its own *staten* or 'states', more or less representative assemblies, along with a states-appointed stadholder. Union competences were exercised by the States-General composed of delegates from the provincial states, who acted on mandates from their home provinces rather than in personal capacity. The stadholder of the powerful province of Holland rose to Union-wide power in the 18th century as the Union's fleet commander. Effectively the stadholdership of Holland became a hereditary office for the descendants of William of Orange, the nobleman who had started the rebellion against Spanish rule in the first place.

In spite of the relative weakness of their central institutions, the United Provinces became a major European naval and merchant power and they obtained numerous colonial possessions. The confederation remained intact until the 1795 invasion by French revolutionary armies. France established a new French-modelled unitary entity called the Batavian Republic (the name refers to the Germanic tribe that historically inhabited the Rhine delta region). In 1806, Napoleon transformed the Batavian Republic into the Kingdom of Holland, a French vassal state under the rule of Napoleon's brother Louis. In 1810, after Louis had increasingly promoted the interests of his Dutch subjects rather than his brother's, Napoleon annexed the Kingdom, incorporating its territory into France proper. After France's defeat, a monarchy was restored as William I, who descended from the last stadholders of Holland, accepted sovereignty in 1813 and a new monarchical Constitution, the *Grondwet*, was adopted in 1814. The house of Orange-Nassau became a royal dynasty. The States-General were established as a unicameral representative assembly and were elected by the 'states', or assemblies, of the provinces.

6.2. The Kingdom of the United Netherlands

The Congress of Vienna insisted on the creation of a strong buffer state against post-Napoleonic France. Therefore the Southern Netherlands, roughly today's Belgium, were merged into the new Kingdom of the Netherlands in 1815. The Kingdom became known as the 'United Netherlands'. The Kingdom's Constitution was amended accordingly by referendum, albeit with limited suffrage and with abstentions counting as votes in favour. Upon the insistence of the Belgian members of the committee that drafted the 1815 amendment, an upper house was added to the previously unicameral States-General. The upper house, called *Eerste Kamer* or First Chamber, would be appointed by the King and was to be a nobility chamber modelled after the British House of Lords. The *Tweede Kamer*, or Second Chamber, would continue to be elected by the provincial assemblies.

The Kingdom of the Netherlands split again when its southern half eventually seceded to form independent Belgium in 1830. The Kingdom's Constitution was updated in 1839 to reflect the secession; the bicameral system was preserved, however. Keeping its official name, the northern rump of the Kingdom of the Netherlands continued to operate under its original Constitution as amended.

6.3. The Dutch Constitution

Formally, the Constitution in force today is still the *Grondwet* for the Kingdom of the Netherlands of 1815. In practice, however, the document is often referred to as the 'Constitution of 1848' or as the 'Constitution of 1983'. These two years saw constitutional amendments so far-reaching that they effectively produced new constitutional texts.

The 1848 amendment, to which King William II agreed in the face of Europe-wide revolutionary movements, marked a decisive step towards a reduction of the personal powers of the monarch to the benefit of parliament. Among other things, political responsibility for government policy was allocated with the ministers, rather than with the King. Gradually, and over a series of political incidents in the middle of the 19th century, this led to a disengagement of the King from active politics. Ministers became more independent vis-à-vis the crown. Crucially, parliament was able to hold ministers to account for their policies, and it became a conventional rule that ministers must resign if they lost parliamentary confidence (see Chapter 5). Thus, the 1848 reform provided the foundation of a parliamentary system. The same reform introduced direct elections to the Second Chamber; the provincial assemblies went on to elect the First Chamber, so that the members of the First Chamber were no longer appointed. The statesman Johan Rudolph Thorbecke is considered the drafter of the 1848 reform, and thus the 'founding father' of the modern parliamentary democracy in the Netherlands. The 1983 amendment, meanwhile, was a general overhaul, designed above all to update and clarify the structure and language of the Constitution. Yet again, technically the document in force is still the (heavily amended) Constitution of 1815.

The Netherlands of today is a constitutional monarchy. The Prime-Minister, who heads the cabinet, is appointed by the King (Art. 43 Dutch Constitution) after a consultation procedure probing likely supportive coalitions between the political parties in the lower chamber, the Second Chamber. The Prime-Minister and the other cabinet members bear responsibility for government action (Art. 42 Dutch Constitution) and are each accountable to the parliament, specifically the Second Chamber; votes of no-confidence are not conditioned (see Chapter 5). The bicameral parliament is called States-General; next to the directly elected Second Chamber it comprises a senatorial house called First Chamber, which is (since 1848) elected by the assemblies of the Dutch provinces (Arts. 50 to 55 Dutch Constitution). The state structure is decentralized but unitary (Chapter 7 of the Dutch Constitution, see also Chapter 3). National legislative power is exercised by the government and the States-General jointly (Art. 81 Dutch Constitution). Legislative initiative and the power of amendment lie with the government and (the members of) the Second Chamber (Arts. 82 and 84 Dutch Constitution). Bills must pass both parliamentary chambers (Arts. 85 and 87 Dutch Constitution); the First Chamber retains a power of rejection but not of initiative or amendment, although in practice it sometimes makes its approval to bills conditional upon their prior amendment (see Chapter 4).

Judicial review of the constitutionality of statutes is prohibited, and there is no constitutional court (Art. 120 Dutch Constitution, see also Chapter 6). Self-executing provisions of international treaties, namely provisions that can be invoked before national courts as being capable of binding individuals, enjoy supremacy over Dutch statutes by virtue of the Dutch Constitution, however (Arts. 93 and 94 Dutch Constitution). A constitutional amendment that would allow judicial review on human-rights grounds has been approved in first reading in 2008, but approval in second reading requires elevated majorities in parliament and the issue remains controversial.

The Netherlands is a founding member of the European Economic Community; transfer of competences to international organizations in general is authorized (Art. 92 Dutch Constitution), yet the Constitution contains no Europe-specific clause. The supremacy of European Union law over national law is accepted without any major friction. The ratification of treaties deviating from the Constitution requires a two-thirds majority of votes cast in both Chambers (Art. 91 (3) Dutch Constitution).

Ordinary constitutional amendment requires two readings in both Chambers, with simple majorities in both Chambers in the first reading to adopt a statute that contains the definitive proposal, followed by new elections of the Second Chamber, and two-thirds majorities of votes cast for that proposal in both Chambers in the second reading (Art. 137 Dutch Constitution). Apart from the different majority requirements, the difference between the first and the second reading is that in the second reading no amendments may be introduced any longer.

> *Two Readings*
>
> The intervening elections between readings in the constitutional amendment procedure are to allow the voters to express their view on the planned amendment, without there being an actual referendum. In practice, however, elections do not take place specifically with a view to legitimize a draft constitutional amendment. Instead, the Second Chamber is dissolved when new elections would have been scheduled anyway, after which the second reading may start.

The Constitution does not provide for nation-wide referendums. A consultative, i.e. non-binding referendum has however been conducted in 2004 for the first time. On that occasion, voters rejected the proposed ratification of the Treaty establishing a Constitution for Europe. Important constitutional amendments of the past include the 1848 reform which limited the powers of the King; the introduction of proportional representation and universal (male) suffrage instead of a district system for parliamentary elections in 1917; and the general overhaul of 1983 when, among other things, social rights were added to the human-rights catalogue and the term of the First Chamber was cut from six years to four so as to match the term of the Second Chamber.

6.4. The Charter for the Kingdom

The Charter (*Statuut*) for the Kingdom represents a de-colonization scheme devised in the 1950s. Rather than separating from what was left of the Dutch colonial empire, the overseas territories of Suriname, in South America, and Curacao, a group of island territories in the Caribbean Sea later renamed Netherlands Antilles, placed their relations with the Netherlands proper on an entirely new footing. The three countries set up a quasi-federal Kingdom wherein both the motherland and the two colonies would become autonomous sub-units, which would only exercise certain powers jointly. After Suriname left the Kingdom to become fully independent in 1975, the number of constituent countries fell to two. In 1986 the island of Aruba gained a separate status, leaving the Netherlands Antilles, bringing the number of constituent countries in the Kingdom of the Netherlands back to three: the Netherlands (Europe), the Netherlands Antilles, and Aruba. In 2010 the Netherlands Antilles were dissolved, with the island of Curacao and the Dutch half of the island of Saint Martin gaining Aruba-like separate status, thereby increasing the number of constituent countries in the Kingdom to four. The other three Antillean islands, which were perceived to be not as economically viable as Aruba, Curacao and Saint Martin, were converted into quasi-municipalities of the European Netherlands.

All four current countries are entities in a system that Dutch doctrine describes as a *sui generis* system with federal characteristics. The countries have a common head of state, which is the Dutch King (Art. 1a Charter for the Kingdom). All three countries furthermore enjoy home rule, each with its own government, parliament, and constitution (Arts. 41 and 42 Charter for the Kingdom). In the case of the overseas countries, this meant far-reaching autonomy from the former Dutch colonial power; in the case of the Netherlands proper, this meant that the Dutch Constitution of 1815 would simply continue to operate for the Kingdom in Europe, the country for which it was devised in the first place, subject to the supremacy of the Charter for the new overarching Kingdom (Art. 5 (2) Charter for the Kingdom). The Charter designates some core powers to be exercised Kingdom-wide through institutions common to the Kingdom's four constituent countries, most notably foreign affairs and defence, as well as matters concerning citizenship and naturalization, extradition and immigration (Art. 3 Charter for the Kingdom). Effectively, the pre-Charter Netherlands proper agreed to transfer these core powers to the new quasi-federal Kingdom.

The Charter stops short of creating entirely new Kingdom institutions for the exercise of Kingdom powers, however. Thus, there is no separate Kingdom parliament alongside the Dutch, the Aruban one and those of Curacao and Stain Martin. Instead, the Charter builds upon the pre-existing Dutch government institutions in The Hague. If a matter is a Kingdom competence, then executive decisions are taken, and legislation is passed, by the Dutch government and parliament in The Hague with the participation of ministers plenipotentiary from Aruba, Curacao and Saint Martin. In effect, when the Dutch council of ministers discusses matters that affect the Kingdom as a whole, the council's membership is simply expanded to include the overseas envoys (Art. 7 Charter for the Kingdom, see also Chapter 5); the meeting is then re-labelled 'Kingdom Council of Ministers'. Similarly, when legislation is to be adopted in The Hague that affects the Kingdom as a whole, and not just the Netherlands, then the overseas envoys are involved in the process and the legislation is labelled *rijkswet*, or Kingdom Statute, rather than simply *wet* (Arts. 15 to 18 Charter for the Kingdom, see also Chapter 4). Overall, the Kingdom is heavily Europe-dominated. Although in practice the Kingdom is ruled by consensus, formally the overseas envoys can delay but not stop the adoption of decisions for the Kingdom in The Hague. In the Kingdom Council of Ministers, the overseas envoys can ultimately be outvoted (Art. 12 (5) Charter for the Kingdom). A proposal for an amendment to the Charter, however, requires an explicit qualified approval from the parliaments of the Caribbean countries (either two-thirds majorities in first reading or simple majorities in two readings) before the Europe-based Kingdom lawmaker can change the Charter by a Kingdom Statute (Art. 55 Charter for the Kingdom).

Chapter 3

FEDERALISM, UNITARISM AND DECENTRALIZATION

1. Overview

Federalism is a principle relating to the territorial distribution of power within a constitutional system. Federalism obtains where the component regions of a state have their privileges, especially their constitutional autonomy, their legislative competences and their participation in federal decisions, enshrined in the national constitution. The opposite of a federation is the unitary state, where power can be devolved to regions but can also be taken back from them by a decision of the central authority without the involvement of the regions themselves. There is no general theory of federalism that would unambiguously define a system as being federal or otherwise. There are many shades of grey, as it were, between a centralized unitary state and a loose association of regions. However, when we observe systems that are considered federal, we can inductively identify certain common characteristics which do distinguish such federal systems from unitary states. Typically, a federal system displays the following characteristics.

Division of Territory
The territory of the state is divided into smaller component territorial sub-units. Federalism is therefore a territorial concept. Other forms of consociation, such as power-sharing between ethnic or religious groups which have no specific regional attachment, are not typically considered to be a form of federalism.

Regional Autonomy
The sub-units possess regulatory powers and separate institutions which are autonomous with respect to the central authority. In a 'pure' federation, regions would therefore be able to set up their own constitutional system and regulate their own affairs without interference from the national capital. Often, however, the federation as a whole prescribes certain minimum standards. For example, both Germany and the US guarantee that each of their respective component States must maintain a republican form of government.

Federal Supremacy
Federal (national) law has supremacy over the law of the sub-units. If federal law does not override conflicting regional law in the areas where the federation is competent, then the regions would be completely autonomous. In that case, there would not be sufficient cohesion to call the state federal, and the system would be rather called a *confederation* of otherwise independent states. Alternatively to federal supremacy, a very strict separation of mutually exclusive competences may apply. If any one power can be exercised by only one level at a time, federal supremacy is not necessary. This principle applies in the Belgian system. Most federations in the world however award supremacy to federal law.

Regional Representation
The sub-units are represented at federal level. This is one of the most crucial criteria, in that federations provide for the participation of their regions in federal decision-making. As a result, the regions are not merely the passive recipients of federal law, and they are not isolated from the national level. Instead, apart from having autonomy for their own affairs, they have a stake in the system as a whole as well. Regional representation in the national capital is typically ensured via an upper chamber of a bicameral parliament. The lower chamber would then represent the population of the federation as a whole.

Codification of Prerogatives
The autonomous powers of the sub-units and their representation at federal level are enshrined in the national written constitution. Regions in unitary states may receive their powers from ordinary national legislation; the insertion of these principles in the constitution ensures that federalism is a fundamental and entrenched feature of the state.

Participation in Constitutional Amendment
The sub-units are involved in the process when the constitution is changed. Without such involvement, the regions would depend on the will of the central authority for the maintenance of their autonomy and prerogatives. Involvement in federal constitutional amendment usually takes the form of a two-chamber approval at national level or of the ratification of amendments in the regions themselves, or both.

Constitutional Court
An independent arbiter resolves conflicts between the central authority and the sub-units over the scope of their powers. Such arbiter is usually the judiciary, more specifically a constitutional court or court of arbitration. Allowing the central authority to unilaterally interpret the scope of regional powers would make the system de facto unitary; allowing the states individually to define their own powers would weaken national cohesion and might tear the federation apart.

1.1. Degrees of Federalism and Devolution

It is difficult or even impossible to define, let alone find, an ideal-type federation. Federations differ in the amount of power they reserve for their component regions. Austria is considered to represent a 'milder' form of federalism compared to, for example, Germany. The Austrian *Bundesrat* or upper chamber is composed of senators who are elected by the regional parliaments, they are not bound by instructions from their home regions, and they can normally only delay but not stop the adoption of federal laws. The German counterpart, which is also called *Bundesrat*, meanwhile represents the regional governments themselves, votes are taken uniformly region by region, and vetoes can be overruled only by higher-than-usual majorities or, in many cases, they cannot be overruled at all because the chamber's consent is required. Austria therefore rather stresses national unity at the expense of regional powers, while Germany features a stronger regional representation. At the same time, the regional governments represented in the German Bundesrat wield varying numbers of votes, depending on their population size. In the US Senate, by contrast, all States, even small ones, are guaranteed two senatorial seats. Federalism is stricter when it emphasizes the notional equality of its component parts. Still, both Germany and the US reserve residual legislative powers to the States: what the constitution does not stipulate as a federal competence automatically belongs to the competence of the individual States. In Canada, for example, the presumption is construed the other way around: competences are federal unless they are assigned by the constitution to the provinces.

Meanwhile, states that are unitary may display features which are actually characteristic of federations. The concept of devolution or decentralization of power, which is found in virtually all states, after all underlies the very concept of federalism. The common idea is that certain types of power should be exercised centrally and for the whole nation, whereas other types of power should be exercised in a decentralized manner. Decentralized decision-making allows diverse regions, or municipalities, to take into account local needs and conditions. Devolution of power from the centre to the regions in, for example, the UK, Italy or Spain, has been significant.

Federalism versus Unity?

To conservative forces in unitary states, the notion that their state should become federal can evoke images that the central authority is weakening and the homeland is falling apart. Often, however, the introduction of a federal structure or far-reaching decentralization is a compromise that is designed to appease and co-opt secessionist movements and in fact keep the state together as a whole. The adoption of federal or quasi-federal models in Spain, Belgium or post-war Iraq was exactly to accommodate autonomy-minded ethnic or cultural groups so as to ease tensions while preserving the country as a whole.

Furthermore, several states feature a bicameral parliament even though they are not considered federal. The Czech Senate is elected in districts, rather than by proportional representation; the French Senate represents the country's territorial subdivisions and is chosen by elected national, regional and local office-holders from the departments; the members of the Dutch First Chamber are elected by the parliaments of the provinces. Of course, the presence of upper chambers in these unitary states can be explained by historical factors. Most notably, having another chamber to provide a counterweight against the lower chamber is often considered desirable by itself. In the Czech case, we may recall that the Senate actually was a proper federal upper chamber when it still represented the Czech and Slovak constituent parts of Czechoslovakia; after the split between the Czech Republic and Slovakia in 1992, however, its federal purpose was lost, and bicameralism in the unitary Czech Republic was preserved for other reasons (Slovakia, incidentally, simply became unicameral). Thus, it might be argued that, without conceding that they are in fact federal, many unitary states subscribe to the same federalist ideas of decentralization and diffusion of power. In fact, it is possible that in certain areas a strongly decentralized unitary state allocates more powers to its regions than a mildly federal system does.

1.2. Types of Federalism and Devolution

Depending on the aspect studied, federal systems can be classified under different headings. One fundamental distinction is that between *integrative* federalism, on the one hand, and *devolutionary* or centrifugal federalism, on the other hand. In some cases, states that used to be independent decide to pool their powers to create a new federal system. Examples of such integrative federalism include Switzerland (whose core cantons united in the 13th century), the United States of America (unification in the 18th century) and Germany (first unification as a nation-state in the 19th century). In the opposite scenario, formerly unitary entities would re-establish themselves as federations or devolve so much power to their regions that they become federal. Examples of newly constituted federations replacing unitary predecessors include post-colonial India, post-colonial Mexico, post-apartheid South Africa and revolutionary Soviet Russia. A prime example of devolutionary federalism in a continuous and originally unitary state is Belgium, which established powerful regions as well as communities along linguistic lines in the late 20th century. Another example is the re-definition of the Kingdom of the Netherlands as comprising the Netherlands proper and the territories in the Caribbean region in a quasi-federal construct.

Another aspect where different federal states have adopted different solutions concerns the symmetry of distribution of power among the regions. In *symmetrical* federations, each component region is considered equal, in that the scope of regional power is the same for all component parts of the territory. In systems of *asymmetrical* federalism, meanwhile, some regions have greater autonomy than others. Also decentralization in unitary states can be symmetrical or asymmetrical. Spain features a system whereby Catalonia or the Basque country have secured greater autonomy compared to the 'autonomous communities' in the Spanish heartland. The territorial units of Russia differ in their degree of autonomy between the status of Russian provinces and so-called autonomous republics. The devolution process in the United Kingdom first accorded Scotland far-reaching autonomy, while Wales was initially granted fewer powers. The French island of Corsica enjoys a slightly different status compared to other French regions. The Kingdom of the Netherlands is heavily asymmetrical in favour of the Kingdom's European part.

The term 'devolution' typically points to a transfer of power, particularly legislative power, to selected regions in an asymmetrical manner. 'Decentralization' has connotations of symmetry and is typically limited to administrative or regulatory powers. The difference between legislative and administrative or regulatory power is that legislation may be passed on certain designated areas in principle freely, while administrative or regulatory power only means the power to implement specific pieces of national legislation.

Even where the scope of power is the same for all regions, symmetrical federations may still differ in the way they award the individual regions national representation. In Germany, the number of votes per State in the Bundesrat depends on population size; while small States are still over-represented, in that respect they are treated differently compared to States in the US which all have the same number of senators.

1.3. *Federalism and the European Union*

Federalist terminology is at times employed in the context of the European Union. If we were to apply, just for a minute, our earlier criteria of a federation to the EU, we would come to observe some striking similarities. The Union has been set up by states that wished to pool their powers and exercise them through common institutions. The Union has a large territory that is made up of smaller sub-units, namely the member states. It has permanent lawmaking institutions whereby one body represents the people of Europe, namely the European Parliament, and one body that represents the governments of the sub-units, namely the Council of Ministers. It is through the Council – and the even higher-ranking European Council which brings together national heads of state and government – that the sub-units are involved in European lawmaking, and European laws (directives and regulations) are applicable and enforced by the courts in the sub-units. European Union law can enjoy supremacy over conflicting national law. The rules of the European game cannot be changed without also involving the sub-units: in fact, in order to set up European institutions and determine and change the scope of their powers, all sub-units have to agree to, and ratify, treaties. The competences of the European institutions are enshrined in these written treaties, and power not conferred upon the European level remains with the sub-units (Article 5 (2) TEU). All sub-units have the same status but some of them, for example, have not adopted the common currency and therefore retain greater autonomy in that field. The Court of Justice of the European Union, finally, controls whether the treaties are observed by all European institutions and by the sub-units. If we were to stick to our earlier definition, we would conclude that the European Union functions along the lines of slightly asymmetrical integrative federalism.

> *A European Super-State?*
>
> To some, the idea that the European Union functions like a federation is associated with a terrifying scenario whereby Europe becomes a gigantic state above the nations, regulating everything centrally and draining its member states of their sovereignty and independence. However, we should note that especially in comparison with other federal systems, the EU secures the position of the several member states to a very high degree. The member states are involved at every turn of the road. In fact, the EU is set up by the member states themselves because they either cannot, or do not want to, act alone. The reforms to improve European supervision of the banking sectors and of the government finances of the member states, which have been tabled and adopted in the wake of the financial crisis and the European debt crisis, for example, were not an attempted power-grab from 'Brussels' but something that the member states wanted themselves. European integration in fact embodies the same idea that ever more countries actually accept for themselves in their own constitutions, namely that it is desirable to have both a central government and regional authorities, each regulating what may be regulated best at their respective level.

1.4. Summary

Both federalism and devolution or decentralization embrace the same underlying idea, namely that some powers should be exercised for the state as a whole while the exercise of some other powers should be left to smaller territorial entities. The difference between federations proper, on the one hand, and decentralized unitary states, on the other hand, lies in the source of power of the territorial sub-units. In federations, the autonomy and prerogatives of the sub-units, notably their legislative autonomy and their participation in federal decision-making, derives from the common constitution. In unitary states, the sub-units such as provinces or regions receive their powers from the national capital, and these powers can in principle be withdrawn, even against the will of these regions themselves, in a move towards greater centralization. As regards the systems under consideration, three are federal or quasi-federal (the US, Germany and the Kingdom of the Netherlands) while three are unitary (the UK, France, and the country of the Netherlands in Europe). Of the three federations, the US is symmetrical, to the point that it does not even allow the national capital to be located in one particular State but, instead, assigns a separate capital territory. Representation in the Senate is equal for all States. Germany is symmetrical as far as the scope of the States' powers is concerned, but the weight of representation in the national upper chamber varies with population size. The Kingdom of the Netherlands is asymmetrical in that it is based on pre-existing Dutch institutions in The Hague, and the country of the Netherlands can overrule the Caribbean islands. The US and Germany are, historically, integrative federations, while the Kingdom of the Netherlands represents a devolutionary setup in a formerly colonial system.

All three unitary states, meanwhile, feature a form of devolution or decentralization. France, which until the 1980s had been considered the arch-type of a centralist state, today features regions as well as greater autonomy for its departments, the traditional territorial subdivisions. A separate devolution process has taken place with respect to the island of Corsica as well as overseas territories. The Netherlands considers itself a decentralized unitary state, where the Constitution attributes legislative power to the national legislature and national legislation in turn assigns powers to provinces and, more importantly in Dutch perception, municipalities. The UK has embarked on a devolution process to assign greater powers to Scotland, Wales and Northern Ireland (whereas attempts to devolve powers to the different regions of England have met with scepticism). Devolution regarding Scotland may even result in a referendum to allow the Scottish population to express its opinion about further devolution or, eventually, independence. All three unitary states considered here are bicameral, but for different historical reasons, and neither upper chamber represents the respective regions as such.

1.5. Further Reading

M. Burgess, *Comparative Federalism: Theory and Practice* (London: Routledge 2006).
A. Gamper, 'A Global Theory of Federalism: The Nature and Challenges of a Federal State', 6 *German Law Journal* (2005), p. 1297-1318.
J. Kincaid & G. A. Tarr (eds.), *Constitutional Origins, Structure, and Change in Federal Countries* (Montreal: McGill-Queen's University Press 2005).
K. Lenaerts, 'Federalism: Essential Concepts in Evolution – The Case of the European Union', 21 *Fordham International Law Journal* (1997-1998), p. 746-798.
L. Thorlakson, 'Comparing Federal Institutions: Power and Representation in Six Federations', 26 *West European Politics* (2003), p. 1-22.
R. Watts, *Comparing Federal Systems*, 3rd ed. (Montreal: Institute of Intergovernmental Relations 2008).

2. The United States

The United States of America is a federal system, comprising a federal authority and originally thirteen, now fifty constituent States. New States can be admitted to the US federation by an Act of Congress (Art. IV (3) US Constitution). All of the current fifty States have their own constitution; they are all republics and have a presidential system of government. They feature State parliaments, which all have, save for unicameral Nebraska, two chambers; the State executives are headed by directly elected governors. Furthermore, each State has its own State court system. The District of Columbia, the federal capital district, is not a State; instead, it is governed directly by federal authorities (Art. I (8) US Constitution). Meanwhile, the federal character of the national level in the US is reflected in all three branches of the federal government (the federal legislature, the federal executive and the federal judiciary) as well as in the separation of powers between the federal level and the States.

2.1. US Federalism: The Senate

As regards the federal legislature, Congress operates as a bicameral federal parliament (Art. I (1) US Constitution). One chamber, the House of Representatives, represents the people of the US. It is elected in nation-wide general elections (Art. I (2) and 14th Amendment US Constitution). The other chamber, the Senate, represents the several States, and each State, no matter its size, is represented by two Senators (Art. I (3) US Constitution). Each Senator is elected within the State that he will represent: originally by that State's parliament, since 1913 by that State's people directly (17th Amendment to the US Constitution). This means that all Senators are accountable to the population of their respective State, while no State is penalized for having a smaller population (see for further details Chapter 4). In the constitutional amendment process, no State may be deprived of equal representation in the Senate against its will (Art. V US Constitution).

The Senate has important prerogatives in the federal government structure. The Senate's consent is always required to pass federal legislation; it cannot be overruled by the House of Representatives (Art. I (7) US Constitution; see also Chapter 4). It is the Senate, not the House of Representatives, that has to give its approval if the President concludes international treaties, and if the President nominates heads of federal agencies, government ministers ('secretaries') and other executive officers, as well as federal judges (Art. II (2) US Constitution). Furthermore, it is the Senate that tries impeachments (Art. I (3) US Constitution). This means that it is the Senate that decides, by a two-thirds majority of members present, whether or not the President, the Vice-President or any other executive officer is guilty of treason, bribery or another high crime or misdemeanor and should be removed from office (Art. II (4) US Constitution; see also Chapter 5), or whether a federal judge has failed to exercise his judicial powers in 'good behaviour' (Art. III (1) US Constitution; see also Chapter 6) and should therefore be removed from office. Thus, the Senate, and through it the several States, have a crucial role in federal lawmaking and in maintaining checks and balances with respect to the federal executive and the federal judiciary.

2.2. Federalism and the House of Representatives

While the Senate is set up to represent the States, the federal character of the United States is also reflected in the election mode of the House of Representatives, the other chamber of Congress. In principle, the House represents the people of the United States, rather than the several States; for this purpose it always was directly elected. The numbers of House members are however allocated per State based on census results, and each State must have at least one seat (Art. I (2) and 14th Amendment US Constitution). The States themselves decide on the borders of the single-member districts that correspond to the seats they are allocated (see also Chapter 4). Thus, even House elections reflect the federal principle: congressional districts never cut across State borders and even very small States are guaranteed one House member, in which case the entire State counts as one congressional district.

2.3. Vertical Separation of Powers

Separation of powers is a crucial concept in the US Constitution: three branches of government, keeping each other in check, are separated from each other by 'barriers'. Apart from this horizontal separation of powers, however, a vertical dimension exists that separates the federal level of government from the level of the States.

In the United States, Congress as the federal legislature cannot simply pass statutes on whichever subject it deems fit. The governing principle is that Congress only has those powers which are explicitly enumerated in the US Constitution. If a matter is not stated in the Constitution as being a federal competence, and as long as it is not prohibited to States by that Constitution either, it remains a competence that the States – or the people – can exercise by themselves (10th Amendment to the US Constitution). The States and people thus have residuary legislative powers, meaning all powers that are not prohibited, or delegated to the federal level, by the Constitution. In those cases where powers are delegated to the federal level, however, federal statutes that are enacted pursuant to the Constitution are, just like the Constitution itself, qualified as the supreme law of the land, overriding State law and State constitutions (Art. VI US Constitution). The supremacy clause ensures the effectiveness of federal law in those areas in which the Constitution grants powers to the federal level.

The core legislative competences of the federal level are enumerated in the constitutional provisions on the powers of Congress, starting out with the formulation 'The Congress shall have power to…' (Art. I (8) US Constitution). Additional explicit competences are conferred upon Congress by other provisions and by subsequent amendments (for example the 14th Amendment to the US Constitution). The US Constitution in turn also provides a number of limitations upon federal competences, explicitly prohibiting Congress to exercise legislative power in certain manners or for certain purposes. Such limitations are contained in the original body of the Constitution (such as Art. I (9) US Constitution) as well as in the amendments (very prominently the 1st Amendment to the US Constitution).

The enumeration of limited powers for Congress, and the retention of the rest of powers with the States or the people, unless prohibited, may appear very restrictive on the federal legislature. However, the open-ended nature of some of the core power-conferring provisions should be taken into account as well. Two clauses stand out in this context: the 'commerce clause' and the 'necessary and proper clause' (both contained in Art. I (8) US Constitution). The 'commerce clause' provides that Congress may 'regulate commerce with foreign nations, and among the several states, and with the Indian tribes', while the 'necessary and proper clause' allows Congress to 'make all laws which shall be necessary and proper for carrying into execution the foregoing powers, and all other powers vested by this Constitution in the government of the United States, or in any department or officer thereof'. Both clauses give rise to federal regulatory and criminal-law competences. Congress has been using both clauses to great success by interpreting very broadly what policy areas affect interstate 'commerce', and what is 'necessary and proper' in order to implement its enumerated powers. The US Supreme Court, interpreting the

Constitution, is in turn prepared to look generously, although not without limits, at the scope of federal powers.

Concerning the necessary and proper clause, the Supreme Court, in the 1819 case of *McCulloch* v. *Maryland* (17 U.S. 316), has ruled:

> 'Let the end be legitimate, let it be within the scope of the constitution, and all means which are appropriate, which are plainly adapted to that end, which are not prohibited, but consist with the letter and spirit of the constitution, are constitutional'.

The case arose from a dispute between the State of Maryland and the newly established US federal bank, whereby Maryland challenged the constitutionality of the incorporation of a federal bank. The Supreme Court noted that, while the US Constitution does not explicitly authorize the setting up of a federal bank, the creation of such a bank can be deemed necessary and proper in order for Congress to collect taxes and support an army. That is, in turn, a power that the US Constitution does confer upon Congress explicitly, so the incorporation of a federal bank is, by extension, authorized as well.

A prominent example of the extensive use of the commerce clause can be found in the upholding of federal civil rights legislation by which Congress addressed racial discrimination in the 1960s. In the 1964 case of *Heart of Atlanta Motel Inc.* v. *United States* (379 U.S. 241), a motel challenged the constitutionality of the Civil Rights Act of 1964, which put a ban on discrimination of black people in public places, including hotels. The Supreme Court held that Congress could impose such a ban since racial discrimination might deter black people from travelling from State to State which would in turn affect interstate commerce. Located strategically at an interstate highway near a State border, the motel in question had mostly out-of-State guests. Even if patrons are mostly from within the State, and therefore have not crossed any State borders, it is sufficient that a substantial portion of the food that a restaurant serves comes from other States, which again affects interstate commerce. Thus, Ollie's Barbecue, a restaurant in Alabama which had previously refused to serve black customers, could not rely on the unconstitutionality of the Civil Rights Act either, as the Supreme Court held, also in 1964, in *Katzenbach* v. *McClung et al.* (379 U.S. 294). Congress therefore could legislate under the commerce clause to combat racial discrimination.

The Power of the Purse

Even if Congress cannot bring regulatory activity under the commerce clause or the necessary and proper clause, it still retains its budgetary spending power (first clause of Art. I (8) US Constitution) as an important tool to achieve its aims. Thus, Congress need not impose directly enforceable federal regulations if it can encourage the States to enact equivalent regulations themselves. For example, Congress secured a nationwide minimum drinking age of 21 years by giving financial incentives to the States to pass State laws and enforce the new (higher) minimum age. The incentive in this case is that, pursuant to the Federal Highway Aid Act (23 USC § 158), States that do not have such a minimum age law lose part of their entitlement to federal road-building

> subsidies for highways. In the 1987 case of *South Dakota* v. *Dole* (483 U.S. 203) the Supreme Court found such a conditionality provision in a federal spending programme a 'relatively mild encouragement' to State action, which is lawful under the federal taxing-and-spending power. States still have the choice to adopt a lower minimum drinking age if they so desire, while Congress, as a federal lawmaker, stays within the limits of the powers that the US Constitution confers upon it.

In spite of its broadness, there are also limits to the extensive interpretation and use of the commerce clause, which was brought home to Congress in the 1995 case of *United States* v. *Lopez* (514 U.S. 549). After half a century of leniency, the US Supreme Court stepped in to declare unconstitutional federal legislation for being outside the scope of the commerce clause. The 1990 Gun-Free School Zones Act had imposed a ban on firearms in and around schools, and the defendant had carried a gun into his high school. The Supreme Court rejected the government's reasoning that the statute was justified under the commerce clause because violent crime, and the distractions caused by guns in a schooling context, would negatively affect the economy and interstate travel. Such reasoning was too far-fetched, in the Court's view, and it was made clear that not everything that might be remotely commerce-related gives rise to federal legislative competence. Otherwise, Congress would at some point acquire virtually unlimited federal legislative powers, and federal authorities would gain general police competences that are so far reserved to the States.

2.4. *Federalism at Presidential Elections*

The federal character of the US system is also reflected in the way the President, the head of the federal executive, is elected. If the President and Vice-President were elected by direct popular vote, it would mean that small States would have fewer votes because of their smaller population size. Instead, the President and Vice-President are elected by electors from the States (Art. II (1) and 12th Amendment US Constitution), whereby differences in size between the States are mitigated. Each State is entitled to have as many electors as it has Senate seats, namely always two, plus the number of seats it has in the House of Representatives, which is at least one. Thus, even a very small State, as well as the capital district (23rd Amendment to the US Constitution), will be entitled to at least three electors. States may and do keep separate voting procedures for their electors and small States are over-represented to balance out differences in size between the States. As an additional federal safeguard, the presidential and vice-presidential candidate on the same electoral ticket must be from different States, since electors are barred from voting for two candidates from the same State.

2.5. *Federalism and the Executive and Judicial System*

As regards the judiciary, the federal character of the US is expressed very prominently. There is a separate system of federal courts which have their own hierarchy;

next to that, each State has its own court system (see also Chapter 6). This means that the US has, in effect, fifty-one judicial systems, corresponding to one nation-wide federal jurisdiction (which is also competent for Washington, D.C.) plus fifty State jurisdictions. Each State decides for itself when and where to set up State courts, such as local court divisions, State courts of appeal and State supreme courts. It is also the States which determine the procedure for the appointment or election of their State judges. Under federal jurisdiction, the United States Supreme Court is the highest federal court, and it is established directly by the US Constitution; lower federal courts are established by federal statute (Art. III (1) US Constitution). State and federal courts are not in principle in a hierarchical relation to one another; instead, they operate in parallel to each other, each within its own jurisdiction, even though jurisdictions sometimes overlap.

The system of a federal court hierarchy next to fifty State court hierarchies resembles the organization of executive agencies. The States have their own agencies to carry out activities under State laws, while in order to execute federal statutes the US has established its very own network of federal agencies and branches across the country. Both systems are in marked contrast with, for example, the German federal system, where States are entrusted to execute federal legislation while State courts, with federal courts on top of the hierarchies, are entrusted to apply federal statutes in judicial proceedings. Similarly, relies on the member states to transpose EU directives into national law and to collect or to enforce EU environmental or work safety standards: in the US such tasks would be carried out by federal agencies. Furthermore, national judges are expected to uphold EU law in domestic court proceedings, there are no separate courts for the application of EU law

3. Germany

The Federal Republic of Germany bears its federal character already in its name. The German territory is composed of sixteen States, called *Länder* (singular: *Land*). Each State has its own constitution, all featuring a republican and parliamentary system of government. All States have their own parliaments, which are mostly called State Diet and which are all unicameral (Bavaria abolished its upper chamber in 1999); State governments are headed by State prime-ministers who are accountable to their State parliament; State courts are integrated, however, into a nation-wide judiciary.

The German Basic Law contains several provisions to express and preserve Germany's federal character. Already the first united German nation-state, the German Empire founded in 1871 and its immediate predecessor, the North German Confederation, were federal in character, be it that Prussia played a dominant role as the overwhelmingly largest State. Under the republican Weimar Constitution of 1919, Germany remained federal. The only period when modern-day Germany as a whole was a unitary state was during the Nazi dictatorship, where the federal States were suppressed and the territory was instead divided into administrative districts. After Germany's defeat in World War II, the restoration of a federal structure in the West, coupled with the splitting up of Prussia into several smaller States, was seen as a safeguard against too great a concentration of power in the national capital. The new democratic (West) German Basic Law, adopted in 1949, explicitly states that Germany is a democratic and social federal state (Art. 20 (1) Basic Law). The German Democratic Republic in the East, by contrast, went on to become unitary: its five States were replaced by administrative districts in 1952, and its Socialist Party-controlled upper chamber convened for one last time in 1958 to approve its own abolition; the five eastern States re-constituted themselves only after the fall of the Berlin Wall. The (West) German federal constitutional principles that now apply to the whole of Germany, the division of Germany into States, and the States' participation in principle in federal lawmaking, are covered by the 'forever clause' and cannot be amended (Art. 79 (3) Basic Law).

3.1. German Federalism: The Bundesrat

As far as German legislative institutions are concerned, the prime expression of federalism, and the involvement of the States at the German federal level, is the institution of the Bundesrat, which translates as 'Federal Council' (see also Chapter 4). The Bundesrat is a co-legislative chamber that operates next to the directly elected parliament, the Bundestag or 'Federal Diet'.

Each State has its own parliament and its own government. All sixteen States function according to a parliamentary system, which means that the State governments rely on the support or tolerance of a majority in their State parliaments. The Bundesrat consists of members of these sixteen State governments – premiers and ministers – or their representatives (Art. 51 (1) Basic Law). The State governments are represented in the Bundesrat on a permanent basis, speaking on behalf of their State. If there is a change of government in a State, for example because the government lost its parliamentary majority after elections, that State's representation is taken over by the new government, which will from then on speak on behalf of that State. The Bundesrat itself keeps operating the entire time. Since elections in the sixteen States do not take place all at once, but all follow their own rhythm, the composition of the Bundesrat is in constant flux, changing every time a State happens to be taken over by a new government.

Each State is allocated a fixed number of votes (Art. 51 (2) Basic Law), roughly reflecting population sizes but mitigating differences between the States by over-representing smaller States. A State can only send as many representatives as it has votes (Art. 51 (3) Basic Law), but the number of representatives present will not influence the number of votes the State is allocated. Thus, contrary to the United States Senate, where Senators are elected on a personal basis in their State for a fixed term, the German Bundesrat is a permanent chamber comprising State governments. The Bundesrat does not have a fixed term, nor can it be dissolved or re-elected, because all sixteen State governments are simply present all the time, only represented by changing people.

It is through the Bundesrat that the sixteen States have a say in the federal legislative procedure. The presence of the Bundesrat next to the Bundestag, the parliament proper, ensures that State governments are not only the passive recipients of federal law, but play an active role, balancing out the majoritarian-democratic element in parliament with a federal element in the Bundesrat. However, whereas in the United States the Senate and the House of Representatives are co-equal as far as the adoption of statutes is concerned, the German Basic Law in principle allows the directly elected parliament to overrule the Bundesrat, unless the Basic Law provides otherwise (see Chapter 4). The federal element thus cedes to some extent to the democratic element of the German constitution.

3.2. Federalism and the Bundestag

While German federalism in the legislative institutions is primarily expressed through the Bundesrat, even the directly elected parliament, the Bundestag, displays a federal element in its composition. Set up to represent the German people as a whole (Art. 38 (1) Basic Law), the Bundestag nevertheless features an electoral system that reflects the fact that Germany is composed of sixteen States, and that political parties have subdivisions in the States as well.

The electoral system of the Bundestag is a mixed-member proportional system (see Chapter 4 for further details). Political parties compete for the proportional allocation of Bundestag seats via party lists that their regional branches draw up State by State. Under the system that applied until 2011, the seats won by political parties based on their share of the vote nation-wide were subdivided between their individual State lists, depending on how many of its votes came from which State. Thus, if a party owed a quarter of its success to votes that were cast for its list in the State of North Rhine-Westphalia, then a quarter of that party's seats were allocated to its list from that State. Under the system as is was introduced in late 2011, Bundestag seats are first divided between States based on their share of total voter turnout, and in each State party lists compete for the seats allocated to their respective State. Either way, party lists are not national lists but State lists, and the system aims to ensure not only proportional representation between political parties but also proportional representation between States, in other words a regional spread in the membership of the Bundestag.

3.3. The Competences of the Federal Lawmaker

The States' prerogatives under the German Basic Law are not limited to their participation in federal lawmaking via the Bundesrat. Federal statutes cannot be passed in all areas in the first place. As far as the internal distribution of power between federation and States in Germany is concerned, the federation legislates only in those areas where the Basic Law so provides. If a power is not enumerated in the Basic Law as being subject to federal legislation in one way or another, this power is retained by the States (Art. 70 (1) Basic Law). Like the US Congress, the German federal lawmaker – Bundestag and Bundesrat – relies on a competence catalogue from which it derives power to legislate, while the States keep residuary legislative competence (see also Chapter 4).

The German Basic Law in fact features two such federal competence catalogues. The first category of federal competences are the exclusive federal competences, where only the federal lawmaker can legislate, unless a federal statute explicitly authorizes the States to legislate as well (Arts. 71 and 73 Basic Law). Areas of exclusive federal competences include, for example, foreign relations, citizenship, and air traffic. The second category are competences for concurrent legislation, where the States can legislate only when and in as far as the federal lawmaker has not legislated already (Arts. 72 and 74 Basic Law). This area includes the law on associations, labour law and waste management. Since 2006, States may adopt legislation that deviates from already existing federal law in areas of concurrent competences, such as hunting, regional planning and admission to higher education (Art. 72 (3) Basic Law). Any areas that are neither exclusive federal competences nor areas for concurrent legislation remain exclusive State competences. The most notable cases where the sixteen States are exclusively competent to regulate on their own, because these cases have been omitted in the two federal competence catalogues, concern cultural policy, primary and secondary education, and ordinary policing powers. In practice, the States coordinate with each other their activities in areas where they are exclusively competent, such as rules on German orthography, the mutual recognition of high school diplomas or the design of police uniforms. Such coordination takes place in regular inter-ministerial conferences.

It should be noted that the degree to which the Bundesrat is involved in federal lawmaking does not depend on whether the federal statute concerns exclusive federal or concurrent competence. As soon as the federal level is involved, the Bundesrat is involved as well, for the Bundesrat is a federal co-legislator. Whether its veto with respect to the Bundestag is suspensive or absolute only depends on whether the applicable constitutional provision states that the Bundesrat's consent is required to pass a statute or not.

3.4. *Federalism and the Election of the Federal President*

The German head of state is the Federal President. The President is elected by an electoral college called Federal Convention (Art. 54 (1) Basic Law, see also Chapter 5). The federal element of Germany's Basic Law is reflected in presidential elections in the way the Federal Convention is composed. The Federal Convention is a single-purpose gathering; it convenes only in order to elect the Federal President. The Convention comprises all the members of the Bundestag, plus an equal number of delegates who are elected by the parliaments of the sixteen States (Art. 54 (3) Basic Law). The distribution of the States' half of Convention seats among the individual States is calculated proportionally on the basis of the States' share of the total German population; the delegates from each State are then elected, again based on proportional representation, by that State's parliament. The composition of the Convention reflects both the majoritarian-democratic principle and the federal principle of the German constitution, by bringing together elected national parliamentarians and delegates from the States in equal numbers.

3.5. *Federalism and the Executive and Judicial System*

The involvement of State governments in federal lawmaking via the Bundesrat is justified in a federal logic, not just because it reflects the fundamental federal principles of the German constitutional order (Arts. 20 (1) and 79 (3) Basic Law). States will have to accept that federal law has supremacy over State law (Art. 31 Basic Law) and, more pertinently, the States are expected to execute federal legislation once it is adopted (Art. 83 Basic Law). The execution of federal statutes by the States stands in marked contrast to the system in the United States, where the federal executive has to set up agencies of its own if it wishes to implement federal legislation. While the US system thus places a strong emphasis on the separation between federal and State authority, Germany puts an emphasis on the cooperation between the States and the federal level, both at the adoption and at the execution stage.

In line with these principles of cooperative federalism, the judicial system of Germany is characterized by a division of court hierarchies into inferior courts, which are State courts, and a layer of supreme courts, which are federal courts (Art. 92 Basic Law). The federal level has set up five main supreme federal courts, one for each main subject-area jurisdiction, plus a number of specialized federal courts (see Chapter 6). As a result, court hierarchies exist within each of the sixteen States, including local, district and appellate levels, with one federal court on top of each hierarchy.

Contrary to the United States, where federal courts and State courts operate in parallel hierarchies next to each other, the German judicial system relies on State courts to apply both State and federal law, under the supervision of a layer of federal supreme courts. The States furthermore participate in the appointment of ordinary federal judges, in a process involving federal ministers and committees that consist of State ministers and members who are elected by the Bundestag (Art. 95 (2) Basic Law); the States are also involved in the appointment of Federal Constitutional Court judges via the Bundesrat, which elects half the judges on that Court (Art. 94 (1) Basic Law, see also Chapter 6).

4. The United Kingdom

'Federalism' is a term that should be used with great caution in the United Kingdom. Since much of UK constitutional law revolves around the sovereignty of Parliament in London, and therefore the supremacy of statutes over all other sources of law, federalism is bound to provoke certain tensions. The UK neither wishes to become federal itself, nor does it wish to become part of a larger European federation (although it already might be, see Chapter 6). Nevertheless, the practical benefits of power-sharing with smaller territorial units and decentralization are increasingly endorsed within the UK. These notions find their most prominent expression in the process that is called 'devolution'.

Devolution means a process whereby Parliament adopts statutes in order to create sub-national authorities, and whereby it hands them over legislative powers that they can exercise for themselves. Thus, under the Scotland Act 1998, Parliament created a separate parliament for Scotland, and the Government of Wales Act 1998 and the Northern Ireland Act 1998 set up a Welsh national assembly and revived a legislative assembly for Northern Ireland, respectively. The Greater London area has also received powers going beyond those of an ordinary local authority, which makes it a beneficiary of devolution as well.

The most far-reaching devolution has initially been conducted with respect to Scotland in 1998. Through its own Scottish parliament, Scotland can in fact exercise all legislative powers for its own territory, unless these powers are reserved to Westminster, or are otherwise forbidden, or until Westminster reassumes its power to legislate for Scotland (Sections 28 and 29 Scotland Act 1998). Powers that Westminster has explicitly reserved for itself are enumerated in a detailed list and include matters of foreign affairs, defence, currency, fiscal and economic policy (but not local taxes for the funding of local expenditure), immigration, intellectual property law and many more (Schedule 5 Scotland Act 1998). What remains as devolved powers are powers that are either not mentioned as being reserved or that are mentioned as being exceptions from a reserve. These include culture, education policy, tourism and health care. Apart from its general overriding competence, Westminster will by convention only legislate for Scotland in a devolved matter if the Scottish parliament has accepted a 'Sewel motion' and has expressly invited Westminster to pass a statute for Scotland. This customary rule is named after Lord Sewel who proposed adhering to it. Sewel motions are indeed not uncommon; usually they do not invite Westminster to pass separate statutes for Scotland but rather request the extension of planned legislation for England and Wales to cover Scotland as well.

> *Sovereignty of the Scottish Parliament?*
>
> When it devolved legislative powers to the Scottish parliament, Westminster Parliament explicitly stipulated that Scottish legislation may not violate European Union law or the rights contained in the European Convention on Human Rights (Section 29 (2) Scotland Act 1998). The latter qualification is noteworthy: Acts of Parliament of the UK cannot be invalidated for an alleged violation of Convention rights; Scottish laws enjoy no such protection. Acts of the Scottish parliament do not enjoy legislative supremacy like UK statutes do, at least as long as Scotland remains a part of the United Kingdom.

What sets UK devolution apart from genuine federal systems is that federal entities derive their power from the constitution itself, whereas devolved entities receive theirs from the central government. Devolution implies a conferral of powers in a top-down manner. This conferral can be enhanced or reversed at will by the central authority. The Scotland Act 1998, for example, explicitly provides that devolution does not prevent Westminster from passing statutes for Scotland anyway (Art. 28 (7) Scotland Act 1998); in fact, such a provision would not even be strictly necessary, because Westminster can just as well revoke the entire Act altogether, either explicitly or by implied repeal. Westminster's discretion is also evident with respect to the other devolved authorities. Thus, the assembly of Wales has at first only received executive powers, not legislative ones; only the subsequent Government of Wales Act 2006 expanded Welsh devolution further. In Northern Ireland, a separate regional parliament had already been set up in 1921, but it was suspended in 1972, the region then being brought under direct rule from London; the powers devolved to the restored Northern Irish parliament in 1998/1999 were again suspended in 2002, when the peace process in the region stalled, and later granted again. Neither Scotland, nor Wales, nor Northern Ireland have a formal say in such devolution decisions, because neither country is represented at the central level as such.

> *The West Lothian Question*
>
> In the course of devolution, especially with regard to Scotland, questions concerning regional representation in the national capital in parallel to devolution do arise. The dilemma is known as the 'West Lothian Question', after the home county of the parliamentarian who first brought it up in the 1970s. It arises from the fact that the UK House of Commons is still elected via constituencies, which include electoral districts that are located in Scotland. The 'anomaly' is that Scottish members of the Commons can help pass laws that apply to England, but, if the matter concerns devolved powers, not to their own home constituents in Scotland; conversely, while Scottish parliamentarians have a vote on statutes affecting England, parliamentarians from English districts, if they accept devolution, cannot in turn pass statutes for Scotland. A far-reaching proposal to address the West Lothian Question would be to create a separate English parliament and expand existing devolution, which would place England, Scotland, Wales and Northern Ireland on an equal footing – although any separate English parliament would dwarf the other regional assemblies by far. An experiment to devolve power to English regions, namely the North-East of England, has been rejected in a referendum held there in 2004. Other options include the exclusion of Scottish parliamentarians from votes that have no bearing on Scotland, or the cutting down of the number of Scottish districts which leads to fewer Scots in the Commons. Arguably, the West Lothian Question cannot be resolved at all as long as there is no clear understanding of what or who exactly is represented in a national parliament. After all, other systems do not have such trouble accepting that devolution and national parliamentary representation can operate side by side.

5. France

The French Republic can be characterized as a moderately decentralized unitary state (Art. 1 French Constitution). Such characterization comprises two elements, namely that fundamental constitutional power is vested in central institutions, while the state also accepts that its administration should be delegated to smaller territorial sub-units. The basic unitary nature of France, and its traditional centralization of power in the capital city of Paris, goes back to the post-revolutionary and Napoleonic regimes. France had been unitary already under the pre-1789 absolutist monarchy, although the local nobility had been exercising power in the countryside. After the Revolution, in an effort of centralization of power, France created a strong national government in Paris. It abolished the historical provinces and replaced them, in 1790, by administrative districts called *Départements*. Departmental borders were deliberately drawn across historical regional borders; departments were named after their prominent natural landmarks and were subsequently numbered to emphasize the unity and homogeneity of the nation and the pure rationality of its subdivisions. Centralism was seen as a logical consequence of, and precondition to, the equality of all people, the rule of law and the exercise of national sovereignty. Departmental and local authorities were charged with implementing national policy within the limits set by national statutory law and the Constitution; the central authority was represented locally through a prefect.

It was in the later part of the 20th century, then, that France in turn embraced a more determined approach to decentralization of power. In 1982, executive powers in the departments were transferred from the prefect to the departmental council president. On the same occasion, regions, originally established in 1972, were given the status of a formal layer of government above the departments, and the regional councils have been elected directly, rather than indirectly, since 1986.

The Constitution provides the legal basis for decentralization, as well as decolonization in the case of overseas territories (Arts. 72 to 75 French Constitution); further details are laid down in statutory law. The furthest-reaching autonomy as regards overseas dependencies has been granted to New Caledonia in the Pacific. The island of Corsica, off France's Mediterranean coast but part of metropolitan France proper, has also received special autonomous powers. Its two departments were disconnected from a mainland region and formed their own region in 1975; this region was reformed into a 'territorial collectivity' in 1991, with a Corsican assembly for a regional council and with slightly greater powers compared to a region proper. A further-reaching possibility of delegation of central legislative powers to Corsica by statute has been declared unconstitutional by the Constitutional Council, however, considering that the Constitution does not permit any such delegation beyond what is expressly allowed (Decision of 17 January 2002, 2001-454 DC).

A constitutional reform in 2003 introduced changes that allowed for further decentralization. Most importantly, decentral authorities are allowed to deviate, on an experimental basis and under tight conditions, and based on a statute or regulation within the limits set by organic statute, from national legislation (Art. 72 French Constitution). These authorities however still remain under oversight from the national government.

Thus, like in other decentralized but unitary states, the competences of the territorial sub-units in France derive from statutes that are adopted in the national capital, without the sub-units having a direct say in their adoption. Based as it is on voluntary devolution of power downwards, French decentralization can be expanded, or taken back, at the discretion of the national lawmaker, within the limits set by the Constitution. Although the Senate is charged with the representation of France's territorial subdivisions (Art. 24 French Constitution), this does not mean that France is federal, since the state is indivisible (Art. 1 French Constitution). Like other senates in unitary states, the French Senate should above all be seen as a counterweight against the lower chamber, in this case one that over-represents the rural population (see also Chapter 4).

6. The Netherlands

The first appearance of an independent Dutch political entity occurred when, in 1579, seven provinces in the lowlands united in their armed rebellion against Spanish rule to form the United Provinces. The United Provinces were a republic, but rather loosely confederal in nature; they lasted until the invasion by revolutionary France in 1795, and the subsequent creation of the unitary, French-modelled Batavian Republic. The land remained unitary as the Kingdom of Holland, a Napoleonic vassal state created in 1806, and in the period following the territories' incorporation into France proper in 1810. After Napoleon's defeat, the Congress of Vienna agreed on the creation of the Kingdom of the (United) Netherlands, an independent unitary state that covered roughly the modern Netherlands and Belgium. It was that state that would, after the secession of Belgium in 1830, become the modern-day European Netherlands. Thus, while originally a 16th century confederal project, the Netherlands emerged from the Napoleonic wars as a unitary state.

6.1. Decentralization in the Netherlands

The Netherlands is a unitary but at the same time a decentralized state. Provinces and municipalities are set up by statute (Art. 123 Dutch Constitution). Dutch doctrine actually considers the municipalities, rather than the provinces, to be the more important level of decentralized power.

The Dutch territory is divided into twelve provinces, which are further subdivided into municipalities. Each province has a directly elected parliament, called 'provincial states'; the municipalities elect municipal councils (Art. 125 Dutch Constitution). The provincial executive is headed by a King's Commissioner who is appointed by the central government; in the municipalities, unusually for a Western democracy, the mayor is appointed by the central government as well (Art. 131 Dutch Constitution). A constitutional amendment to abolish the appointment of mayors, and to allow for elections instead, has been narrowly rejected by the First Chamber in second reading in 2005.

The Constitution allows the provinces, as well as the municipalities, to regulate 'their local affairs' (Art. 124 (2) Dutch Constitution), although that is a very flexible term. The details regarding the scope of provincial and municipal powers are defined by ordinary statute. Provincial powers lie mostly in the area of zoning and infrastructure. Local and regional power extends only to regulation, which does not mean legislation but only the implementation of legislation. Legislative powers proper are reserved to the central lawmaker. Thus, local and regional regulation is always subordinate to national legislation. Crucially, the Constitution allows for the central government to exercise supervision over the provinces and municipalities, both under 'preventive supervision', meaning approval of local or regional decisions before their adoption, and 'repressive supervision', meaning the annulment of decisions already adopted (Art. 132 Dutch Constitution).

Next to territorial decentralization, the Netherlands also features functional decentralization of power, the most prominent functionally decentralized entities being the water boards which manage surface waters (Art. 133 Dutch Constitution). Again, the shape and power of decentralized entities are fixed by ordinary national statute.

It is true that the Dutch senatorial First Chamber is elected by the members of the Dutch provincial assemblies, which might at first glance resemble a system of federal bicameralism. However, the First Chamber does not turn the Netherlands into a federation. Senators do not represent a specific province, as the votes from provincial parliamentarians are counted on a nation-wide basis under proportional representation (see also Chapter 4). The election by provincial parliamentarians, introduced in 1848, is simply the more democratic alternative to the previous system, whereby the members of the First Chamber were appointed by the King for life. Both Chambers of the Dutch parliament retain a mandate to represent the entire Dutch people (Art. 50 Dutch Constitution).

6.2. The Overarching Kingdom

In 1954, the Netherlands, which during the 'golden age' as the United Provinces had acquired a significant trade-driven colonial empire, implemented a far-reaching de-colonization measure. The last remaining overseas possessions that wished to keep their ties with Europe, Suriname and the Curacao island territories (later renamed Netherlands Antilles), entered into a quasi-federal order with their former colonial motherland. Together, the Netherlands and the two overseas countries set up an overarching Kingdom of the Netherlands governed by the Charter for the Kingdom. Essentially, the term 'Kingdom' was redefined: originally the Kingdom was the Netherlands, and the colonies were akin to mere 'appendages'; now the Kingdom is an overarching legal construction comprising the Netherlands and the overseas territories alike. Since the founding or rather the re-definition of the Kingdom, Suriname became fully independent, and the current Caribbean countries are Aruba (which became a separate constituent country next to the Netherlands Antilles), Curacao and Saint Martin (which in turn emerged as separate countries when the Netherlands Antilles were completely dissolved in 2010). The remaining Antillean islands, the so-called BES islands (Bonaire, Saint Eustatius and Saba), became, also in 2010, de facto municipalities of the Netherlands in Europe, and are therefore not constituent countries of the Kingdom.

United by the Dutch King as hereditary head of state, the Kingdom exercises a number of core competences, including defence, foreign affairs and citizenship, for its constituent countries jointly (Art. 3 Charter for the Kingdom); for the rest, the constituent countries are autonomous, possessing their own governments, parliaments and constitutions (Arts. 41 and 42 Charter for the Kingdom). The federal Kingdom is Europe-centered rather than symmetrical, however. Instead of maintaining a separate government and parliament, the Kingdom's executive and legislative powers are in fact exercised by the Dutch institutions in The Hague, albeit in special configurations and with qualified procedures involving representatives from the overseas countries. These representatives, called ministers plenipotentiary, participate in Dutch cabinet meetings (Art. 7 Charter for the Kingdom, see also Chapter 5) and in lawmaking (Arts. 14 to 18 Charter for the Kingdom, see also

Chapter 4) whenever overall Kingdom interests are concerned. Whenever these Kingdom procedures apply, the institutions act as Kingdom institutions and are named as such: the government turns into the Kingdom Council of Ministers, with its membership expanded to include the overseas representatives, for example, and the advisory Council of State, also with expanded membership, acts in its capacity as Council of State of the Kingdom.

> *The Autonomy of the Overseas Countries*
>
> Compared with France's and Britain's dependencies in the Caribbean region, Aruba, Curacao and Saint Martin enjoy far-reaching autonomy from their motherland; even decisions that are taken in Europe are based on consultation and consensus. In order to explain this arrangement, it is helpful to note that the Charter for the Kingdom had originally been intended to keep the far larger colony of Indonesia within the realm. Accordingly, the concessions from the motherland to the colonies were extensive. In the event, Indonesia declared itself fully independent from the Kingdom anyway; the tiny colonies in the Caribbean region, however, were more than happy to accept their new status under the Charter.

Chapter 4

PARLIAMENTS AND LAWMAKING

1. Overview

A system of representative democracy is based on the idea that citizens do not take all decisions on their public affairs themselves. Instead, persons or institutions elected by the citizens take these decisions on the citizens' behalf. Parliament, a central elected lawmaking assembly, plays a crucial role in ensuring that the rulers are still the representatives of the ruled. In that context, parliament exercises two core tasks under constitutional law: *legislation* (taking decisions that bind the citizens on the citizens' behalf, including the budget) and *control* (scrutinizing, again on behalf of the citizens, other government institutions, especially if the latter are not directly elected). Underlying both functions, since parliaments are elected multi-member forums with shifting majorities and minorities, is a representative and communicative function in society. Thus, even groups that are opposed to a piece of legislation are duly heard in a process of public deliberation. Minority input is in fact crucial for holding the majority, and majority-supported institutions, to account. Elections at regular intervals are to ensure that the parliament keeps reflecting popular preferences, that minorities have a chance to become majorities, and that the members of parliament remain accountable to the citizens they represent.

Although it might be convenient to treat 'parliament' and 'legislature' as synonyms, or to generically call parliamentarians 'lawmakers', the notion that parliament makes laws should be understood rather critically. First, often parliament does not in fact initiate and draft laws by itself. In parliamentary democracies, legislation is usually prepared and introduced by the government, which has at its disposal the ministerial civil service with its technical expertise. Nevertheless, since this legislation then still has to pass a parliamentary process and in principle requires the approval of a parliamentary majority, parliament does provide democratic legitimacy for new laws through its consent. Second, often parliament is not the only lawmaker. In a federal system legislative powers may be assigned to the regions (although in that case there will be regional parliaments to carry out legislative tasks). Usually the government is allowed to enact detailed regulations, or ordinances, in order to implement laws. Referendums, where they exist, may repeal and replace laws made by parliament, and so may courts, to the extent that they are assigned the power to quash or even alter legislation found incompatible with, for example, the constitution. In constitutional monarchies, the lawmaker is often defined as the monarch and his government acting *together* with parliament; that is the case in the Netherlands and Belgium, and in the United Kingdom where technically the lawmaker is the King-in-Parliament as the monarch gives assent to bills passed by Parliament. In member states of the European Union, binding European legislation, most notably directives and regulations, can override domestic legislation. Since the national parliaments' approval is not required for their adoption, parliamentarians who wish to stay involved in the European legislative process will need to rely on other means to extract timely information, provide input and hold the decision-makers to account. At the same time, while national parliaments are not lawmakers at EU level, most EU legislation requires the approval of the European Parliament, which is to a large extent modelled after national parliaments and which is elected to represent the citizens in EU decision-making, even though it does not necessarily function in the way that domestic assemblies do.

> *The Mother of all Parliaments*
>
> The term 'parliament' derives from the French *parler* (to talk) and describes an assembly where policies are debated. The term originates in 13th century England when the King would summon landowning nobility, senior clerics as well as representatives of towns and boroughs to discuss and approve new taxes. The UK Parliament at Westminster, though it is not the oldest in the world, has been a prototype for parliaments around the world in many respects. A parliamentary system where the majority forms the government is in fact called the 'Westminster model'. Furthermore, Westminster Parliament is a prototype for a bicameral system, comprising a 'lower' chamber which is directly elected and an 'upper' chamber which is unelected, elected indirectly, or at least elected differently from the lower chamber.

In spite of all these practical qualifications, legislation passed by the central parliament enjoys a crucial role in constitutional systems. Many constitutions stipulate that a certain area may only be regulated by statute. Such a 'legislative reserve' typically applies to human rights, meaning that a limitation on such rights is permissible only if it is adopted by the legislature. This notably excludes limitation by a simple government order. The Dutch Constitution, for example, distinguishes between limitations on fundamental rights *by* statute and *pursuant to* statute, the former meaning that the limitation must be laid down in legislation while the latter allows for legislation to delegate regulatory authority for such limitation. A legislative reserve ensures that certain sensitive matters are regulated in the highest-ranking norm under the constitution, namely statute, and that they are discussed in an open forum involving parliamentary minorities. To draw a stark contrast, the German Nazi Party secured the passage of an Enabling Act in 1933 which allowed the government to henceforth adopt legislation on its own, without parliamentary approval, even if it deviated from the Constitution. This move consolidated the legal basis for the Nazi dictatorship. The modern Basic Law, among other safeguards against any future dictatorship, prescribes that constitutional amendments must be passed explicitly, not by way of a *carte blanche*.

Once adopted, statutes, or acts of parliament adopted by the democratic legislature, typically enjoy stronger immunity from judicial review compared to delegated legislation or government decrees. German judges, for example, can check the constitutionality of government ordinances and set them aside on their own if they violate the Basic Law; statutes, however, must be referred to the Constitutional Court. The same principle applies to all Kelsenian systems where a special constitutional tribunal is set up to review legislation (see also Chapter 6).

As regards a parliament's controlling function, again its character as a forum should be stressed. It is convenient to juxtapose *the* parliament as against *the* government as a matter of constitutional law. The logic of a parliamentary system, where the government relies on parliamentary confidence or tolerance to stay in office, hinges on the possibility for parliament to, in return, hold the government to account and to sanction it. Still, in reality we should note that parliaments consist of individual parliamentarians who are typically organized in political party groups. If a party group provides the government, or is in a coalition with other party groups to provide a government, then these 'government' parliamentarians must reconcile a critical attitude with a task to keep their own ministers in office. After all, their party has been elected with a view to form and support a stable government. Parliamentary dynamics instead thrive on minority input: political parties that are in opposition to the incumbent government are the ones who in reality contest and question the government most incisively. In presidential systems, incidentally, parliamentarians tend to be more independent from the government since their respective tenures are not as directly intertwined. Parliament's refusal to support the government will not automatically lead to a fall of the government; and a crisis in the executive administration will not automatically lead to new general elections. The US Congress has a reputation of being more independent and less bound by party discipline compared to European parliaments, where the majority is at the same time the power-base for the executive.

Party Discipline

Many systems recognize a certain tension between the independent mandate of an elected member of parliament, on the one hand, and the coherence of political parties, on the other hand. Especially in parliamentary systems, where the cabinet relies on parliamentary support to stay in office, party discipline forces parliamentarians to vote according to their party line. Party discipline may be justified by the legitimate expectations of voters that the party they support will act in a predictable manner; in Germany, parties are even constitutionally recognized as important institutions to contribute to national will-formation (Art. 21 Basic Law). The party system in the Parliament of the UK is famous for having 'party whips', individual members assigned by their party leadership to enforce uniform voting according to party line; on important votes, such as on ethical questions, parties however at times

> explicitly waive party discipline and allow each member of parliament to make up his own mind. In the US Congress, whip functions are exercised by the respective majority and minority leaders, but there party discipline is less pronounced: not only is the majority, due to the presidential system, not expected to keep the executive in office; the constituency-based election system and primary-based candidate selection process also gives strong incentives for individual members to seek benefits or exceptions for their home State (Senate) or their home district (House) before much else.

1.1. *Principles of Elections*

If the members of parliament are to represent the citizens, then a method must be devised how to actually translate voter preferences into the composition of parliament. Yet while it is tempting to focus immediately on the technical details of different election systems, we should first consider some fundamental principles underpinning the election process in a representative democracy. Having a parliament does not automatically mean having free and fair elections. Authoritarian one-party states may well sport a parliamentary assembly, but there the seats are contested in sham elections which do not leave voters an actual choice. In dictatorial regimes, the incumbent may resort to violence, intimidation of the opposition and vote-rigging in order to stay in power. Election systems are therefore only meaningful if certain fundamental principles are observed, which are often indeed summed up in the demand that elections be free and fair.

The German Basic Law provides an oft-quoted catalogue of five election principles, namely that parliamentary elections must be general, direct, free, equal and secret. These principles are also expressed in, for example, Art. 14 TEU, which stipulates that elections of the European Parliament must take place by direct universal suffrage in a free and secret ballot. The principle of *general* elections, or universal suffrage, means that the entire voting population must be entitled to participate in the vote. Since the 19th century and into the first half of the 20th century, Western democracies have one by one expanded the franchise so as to give women an equal right to vote: New Zealand in 1893, Finland in 1906, the US in 1920, and many more countries during the inter-war period and immediately after World War II. In Europe, Appenzell Innerrhoden was the last Swiss canton to enfranchise women in 1990. Similarly, universal suffrage has been introduced to replace limited suffrage systems whereby only wealthy or tax-paying citizens could vote. In the Netherlands, wealth or taxation was a condition for enfranchisement until 1917; the UK abolished all property requirements and thus introduced universal suffrage in 1928. A restriction on the right to vote still common today is the imposition of a minimum voting age, the exclusion of resident foreigners from the vote, as well as the exclusion of nationals living abroad; an example of the disenfranchisement of individuals relates to the removal of voting rights for convicted criminals, which many countries prescribe or allow.

> *Hirst v. United Kingdom*
>
> In a judgment of 6 October 2005, the Grand Chamber of the European Court of Human Rights (no. 74025/01) ruled that a blanket deprivation of voting rights of all convicted prisoners, irrespective of individual factors such as the gravity of their offence or the length of their sentence, as then practiced by the UK, is incompatible with the right to vote as guaranteed by Article 3 of Protocol no. 1 to the European Convention on Human Rights. This does not mean that all convicted prisoners must therefore be given the right to vote, and the Court indeed noted that a great diversity of approaches exists among European states in this matter; but, according to the Court, 'automatic and indiscriminate' disenfranchisement goes beyond the states' margin of appreciation, i.e. the room within which they are free to adopt their own solutions.

Directness of the vote, or direct suffrage, means that votes must be cast for contestants immediately, rather than for electors who would then go on to cast the actual vote (as had been the case in 19th century Prussia). *Freedom* of the ballot allows each voter to make up his own mind without interference. In Germany this also means that a voter may decide not to vote at all, whereas in Belgium citizens are actually legally obliged to participate in the vote as a civic duty (although there they can tick an 'abstention' box or cast an invalid vote). *Equality* of the vote is often expressed in the 'one-person-one-vote' principle. This means that each vote carries the same weight. In the past, some systems for example distinguished between voters based on their wealth. The parliament of Prussia in the 19th century was divided into three equal sections, each section being elected by citizens falling in a corresponding tax bracket. This meant that wealthy citizens were over-represented because they constituted far less than a third of the population. In the UK, graduates of certain universities could cast two votes rather than one up until 1948: one for their geographical constituency and one for their university constituency.

> *Votes of unequal weight*
>
> A recurring problem in certain types of election systems, notably single-member and multi-member constituencies, in other words district systems, is that even when each voter has one vote, their votes carry unequal weight depending on the seat-to-voter ratio. If two districts elect the same number of parliamentarians but one district is twice as populous as the other, then each vote from the smaller district carries twice the weight of a vote from the larger district. Similar effects are observed if the number of seats is roughly but not directly proportional to population size. In the European Parliament, where EU member states essentially count as electoral districts, large member states have fewer seats than they would be entitled to if their shares of total seats were proportional to their share of the total EU population, while small member states are over-represented. As a result, a German member represents many times more voters than a Maltese member, but both have equal voting rights in the European Parliament. And even where the number of seats is proportional to population size, votes from districts where few voters actually do participate in the elections will carry more weight than votes from districts with a high voter turnout.

Secrecy, finally, prescribes that a person's voting behaviour must not be made public, that votes are cast in closed booths rather than by hand-raising, and that no-one may be forced to reveal for whom he voted. In that sense, secrecy of the ballot is important to safeguard the freedom of the vote.

1.2. Election Systems

The question how to actually devise an ideal election system has occupied many political philosophers and mathematicians in the course of history. Cynics may point out that election systems can be designed to fit certain preferences and guarantee or at least favour certain outcomes. Either way, a broad variety of electoral systems exists throughout the world. Most election systems fall into one of two broad families of systems: majoritarian systems and proportional representation. In a *majoritarian system*, a contested seat is awarded to the candidate who wins a defined majority of votes in a certain constituency, or district; under *proportional representation*, the number of parliamentary seats that a political party wins relates to its share of the vote.

The simplest form of a majoritarian system is the first-past-the-post system as applied to single-member constituencies. In such system, the territory of a state is divided into electoral districts, or constituencies, which elect one parliamentarian each. The number of districts then equals the number of seats in the parliamentary chamber. In each district, the candidate who obtains a plurality, or relative majority, of votes cast wins the respective seat. It is then not necessary for the winning candidate to reach any minimum percentage of the vote; what is decisive is that he has obtained one vote more than the second-strongest candidate. The UK House of Commons and the US House of Representatives are elected via such a first-past-the-post system in single-member constituencies. A more sophisticated form of a majoritarian single-member constituency system is a system whereby a candidate must receive an *absolute* majority of votes, instead of merely a relative majority. An absolute majority means more than half of the total votes, and therefore more than the votes for all other candidates combined. Such an absolute majority single-member constituency system however needs to provide for a solution in case no candidate receives the required share of the vote. The system used for elections of the National Assembly of France, for example, relies on a runoff system. If no candidate receives an absolute majority representing a quarter of registered voters in their single-member constituency in the first round, a second round, or runoff, is held whereby the strongest candidates from the first round, namely those whose vote shares represent one-eighth of registered voters, may run and whereby a relative majority suffices to win. In an alternative vote system, by contrast, as it is used for the Australian House of Representatives, there is no runoff after the first round. Instead, voters can rank the candidates on their ballot paper by order of preference, and if no candidate obtains an absolute majority, the second and subsequent preferences of voters who had supported losing candidates are transferred to the other candidates until one of them does. The idea is still the same as in a runoff system, however, in that it is required that, at the end of the process, any winner in a single-member constituency is supported by more than half the voters. The alternative vote system had been proposed in the UK as well but was rejected in a nation-wide referendum in 2011.

> *Rejecting AV*
>
> The alternative vote system had been advocated in the UK to ensure that the composition of the House of Commons, while still not based on proportional representation, might be more representative with respect to nation-wide election results, and that smaller parties would stand a more realistic chance of being represented in Parliament. After all, whereas in a single-round first-past-the-post, or FPTP system small-party supporters would fear wasting their votes on unsuccessful candidates, forcing them to tactically support a big-party candidate, AV allows them to express their true first preference while still indicating their second choice. In the run-up to the 2011 referendum on this issue, the movement against AV mainly claimed that the proposed system was more complicated than FPTP and that it would not definitively solve its problems, notably the wasted votes phenomenon; in the end, a widely held view was that while FPTP was far from perfect, AV was not the better alternative solution, and that ultimately the choice should be between FPTP and proportional representation.

In a system of proportional representation, several or all seats in parliament are contested at once. While a number of mathematical models exists how to assign seats to competing political parties, the fundamental principle remains that, for example, twenty percent of the votes should roughly translate into twenty percent of contested seats. Three main types of proportional representation systems can be distinguished. One is the list system, which is for example used in Israel, allowing voters to cast their votes for political parties which then go on to fill the parliamentary seats they have won from their pre-established list of candidates. The single transferable vote system, as used for example in Ireland, meanwhile relies on multi-member constituencies where voters can rank-order their candidates of choice. The system re-allocates surplus votes from candidates who have safely won a seat, and the votes from those who have been eliminated, to the remaining candidates of second choice until all seats in the multi-member constituency are distributed. Mixed-member proportional systems such as the German one, finally, include combinations of proportional representation and single-member constituency systems, so as to benefit from the advantages of both systems. The Netherlands uses proportional representation for the elections of both of its chambers.

Broadly speaking, single-member constituency systems ensure a direct and personal link between a parliamentarian and his voters – citizens can approach 'their' member of parliament to express local grievances – but it can lead to a distortion of overall popular preferences. After all, much depends on the size and shape of the districts; a party that narrowly wins small districts, and loses by a huge margin in large districts, can eventually have a smaller number of votes nation-wide but still win a majority of seats in parliament. Furthermore, since voters are aware that only the winning candidate will receive a seat and the other candidates will receive none, an effect called 'winner-takes-all', they will be wary to 'waste' their votes on small-party candidates and instead only support promising candidates. This typically leads to the emergence of a two-party landscape, with candidates of either one or the other large party winning districts. This typically ensures stable governments, as cabinets are formed by alternating absolute majorities – although the 2010 elections in the UK proved that even a first-past-the-post system can yield a 'hung parliament', when no party had an absolute majority so that two parties had to enter a coalition to form one. Still the system under-represents smaller parties, especially if their supporters are geographically dispersed and constitute minorities in many districts rather than majorities in a few.

In systems of proportional representation, meanwhile, the distribution of seats reflects overall public opinion more faithfully, and fewer votes are 'wasted'. When the system relies on party lists for the allocation of seats to candidates, however, the personal element in popular representation suffers somewhat. After all, a purely list-based system allows political parties to rank their candidates in advance of the ballot, giving voters only a say about their party of choice but not about their preferred individual candidates. Some proportional representation systems therefore introduce additional personal elements. The Netherlands allows voters to vote for specific candidates further down the party list, and to break the party ranking.

Proportional representation tends to lead to a multi-party parliament where also smaller parties are represented according to their share of the vote, and where no single party commands an absolute majority of its own. To keep parliament from fragmenting excessively, many systems operate a form of electoral threshold, a hurdle that parties have to clear in order to win seats. This helps keep small parties out. The hurdle can be rather high (ten percent of the vote in Turkey), medium (five percent in Germany), low (two percent in Israel) or very low (one full seat, or roughly 0.6% of the vote, in the Netherlands). Yet even with a hurdle in place, coalition-building is typically necessary to form a cabinet in a parliamentary system. Thus, two or more parties have to agree to form a majority-backed cabinet, which means compromises and possibly a dilution of voter preferences. Single-member constituency systems, meanwhile, to the extent that they give rise to a two-party landscape, are expected to produce single-party governments. The French Fifth Republic deliberately replaced proportional representation with single-member constituency voting so as to consolidate the party landscape in the National Assembly and to stabilize the cabinet.

1.3. *Bicameralism*

Discussions about direct elections and democratic representation through parliament usually focus on unicameral parliaments or the lower chambers of bicameral parliaments. Many parliaments in the world are indeed *bicameral*, meaning that they are not a single assembly but comprise two assemblies, or chambers, next to each other. The 'lower' chamber is then usually directly and democratically elected, and it is the more important one politically and the more powerful one constitutionally. The upper chamber is then typically the additional chamber that complements the lower chamber. The reasons why a parliament has such an additional upper chamber differ from one system to another.

Bicameralism originates in England, where since the 14th century the Commons (representing the citizens of towns and boroughs) would sit separately from the Lords Spiritual and Temporal (clergy and feudal nobility). The feudalistic distinction between Commons and Lords is also the basis for speaking of 'lower' and 'upper' chamber or, as in the Netherlands, of 'first' (upper) and 'second' (lower) chamber. Again, in most bicameral systems, including the UK and the Netherlands, the 'lower' or 'second' chamber is in fact dominant. The historical reason for bicameralism in the UK is to stress the separation of the different estates. As the relevance of feudal nobility diminishes, the future of the House of Lords is a subject of debate, however. Possible options range between turning the Lords into a fully elected chamber and its complete abolition. In federal systems, the upper chamber is typically used to represent the constituent parts of the state as such, next to the lower chamber which is elected in nation-wide elections. The senates of the US and Australia, or the Bundesrat of Germany and Austria, respectively, specifically ensure that representatives from the regional subdivisions, or senators elected within these subdivisions, can participate in federal lawmaking. Arguably, the European Union's legislative institutions are modelled after federal bicameralism as well, where the European Parliament represents the citizens and the Council represents the (governments of the) individual member states.

Several other systems which are neither feudalistic nor federal have adopted or retained bicameralism for more complex historical reasons, often for its own sake. A two-chamber system is often perceived as a means to ensure that decisions are not taken too hastily, and that a counterweight to the majority of the day exists. The very term 'senate' may justify such an approach. The Roman Senatus, from the Latin word *senex* (old), was originally a council of elders. Many modern-day senates are noted for their claim to higher dignity and a calmer working style. They often sit for a longer term, have fewer members and indeed a higher minimum age for membership. The senatorial First Chamber of the Netherlands sees itself as a *chambre de réflexion* or 'chamber of second thoughts' as opposed to the hectic lower chamber. Other countries which have set up, kept or re-introduced a two-chamber system in spite of being unitary states include Poland, the Czech Republic, Ireland and France. The French Senate has been set up intentionally as a counterweight to the National Assembly, with a bias towards the countryside population, and following examples set by earlier periods of bicameralism in French history. Unicameral parliaments are often found in relatively small and ethnically homogenous unitary states, such as the Nordic states in Europe (Denmark and Sweden abolished their upper chamber in the 1950s and 1970s, respectively), Portugal, Greece, and many states in Eastern Europe and Central America.

1.4. *The Legislative Process*

Lawmaking is a crucial task for a parliament and its chambers, but the details of how this task can be exercised differ between systems. The powers that are particularly relevant to a parliament or chamber are:

- the right of initiative (the right to propose legislation);
- the right of amendment (the right to propose changes to draft legislation); and
- the right of veto (the right to stop, completely or subject to an override, the adoption of legislation).

The power of initiative may seem relatively trivial, yet without a proposal there can be no statute. Furthermore, the one who proposes statutes is also the one who decides what is discussed and when: initiative therefore means agenda-setting. In order to shift this prerogative out of international bargaining between the member states, the European Union's ordinary legislative procedure places the exclusive right of initiative with the European Commission (Art. 294 TFEU). Veto power, by contrast, may seem a strong tool; however the total rejection of a proposal is a heavy-handed measure if actually only slight changes to the proposal are desired. Thus, veto power without a power to propose amendments means being confronted with take-it-or-leave-it choices.

> *Parliament Votes*
>
> How does a parliament take a decision? Since a parliament is a multi-member assembly, it needs to be determined how many out of how many members must approve a proposal so that it may be considered to have received overall parliamentary approval. The usual procedure is simple majority vote. Thus, if a parliament has 100 members, and 75 members actually participate in the vote, then a bill, for example, is passed if more members vote 'yes' than vote 'no'. Abstentions count as neither for nor against. The bill is adopted if it receives, for example, 36 votes in favour, with 34 against and five abstentions. The minimum number of members that have to be present at the vote for it to be valid is called quorum. A tougher requirement than simple majority, or plurality, is absolute majority. That is the majority of the members of the parliament rather than a majority of votes cast. In a parliament of 100 members, 51 must actually support a motion or a bill if an absolute majority is required. Even tougher than absolute majorities are qualified or super-majorities, for instance three-fifths or two-thirds of members or votes cast. The graver and more important the decision, the higher the threshold tends to be. Thus, constitutional amendments under rigid constitutions require bigger majorities than ordinary statutes do.

Systems where both chambers of a parliament are co-equal, especially where a bill requires the approval of both chambers to become law, are called *perfect bicameralism*. This means that the upper chamber has an absolute veto as against the lower chamber because it can withhold its approval and thereby stop a bill; that is the case in the US, as well as in the Netherlands. Even these systems are not perfectly bicameral in a strict sense, though, for example because the Senate of the US has a slightly limited power of initiative compared with the House of Representatives and the senatorial First Chamber of the Netherlands does not have that power at all. Indeed, in most bicameral systems the upper chamber's powers of initiative, amendment or veto are restricted. Usually, a veto from the upper chamber can be overruled by the lower chamber, so that the bill may become law even against the will of the upper chamber. In cases of disagreement between the two chambers, a bill may either continue, in principle, to go back and forth until there is an agreement (like in the UK or France) or the process may end after a certain number of readings (US, Germany, the Netherlands). In some systems, a conciliation committee may be established to seek a compromise (Germany, France, US). A veto that cannot be overruled is called an *absolute* veto; a veto that merely delays the adoption of a law is called a *suspensive* veto.

The requirements for a lower chamber to finally overrule the upper chamber differ between systems, too. In Austria, the lower chamber may in most cases simply re-approve the bill in question for a second time to insist on its adoption. In the UK, most bills may be referred for royal assent after a waiting period if the Lords refuse to agree; in France, the government may break an impasse by letting the National Assembly cast the final vote. In Germany, the Bundestag requires a higher majority to overrule the Bundesrat depending on the majority by which the Bundesrat has rejected the bill in the first place, but the Basic Law may also provide that the consent of the Bundesrat is needed so that it cannot be overruled. The Netherlands allows the senatorial First Chamber to approve or reject bills in an absolute manner, but not to propose amendments (although in practice the Chamber does suggest amendments as a precondition for approval); the German Bundesrat may not propose amendments itself either, but can call for the establishment of a conciliation committee which in turn may propose amendments. As noted, the US does not allow either chamber to overrule the other, since the consent of both is required for the adoption of bills. Compromises are facilitated through the establishment of a joint conference committee that has the task to prepare texts acceptable to both chambers. The European Union's ordinary legislative procedure also envisages bicameral approval in the European Parliament and the Council, except that there are still areas where the Council can act without the consent of the European Parliament; in a proper state, legislation with the approval of only the senate and without the consent of the lower chamber would be highly unusual, but then again the European Union is not a state.

1.5. Referendums

One of the rules that underpin a representative democracy is that once the voters have elected their representatives for a certain term, the decisions taken by these representatives cannot be repealed by voters. In many systems this rule is, however, not fully implemented, in that a feature taken from direct democracy is added to an otherwise representative democratic system: the referendum. A referendum is a popular vote on a decision already taken or yet to be taken, which may include the decision whether a draft law should enter into force or whether an already existing law should be repealed or not. The availability of referendums puts constraints on the power of the lawmaker to decide autonomously.

Generally a referendum can be mandatory or optional. In case of a mandatory referendum, a popular vote *must* be held to approve a certain type of decision. For example, in Ireland a constitutional amendment requires a referendum, in which the proposal must be approved, otherwise the proposal is deemed rejected. An optional referendum may, but does not have to be called. Whether it is mandatory or optional, a referendum can be either binding or consultative, which relates not to the question whether to hold one but to the question whether the outcome produces binding effects. In a binding referendum, for example, a proposed decision – such as, again, a constitutional amendment – may not be taken if it is rejected. The outcome of a consultative referendum, by contrast, indicates voter preferences but legally allows representative decision-makers to nevertheless decide otherwise.

Supporters of referendums value the opportunity for voters to express their own opinion without its being translated through representatives whose preferences are not always perfectly aligned with those of the citizens they represent. Detractors are either distrustful of the capacity of referendums to capture complex problems in a simple yes-or-no question, or of the capacity of voters to have a full grasp of complex problems in the first place, or both. While referendums might promote civic responsibility, they might also be abused as a tool for populist movements seeking a crass simplification of policy choices. Cynics might point out that government-initiated referendums are sometimes held to legitimize decisions already taken; in international negotiations, governments might threaten to hold a referendum in their home country as a threat to resist decisions that they oppose anyway; where the government favours a decision that is unpopular, referendums are often avoided, or repeated until the result conforms to the government's wishes.

Of the five systems discussed here, France relies most heavily on referendums as a constitutionally mandated expression of the popular will (Art. 3 French Constitution). In France a national referendum is in principle mandatory to approve constitutional amendments (Art. 89 French Constitution) and the French consent to admit new member states to the European Union (Art. 88-5 French Constitution), even though in both cases a joint session of parliament may be held instead to approve such decisions by super-majority. In addition, the President may call referendums to approve laws under Article 11, which has been used in the past to approve constitutional amendments as well, and to approve the ratification of treaties affecting the functioning of national institutions; since 2008, parliamentary minorities may initiate a referendum as well under Article 11. Germany, by contrast, is historically sceptical of allowing popular input to lawmaking for fear of a populist threat, even though referendums can be, and are, conducted at State and local level. The only cases where the Basic Law envisages referendums for federal purposes relate to the realignment of State borders (Art. 29 Basic Law) and the popular approval of an entirely new constitution to replace the Basic Law (Art. 146 Basic Law). Demands for ordinary federal referendums are sometimes dismissed arguing that the Basic Law does not envisage them, although many scholars point out that strictly speaking it does not prohibit them either. The US Constitution does not feature any nation-wide referendums, which can be explained by the fact that the federal system was historically built upon an association of individual States, each with its own people, rather than upon the idea of a unitary sovereign nation, as it is understood in France. The US States themselves can and do hold referendums, though, a most prominent example being California with a relatively high number of ballot initiatives. The Dutch Constitution does not include any referendums either, although it came into force with the approval of the monarch and with the endorsement in a national referendum; a nation-wide optional consultative referendum has been conducted once, in 2004, in order to seek the endorsement of the ratification of the Treaty establishing a Constitution for Europe (a Treaty which was rejected and which was then replaced by the Treaty of Lisbon). The UK Parliament is free to call for binding or non-binding referendums, without of course limiting its power to ignore the results of consultative referendums or to later repeal statutes approved, or enact those rejected, in binding ones. Nation-wide referendums have been held twice: a consultative one on continued membership of the European Economic Community in 1974, and a binding one in 2011 on a new election system.

1.6. *The Government and the Head of State*

As noted at the outset, it would be deceiving to speak of parliament as the sole lawmaker. Especially in a parliamentary system, the government takes an active role in the legislative process. First, almost all bills are drafted and tabled by the government; second, the rejection of an important government bill in parliament may lead to a cabinet crisis, since it means that the government cannot count on a loyal parliamentary majority. For example in the UK it is considered embarrassing if a government bill is only adopted because the opposition votes in favour while the government's own rank-and-file votes against. Finally, the head of state may participate in the legislative process, in that he signs the bills into law but in some systems might also refuse to sign them.

As regards the introduction of bills, the presidential US system does not grant the President the right of initiative. Nevertheless, he may communicate to Congress his wishes, for example in the form of a request for a budget, or may otherwise let his allies in Congress introduce bills for him. The French President can, depending on his personality and the political constellation, steer the government's legislative agenda as he presides over the council of ministers, so that the prime-minister may in turn introduce bills in parliament. Usually, parliamentary systems simply accord the government the right of initiative. The passage of a bill may at times be explicitly made a matter of parliamentary confidence in the government. This is a means to discipline the government parties and to 'blackmail' parliament into approving a bill, for otherwise a cabinet crisis would be triggered, possibly followed by early elections. In France, if the government makes a bill a matter of confidence, it will even be deemed approved by the National Assembly automatically unless the Assembly brings the government down (although the use of this option has been restricted in 2008).

As regards the veto powers of heads of state, the situation also differs per country. In constitutional monarchies, lawmaking is historically an interplay between parliament and the King. In practice, the crowned heads in modern constitutional monarchies either may not or will not refuse to sign bills into law, however. In the UK it is sometimes said that the King will even have to give royal assent to his own death sentence; a rejection is not inconceivable, but would certainly trigger a constitutional crisis. In Belgium, King Baudouin I in 1990 objected to an abortion law on ethical grounds; he agreed to be declared incapacitated for a few hours so that the bill could enter into force without him having to sign it. In 2008 Grand-Duke Henri of Luxembourg similarly objected to signing a euthanasia law, but this was then followed by a unanimous vote in parliament, which was approved by the Grand-Duke himself, to simply abolish royal assent. In other words, his approval is no longer needed; instead he is constitutionally obliged to sign all bills within three months. In France, the President can refer a bill for constitutional review by the Constitutional Council, and ask for one more parliamentary debate, but will ultimately have to promulgate it within fifteen days. The German President does not possess any explicit veto power, but he conventionally reviews the constitutionality of bills and may, in fact must, refuse to sign bills deemed evidently unconstitutional. The US President does possess an explicit veto power, not just on grounds of unconstitutionality but on any grounds, including policy reasons; his veto may however normally be overruled by super-majorities in Congress. It is then incumbent upon the legislature and the executive to resolve the deadlock in case the opposition to the President does not command the necessary super-majorities in Congress; the need for such resolution is particularly urgent where the President has vetoed the annual budget.

1.7. Summary

The five systems under consideration illustrate the diversity of constitutional arrangements regarding parliaments. All five systems are bicameral, but for different reasons: federal representation (US and Germany), feudalist heritage (UK) and a historical tradition of having an upper chamber as a counterweight to the majority of the day (France and the Netherlands). Four systems use single-member constituencies to elect their lower chamber, but the details differ: first-past-the-post (UK Commons and US House of Representatives), first-past-the-post in a mixed member proportional system (German Bundestag) or a run-off between the strongest candidates from the first round (French National Assembly). Proportional representation is used exclusively in the Netherlands, and in combination with single-member constituencies in Germany. The upper chambers have the power of initiative in four systems (UK Lords, French Senate, German Bundesrat, US Senate except for tax bills) and an amendment power of their own in three systems (UK Lords, French Senate and US Senate). The upper chamber's approval is required for all bills in two systems (US and the Netherlands), while in the other systems the lower chamber can in some or most cases overrule the upper chamber. The head of state has a veto in the legislative process in the US, he has no veto in France, he may only reject unconstitutional bills in Germany, and he will conventionally not refuse to sign bills in the UK and the Netherlands.

1.8. Further Reading

R.L. Borthwick, 'Methods of Composition of Second Chambers', 7 *The Journal of Legislative Studies* (2001), issue 1, p. 19-26.
Ph. Laundy, *Parliaments in the Modern World* (Dartmouth: Ashgate 1989).

A. Lijphart, *Electoral Systems and Party Systems: A Study of Twenty-Seven Democracies 1945-1990* (Oxford: OUP 1994).
A. Lijphart, *Patterns of Democracy: Government Forms and Performance in Thirty-Six Countries* (New Haven: Yale University Press 1999).
B. Manin, *The Principles of Representative Government* (Cambridge: CUP 1997).
Ph. Norton, 'Playing by the Rules: The Constraining Hand of Parliamentary Procedure', 7 *The Journal of Legislative Studies* (2001), issue 3, p. 13-33.
Ph. Norton (ed.), *Parliaments and Citizens in Western Europe* (London/Portland: Frank Cass, 2002).
S. Patterson & A. Mughan (eds.), *Senates: Bicameralism in the Contemporary World* (Columbus: Ohio State University Press 1999).
D. Shell, 'The History of Bicameralism', 7 *The Journal of Legislative Studies* (2001), issue 1, p. 5-17.

2. The United States

The US Constitution stipulates that federal legislative power is vested in Congress, a bicameral parliament comprising the House of Representatives and the Senate (Art. I (1) US Constitution). The House is to represent the people of the US; Senators represent the individual States at federal level. House membership roughly but not exactly proportionately reflects population sizes within the States, while the number of Senators is the same for each State, namely two. Both chambers reside in the Capitol building in Washington, DC.

2.1. The House of Representatives

The House of Representatives is a directly elected assembly. It is elected for a term of two years. Seats in the House are apportioned to the individual States based on their population statistics. Once every ten years, a census is conducted to determine population numbers, and distribution is based on proportionality; each State is entitled to at least one representative, however (Art. I (2) and 14th Amendment US Constitution). The precise number of seats per State is regularly determined in apportionment bills, yet the total number of House seats is fixed by statute at 435. States were in principle free to determine themselves how to have 'their' House members elected (Art. I (4) US Constitution); however, federal legislation has already prohibited State-wide elections for the entire House delegation and instead prescribes a system of single-member constituencies (2 USC § 2c). For the purposes of House elections, therefore, the territory of a State with more than one House seat is parcelled into congressional districts, with each district electing one member to the House. In States that are entitled to one seat only, such as Alaska or Delaware, the whole State territory coincides with its congressional district territory. The State with the largest population as of 2010, California, has 53 congressmen and therefore 53 congressional districts.

> *Gerrymandering*
>
> While the number of congressional districts for a State is fixed under apportionment rules, the borders of the districts are set by the States themselves. Control of the State parliaments is therefore important for a political party's chances of success in federal House elections. When in charge of drawing district borders, a party may resort to a practice called gerrymandering: borders are then drawn tactically to put the opponent at a disadvantage. This is done by 'packing' opposition-friendly population into huge districts (so that they win only one seat each) while 'cracking' the remaining opposition-friendly population into several districts that are each dominated by incumbent-friendly majorities. Eventually, rather than being rectangle-shaped, districts may resemble snakes criss-crossing the State in order to 'catch' relevant populations – snakes or, indeed, salamanders, like the congressional district devised by 18th and 19th century politician Elbridge Gerry to whom the term gerrymandering refers. Thanks to tactical districting in the States, most incumbents in the House are relatively secure in their seats, and few districts are genuinely contested in close races. The US Supreme Court ruled that malapportionment (excessive differences in population sizes between districts) as well as gerrymandering on racial grounds (such as to disenfranchise black minorities) is unconstitutional. Partisan gerrymandering to put political opponents at a disadvantage is not unconstitutional, however.

In order to win a district, a candidate must obtain a plurality of votes. In other words, he must obtain at least one vote more than the second-strongest candidate did. The States determine the procedure for resolving ties between two or more strongest contenders; mostly a lot is drawn.

2.2. The Senate

Unlike the House of Representatives, which represents the people of the US via a district system, the Senate represents the individual States at federal level. It consists of two Senators from each State no matter its size, and thus of a total of 100 Senators.

Originally, Senators were appointed by the parliaments of their States (Art. I (3) US Constitution). This provision was superseded by the 17th Amendment of 1913, however, stipulating that Senators are to be elected by the populations of their States. Senate elections are, like those of the House, based on a single-member constituency principle. Each State is one constituency. Each State decides for itself how to elect its two Senators; most use a first-past-the-post system, however. Thus, to be elected Senator for his State, a candidate must secure a plurality of votes cast in that State. Some States, such as Texas, Georgia or Arkansas, prescribe a run-off between the two strongest candidates if no candidate has achieved an absolute majority in the first round.

The term of office of each individual Senator is six years. A majoritarian system for the Senate is sustainable even though there are two Senators per State, because the Senate is not re-elected all at once. Instead, one-third of the Senate is re-elected once every two years. This means that political change is translated into the composition of the Senate gradually, rather than abruptly. It also ensures that at no point both Senate seats of the same State are contested at the same time. After one Senator is elected (with a majority in his State), the second Senator will be elected or re-elected either two or four years later (again with a majority in that State), but not six years later since that is when the first Senator may run for another term.

> *Two-Party System*
>
> Since both the US Senate and the House are elected in majoritarian systems with single-member constituencies (in the Senate each State is one constituency, for House elections a State may have more than one district), voters tend to back only promising big-party candidates in order not to 'waste' their votes on unsuccessful ones. A two-party landscape emerges, independents or small-party politicians in office are rare. At the same time, candidates tend to be less aligned with their party than they are in European systems. One of the reasons is that even outsiders can become a candidate through the relatively open system of primaries, which are elections held by each party to select candidates who then go on to run in subsequent elections. In European systems candidates are usually nominated in less open internal party conferences.

The Senate is presided over by the Vice-President of the US. The Vice-President has no vote, but his vote does decide in case a Senate vote is tied (Art. I (3) US Constitution). The Senate usually votes by simple majority, but for controversial bills the effective threshold is 60. That is the number of votes required to break a filibuster (a practice whereby Senators would talk endlessly in order to delay the vote) and to actually call for a vote. The filibuster rule is eccentric in a comparative perspective, but despite calls to abolish it, it is still cherished and kept in place as an important minority right.

2.3. Federal Lawmaking

Senate and House together form a bicameral legislature. Federal legislation may be passed only in those areas where the Constitution assigns federal legislative competences (10th Amendment to the US Constitution, see also Chapter 3). Bills, that is legislative proposals, may be initiated by members of both the Senate and the House, but the House enjoys the sole power of initiative for tax bills (Art. I (7) US Constitution). In line with the principle of separation of powers, the President as the head of the executive may not introduce bills (although he can encourage fellow party members in Congress to introduce them for him). All bills must receive the approval of both chambers, no chamber can overrule the other. This 'bicameralism clause' in the US Constitution effectively gives both the House and the Senate an absolute veto in the legislative process.

Furthermore, both chambers have the power of amendment. Within the two chambers, bills are referred for detailed consideration in a committee and are then subjected to further debate, amendment, and a final vote on the floor. If adopted, the bill is referred to the other chamber. If a bill is amended with respect to the previous version as adopted by the other chamber, it is referred to a joint committee of both chambers, called 'conference committee'. The committee can propose further amendments to reach a compromise, to be again voted on in both chambers separately.

2.4. The President

Once a bill has passed Congress, it is presented, under the 'presentment clause', to the President of the US (Art. I (7) US Constitution). As head of state, it is the President's task to sign bills into law; in line with the principle of checks and balances, however, the President can also veto bills passed by Congress. In that case he refers the bill back to Congress, together with his objections. The Congress, in turn, can override the President's veto and insist on the bill's adoption. For that, the chamber where the bill has originated in the first place has to vote again, only this time by a two-thirds majority of members present; if the bill passes, the chamber sends the bill to the other chamber, which also must approve it with at least a two-thirds majority of members present. If no chamber or only one of them musters the required two-thirds majority, the adoption of the bill has failed. It should be noted that the President can only veto a bill as a whole, not individual parts of it.

In case the President neither signs the bill nor vetoes it, he exercises a 'pocket veto' (by putting the bill into his pocket). The bill then becomes a law anyway after ten days excluding Sundays. A pocket veto can however also effectively stop the bill, namely if Congress has adjourned within ten working days after its adoption. After all, a veto strictly means making known to Congress what the President's objections are. However no objections could possibly be transmitted for reconsideration if Congress is no longer in session. Therefore, if the President does not sign the bill and has, because of the adjournment of Congress, no chance to send it back either, the bill does not become a law and the adoption has failed. It would then have to be re-introduced anew. Congress can avoid fatal pocket vetoes by not deferring controversial votes until the very end of a session.

> *Pocket Veto*
>
> Remaining inactive and neither signing nor objecting to a bill passed by Congress can be a political tool for the US President. By letting the bill enter into force after ten working days by default, he can make symbolically known that he does not support the bill, or at least parts of it, but does not find it worth rejecting altogether. However, if an adjournment of Congress is scheduled within ten working days, the President escapes the possibility of being overruled. He then has effectively an absolute veto which he normally would not have.

The execution of federal statutes that have entered into force becomes a task of the executive branch headed by the President and for the federal executive agencies (see Chapters 3 and 5). Its application in judicial disputes is a task for the courts (see Chapter 6).

3. Germany

Germany features a bicameral system for the adoption of federal legislation. On the one hand, legislation must pass the Bundestag, the directly elected chamber and the parliament in the strict sense. On the other hand, the Bundesrat, the representation of State governments at federal level, exercises a co-legislative function.

3.1. *The Bundestag*

The Bundestag, or Federal Diet, is Germany's parliament proper. Its name was chosen to replace the imperial-sounding name *Reichstag*, which had been in use under the Weimar Republic. Already the 19th century German Confederation featured a *Bundestag*, yet that body was not elected in nation-wide elections and was rather a representation of the several German principalities. The modern Bundestag first resided in Bonn, West Germany, and since the reunification and the move of the capital in the 1990s resides in the renovated Reichstag building in Berlin.

Representing the German people, the Bundestag is elected for a term of four years (Art. 39 (1) Basic Law). It has a statutory size of 598 members. The elections are based on a mixed-member proportional system: voters cast a vote for a party list under proportional representation, which determines the initial distribution of seats, and a vote for a local district candidate in their single member constituency (there are 299 constituencies in total), where a plurality of votes is required to win; district winners are first to take proportionally allocated seats while any remaining seats are filled from party lists (§§ 1-7 Federal Elections Act). This way in principle half of the Bundestag's statutory seats are filled by candidates from party lists and the other half by members who have won single-member constituencies. Since it is proportional representation that is decisive for the relative strength of political parties and their regional branches, the system is not a mixed system in the strict sense but rather a special form of proportional representation.

In 2008 the Federal Constitutional Court had ruled a core aspect of the previous election system unconstitutional. That was because the system allowed for a mathematical anomaly whereby political parties could win more seats by winning fewer votes and vice versa. The legislature had been given time until 2011 to introduce a new system that would comply with the Court's ruling and, thereby, with the Basic Law. With some delay, a new electoral system was enacted in late 2011. The following paragraphs shall describe the new system, but with occasional references to the old system to illustrate relevant flaws and the reasons for subsequent changes.

3.2. *Election System*

According to the election system adopted in 2011, and just like it was the case before, voters may cast two votes each. Via their 'first vote', on the left-hand side of the ballot paper, voters can choose a particular local candidate to represent their district. Germany is divided into 299 single-member constituencies for that purpose. In order to win a district, a candidate must obtain a plurality of votes in a first-past-the-post system. This means that a candidate must get more votes than the second-strongest candidate. The returning officer, the official in charge of the ballot, draws a lot in case of a tie. Via their 'second vote', on the right-hand side of the ballot paper, then, voters may choose a political party under the principle of proportional representation. For that purpose, the parties' federal subdivisions in the States draw up party lists, ranking candidates by priority: the higher up on the State list a candidate is, the higher his chances of getting a seat in the Bundestag. A voter in the city of Dresden in the State of Saxony can thus choose between several candidates running for his Dresden district, and between several political parties which have drawn up Saxon party lists. Voters are by no means obliged to support the State party list corresponding to their choice of district candidate or vice versa: they can vote for a district candidate of one party but support the State list of another.

3.2.1. Seat Distribution

Under the system introduced in late 2011, Bundestag seats are initially allocated to the States proportionally to their share of voter turnout. Thus, if fifteen percent of the total votes cast nation-wide came from Bavaria – irrespective of which party got voted for or whether the votes were valid or not – then roughly fifteen percent of Bundestag members will be Bavarians. Afterwards, each State's seat contingent is divided proportionally between political parties that ran in that State. If party A won half the 'second' or list votes in Bavaria, it will receive half the Bavarian seats. It will first fill them with its candidates who have won a district in Bavaria; if it has empty seats left, it will fill them with candidates from its State party list by order of their rank on the list. If in Bavaria the party won more districts than there are seats allocated to it in that State, extra Bundestag seats, or 'overhang mandates', are created to make room for all district winners. This means that seats are not subtracted from other parties or other State seat contingents; instead, the number of Bundestag seats is expanded

Because of the overhang seats, the size of the Bundestag varies from one election to another, and typically it includes one or two dozen overhang seats on top of the statutory number of 598. In addition to the overhang mandate, a new type of extra seat has been introduced in 2011, the 'supplementary seat'. Supplementary seats are compensatory seats designed to slightly increase the size of party groups which did not generate any overhang, thereby partly matching the other parties' overhang mandates. After all, overhang seats increase the strength of party groups out of the usual proportion to their share of the vote. In each State, by dividing the number of votes cast there by the number of seats a State is allocated, a calculation is made how many votes are mathematically needed to win one seat. If party A won more votes than it mathematically would have needed to win the number of seats it received, which is possible due to the inaccuracies resulting from rounding off figures, then it is established that it has a number of so-called 'positive rest votes': surplus votes beyond what it needed to win the seats the party received, but not enough to win additional seats. The party's positive rest votes from all States are added up and are divided by the number of votes a party mathematically needs to win one Bundestag seat, namely the total number of votes cast nation-wide divided by the total number of contested seats in the Bundestag. For each whole number that results from the division, the party is awarded one supplementary seat. These seats are awarded to the party's State subdivisions, whereby in principle those which account for the most positive rest votes are the first to receive a supplementary seat, but by priority supplementary seats go to those State lists which have generated overhang mandates. If a State list which has overhang seats receives a supplementary seat, the latter is not added to the former but discounted: the supplementary seats are added before the district winners are accommodated. This is to make sure that parties which already have overhang seats do not grow even further, whereas parties that do not can obtain supplementary seats.

3.2.2. The Threshold

In order to be entitled to proportional representation, a party must receive at least 5% of the national vote for proportional representation, or, alternatively, win three districts. With anything short of that, a party will either not be represented in the Bundestag at all, or only with its one or two districts winners. The 5% hurdle is intended to keep small and potentially radical parties out; the Federal Constitutional Court has ruled that while the measure as such is anti-democratic, as it deprives a share of voters of parliamentary representation, it serves the legitimate long-term goal of stabilizing democracy overall. Against the backdrop of the ill-fated Weimar Republic with its fragmented parliament and no nation-wide hurdle, the minimum threshold is seen as a means to secure, rather than undermine, the democratic system.

> *Clearing the Threshold*
>
> Parties that are small and have geographically dispersed supporters are in Germany particularly dependent on clearing the 5% hurdle for proportional representation. They might encourage voters of their likely big coalition partner to 'borrow' them their 'second votes' in order to get into parliament. They know that they will not win any districts anyway: voters tend not to 'waste' their 'first votes' on small-party candidates in a first-past-the-post system. Big-party voters meanwhile also know that without a coalition partner, their party will not be able to form a government, since proportional representation, via 'second votes', rarely produces any absolute majorities. The small-party tactic of borrowed votes seeks to picture 'second votes' as being less important so that they can be given away – yet of course it is the 'second vote', for a party list, that determines overall party strength under proportional representation. Small parties are in fact eating into their big brothers' vote. Meanwhile, parties that are too small nation-wide to clear the 5% hurdle but that are regionally concentrated have an interest in obtaining three districts. That, after all, entitles them to proportional representation nonetheless. With 4% of 'second votes' and two districts, a party will only get two Bundestag seats, reserved for the two district winners; with 4% and three districts, however, the party will get not just those three seats, but roughly 4% of the total, which can be about two dozen seats.

3.2.3. Unconstitutionality

The German election system is relatively complex because it seeks to pursue several goals at the same time: it must ensure proportional representation, but also regional representation, as well as a direct link with voters via single-member constituencies. The implementation of these goals has led to mathematical anomalies that constituted a violation of the Basic Law. One problematic aspect are the overhang mandates, which can boost the number of a party's seats out of proportion to its share of the national vote if in a particular State it won more districts than it has seats under proportional representation. The other aspect is the 'negative vote value', which the Federal Constitutional Court in its judgment of 3 July 2008 (2 BvC 1/07/2 BvC 7/07) identified as an anomaly that violates the principles of directness and equality of the vote (Art. 38 (1) Basic Law). Negative vote value means that political parties can gain more seats by winning fewer votes and vice versa.

Under the system as it applied at the time, seats were first allocated proportionally to political parties based on their share of the national vote, and these party seats were then subdivided among their State lists. Assume that in Saxony a party has generated an overhang mandate by winning more districts than it has seats. If *more* people had voted for that party's list in Saxony, the party as a whole could have potentially *lost* a seat. The Saxon State list would have grown by one seat at the expense of another State list of the same party, say Brandenburg, but with one regular seat gained it would no longer have needed an overhang mandate to accommodate all its district winners. The overhang mandate, and therefore an extra seat already secured, would have been lost; the party as a whole would have shrunk since a seat was internally transferred from the Brandenburg list, which would have needed that seat to keep its size, to the Saxon list, a list that did not need it. Conversely, *fewer* votes in Saxony and relatively more votes for the party in Brandenburg may have *benefited* the party as a whole: it would have meant that the Saxon list would have lost a regular seat to the Brandenburg list (which would have grown by one seat), without however shrinking itself due to the excess number of district winners it had already won by winning Saxon districts. While in principle these effects can only be calculated in retrospect, the system can – and has been – manipulated if there are by-elections in a district after overall election results have already been published. Parties would then, bizarrely, campaign for supporters *not* to vote for them.

In its 2008 ruling the Federal Constitutional Court allowed the lawmaker until 30 June 2011 for the adoption of a system that complies with the Basic Law. Declaring the system void immediately would have left the country without an election system; demanding a reform already for the following elections scheduled for 2009 would have left the political parties too little time to consider all possible far-reaching effects of even minor changes to the calculation model and to inform voters, according to the Court. The new election system entered into force with a delay of several months, in December 2011. It seeks to minimize the occurrence of negative vote value by swapping the order of the proportional allocation of seats: seats are first divided between States based on their share of voter turnout, and are then subdivided between party lists within the States according to their share of the vote within the individual States. There is now only competition *between* parties for seats allocated to States, and regional branches *within* parties no longer compete against each other as they did before. Critics including Bundestag opposition parties have argued, among other things, that the new system does not eliminate negative vote value. It can still occur: fewer votes for a party in Saxony can still translate into more seats overall. That is because they can lead to a lower Saxon voter turnout and the transfer of one Saxon seat to another State, let us again say Brandenburg; that marginal Saxon seat does not necessarily have to be subtracted from the party itself but can, by chance, be subtracted from another party; the party as a whole will win a seat if the transferred seat happens to be allocated to its own list in the receiving State of Brandenburg. In fact, now even without overhang mandates a negative vote value can arise. Constitutional challenges have been launched on these and other grounds, and the Court is expected to rule on the constitutionality of the new election system.

3.3. The Bundesrat

Next to the directly elected Bundestag, the Bundesrat operates as a co-legislative chamber. Its historical origins lie in the co-legislative chamber of the 19th century North German Confederation. The institution representing State governments has been retained in the 1871 Empire and during the Weimar Republic, and has been re-established in 1949. Since reunification and the move of the capital from Bonn to Berlin, the Bundesrat resides in Berlin, in the former building of the Prussian upper chamber.

The Bundesrat is composed of premiers and ministers of the governments of the sixteen States; it is determined by State government decision who exactly will be designated Bundesrat member for the respective State (Art. 51 (1) Basic Law). The Bundesrat thereby is the permanent representation of the States at federal level. It has no fixed membership, as it is not individual people who sit there but (representatives of the governments of) the States. Accordingly, there is no single election date, no term of office, and no possibility to dissolve the Bundesrat. If the State of Rhineland-Palatinate holds elections as a result of which party A loses its majority in the State parliament to party B, then party B will take over that State's government and henceforth represent the State in the Bundesrat. The government will have changed, but the State remains.

In a proper parliament, the important question would be how many seats a party has. In the Bundesrat, the important question is how many votes a State has. Each State is entitled to a minimum of three votes; States with over two million inhabitants have four; States with more than six million inhabitants have five; States with more than seven million inhabitants have six votes (Art. 51 (2) Basic Law). While population size does matter, this system pays tribute to the equality of States in the overall federation, because it mitigates differences in population sizes by over-representing smaller States. Again, it is States not people that count. Who exactly speaks for the State is irrelevant as long as he is government-authorized to speak for his State; how many people sit in the delegation is irrelevant, since a larger delegation will not get the State any extra votes. A State must have at least one representative present to cast the State's votes, so a plenary session with all States represented comprises at least sixteen members; the maximum total membership of the Bundesrat in terms of persons is 69, because each State can only send as many representatives as it has votes (Art. 51 (3) Basic Law) and 69 is the sum of all the States' votes added together.

The Bundesrat acts by defined shares of its total votes, yet at least by absolute majority (Art. 52 (3) Basic Law). An absolute majority is more than half of the total votes, meaning 35 out of 69. A two-thirds majority of the votes in the Bundesrat, as it is needed for instance to approve a constitutional amendment, means that several States have to vote in favour of the proposal so that between them they muster 46 out of 69 votes.

Each State has to vote *en bloc*, which means that it either casts all the votes that it has in favour of a proposal, or all against, or it abstains. A splitting of votes is not permitted. Votes that are not cast clearly and uniformly, for example if no coherent State opinion exists because the State government is composed of coalition parties which are in open disagreement with each other, are invalid. This the Federal Constitutional Court affirmed in its 2002 decision (18 December 2002, 2 BvF 1/02) regarding the validity of a controversial Bundesrat voting where the members of the delegation from Brandenburg had shouted conflicting statements and the president of the Bundesrat, having asked the State premier to clarify the State's opinion, in the end counted the vote as a 'yes'. The Court held:

> 'The Bundesrat president who conducts the vote is in principle entitled, in case of an unclear situation in the course of the voting, to bring about a clarification with appropriate means and to encourage a valid voting by a State. The right to an inquiry however lapses if a uniform State opinion evidently does not exist and if in the light of the overall circumstances it is not to be expected that such uniform opinion might emerge during the voting'.

Thus, States either vote uniformly, or they do not vote at all. The voting takes place in the open: delegates either raise their hand, or the leading State delegates are called up one by one in alphabetical order of State names to say out aloud 'yes', 'no' or 'abstention'. Then, depending on the State that the delegates represent, three, four, five or six votes are placed in the 'yes', 'no' or 'abstention' camp.

3.4. *Federal Lawmaking*

Federal statutes can be adopted in as far as the Basic Law attributes legislative power to the federal level. Residual legislative competence, that is all powers not explicitly stipulated as being federal, lies with the individual States (Art. 70 (1) Basic Law). Matters for federal competence are enumerated in two different competence catalogues, one for each type of federal competence. First, federal competence can be exclusive, so that only the federal lawmaker can legislate; the States may not legislate there unless a federal statute explicitly allows them to (Arts. 71 and 73 Basic Law). Second, federal competence can be concurrent with State competence; here the States can legislate only when and in as far as the federal lawmaker has not legislated already (Arts. 72 and 74 Basic Law). Framework legislation, which used to be a third type of federal competence, has been abolished in 2006; the same reform allowed the States to deviate from earlier federal legislation in certain matters of concurrent power (Art. 72 Basic Law). Subject-matters that are covered by neither exclusively federal nor concurrent legislation fall under exclusive State competence (see Chapter 3 for examples). Since Germany is a member state of the European Union, federal and State legislative competences can be exercised only in as far as European law has not already limited, pre-empted, conditioned, or superseded German law (see Chapter 6). The Bundestag and the Bundesrat both may issue a reasoned opinion in case they believe that an EU legislative proposal violates the principle of subsidiarity, meaning that the European Union should not exercise its competences because it is not established that member states cannot achieve an EU measure's aims themselves or that the Union could achieve them better (Arts. 6 and 7 of Protocol No. 2 TEU/TFEU). In addition, both chambers may trigger an annulment action before the Court of Justice of the EU in case they believe that already adopted EU legislation breaches the principle of subsidiarity (Art. 8 of Protocol No. 2 TEU/TFEU, Art. 23 (1a) Basic Law). In the case of the Bundestag, the action is triggered upon the initiative of a quarter of its members. Which turns the procedure into a minority right.

3.4.1. The Legislative Process

Legislative initiative for federal statutes, no matter what type of federal competence, lies with the members of the Bundestag, with the Bundesrat, and with the federal government (Art. 76 (1) Basic Law). Bundestag rules of procedure specify the minimum number of Bundestag members needed to launch a legislative proposal: it must be tabled by a political party group or by 5% of members (§ 76 Bundestag Rules of Procedure). Legislative proposals from the Bundesrat must be adopted by the chamber as a whole, acting by absolute majority of its votes. In practice, most bills by far are drafted and introduced by the government.

It is the Bundestag where bills have to be introduced, and it is the Bundestag that actually votes on proposals first. Proposals stemming from the Bundesrat are for that purpose forwarded via the government to the Bundestag (Art. 76 (3) Basic Law). The government's proposals must first be submitted to the Bundesrat, for a preliminary consideration, before being submitted to the Bundestag (Art. 76 (2) Basic Law). This preliminary round in the Bundesrat is not an official introduction of a bill with a view to its adoption or rejection there, but rather an early opportunity for the State governments to express their opinions: the actual introduction of a bill to start the parliamentary process proper takes place in the Bundestag.

The Bundestag normally considers bills in three readings (§§ 75-86 Bundestag Rules of Procedure). In the first reading, the bill's main features are discussed and the bill is referred to a Bundestag committee for further consideration; in the second reading, committee reports and proposals for amendments are debated and voted on; in the third reading, final amendments and, ultimately, the bill as a whole is voted on. The right to table amendments during the Bundestag process lies with the members of the Bundestag. To pass in the final reading, a bill requires a simple Bundestag majority (Art. 42 (2) Basic Law).

3.4.2. The Bundesrat

Once the Bundestag has passed a bill, it is forwarded to the Bundesrat (Art. 77 (1) Basic Law). The influence of the Bundesrat now depends on whether the ordinary legislative procedure applies, or whether the Bundesrat's consent is required. The Basic Law may provide that the Bundesrat's consent is needed in order to pass a federal statute, which is the case whenever an Article in the Basic Law explicitly states that 'this statute requires the consent of the Bundesrat', or includes a variation of this formulation. Otherwise, the ordinary procedure applies.

If the ordinary procedure applies, then the Bundesrat's active consent is not needed. It will pass immediately if the Bundesrat either endorses it or votes not to request the convention of a conciliation committee. If the Bundesrat opposes the bill, it can object to it but it must first appeal to a conciliation committee in order to seek a compromise with the Bundestag. While the Bundesrat itself has no power of amendment, the conciliation committee can suggest amendments to the bill (Art. 77 (2) Basic Law). If the conciliation has failed, the Bundesrat may object to the bill; if after the conciliation the Bundestag has voted again to approve it, the bill is again referred to the Bundesrat, and it may object to it at that stage.

If the Bundesrat objects to the bill with an absolute majority of votes, it is sent back to the Bundestag; the Bundestag can then vote again and, this time with an absolute majority of its members, reaffirm the bill, in which case the Bundesrat gets overruled and the bill passes anyway. If the Bundesrat has objected to the bill with a two-thirds majority of its total votes or more, the Bundestag requires a two-thirds majority of votes cast, representing at least an absolute majority of its members, in order to overrule that objection (Art. 77 (4) Basic Law). Thus, if the Bundesrat does not muster an objecting majority, the bill is passed; if it does, and the Bundestag does not muster the required majority for a counter-vote, the bill fails. A bill that does not require the consent of the Bundesrat passes if the Bundesrat (eventually) approves the bill as adopted by the Bundestag, or if does not object to it within two weeks of receipt, or if it objects but then withdraws its objection, or if it does object but that objection gets overruled by the Bundestag, or if it does not appeal to the conciliation committee in the first place (Art. 78 Basic Law).

If the Bundesrat's consent is required, the bill passes only if the Bundesrat approves it with at least an absolute majority of total votes, or two-thirds where the Basic Law so provides. An important example of bills that require Bundesrat consent are constitutional amendment bills, which need the approval of both the Bundestag and the Bundesrat acting by a two-thirds majority of members or votes, respectively (Art. 79 (2) Basic Law). Statutes on taxes the revenue from which is wholly or partly intended for the budgets of the States or municipalities (Art. 105 (3) Basic Law) also require bicameral approval. Until 2006, the adoption of statutes the execution of which is delegated to the States and whereby the federal level adopts administrative guidelines also required Bundesrat approval (Arts. 84 and 85 Basic Law); as a result, more than half of bills required Bundesrat consent which meant, if the opposition controlled the Bundesrat, the country could be paralyzed.

> *The Joint Decision-Making Trap*
>
> As citizens become dissatisfied with an incumbent government, they often vote, in protest, for the opposition at their next State elections. Thereby they help the opposition, forming ever more State governments, to gradually take over the Bundesrat. Whenever this happens, Bundestag and Bundesrat, government and opposition, are locked in the so-called 'joint decision-making trap' of two chambers with opposite majorities. The result is that the government can be held hostage by the opposition and Germany is effectively governed via the conciliation committee that works out compromises between the two. The general trend in constitutional reform is therefore to grant the States more autonomous powers of their own, and in return loosen their grip on federal lawmaking by making fewer bills subject to absolute Bundesrat vetoes. Still, it should be noted that federalism and bicameralism are exactly intended to slow processes down, and to avert a concentration of power and the adoption of extremist or erratic policies.

A constitutional amendment of 2006, dubbed 'federalism reform', sought to disentangle federal and State competences. A number of subject-areas were transferred to either exclusive federal or exclusive State jurisdiction. In return for greater autonomy and the right to deviate from federal law in certain areas, the States agreed to bring back the number of absolute veto provisions. Most notably, Article 85 was stripped of the Bundesrat consent requirement for statutes that allowed the Federation to adopt administrative guidelines, although the provision now allows the States to deviate from such federal guidelines (unless the statute provides that they may not deviate, in which case the statute does require Bundesrat consent).

> *Mind the Default*
>
> In the ordinary legislative procedure in Germany, where Bundesrat consent is not needed to pass a bill, a State's abstention counts as a non-objection, and therefore as approval by default; if Bundesrat consent is required, however, abstentions count as non-support and therefore as votes against the bill. In 2008 a frustrated federal minister of the interior suggested to change the Basic Law so as to calculate majorities of votes actually cast. He argued that States which abstain because there are internal disputes within their government coalition should not be allowed to paralyze the system. The suggestion was widely criticized as anti-federal.

To seek a compromise in case of disagreement over a bill that requires its consent, the Bundesrat again can appeal to the conciliation committee, which in turn can propose amendments to be voted on by the Bundestag. Yet ultimately, without Bundesrat approval, the bill is not passed. If no 'Bundesrat consent' formula appears in the relevant constitutional provision, the normal procedure applies and the Bundesrat can be overruled in accordance with Article 77 (4) of the Basic Law.

3.4.3. The President

Bills that have passed the legislative process involving Bundestag and Bundesrat are submitted to the Federal President. The President as head of state signs bills into law after they have been countersigned by government members (Art. 82 (1) Basic Law). The President retains a task of constitutional review, however, meaning that he may, and in fact must, refuse to sign legislation that he deems to violate the Basic Law, or that has been adopted in an unconstitutional manner. Bills adopted in a process that suffered from procedural defects may not be signed by the President since Article 82 (1) only speaks of statutes 'completed in accordance with the provisions of this Basic Law'. As regards substantive defects, the Basic Law does not explicitly provide for any presidential veto. It exists, however, as a matter of constitutional convention derived from Articles 1 (3) and 20 (3) of the Basic Law which commit state authority to respect for human rights and the constitutional order. Thus, the President may not carry out acts that violate the Basic Law, nor sign and approve acts that do.

Veto or No Veto?

Germany is not the only system whose constitution remains ambiguous regarding whether the head of state is obliged to sign bills or whether he may refuse to sign. The formula would only state, roughly, that bills become law after they have been signed. The Dutch Constitution is such an example of ambiguity, the text implies a choice and only convention dictates that the monarch is not actually expected to withhold signature. An internationally noted example of ambiguity is the Czech Republic, where in 2009 the president interpreted the constitutional clause which makes his signature a necessity as allowing him to not ratify the European Union's Treaty of Lisbon, thus making his country the last member state to ratify the text.

The presidential constitutional review power is not entirely uncontroversial, though, especially as regards alleged substantive as opposed to procedural defects. As a matter of principle, and in contrast to the Weimar Republic, the Basic Law does not stipulate a strong presidency. In practice, a President's refusal to sign unconstitutional legislation remains an exceptional measure, if the violation of the Basic Law is obvious and if it would create far-reaching and possibly irreversible effects. A presidential veto for purely political reasons does not exist (see also Chapter 5).

4. The United Kingdom

The Parliament of the UK is bicameral. It consists of the House of Lords, which is an unelected upper chamber, and the House of Commons, which is the directly elected lower chamber. Parliament evolved from the medieval King's Council, a feudalist advisory assembly convened by the monarch; the two chambers have been meeting separately since the 14th century. Both chambers reside in Westminster Palace in London, and the Parliament is therefore known as Westminster Parliament.

4.1. The Commons

The House of Commons represents the people of the UK. The name refers to the 'communes', or territorial communities, as opposed to the feudal nobility and clergy which originally sat in Parliament and which later went on to convene separately in the House of Lords. The commons have first been summoned to Parliament in the late 13th century, and were included in the Model Parliament called by Edward I in 1295 (see also Chapter 2). Originally the Commons comprised representatives of the various counties, towns and boroughs. The franchise was gradually expanded since the 1830s, so that a larger share of the population was actually represented. The Representation of the People Act of 1832 reduced the minimum property status a person had to hold in order to gain the right to vote, and it distributed voting districts more fairly; women were granted the right to vote in 1918; property requirements for the franchise were abolished, and the same minimum voting age for women and men was introduced, in 1928.

The House of Commons is elected for a statutory period of five years; to extend its term, the Commons must pass a statute that also receives the approval of the Lords (Parliament Act 1911). Early elections before the end of the five-year term can be called only if the House of Commons passes a motion to that effect with a majority representing two-thirds of its total seats including vacant seats, or if a vote of no-confidence is not followed, within 14 days, by a vote of confidence in the government (Section 2 Fixed-Term Parliaments Act 2011, see also Chapter 5). The previously applicable royal prerogative of dissolving Parliament when the Prime-Minister so advises has thereby been abolished through statute.

For the purposes of elections of the Commons, the UK territory is divided into single-member constituencies. The number of districts, as well as district borders, are fixed by statute. The Commons has 650 members, each representing one constituency. In order to win a constituency, a candidate must gain a plurality of votes there. The returning officer, the official in charge of the ballot, draws a lot in case of a tie between two or more strongest contenders.

Constituency

Systems such as France, but also Belgium and the Netherlands, stress that the entire parliament represents the population as a whole, not that individual members represent individual voters. The UK tradition is different: members are closely associated with the constituency they are from. In fact, members of the House of Commons address each other during debates as members from the district they represent.

In 2011 a statute called for a national referendum to replace the first-past-the-post system with the alternative vote system. In such a system, candidates in single-member constituencies need an absolute majority rather than a mere plurality of votes to win, and voters may rank candidates by order of preference. If no candidate reaches an absolute majority based on first preferences, the least successful candidate is eliminated and it is examined what his supporters' second choices were; their votes are transferred to the candidates of second choice and are added to the votes which they originally received. The votes of those voters who had not indicated any subsequent choices, and who had only indicated their first preference, are not transferred to other candidates. If after this distribution of votes from the weakest to the other candidates still no-one has reached an absolute majority, a second transfer takes place: the next weakest candidate is eliminated and his votes are again transferred to the candidates of second choice, and the votes that he had just received from the first transfer go to the candidates of third choice. This process of elimination and vote transfer is repeated until one of the remaining candidates reaches an absolute majority. The system was rejected in the 2011 referendum, however, so that the old first-past-the-post system continues to apply to the House of Commons.

4.2. The Lords

The House of Lords is not an elected assembly. Its membership comprises two categories: Lords Spiritual and Lords Temporal. The Lords Spiritual are the two archbishops, three specific bishops and a further twenty-one senior bishops of the Church of England (Bishoprics Act 1847). Anglican bishops are appointed by the King on the advice of the Prime-Minister. Lords Temporal are the non-clerical peers. There are two types of non-clerics in the Lords: life peers and hereditary peers. The difference is that hereditary peers inherit their title and seat in the Lords and pass it on to the next generation, while life peers are appointed in their own lifetime and do not pass on their title and seat. Hereditary peers were historically the most important and, at about 700 members towards the end of the 20th century, also the most numerous category of peers. The House of Lords Act 1999 abolished hereditary peerages as an automatic entitlement to seats, however, allowing only 92 sitting hereditary peers to keep their seat until the next stage of House of Lords reform. All peerages are awarded by the King upon the advice of the Prime-Minister; peers may choose not to actually participate in the work of the House.

> *The Award of Peerages*
>
> Since it is effectively the Prime-Minister, rather than the monarch, who decides on who receives a life peerage, there is a danger that peerages may be awarded in return for favours, such as donations for the government party. This is one of the arguments to reconsider the composition or at least the appointment process of the Lords.

The House of Lords was, historically, also the highest court in the UK (see Chapter 6). To underline the distinctness of legislative and judicial work, judicial functions were exercised by Law Lords, or 'Lords of Appeal in Ordinary'. Judges could be awarded life peerages so that they could join the House as Law Lords. Convention dictated that Law Lords would not participate in the consideration of legislative proposals. To separate judicial and legislative functions even more strictly, however, the UK set up a proper Supreme Court. The House of Lords lost its judicial task. The first Supreme Court of the UK was staffed by the Law Lords who were extracted from the House of Lords and housed in a separate building (Constitutional Reform Act 2005).

> *Reform of the House of Lords*
>
> A reform process is ongoing to adapt the UK Lords, in essence a traditional nobility chamber, to more modern constitutional standards. Already in 1911 the Lords were deprived of their general absolute veto in the legislative process, but reform of the Lords continues into the 21st century. As of 1999, the number of hereditary peers entitled to a seat in the House of Lords was severely cut. As of 2005, the judicial function of the Lords was abolished. The Lord Chancellor is no longer the speaker of the House of Lords (historically, the Lord Chancellor was a government minister, and the speaker of the House of Lords, and the chief Law Lord – a merger of executive, legislative and judicial tasks in a single office). Debate about the role of the Lords continues: questions are raised as to how peers should be selected; whether they should simply be democratically elected; or whether they might come to represent the UK regions in one form or another. Ultimately, the question is whether the Lords might be abolished altogether. Yet the Lords are deeply entrenched in UK history and society. Their role as an additional check on the government has come to be cherished, so that abolition looks highly unlikely.

4.3. The Legislative Process

Legislative power in the UK is exercised by Westminster Parliament, passing statutes that receive the King's royal assent. Technically, therefore, the UK legislature is referred to as the King-in-Parliament, the monarch acting with the advice and consent of the Lords Spiritual and Temporal and Commons. In practice, the monarch does not refuse assent, and Parliament is effectively the lawmaker. More specifically, since in almost all cases the Commons can refer a bill for royal assent even without the Lords' approval (Parliament Acts 1911/1949), the House of Commons is the crucial legislative chamber.

The legislative powers of Parliament are, in accordance with the notion of parliamentary sovereignty or legislative supremacy, in principle unlimited. Parliament can make any law, and only Parliament can repeal its own laws. The remnant of the King's autonomous discretionary power is called the royal prerogative. Royal prerogative covers those areas which have not yet been regulated by statute. In practice, the King exercises royal prerogatives with the advice of his cabinet, which effectively means that the government decides and bears responsibility for it. Important areas of royal prerogative, and thus government power outside statutory law, are the internal organization of the civil service, the decision to declare war and make peace, the decision to conclude a treaty, and the appointment of ministers and peers. Once a statute is adopted in such area, it displaces royal prerogative. The decision to dissolve the Commons and call early elections, for example, was a royal prerogative, exercised with the advice of the Prime-Minister, until the Fixed-Term Parliaments Act 2011 by statutory provision regulated the possibilities to call early elections and therefore suppressed royal prerogative in that field.

As the UK is a member state of the European Union, national legislative competences can be exercised only in as far as European law has not already limited, pre-empted, conditioned, or superseded UK law (see Chapter 6). The Commons and the Lords may both issue a reasoned opinion in case they believe that an EU legislative proposal violates the principle of subsidiarity, meaning that the European Union should not exercise its competences because it is not established that member states cannot achieve an EU measure's aims themselves or that the Union could achieve them better (Arts. 6 and 7 of Protocol No. 2 TEU/TFEU). In addition, Article 8 of Protocol No. 2 TEU/TFEU gives the Court of Justice of the EU jurisdiction to hear annulment actions notified by the UK government on subsidiarity grounds, acting where appropriate on behalf of the UK Houses of Parliament.

Proposals for UK statutes of general application are called public bills. Public bills can be introduced both in the Commons and in the Lords; conventionally, however, bills regarding finances are introduced in the Commons. As regards the House of Commons, bills may be initiated by the government or by individual members of the Commons. The former proposals are then called government bills, the latter private member's bills. Bills proceed through three readings. In the first reading, the House of Commons is merely given notice of the bill's being filed. In the second reading, the bill's main features are debated, yet no amendment on the substance or vote takes place. The bill is then referred to committees for detailed scrutiny and amendment. Committee reports are considered by the whole House, proposed amendments being approved or rejected if there are any. In the third reading, then, the bill is finally voted on. Bills adopted in the Commons are referred to the House of Lords, where they pass a largely similar process of readings. Bills originating in the Lords are approved by the Lords first and are then sent to the Commons.

Parliament had originally been unicameral, as Commons and Lords sat together. After they began to sit separately in the 14th century, the consent of both Houses was necessary to pass an Act of Parliament. The principle that bills require the consideration of both Houses still applies today, although in most cases a non-adoption of bills by the Lords can lead to a referral for royal assent anyway. Apart from that, if one chamber proposes amendments to the other chamber's bill, the bill is referred back and forth until a compromise is reached. If both the Commons and the Lords approve the bill, the bill is referred to the King for royal assent.

4.3.1. Royal Assent

Acts of Parliament require royal assent to become law. By convention, the King does not refuse to give royal assent. The last monarch to refuse to give royal assent to a bill passed by Parliament was Queen Anne, in 1708. A future rejection of a bill by a monarch is not inconceivable, perhaps in an emergency situation, but will not take place under normal circumstances. After all, it should be remembered that the deposition of a King, or an abolition of the monarchy altogether as a reaction to an unjustified royal veto, is not inconceivable either.

4.3.2. The Lords

While in principle both chambers must pass a bill before it is submitted to the monarch for assent, ultimately the government in the Commons may decide to override the Lords. The Parliament Acts 1911 and 1949 stipulate that bills not adopted by the Lords will, after a certain time period, be referred for royal assent unless the Commons decide otherwise. Concretely, under the Parliament Acts, a bill that has originated in the House of Commons can be referred for royal assent even without the approval of the Lords, if the Commons adopt it in two consecutive parliamentary sessions with at least one year having passed between the second reading in the first place and final adoption. 'Money bills', which according to the assessment of the speaker of the Commons deal only with finances and taxation, can be referred for royal assent if the Lords have not approved them within one month. Bills that have originated in the Lords in the first place cannot be adopted without the Lords' approval, however; the same applies to 'life-prolonging' bills that would extend the maximum period between general elections beyond the current five years. For the rest, the veto power of the Lords is suspensive, as it may delay legislation but not stop it from entering into force.

The Parliament Acts originate in the early 20th century, when the government pushed for a restriction of the absolute veto power of the Lords. After the conservative-dominated Lords had rejected a proposed tax reform, the government under the Liberal Prime-Minister Herbert Henry Asquith tabled a constitutional reform allowing the Commons to overrule the Lords. The Act by which this might be achieved however required the approval of the Lords in the first place. The government asked King Edward VII to create so many new government-friendly peers that the political balance in the Lords would tilt in the government's favour. The King agreed to support the government if it obtained the people's approval for the plan in general elections. The government indeed stayed in power after the following elections. Edward's successor, King George V, complied and threatened to create hundreds of new Liberal peers. To avoid this, the Lords approved the Parliament Act 1911.

> *Packing the House of Lords*
>
> The threat to create massive numbers of government-friendly peers had already been used in the 1830s to secure the Reform Act, which sought to democratize the election system to some extent. The Parliament Act 1911 was secured in largely the same way. The 1911 Act had however far-reaching consequences, in that from that moment onwards the Lords could theoretically be ignored altogether. It is therefore no longer necessary to threaten to create additional peerages.

The Act allowed for most bills to be referred for royal assent without the Lords' approval after three parliamentary sessions over two years. After World War II, the Labour government of Clement Attlee called for a further reduction of the power of the Lords. Thus, the Parliament Act 1949 was tabled to allow for royal assent without the Lords' approval already after one year, rather than two years. The 1949

Act was actually passed without the approval of the Lords, as the government did not need their approval any longer. Invoking the 1911 Act, the government simply referred it for royal assent after two years. Since then, the Lords' suspensive veto lasts one year.

To avoid being overridden under the Parliament Acts, by convention the House of Lords does not object to money bills. Furthermore, under a custom called Salisbury Convention, the House of Lords does not obstruct the passing of bills that implement the electoral manifesto of the government, and which are therefore democratically legitimized in a strong manner. For the rest, the Lords feel free to table amendments or reject bills, even if they risk being overruled.

5.   France

The French parliament is bicameral, comprising the National Assembly and the Senate. The former is elected directly in single-member districts by absolute majority with run-offs; the latter is elected indirectly, via a body of electors who themselves hold elected offices. A Senate existed in many of France's constitutions, first set up under the Directory of 1795 and retained in various forms and under various names by later constitutions. The Second Republic of 1848, by contrast, was unicameral. The Senate under the Fifth Republic represents the territorial subdivisions of France and, historically, French citizens living abroad (Art. 24 French Constitution); since the constitutional reform of 2008, French expatriates are represented in both the Senate and the National Assembly.

5.1.   *The National Assembly*

The National Assembly is the lower chamber of the French parliament. It resides in the Palais Bourbon in Paris. The chamber has its historic origins in the 1789 Revolution, when the Third Estate convened by King Louis XVI declared itself a single and unicameral National Assembly.

The National Assembly is elected directly (Art. 24 French Constitution) for a term of five years (Art. LO 121 Electoral Code). The Assembly comprises 577 seats (the maximum number has been inserted in Article 24 in 2008). The electoral system applied is based on single-member constituencies with a run-off. For that purpose, each Département, and overseas equivalent of this territorial unit, is divided into electoral districts, and each district is represented by one parliamentarian.

The electoral system is laid down in statutory law (Art. L 162 Electoral Code): Article 25 of the Constitution stipulates that some rules, such as the electoral term, must be laid down in organic statutes, a special type of statutes designed to implement details of constitutional provisions, while Article 34 provides that the election system proper is to be regulated by ordinary statutes. In order to win a district in the first round, a candidate must obtain an absolute majority of votes cast, representing a quarter of registered voters in the district. If no candidate gains an absolute majority in the first round, then all candidates who have received votes corresponding to at least 12.5% of the number of registered voters in the first round move on to a second round. In the second round, a plurality suffices in order to win.

Assume, for example, that in a district turnout was 70% of registered voters. Of the votes actually cast, candidate A obtained 40%, candidate B 30%, candidate C 20% and candidate D 10%. A second round will have to be held, since no candidate managed to win an absolute majority of votes cast. In the second round only candidates A, B and C will be running, having secured shares corresponding to 28%, 21%, and 14% of registered voters, respectively, and therefore more than 12.5% each. Since D has obtained a share equal to less than 12.5% of the number of registered voters in the first round, he does not move on to the second round. If in the second round candidate A again wins 40% of votes cast while B and C win 30% each, candidate A will have secured a plurality and is elected.

> *Run-Off Voting*
>
> A single-member district system using a single ballot for a first-past-the-post contest normally punishes small parties as voters are reluctant to 'waste' their votes on small-party candidates and to eat into the vote of promising big-party ones. The run-off, however, allows voters to choose more freely and less tactically, knowing that in all likelihood there will be a second vote anyway. Even if their favourite candidate does not qualify for a second round, voters have another opportunity to opt for their second choice. The run-off also allows parties to strategically withdraw their candidates in selected districts and to endorse an ally of a similar political colour. In the end, since smaller parties have a chance to unfold their potential, and even though two big party alliances tend to emerge, the French National Assembly is not a two-party parliament but has a multi-party landscape.

If only one candidate obtains the minimum share to proceed to the second round, but no absolute majority, he and the second-strongest candidate advance to the second round; if the minimum share is not obtained by any candidate at all, the two strongest candidates advance. If votes are tied in the second round, the older candidate is elected (Art. L 126 Electoral Code).

> *Proportional Representation*
>
> In the 1980s, the Socialist government introduced proportional representation as a fairer way of electing the National Assembly. Ironically, the system immediately allowed a small far-right party to enter parliament. The conservatives, who had narrowly won these first proportional representation elections, favoured a return to single-member constituencies as well. The reform was therefore quickly reverted, so that now the single-member constituency system continues to apply.

5.2. The Senate

The French Senate is an indirectly elected upper chamber. It resides in the Palais de Luxembourg in Paris. Until 2004, Senators were elected for nine-year terms with one-third of the Senate being re-elected once every three years. A statute of 30 July 2003 (Statute no. 2003-696) set in motion a reform process which concluded with the senatorial elections of 2011. As of 2011, Senators are elected for six years, with half of the Senate being re-elected once every three years. The statutory number of Senators increased to 348, and since the constitutional amendment of 2008 Article 24 of the French Constitution explicitly caps the number of Senators at 348.

The Senate is elected by a body of roughly 150,000 electors. These electors do not meet all at once, however, but cast their votes at the level of France's territorial sub-units, more in particular within those sub-units whose Senators are facing re-election. The Senate is after all to represent French territorial subdivisions (Art. 24 French Constitution). Most Senators by far are elected within the Départements, the administrative districts, of metropolitan France (continental France and Corsica) as well as the overseas departments. As of 2011, this category comprises 326 out of 348 Senators. Other overseas dependencies keep electing between one and two Senators each. Twelve seats are, as before, reserved to represent French expatriates.

As far as metropolitan France, overseas departments and other overseas dependencies are concerned, separate electoral college votes take place at the level of the departments. Within each department, the electoral college comprises: the members of the National Assembly whose constituency lies in that department; the members of the elected council of the department; and the members of the council of the Région, the higher regional unit to which the relevant department belongs, who are elected within that department; the other 95% of the electoral college are made up of delegates from elected municipal councils within that department. The number of delegates per municipal council is related, but not proportional, to the municipalities' population size. Councils of municipalities with less than 9,000 inhabitants delegate between one and fifteen of their members to the electoral college, depending on the size of the municipal council; in the case of municipalities with at least 9,000 inhabitants but less than 30,000 inhabitants, all council members are electors; in the case of municipalities of 30,000 inhabitants or more, the delegation consists of all council members plus one additional delegate per 1,000 inhabitants in excess of 30,000 (Arts. L 284 and L 285 Electoral Code).

The number of Senators to be elected within each department and overseas dependency is fixed by statute, roughly reflecting its population size. The election method depends on the number of Senators. In departments electing three Senators or less, an absolute majority vote with a plurality run-off is held for each post to be filled during partial re-elections of the Senate; proportional representation is applied in departments electing four Senators or more.

The Senate's Bias

Overall, the composition of the electoral body of the French Senate is heavily biased towards small-town municipalities. Delegates of municipal councils make up the overwhelmingly largest single category of electors, and therein small rural councils are grossly overrepresented with respect to big-city councils when taking into account population size. For decades this helped ensure that while National Assembly majorities shifted, the Senate would remain dominated by conservatives. Remarkably, and perhaps ironically, parties of the political left gained control of a majority in the Senate for the first time in 2011.

The twelve Senators who are elected to represent French citizens living abroad are elected via proportional representation by the 150 elected members of a special council; these council members are in turn elected by French expatriates in French consulates outside France.

5.3. The Legislative Process

Statutes may be passed by the French parliament in as far as they concern subject-areas that are explicitly listed as being matters for statute (Art. 34 French Constitution). These parliamentary statutes are then called *Lois*. Subject-areas not listed as falling under parliamentary competence remain subject to regulation or *Règlement* by the government (Art. 37 French Constitution). Since France is a member state of the European Union, French legislative competences can be exercised only in as far as European law has not already limited, pre-empted, conditioned, or superseded French law (see Chapter 6). The National Assembly and the Senate may both issue a reasoned opinion in case they believe that an EU legislative proposal violates the principle of subsidiarity, meaning that the European Union should not exercise its competences because it is not established that member states cannot achieve an EU measure's aims themselves or that the Union could achieve them better (Arts. 6 and 7 of Protocol No. 2 TEU/TFEU, Art. 88-6, first paragraph, French Constitution). In addition, both chambers may trigger an annulment action before the Court of Justice of the EU in case they believe that already adopted EU legislation breaches the principle of subsidiarity (Art. 8 of Protocol No. 2 TEU/TFEU, Art. 88-6, second paragraph, French Constitution). The action is triggered upon the initiative of 60 deputies or 60 senators.

Legislative initiative for statutes within national competence lies with the Prime-Minister, the National Assembly and the Senate (Art. 39 French Constitution). Government bills are first presented to the Council of State, an advisory body, for an opinion; the constitutional reform of 2008 allowed for private member's bills to be referred to the Council of State as well. Once introduced, a bill must in principle pass both chambers in order to be adopted (Art. 45 French Constitution). The Prime-Minister may choose in which chamber to introduce his bills first; however, bills dealing primarily with France's territorial subdivisions must first go to the Senate while finance and social security financing bills first go to the National Assembly. Government and government-endorsed bills are set on the parliamentary agenda with priority, yet since the 2008 reform that rule only applies to two out of four weeks (Art. 48 French Constitution).

The power of amendment lies with the government and, in principle, with the members of the two chambers of parliament (Art. 44 French Constitution). However, parliamentarians are barred from tabling amendments or proposing bills of their own if such bills or amendments would raise public expenditure or decrease revenue (Art. 40 French Constitution). Furthermore, the government may declare parliamentarians' bills and amendments inadmissible if they concern non-statutory areas or areas of legislation already delegated to the government; the Constitutional Council rules in case of disagreement (Art. 41 French Constitution). Government bills are first discussed in their original version (Art. 42 French Constitution). All bills are referred for detailed scrutiny to a parliamentary committee, which can propose amendments (Art. 43 French Constitution); the government can object to parliamentarians' amendment proposals if these proposals have not first been referred to a committee (Art. 44 French Constitution). The government can rule out parliamentary amendments altogether by insisting on a single vote or *vote bloqué*: the respective parliamentary chamber must then vote on the entire bill as a whole, or a selected part of the bill, and only with those amendments that the government has accepted or introduced itself (Art. 44 French Constitution). Otherwise, each chamber votes on proposed amendments and draft provisions one by one, and finally on the bill as a whole.

Next to invoking the take-it-or-leave-it option of the single vote, when a bill is before the National Assembly, the Prime-Minister may also make the passing of a bill a matter of the National Assembly's parliamentary confidence in his government. In that case, the bill is considered adopted unless the National Assembly brings down the whole government by a motion of censure (Art. 49 French Constitution, see also Chapter 5). Since 2008, this procedure is limited to financial and social security bills and, apart from that, to one bill per session.

Generally, the 2008 reform lifted some of the traditional restrictions on parliament. Extended waiting periods (Art. 42 French Constitution) ensure that bills cannot be pushed through too hastily; autonomous agenda-setting is expanded (Art. 48 French Constitution); the approval-by-default procedure in the National Assembly under Article 49 has been restricted. In addition, parliament is allowed to initiate a referendum (Art. 11 French Constitution) and to veto certain important presidential nominations (Art. 13 French Constitution, see also Chapter 5). Generally, however, at least as far as constitutional rules are concerned, the French parliament remains rationalized, i.e. restricted, compared with the parliaments of many other Western democracies. Parliamentary agenda-setting is still not completely autonomous, amendment powers remain restricted, the budget can still be enacted without parliamentary approval and the procedure for approval by default still exists.

5.3.1. The Senate

In case the National Assembly and the Senate are in a disagreement with each other over a bill, and do not adopt it in identical terms, the bill is referred back and forth in a procedure called *navette* or 'shuttle' until a compromise is found or the bill is abandoned. The Prime-Minister may, however, also convene a joint committee of seven members of each chamber; this he can do after two unsuccessful readings in both chambers, or, if the government has declared the matter urgent, already after one reading. Reading here means the entire process of one consideration of a bill in one chamber. Since 2008, the presidents of the two chambers may jointly oppose the application of this accelerated procedure. If convened, the joint committee's task is to draft a compromise, but it cannot propose any amendments against the government's will. If the conciliation process fails, the government may after one more inconclusive reading in both chambers ask the National Assembly to decide in last instance, thus overriding the Senate (Art. 45 French Constitution).

Should the National Assembly fail to adopt a finance bill, for example the budget, within forty days, the government may expedite the process by referring the bill to the Senate, which must rule within fifteen days, and by then convening a joint committee. If after seventy days there is still no agreement, the government may enact the bill by way of government ordinance (Art. 47 French Constitution). The same applies to social security financing bills, only here the government may refer bills to the Senate already after twenty days and enact them itself after fifty days (Art. 47-1 French Constitution).

5.3.2. Organic Statutes

Some statutes are qualified by the Constitution as 'organic statutes' or *Lois organiques* (Art. 46 French Constitution). These are statutes regulating important institutional matters which are not regulated in detail by the relevant constitutional provision itself. For example, the exact size of the two chambers of parliament (Art. 25), the specifics how to table government bills (Art. 39) or the details of the procedure by which the Constitutional Council can check the constitutionality of statutes in force (Art. 61-1) are to be regulated by organic statute. The process of parliamentary consideration of organic statutes is in principle the same as for ordinary statutes. The first difference, though, is that a cooling-off period of six weeks in the first chamber seized or four weeks in the second chamber seized must lapse before plenary debates and voting on the bill may start; if the government starts the accelerated procedure, the period in the first chamber seized is fifteen days. Second, when the two chambers are in disagreement with each other about an organic statute, and the usual joint-committee procedure has failed, the National Assembly requires an absolute majority of members to override the Senate in final instance. Third, organic statutes that relate to the Senate require the consent of the Senate itself, and thus the National Assembly cannot make the final decision in these cases. Fourth, organic statutes must always be cleared by the Constitutional Council as being compatible with the Constitution before they may enter into force.

5.3.3. The President

Bills adopted by parliament in one way or another are referred to the President for promulgation. The President must sign all bills within fifteen days; he may request only one reconsideration of the bill in parliament (Art. 10 French Constitution), but he has no veto. As long as they are not promulgated, bills regarding ordinary statutes may be referred to the Constitutional Council for a review of their constitutionality; bills for organic statutes, along with draft parliamentary rules of procedure and proposals resulting from a parliamentary initiative for a referendum, must always be checked by the Constitutional Council before they may enter into force or be promulgated (Art. 61 French Constitution).

> *Presidential Disapproval*
>
> In 2006, President Jacques Chirac was confronted with an unpopular bill on labour market reform which had provoked mass protests on the streets. After he had exhausted his means to delay promulgation, and the Constitutional Council found the bill as such constitutional, he was forced to sign it. He added that he did not want the law to be applied in practice, though. This was considered a helpless and disgraceful appeal.

5.3.4. The Constitutional Council

The Constitutional Council is a body that plays an important role in the French legislative process. The Council is composed of nine appointed members (Art. 56 French Constitution). Three of these members, including the chairman, are appointed by the President of the Republic, three are appointed by the president of the National Assembly, and three by the Senate president. The members serve non-renewable terms of nine years each; three of the members are replaced once every three years, meaning that once every three years the President and the two speakers get to appoint one new member each. Since the 2008 reform the Constitution allows parliamentary committees from both chambers to be involved in presidential nominations, and stipulates that the nomination is deemed vetoed if three-fifths of the added total votes cast by both committees are against the nomination (Arts. 13 and 56 French Constitution). In addition to the appointed members, former Presidents may join the Council as life members. When the number of Council members is even and votes are tied, the vote of the Council chairman decides.

Traditionally, the main tasks of the Constitutional Council are to check the validity of elections and referendums, and to control the constitutionality of bills adopted by parliament before they enter into force. The setting up of the Council may be seen against the backdrop of the rationalization of parliament in the Fifth Republic: parliament is no longer the judge of its own elections, and its bills are subjected to further scrutiny as regards their compliance with the Constitution. Since 2008, the Constitutional Council is also charged with the review of the constitutionality of statutes already in force (see for details Chapter 6). This is a novelty in French constitutional law; the idea behind the establishment of the Council in the first place was indeed the ex ante review of bills *before* they became law.

Originally, constitutional review of bills before promulgation mainly concerned the question whether or not parliament had stayed within its competences to legislate in the first place. It was thus a check on parliament via a review of the formal constitutionality of bills. In 1971, however, the Council expanded the scope of its review powers so as to include fundamental freedoms. While the French Constitution itself contains no human-rights catalogue against which to check bills, the Constitution's preamble does contain a reference to human rights as enshrined in the Declaration of the Rights of Man and the Citizen of 1789 and the preamble to the constitution of the Fourth Republic of 1946. Controlling the constitutionality of a bill that would have restricted the right to form associations, the Council held that, via the preamble, the revolutionary bill of rights and the preamble of the predecessor constitution formed an integral part of the current Constitution. As a result, bills must not only comply with formal rules on competence allocation but also with substantive human-rights standards. The disputed part of the bill in question was declared unconstitutional for a violation of the freedom of association (Decision 71-44 DC of 16 July 1971). In 2008, the review of fundamental rights as guaranteed by the Constitution was explicitly inserted into Article 61-1, which deals with the review of legislation in force. The reference formally codifies the review grounds which are applied in practice.

The Constitutional Council engages in constitutional review of bills in two cases, namely via compulsory and optional review. Draft organic statutes, draft rules of procedure of the two chambers of parliament and parliament-sponsored bills to be submitted to a referendum must always be checked for their constitutionality before they can become effective. All other draft statutes can be checked upon request. Such a request can be made by the President, the Prime-Minister, the president of the National Assembly, the president of the Senate, a group of sixty members of the National Assembly and a group of sixty members of the Senate (Art. 61 French Constitution). The President may not promulgate statutes pending constitutional review; the Council must decide within one month or, if the government declares the matter urgent, within eight days. If the Constitutional Council holds that the bill complies with the Constitution, the President promulgates it and the statute enters into force. If the Council finds a violation of the Constitution in the bill examined, however, the bill, or the unconstitutional parts of it, may not enter into force (Art. 62 French Constitution). The other actors in the lawmaking process are then confronted with the choice of either passing a new bill that is constitutional, or abandoning the project, or trying to amend the Constitution itself. The Council may also declare bills constitutional provided they are interpreted in a certain way; typically this interpretation is respected.

The Constitutional Council and the Opposition

Originally, the only functionaries who could refer bills to the French Constitutional Council were the President, the Prime-Minister, and the presidents of the two chambers of parliament. The possibility for sixty members of either chamber to refer bills was created via a constitutional amendment in 1974. Thus, parliamentary minorities since then have at their disposal a tool to have bills checked that may have been adopted by the ruling majority against their will. However, since the Constitutional Council can only start ex ante review of bills between the moment of their adoption in parliament and their promulgation by the President, the opposition may have to be quick on their feet: the President is not obliged to wait for any references to the Council. Thus, if the President signs the bill before a reference is made, the statute enters into force, and the opportunity for ex ante constitutional review is gone. Since ex post review is allowed pursuant to the 2008 reform, the urgency might diminish somewhat.

Traditionally it was problematic to consider the Constitutional Council a constitutional court. Although many members of the Council are law professors in practice, they do not necessarily have to be lawyers; although Council procedures in ex ante review resemble adversarial proceedings for and against a bill, such as opposition versus government, strictly speaking there is no defendant, and the review is completely abstract. Individuals cannot bring cases for constitutional review before the Council, and until 2008 the Council did not hear any judicial disputes between private parties, neither via preliminary references nor on appeal. Since 2008, or at least starting with the entry into force of the organic statute pursuant to Article 61-1, the Council has acquired rather more court-like characteristics, in that it now may hear preliminary references from the two supreme courts on whether a statute in force is constitutional (see Chapter 6). As it now also exercises a task readily associated with a constitutional court, namely constitutional review of legislation triggered by concrete adversarial court proceedings, the French Constitutional Council can now be placed with greater confidence in the larger family of European constitutional courts, even though it is still not called a court.

6. The Netherlands

The States-General are the bicameral parliament of the Netherlands. It comprises the directly elected Second Chamber, or lower house of parliament, and an indirectly elected First Chamber. In English-language publications they typically refer to themselves as 'House of Representatives' and 'Senate', respectively. Both Chambers reside in the Binnenhof, a castle-like complex of medieval and early modern buildings, with modern extensions, in The Hague. Bicameralism has been introduced in 1815, when the Belgian members of the constitution-drafting committee insisted on the creation of a nobility chamber for the United Netherlands; after Belgium seceded from the Kingdom, the States-General remained bicameral. The government elected in 2010 pledged to cut the size of the States-General by one-third, reducing the number of seats from 150 to 100 in the Second Chamber and from 75 to 50 in the First; this, however, requires a constitutional amendment the successful completion of which – since it requires bicameral approval, intervening elections and again bicameral approval with super-majorities in the second reading – is far from certain.

6.1. The Second Chamber

The Second Chamber consists of 150 members, who are directly elected for a term of four years in a system of proportional representation (Arts. 51 (2), 52, 53 and 54 Dutch Constitution). Twenty percent of votes for a political party will roughly correspond to twenty percent of seats. A threshold of 1/150th of total votes cast is applied, since a party must gain at least one full seat in order to be represented (Art. P7 (2) Elections Act); voters vote for party lists but may cast preference votes for individual candidates on the list of their choice.

To translate votes into seats, the Netherlands uses the d'Hondt method of largest averages. First, an electoral divisor is established, namely the total number of votes cast nation-wide divided by the total number of available seats in parliament. The divisor represents the number of votes needed to obtain one seat. It is then established how many times the divisor fits into each party's number of votes. After seats are distributed based on whole numbers, some seats will usually remain unassigned. These rest seats go to the parties that have the highest average number of votes per seat if they had one seat more than they actually have so far.

For example, assume that party A has won 3,487,209 votes, party B 2,089,476 and party C 1,034,126, out of the total 9,523,760 votes cast nation-wide. The electoral divisor is 9,523,760 / 150 = 63,491.733. This leads to the following initial distribution of seats:

Party A: 3,487,209 / 63,491.733 = 54.923...
Party B: 2,089,476 / 63,491.733 = 32.909...
Party C: 1,034,126 / 63,491.733 = 16.287...

Based on whole numbers, party A has won 54 seats, party B 32, and party C 16 out of 150 seats in the Second Chamber. Assume rest seats are left unassigned, because numbers did not divide decimal-free. One seat is added, for calculation purposes, to the seats that the parties have already obtained, and the sum is divided by the party's total number of votes. For the parties in the example, this means:

Party A: 3,487,209 / (54 + 1) = 63,403.8
Party B: 2,089,476 / (32 + 1) = 63,317.45
Party C: 1,034,126 / (16 + 1) = 60,830.94

If we only look at the three parties in the example, then the first rest seat goes to party A, because it has the highest average number of votes per seat after one seat has been added to its seats so far; the second rest seat goes to party B with the second-highest average, etc. The process is repeated until all 150 seats are distributed.

Only parties that have a number of votes that is at least equal to the electoral divisor may participate in the race for rest seats. Thus, if party D has won 62,000 votes nation-wide, then it will not get a full seat based on whole numbers (because 62,000 is lower than 63,491), and it will not be entitled to rest seats via highest averages either. The electoral threshold is thus the electoral divisor, or one full seat, corresponding to 1/150th or about 0.6% of the national vote.

Parties rank their candidates on lists in advance of the vote. If a party wins 35 seats, then its top 35 list candidates will in principle move in to occupy them. To a certain extent, voters have a say over party ranking at elections, however. Instead of voting for number one on the list, which is typically the party leader, they may cast a 'preference vote' for a lower-ranking list candidate of the party of their choice. For overall seat distribution, the vote still counts as a vote for the party, no matter which candidate is preferred. List candidates can be elected via preference votes if they obtain 25% of the electoral divisor, as long as their party is represented in the Second Chamber in the first place (Art. P15 (2) Elections Act). In the above scenario, if a list candidate obtains at least 15,872 votes (a quarter of the divisor), he can get a seat via preference votes even though his party had ranked him too low to get into parliament via the list order; higher-ranking candidates with fewer preference votes move one place down on that list.

> *Preference Votes*
>
> Preference votes as used in Dutch Second Chamber elections may help reveal the relative popularity of a party's politicians. Low-ranking but popular list candidates can gain attention and clout this way. It may even be that the party's number two on the list gets more preference votes than the leader on place one for whom most people vote by default. The practical impact of preference votes is limited, however. Very few candidates have ever received a seat via preference votes that they would not have received anyway via their list ranking. Introducing a stronger personal element to parliamentary elections remains an item of Dutch long-term constitutional reform debate. A German-style mixed-member system that is still based on proportional representation is at times considered: voters could cast one vote for a party list and another vote for a local district candidate. However, since the German system includes the possibility of overhang mandates, it could no longer be guaranteed that the number of Second Chamber seats would stay at 150. That number is fixed in the Constitution, though, so an amendment might be necessary.

6.2. *The First Chamber*

The First Chamber of the States-General is a senatorial assembly. It consists of 75 members elected for a term of four years (Arts. 51 (3) and 52 Dutch Constitution). The members of the First Chamber are elected all at once by all the members of the parliaments of the twelve Dutch provinces via a system of weighed proportional representation (Arts. 53 and 55 Dutch Constitution). The provincial parliamentarians meet within their own province. Each provincial parliamentarian has one vote, which is then multiplied by a factor that is to reflect his province's population size. The factor is established by dividing the province's population number by a hundred times the number of parliamentarians in that province (Art. U2 Elections Act). Assume that 30 of the 51 members of the parliament of province X vote for party A, and that province X has 740,124 inhabitants. The province's population factor is 740,124 / (51 × 100) = 145.12, so the 30 votes count as 30 × 145 = 4,350 votes for party A from province X.

The proportional distribution of First Chamber seats among political parties follows the same principle that is applied to Second Chamber elections. Thus, the total number of (weighed) votes is divided by the number of First Chamber seats; each party's number of votes is divided by the resulting divisor to distribute seats based on whole numbers; rest seats are awarded to parties that have the highest average number of votes per seat if they had one seat more than they actually have; that last procedure is repeated until all 75 seats are distributed; members can be elected via preference votes if they have obtained 50% rather than 25% of the electoral divisor.

> *The Purpose of the First Chamber*
>
> Since the Netherlands neither needs a 'House of Lords' nor federal representation, the rationale of keeping a senatorial chamber is contested. Generally, bicameralism is

accepted as desirable for its own sake. The First Chamber may take more time to reflect on the quality or constitutionality of bills. It also invests more energy into the scrutiny of European legislative proposals, which are important but often attract little interest in the Second Chamber because the national parliament will not vote on them itself and the proposals seem far removed from voters' concerns.

6.3. The Legislative Process

The lawmaker in the Netherlands is defined as the government and the States-General acting together (Art. 81 Dutch Constitution). The government is the King and his ministers; the States-General are the Second Chamber and the First Chamber. The Dutch lawmaker passes statutes for the Netherlands proper (including the three Caribbean islands that form part of it) and, in a qualified procedure, for the overall Kingdom (including the three other countries in the Caribbean). Since the Netherlands is a member state of the European Union, Dutch legislative competences can be exercised only in as far as European law has not already limited, pre-empted, conditioned, or superseded Dutch law (see Chapter 6). The Second Chamber and the First Chamber may both issue a reasoned opinion in case they believe that an EU legislative proposal violates the principle of subsidiarity, meaning that the European Union should not exercise its competences because it is not established that member states cannot achieve an EU measure's aims themselves or that the Union could achieve them better (Arts. 6 and 7 of Protocol No. 2 TEU/TFEU). In addition, the Dutch government has agreed to transmit annulment actions before the Court of Justice of the EU in case the Chambers pass motions expressing the belief that already adopted EU legislation breaches the principle of subsidiarity (Art. 8 of Protocol No. 2 TEU/TFEU).

6.3.1. Statutes for the Netherlands in Europe

Legislative initiative for statutes (*wetten*) lies with the government ('by or on behalf of the King') as well as the individual members of the Second Chamber (Art. 82 Dutch Constitution). Bills are referred to the Council of State, an advisory body, for an opinion (Art. 73 (1) Dutch Constitution). The bill can then be amended, rejected, or adopted by the Second Chamber; the government also retains a power of amendment (Art. 84 Dutch Constitution). Bills are considered in committees and are finally debated and voted upon on the floor. Once the Second Chamber has passed a bill, it is referred to the First Chamber (Art. 85 Dutch Constitution).

Bills must be passed by the States-General, meaning both Chambers (Art. 87 Dutch Constitution). The Constitution does not provide for any rules on what happens in case of a conflict between the two; thus, since bills require bicameral approval, the First Chamber has the power of absolute veto. The First Chamber does not have the power of initiative or amendment, however. To compensate for its lack of amendment power, a practice emerged whereby the First Chamber would indicate that it expects the bill to be changed before it will approve it. The government, which is typically the initiator of bills, may then introduce a *novelle*, a supplementary amendment, in the Second Chamber while the bill is actually already before the First Chamber. If the Second Chamber passes the supplement, the First Chamber may adopt the bill including that supplement. Thus, while the First Chamber can formally only approve or reject bills, it can exercise a 'hidden' right of amendment in practice. The *novelle* has been criticized as being technically unconstitutional, but it exists as a matter of convention and therefore as a matter of constitutional practice.

6.3.2. The King

Bills adopted by the two Chambers must be signed by the King and countersigned by cabinet members in order to enter into force. Conventionally, the King does not withhold his signature. If he were to reject a bill personally, the cabinet would bear responsibility for such action and would face the political consequences in the Second Chamber. The monarch exercises restraint in matters of day-to-day politics. It is possible that the cabinet itself rejects a bill, and without cabinet countersignature the King cannot approve the bill even if he wanted to (Art. 47 Dutch Constitution). Yet again, the cabinet would face the repercussions and might have to resign for ignoring the will of parliament. In practice, government refusal to sign bills in one way or another does not take place since most bills originate in the government in the first place. It might be a threat with respect to bills launched by parliamentarians, but if a majority in the Second Chamber were to endorse a bill deemed fundamentally unacceptable by the cabinet, then the cabinet would probably have interpreted this as a vote of no-confidence and would have resigned long before it even came to signatures.

6.3.3. Statutes for the Overall Kingdom

The lawmaker of the overarching Kingdom of the Netherlands (the Netherlands proper including three Caribbean island territories plus the other three constituent countries of Aruba, Curacao and Saint Martin) is, simply, the (European) Dutch lawmaker, except that it acts by qualified procedure. Matters that fall under the competences of the Kingdom but that are just to apply in the Netherlands in Europe are regulated by ordinary Dutch statutes; matters that fall under the competences of the overall Kingdom and that are to apply beyond the Netherlands proper are regulated by *rijkswetten* or Kingdom Statutes (Art. 14 Charter for the Kingdom). Proposals for Kingdom Statutes can be introduced in the Second Chamber by the King (meaning the government) and by members of the Second Chamber; the ministers plenipotentiary, who represent their respective overseas countries in The Hague, may suggest to the Second Chamber to propose a bill (Art. 15 Charter for the Kingdom). The ministers plenipotentiary may participate in Second Chamber deliberations and have the power of amendment (Art. 18 Charter for the Kingdom). If a minister plenipotentiary objects to a bill, the Second Chamber can vote on it anyway. The bill is then adopted if it receives a three-fifths majority of votes cast; if the bill receives a simple majority but less than three-fifths, the legislative process is suspended and the matter is referred for further consultation in the Kingdom Council of Ministers (Art. 18 Charter for the Kingdom).

The Kingdom Council of Ministers is, in fact, the Dutch council of ministers, but in an expanded composition: it includes the three overseas ministers plenipotentiary next to the Dutch Prime-Minister and his ministers. After exhaustion of conciliation procedures with no compromise reached, the Kingdom Council of Ministers decides by majority (Art. 12 (5) Charter for the Kingdom). The same applies if ministers plenipotentiary declare that their country does not wish to be bound by envisaged measures. Since the Kingdom Council of Ministers is dominated by 'European' ministers, the overseas envoys can be effectively outvoted. The Dutch executive and lawmaker therefore remain largely in charge of the overall Kingdom. The overseas representatives participate in the process, and in practice rule by consensus is desired rather than adversarial vote-counting; still, constitutional law does not allow the overseas representatives to veto Kingdom measures.

Chapter 5

GOVERNMENTS, THEIR PARLIAMENTS AND THEIR HEADS OF STATE

1. Overview

What is the difference between head of state and head of government? In Western parliamentary democracies, the head of government – the prime-minister or chancellor – usually holds the more powerful executive office while the head of state – the king or president – is often considered to be the country's ceremonial figurehead. But how exactly are the two offices divided? Where does this distinction come from? Does it always have to be there? And what is then the relation between head of state, head of government, and the parliament?

1.1. Heads of State and Government

To illustrate the origins of the distinction between head of state and head of government, it is useful to consider modern-day European constitutional monarchies. It is in their constitutional traditions that the historical origins of modern constitutional arrangements are visible most clearly. For traditions like the monarch's speech from the throne to the assembled members of parliament are ceremonial only today – they once were a part of real-life politics. They are also relevant for republican systems, because the distinction between head of state and head of government in republics often follows the original monarchical blueprint.

Historically, the King or other crowned monarch of a European country would be the head of his state and the chief of his government himself. In governing, he would be assisted by his cabinet, comprising ministers for different subject-matters like finances or war. Ministers are thus called because they *minister*, or serve and assist, the monarch; a cabinet is, originally, a small room where the monarch could hold private meetings with his advisors. Gradually, a system emerged whereby one of the ministers would assume a guiding and coordinating role with respect to the other ministers. He would thus become the monarch's 'first' minister: the *premier ministre*, or prime-minister. Depending on the personality of the office-holders involved, prime-ministers could rise to political prominence and direct much of policy even in an otherwise autocratic monarchy. Famous examples include Cardinal Richelieu, chief minister to the French King Louis XIII; Count Bismarck, prime-minister and chancellor to a succession of Prussian Kings and German Emperors in the second half of the 19th century; and Pyotr Stolypin, prime-minister to the last Russian Tsar Nicholas II.

Meanwhile parliaments, the representation of the citizenry, asserted their rights as against the monarch and his ministers. One after another, in continental Europe especially in the course of the 19th century, parliaments would insist that no ministers be appointed who were not supported by a parliamentary majority. Consequently, the monarch should dismiss any minister who lost the trust of parliament. This meant that while the prime-minister and the other ministers were still appointed and dismissed by the monarch, their political fate was now effectively tied to the will of parliament. For the Kingdom of the Netherlands, that moment of truth came in 1867, when the cabinet stepped down under pressure from parliament and the King, rather than dissolving parliament, accepted the cabinet's resignation. In the Kingdom of Denmark, that moment came in 1901, when the King agreed to appoint a leftist cabinet in line with the composition of parliament. In Britain, the cradle of this Westminster model of parliamentary government, Parliament had asserted its independence from the crown and the supremacy of statute over royal prerogative already in the 17th century. It has been a constitutional convention since that period that the King would only appoint and keep in office ministers who enjoyed parliamentary support: the last British Prime-Minister appointed against the preferences of a Commons majority came to office, and then had to quickly resign, in 1832.

The introduction of the parliamentary confidence rule (meaning that the cabinet must be at least tolerated in office by a parliamentary majority), and therefore the emergence of a parliamentary system, made the office of the prime-minister much more independent from the crown than it had been. In effect, the monarch would no longer be the acting head of government: the prime-minister had taken over the role of guiding policies, with democratic support from parliament, and of being responsible for these policies. The monarch was 'reduced' to the function of head of state, and was only notional head of government at best.

The core *external* function of a head of state is formal international representation of the state. According to Article 7 (2) of the Vienna Convention on the Law of Treaties, heads of state are listed among those officials who are considered to be representatives of their country. International treaties are therefore typically concluded either by the head of state or on his behalf. The Treaty on European Union of 1992, for example, starts out by reciting that it has been agreed by the monarchs and presidents of the contracting states: His Majesty the King of the Belgians, Her Majesty the Queen of Denmark, the President of the Federal Republic of Germany, etc. Of course, the signatures at the end are those of prime-ministers and foreign ministers, acting for the government, but on behalf of the head of state. *Internally*, heads of state usually serve an integrative function in society as 'figureheads' who remain above day-to-day politics and add a measure of dignity to the state order. Often they are perceived to embody continuity and national unity.

Republics that come to replace monarchies would normally not abolish the division between head of state and head of government. Instead, the office of prime-minister would be kept in place as head of government, while the monarch would be replaced by a republican head of state, typically a president, carrying out largely the same function as a monarch would. The French Second Republic, for example, created a presidency to replace the monarch in 1848; so did the Third Republic after 1870 when Napoleon III had lost his power. The German Weimar Republic in 1919 and the First Austrian Republic of 1920 also established the office of a President to replace the office of the Emperor. Italy created a President to replace the role of the King in 1947. Newly independent states establishing a democratic republican order from the outset also often create both a presidency and a prime-minister's office, like Israel in 1948, India in 1950 or Slovenia in 1991. In all these cases, the president would be head of state while the prime-minister would be head of government. Like in constitutional monarchies, the head of state would formally appoint and dismiss ministers, even though he has a limited choice at best in whom to appoint and merely gives his ceremonial blessing to choices made by others.

It should be noted that not all systems actually separate the offices of head of state and head of government. In presidential systems, such as the United States and most Latin American countries, the President is elected to be both head of state *and* head of government. South Africa equally unites the functions of the head of state and the head of government in one office, namely the President, only here the President is elected and dismissed by parliament like a prime-minister. From a European perspective one could say that the US has a president who is also head of the government while South Africa has a prime-minister who also functions as a president (and who is called president, too). Some systems do not attribute the function of head of state to a single person, but to a collective body: from 1974 onwards, the Yugoslavian presidency was exercised by a council chaired at first by Josip Broz Tito and, after Tito's death in 1980, by different chairmen holding one-year terms. Switzerland does not have a head of state at all: the external functions normally attributed to a head of state are exercised by the government collectively. The States that together constitute modern-day Germany do not have the equivalent of heads of state either, only prime-ministers. Until 1918, however, German States did have heads of state, too, such as the King of Bavaria or the King of Saxony. State premiers in Germany are therefore neither actually nor ceremonially appointed by a head of state: instead they are directly and unambiguously elected by the State parliament itself.

There are also systems, mostly non-Western ones, where a distinction between head of state and head of government cannot easily be applied at all because the distribution of functions is either based on different premises or is rendered irrelevant in practice. In the Soviet Union, for example, the head of government would technically be the chairman of the council of ministers. However, since the Stalinist period real executive power lay in the hands of the secretary-general of the central committee of the communist party. The secretary-general would be usually called the Soviet 'premier' in the West, whether he actually was chief minister or not. The figurehead functions of a head of state were exercised by the chairman of the presidium of the Supreme Soviet, a legislative assembly; however, all party secretary-generals since Leonid Brezhnev held terms as chairmen of the Supreme Soviet presidium as well. In the present-day Islamic Republic of Iran, head-of-state functions and executive functions are carried out by both the President, who is directly elected, and the Supreme Leader, the highest cleric who ranks above the President. The office of prime-minister also existed in Iran, next to the President and the Supreme Leader, until it was abolished in 1989. The European Union, too, features several presidencies: apart from the fact that it is not actually a state, it is difficult to pinpoint what would be its closest equivalent of a head of state. The President of the European Commission presides over a mostly executive apparatus. Before the entry into force of the Treaty of Lisbon in 2009, the European Council of national heads of state and government was chaired by rotating presidencies, whereby member states would take turns to steer the agenda for six months, and whereby the leader of the member state holding the presidency would be effectively president of the European Council. Since 2009 the European Council is presided over by a permanent President serving terms of two and a half years (Art. 15 (5) TEU), yet depending on the incumbent's personality his role can be to chair meetings and to mediate rather than to actually lead the Union. Arguably the EU has a collective head of state, with the European Council as its paramount permanent institution. Rotating presidencies still exist for most configurations of the Council of Ministers, though.

1.2. *The Rank of the Prime-Minister*

Because of the office's historical background, the constitutional position of the prime-minister in a parliamentary monarchy is usually more subtle than it is in a republic. First, even though in Western democracies prime-ministers enjoy a high concentration of power, in the United Kingdom and in the Netherlands they are – as a matter of constitutional doctrine – still considered to be the first among equals. After all, a prime-minister is what he is: the 'first' in a group of officials who are all ministers to the crown. UK statutory law barely acknowledges that the office of prime-minister even exists, the post is almost completely conventional (although it de facto exists since the early 18th century); the Dutch Constitution explicitly mentions the prime-minister, a political reality since the middle of the 19th century, only since 1983. Second, again as a matter of doctrine, prime-ministers in a monarchy are not technically head of *government* but the head of the *cabinet*. It is the monarch who continues to be the head of government, if only in a purely formal sense. Sweden is exceptional in not even according notional government chairmanship to the King.

It is fair enough to collectively refer to prime-ministers as 'heads of government' in everyday speech, because this is what they effectively are. They steer government business because the monarch is not involved in day-to-day politics, and they do establish the course for the other ministers to follow. The European Council, for example, a supreme body of the European Union, brings together heads of state and government of the EU member states. The Dutch Prime-Minister is the one attending as head of government of the Netherlands, even though technically he is not head of government; nor is he, technically, in any clearly superior position with respect to the other ministers. Indeed, the Prime-Minister's membership in the European Council is one of the factors that contribute to the concentration of power in his hands in reality. In the case of France, by contrast, it is possible for the Prime-Minister and the President to attend European Council meetings together since both enjoy executive and foreign-policy powers, especially in situations when the two offices are held by persons from different political parties.

Even if 'head of government' is a convenient if sometimes inaccurate label for a prime-minister, the monarch in a parliamentary monarchy is still constitutionally entitled to speak of 'My Government'. This is what the monarchs of the UK and of the Netherlands do when ceremonially addressing their parliaments to outline government policy. In republics, the president is not usually considered part of the government itself (unless the system is presidential or semi-presidential). Having received the support of parliament, the prime-minister is head of government in both real and academic terms. He then only receives his appointment from the head of state, but the latter's involvement in government policy does typically not extend any further than that. The German President under the Basic Law of 1949 is, for instance, sometimes referred to as a sort of notary, who only ceremonially hands out appointment certificates. Also the prime-minister's steering function within the cabinet is usually more clearly expressed if he is actively and individually elected by parliament to be head of government.

1.3. *Parliamentary Investiture*

The historical background of a republican or monarchical constitution has a concrete impact on the process of cabinet formation. Even where the head of state formally appoints the cabinet members, some systems feature a process of parliamentary investiture while others do not. Investiture is the act by which public power is conferred on a person: one is *invested* with an office. The difference here lies in whether a new prime-minister, before his formal appointment, is first approved by parliament or not.

In republican systems embracing the concept of popular sovereignty, the cabinet formation process tends to be construed from the point of view of parliament, the locus of popular representation. In Germany, for example, the sequence of events leading up to the establishment of a new government is quite clear: first, parliament elects a Chancellor, and only then does the President appoint him as such. The same holds true in constitutional monarchies that were established by, or that are derived from, popular will. Japan, even though it is indeed a constitutional monarchy, does feature parliamentary investiture, compelling the Emperor to appoint any prime-minister elected by parliament. Also in the Kingdom of Spain, although the King presents a candidate for the prime-minister's office first, election by parliament precedes the actual royal appointment.

In the United Kingdom, the Netherlands, Luxembourg or Denmark, however, the process is construed from the point of view of the monarch. Thus, the monarch would appoint a new prime-minister, and he keeps him in office as long as parliament has not expressly rejected the appointee. The choice of prime-minister then effectively depends on the composition of parliament, and, if necessary, on the outcome of prior political negotiations between political parties which have a sufficient number of seats there to form a workable coalition. Thus, a monarch will not appoint a prime-minister if it is certain that the appointee will immediately be confronted with a vote of no-confidence from parliament. Still, constitutional thinking in these systems affects the procedural order. In the Netherlands, for example, a newly appointed prime-minister gives a speech before parliament, but he does not ask for a vote of confidence: his cabinet survives if it is not brought down. A similar logic applies in the UK, where a prime-minister must first of all survive the parliamentary debate on the speech from the throne, which he had written and for which he is responsible before Parliament. Furthermore, a Dutch cabinet minister, once in office, has a certain amount of freedom to interpret unfriendly parliamentary motions as either a rebuke for a specific policy failure – which means he may stay in office – or as a total and irreparable loss of confidence – in which case he tenders his resignation with the monarch.

> *The Head of State during Cabinet Formation*
>
> Even in systems where the head of state is a largely ceremonial figure, his influence may be considerable in the process that leads to the formation of a new cabinet. This is especially the case where parliament comprises many political parties and several coalitions are possible theoretically. In Israel and Belgium, for example, it may matter greatly whom the head of state charges with putting together a coalition first.

Needless to say, the above distinction regarding parliamentary investiture only applies to parliamentary systems of government. In presidential systems, parliamentary investiture in the 'European' sense is not part of the regular government formation process because regularly the head of government has a mandate from the electorate itself. Still, one should consider whether the United States, a presidential system, may not resemble European republics somewhat. First, in the US, the two chambers of Congress go on to choose a President and Vice-President if no single candidate has obtained the necessary absolute majority of electoral college votes. Second, the President's nominees for cabinet posts and federal judgeships require the consent of the Senate. This is not quite the same as parliamentary investiture: the former procedure is a default, not the rule, and the latter procedure has more to do with checks and balances than with any supremacy of parliament. Nevertheless, these features of US constitutional law should be enough to conclude that the United States is not a *pure* example of a presidential system. In a purely presidential system, cabinet formation would be independent from Congress altogether.

1.4. *Ministerial Accountability*

The key difference between a parliamentary and a presidential system of government is whether or not the government is accountable to parliament. Accountability should be understood in a strict sense here: can parliament dismiss the government if it is dissatisfied with its performance or not? If it can, then the system under consideration is a parliamentary one. Accountability in the strict sense used here thus entails not only the duty for the government to explain and justify its policies, but also the possibility of a sanction in the form of a removal from office if parliament finds the justification wanting.

There is some ambiguity concerning the terms 'accountability' and 'responsibility', and not all languages draw the same distinctions. In British parlance, the key word is 'ministerial responsibility', which is also the equivalent of the term used in Dutch scholarship. Historically, ministerial responsibility was a constitutional breakthrough in monarchical systems, shifting responsibility for policy decisions to the ministers and away from the King. In the Netherlands, the concept was introduced in 1848, when the King was separated from the cabinet through the formula 'The King is inviolable, the ministers are responsible'. Before the change, the King took ultimate responsibility for government policy himself, which meant, since the King was the unassailable monarch, no-one could actually be blamed for failures in a political sense. Now the ministers can be. Accountability, meanwhile, revolves around the actual process of rendering account and the consequences attached thereto. At first, ministers were accountable to the monarch; at a later stage, it became established that ministers are accountable to parliament for everything for which they are responsible, and thus could be *held* accountable. This implies that ministers must inform parliament, justify conduct, and remain subject to dismissal by parliament. The crucial instrument that a parliament wields in this context is the right to ask questions, to conduct investigations or inquiries, and to censure ministers.

> *The Limits of Responsibility*
>
> It is not always easy to hold ministers accountable for things they had no control over, for example the conduct of an individual civil servant whom the minister has never even met. In that case, ministers might claim that they are not personally to blame. Such arguments are usually dismissed: ministers are ultimately responsible for the functioning of their civil service, including its staff. In that sense, ministerial responsibility may be said to be something of a fiction – a legal construction that does not depend on personal blameworthiness. A similar argument sometimes invoked to escape responsibility, and also one that is routinely rejected, is a minister's claim that he personally disagreed with a controversial government policy. The answer then is that collective ministerial responsibility implies that all ministers support the government line, and that they are expected to resign if they do not.

The option for parliament to dismiss a sitting cabinet may be laid down in a constitution or it may be conventional. In constitutional monarchies, it is often conventional: the prime-minister understands that he must tender his resignation if he has been defeated in a parliamentary confidence vote. In republics, the dismissal procedure by which a government may be ousted is typically made more explicit – i.e., it is laid down in the constitution. To stabilize the government by making it harder to oust, the right of dismissal may then also be procedurally conditioned. Well-known conditions are cooling-off periods before parliament may vote on a no-confidence motion; elevated majorities for such a vote to succeed; and the German-style constructive vote of no-confidence procedure, whereby parliament may oust a prime-minister only by electing a new one to take his place. It should be noted that not all monarchies have purely conventional no-confidence vote procedures: in Belgium, votes of no-confidence must be constructive, too, and the person elected to replace an incumbent prime-minister will then be charged by the King with forming a new cabinet.

> *The Terminology of Parliamentary Government*
>
> A cabinet in a parliamentary system is considered politically stable if it commands an absolute majority of seats in parliament or, in bicameral systems, usually its lower chamber. This means that the opposition cannot bring the cabinet down because the cabinet already controls more than half the votes. If a political party has such a majority on its own, then it can *govern alone*. If it does not, it usually enters into a *coalition* with other parties so as to jointly gain an absolute majority; the partners in the coalition will then receive ministerial posts, the largest party typically provides the prime-minister. If the prime-minister's party, or coalition, does not command an absolute majority, or loses it after one of its coalition partners withdraws from the government, then the cabinet is or becomes a *minority government*. It may not necessarily fall or ask for new elections if it can continue to govern pragmatically and seek allies on a day-to-day basis, or if it is explicitly tolerated in office by a supportive party which does not join the coalition itself. If the cabinet does fall, then until the next elections take place or until the next government is sworn in, the incumbent stays in office as a *caretaker cabinet*. It will usually only manage daily business and refrain from taking far-reaching decisions. A coalition comprising the two overwhelmingly largest parties, such as the main left-of-centre and the main right-of-centre party, is called *grand coalition*. A coalition including *all* parties represented in parliament is referred to as a *government of national unity*, and is often assembled in transition periods following civil war and other crises.

Conditions on no-confidence votes mean a restriction on parliamentary prerogatives. However, they are seen as a measure to ensure the stability of the government. In the French Fourth Republic, the current Fifth Republic's immediate predecessor from 1946 to 1958, cabinets had an average lifespan of half a year; after 1930, the German Weimar Republic saw three different cabinets in as many years before the Nazi takeover. The perceived problem in both systems was that no-confidence votes were not conditioned, and that a majority in parliament sufficed to bring a government down. Such possibilities are limited in both the French Fifth Republic and in the present Federal Republic of Germany. By contrast, post-war Italy has for decades been a prominent example of what may happen if parliament remains fragmented among many small political parties and may bring down a government relatively easily: between 1946 and 2006, Italian prime-ministers statistically stayed in office for just under one and a half years. Of course, procedure is not all that matters. The Netherlands has proportional representation with a very low electoral threshold, which means also small parties can obtain parliamentary seats, and no-confidence votes are not conditioned either. As a result, while Dutch cabinets tend to be relatively stable, far fewer of them survive until the next regularly scheduled parliamentary elections compared with those in systems where no-confidence votes are limited.

> *Government Defeated*
>
> Constitutional rules stipulating a vote of no-confidence against an incumbent cabinet in a parliamentary system may suggest that a parliament that used to support a cabinet may suddenly lose trust in it. In reality, however, cabinets do not have to enjoy the support of the entire parliament to begin with: it is enough that they are supported by a majority. A loss of that majority support, in turn, does not necessarily imply a change of opinion in the majority party either. In reality, the most likely cause for a loss of majority support is the withdrawal of a coalition party from the government. Coalitions are, after all, concluded in order to jointly reach majorities that the governing party (i.e. the one providing the prime-minister) would not be able to command on its own. If the coalition breaks apart, the majority is lost; if the withdrawing coalition partner goes on to join the opposition to actively challenge the government, which has now become a minority government, a vote of no-confidence may be likely to succeed.

If parliament is unicameral, ministerial accountability is owed to the plenary. If parliament is bicameral, accountability is usually owed to the directly elected lower chamber. A cabinet may resign after having been defeated in the upper chamber, but that is typically a political choice rather than a constitutional requirement. Italy is exceptional in that it provides that the cabinet, although it is based on party groups in the lower chamber, is accountable to both the lower chamber and the senate and may be brought down by a censure motion from either chamber.

Ministerial accountability itself may be either individual or collective. Collective ministerial accountability means that the cabinet as a whole is accountable to parliament, in the sense that it can be brought down as a unit. If individual ministerial accountability is in place as well, then parliament may also oust individual ministers. It should be noted that individual accountability *complements* the collective one. Thus, even where ministers are individually accountable, they cannot hide behind their individualism to escape responsibility for government policy as a whole.

In the European Union, incidentally, the relation between the European Parliament and the European Commission is to a large extent modelled after government-parliament relations in a parliamentary system at member state level as well. While the President of the Commission and the Commission as a whole are nominated by the European Council, they must receive the approval of the European Parliament before they can take office (Art. 17 (7) TEU). Once in office, the European Parliament can again oust the Commission (Art. 17 (8) TEU and Art. 234 TFEU). The no-confidence vote does not have to be constructive, but it is still heavily conditioned in that three days must pass between the tabling of the motion and the vote, in that only the Commission as a whole can be brought down, and in that a motion of censure requires a two-thirds majority of votes cast representing a majority of the component members of the European Parliament.

Generally there is a correlation between the existence of individual ministerial accountability and whether a cabinet comes into office by parliamentary investiture or not. In the United Kingdom, the Netherlands and Denmark, the monarch appoints cabinet members as notional equals, expecting that parliament will not reject any one of them. In Germany or in Spain – which although it is a constitutional monarchy does feature parliamentary investiture – the focal point for parliament is the prime-minister. As the prime-minister is elected by parliament individually to lead the government, his position stands out. Only the prime-minister may be ousted again in these systems while individual ministers cannot. In France, by contrast, the prime-minister is appointed without parliamentary investiture being prescribed, but ministerial responsibility is collective: after a successful vote of no-confidence, the government falls as a whole.

Forced Resignation

The fact that a constitution does not provide for individual ministers to be ousted does not mean that ministers stay on for the entire tenure of the government. Even where the focus is put on the responsibility of the government as a whole, or on the responsibility of the government leader, individual ministers may still become politically untenable. Parliamentarians may then demand of the minister that he resign voluntarily, or may call upon the prime-minister to ditch him. A no-confidence vote against the entire government over one single minister is in reality a 'nuclear option', but an option nonetheless. Prime-ministers regularly reshuffle their cabinets to defuse political pressure, transferring, demoting or firing ministers who have become a political liability.

In presidential systems, ministerial accountability to parliament in the strict sense is – by definition – not present. The possibility for the US Congress to remove the President in an impeachment procedure is not comparable to a parliamentary no-confidence vote. Impeachment is a quasi-criminal procedure for an enumerated number of grave offences. In a parliamentary system, a vote of no-confidence against a prime-minister does not have to be based on a criminal charge; in fact, parliament does not need to justify at all why exactly it has lost confidence in the incumbent premier. In presidential systems, accountability may only exist in a broader sense, in that the government may be compelled to answer questions and justify its conduct, without, however, being subject to a confidence rule with respect to parliament.

1.5. National Parliaments and the European Union

In presidential systems, congressional oversight over the executive is an important part of the overall system of checks and balances between the different branches of government. In parliamentary systems, parliamentary oversight over the government is in fact crucial, because the government is democratically legitimized through parliament, not through direct elections. The simplified construction in a parliamentary system is that the citizens have delegated power to parliament, which in turn delegates power to the government. The construction is called chain of delegation. A chain of accountability must run in the opposite direction: the government must be accountable to parliament while parliament is accountable to the citizens.

Already in a purely domestic setting, the chain of accountability can be stretched very far and become largely fictitious in practice. That is because regulation in a complex society takes place in a complex and diffuse manner including both public and private actors and specialist working groups across several layers of government. In that case it is hard to identify who is to be held responsible for a certain decision, and blame can be easily shifted.

A problem of its own arises in the context of the European Union. Through its seat in the EU Council of Ministers, national governments are able to participate in European lawmaking. These laws (above all directives and regulations) become binding upon the member states and their citizens; national parliaments must transpose European law into national law where applicable. The Council as such is however not directly elected, nor is it accountable as such to any single parliamentary body. Only the individual ministers, if their home member state has a parliamentary or at least semi-parliamentary system (which all EU member states except Cyprus do have), are individually accountable to their national parliament. However it is difficult for a national parliament to hold ministers to account for their EU action. Some parliamentarians wish to engage in oversight over, or even participation in EU decision-making, but most do not because it requires time they do not have while voters tend to be interested in matters closer to home. Europe-friendly parliamentarians often do not wish to disturb the smooth functioning of the EU with any domestic interventions. Even if the political will is there to exercise tighter control, EU decision-making is often opaque as civil servants prepare the actual decisions in more or less informal consultations. Some national parliaments, notably the Nordic ones, insist on briefing a minister before he travels to Brussels for a Council meeting and on giving him instructions on how to negotiate and vote. However usually by the time a proposal actually reaches the Council, most deals have already been struck; and if the Council votes by majority, which it can do in most cases, a minister may be outvoted even if he sticks to his instructions.

The phenomenon that, in the course of European integration, national parliaments lose lawmaking power while the European Union itself does not have, and possibly cannot have, a democratic character that we are used to at national level, is called 'democratic deficit'. Parliament-oriented proposals to remedy this deficit set in at different angles. Some argue that the democratic deficit must be remedied by strengthening the European Parliament, which is in fact the only directly elected EU institution. Already now, the approval of the European Parliament is required for most European laws, but voter interest remains low. Others insist that national parliaments should be strengthened in holding their governments to account and in checking EU legislation before it is adopted. Furthermore, national parliamentarians might be encouraged to debate European issues more passionately and to cooperate more closely with each other. The Treaty of Lisbon includes provisions by which European legislative proposals must be sent to national parliaments so as to keep them informed, and which allow national parliaments to raise objections against such proposals. Some parliaments already do scrutinize proposals as a matter of routine. Ultimately, it is up to each parliament itself what to do with the power it has.

1.6. The Immunity of the Head of State

While we discuss the modes by which prime-ministers and their cabinets can be held to account and brought down in a parliamentary system, we should be aware that these modes do *not* concern the head of state. The monarch, or the president in a republic, does not depend on continued parliamentary confidence to stay in office – only his ministers do. Absolute or autocratic monarchs would convene and dissolve a parliament, not subject themselves to judgment from parliament, and this principle is retained in constitutional monarchies and republican systems. The parliamentary minority in the United Kingdom, for example, is known as 'His Majesty's Loyal Opposition', meaning that it opposes the incumbent cabinet but not the monarch.

Heads of state do, of course, perform certain official actions; however, Western democracies typically make the acts of the head of state subject to countersignature. Thus, a royal decree or presidential decision takes effect only if it has also been signed by the prime-minister or other ministers. The purpose and effect of counter-signature is twofold. On the one hand, the head of state is stripped of his discretion if he cannot act on his own. The introduction of the countersignature requirement in the Netherlands in 1840 marked a dramatic step from autocratic monarchy towards liberal parliamentarism: the King was no longer the monarch in a personal sense, but a constitutional office comprising the monarch and his ministers acting together. Second, the cabinet, if it signs and thus consents, takes over responsibility for acts of the head of state. This allows parliament to allocate blame with the cabinet, which may be forced to resign, rather than the head of state who is politically immune. Thus, while the discretion of the head of state is restricted, his dignity and unassailable status as the country's figurehead is enhanced because responsibility for actual policies remains with the ministers. This mechanism is upheld even if it sometimes results in bizarre situations: the act by which the Dutch monarch appoints a new prime-minister is a royal decree, which must also be signed by the new prime-minister himself in order to be valid.

The head of state is separated from parliament and parliamentary politics also in other, more symbolic ways. The monarch in the United Kingdom, for example, may not enter the House of Commons and instead addresses the two houses of Parliament jointly, in the House of Lords, to ceremonially open a new parliamentary session. Afterwards, even though the monarch has just outlined his government's policy priorities (the speech is written under the responsibility of the Prime-Minister and is only read out by the monarch) the two houses first go on to debate a completely unrelated bill before discussing the speech. This is meant to underline that Parliament chooses itself what to discuss and when. In France, until 2008 the President could address the parliament only in written statements which were read out aloud and which could not be followed by a debate. Since 2008, the President may address the parliament himself, but only in joint session, and a debate may follow but only once he has left and no vote may take place after the debate. These rules underline, among other things, the unassailable role of the head of state as standing above politics. It is the cabinet, not the president or monarch, which has to engage in the political process and be subject to removal on political grounds.

Incidentally, it should be noted that in some systems, such as Israel and Turkey, the head of state is elected by parliament. This however does not make these systems presidential, nor does it make the head of state subject to sustained parliamentary confidence. For there the president is not elected to lead the government (that task is fulfilled by the Prime-Minister); and once in office, the president may only be removed again in impeachment-type procedures for serious crimes or misconduct. Thus, the head of state remains above politics, and only in his coming to office does he need initial parliamentary approval, presumably because the alternatives, in particular direct elections or a vote by an electoral college, were not deemed desirable and the president must be chosen somehow.

To ensure that heads of state are not completely irremovable, notably in cases where they commit crimes, different systems do feature special impeachment procedures. Definitive removal from office is also relevant if the head of state is incapacitated in one way or another. In Germany, an action for removal from office against the President may be brought before the Federal Constitutional Court by super-majorities in the Bundestag or Bundesrat; in France, parliament would sit as a high court to try the President; in the United States, the House of Representatives may impeach the President which leads to a trial before the Senate. In neither case is the removal procedure comparable to a no-confidence vote, like it may be raised against a prime-minister, because it is meant as a form of criminal prosecution rather than a sign of ordinary disapproval.

1.7. *Dissolution of Parliament*

In order to keep representing the will of the people, a parliament is elected for a set term at the expiry of which new elections are held. Most Western-style parliaments are elected for terms of four or five years (the term of the US House of Representatives is, at two years, unusually short). There may however, depending on the system, be circumstances where early elections are called for. In European monarchies, parliament is convened and dissolved by the monarch. Notionally at least, it is *his* parliament: an advisory assembly to the crown. Also in republics, if anyone is entitled to dissolve parliament, apart perhaps from parliament itself, then it is the head of state – the functional successor of the monarch.

On the one hand, dissolution of, or refusal to convene parliament may be an anti-democratic measure taken in order to suppress opposition and restrict popular participation. In 17th century England, for example, King Charles I refused to convene Parliament for over a decade in an ultimately failed attempt to maintain self-rule. Tsarist Russia saw its first-ever modern parliament summoned only in 1906. Similarly, when dictatorial regimes come to power, a permanent dissolution of parliament is often among their first moves. This is what occurred in Austria in 1933, when Engelbert Dollfuss had parliament dissolved and prevented its reconvention; or in Greece when, in 1967, a military junta, upon assuming power, suspended the constitution. On the other hand, within a functioning democracy with stable institutions, a dissolution of parliament may be a measure to break a political deadlock. In that case, dissolution of parliament simply means fresh elections. Such a situation may occur if, for example, after elections political parties cannot agree to form a workable government coalition, or if a sitting government loses its parliamentary majority because one of the coalition partners leaves and joins the opposition. The (acting) prime-minister would in that case request the head of state to dissolve parliament and to call new elections. The degree to which the head of state then has actual discretion to reject or comply with the request differs from one system to another.

Some systems, especially republics, which tend to be sensitive to the fact that parliament represents the people and should therefore not be dissolved arbitrarily, restrict the possibilities to dissolve parliament. Germany is a case in point: the President may dissolve the Bundestag only after the Chancellor has lost a vote of confidence, but not if parliament has already elected a new Chancellor in the meantime. The German Bundestag cannot dissolve itself either, for otherwise the government, through its loyal parliamentary majority, could nevertheless have elections take place at will. In France, the President may dissolve the National Assembly, and at discretion – meaning alone and without countersignature from ministers – but not more than once a year. The European Parliament, which in many ways is modelled after national parliaments within parliamentary democracies, cannot be dissolved at all: elections take place at the end of each regular five-year term.

Other systems, notably constitutional monarchies, place no such limitations on the head of state, or on the government, for that matter. In the Netherlands, parliament is dissolved by royal decree, which means that the government decides and that constraints on the frequency of dissolutions of parliament are political rather than legal in nature. Convention however does restrain the government in that the parliament may be dissolved only once over the same conflict. In the Netherlands, fresh elections typically follow the fall of a cabinet, which allows the electorate to decide on who must take the blame for the preceding crisis and who should form the next cabinet. Strictly speaking, however, in a parliamentary system a fall of a cabinet does not necessarily require early elections, at least as long as a new cabinet can count on the support of the members of the same parliament. The United Kingdom traditionally had a similar arrangement whereby the dissolution of Parliament was a royal prerogative that was in effect exercised by the Prime-Minister at discretion. Therefore, it was the Prime-Minister's choice at which point new elections should be held, as long as he did not exceed the statutory maximum length of Parliament of five years. Since the entry into force of the Fixed-Term Parliaments Act 2011, however, statute provides that the five-year term is in principle fixed and early elections may be called only if the House of Commons itself adopts a motion to that effect with a super-majority representing two-thirds of total seats, or if a vote of no-confidence in an incumbent cabinet is not followed, within 14 days, by a vote of confidence in a (new) cabinet. Other opportunities for a dissolution of Parliament are now excluded, and royal prerogative displaced.

In presidential systems, a dissolution of parliament by the head of state is not possible, because parliament is not constitutionally subordinate to the president. The reverse also holds true: parliament cannot oust the president in a no-confidence vote, because the president does not rely on parliamentary support to stay in office. Since both have independent mandates of their own, both remain in place for their respective term.

1.8. Summary

Many details of government-parliament relations in a given system depend on whether the system is parliamentary or presidential, and on whether a parliamentary system is situated in a monarchy or a republic. The US is presidential and combines the functions of head of state and government in the President. France is semi-presidential, meaning that the head of state is elected with an independent mandate of his own but also shares executive functions with a prime-minister. The other systems under consideration are parliamentary democracies, which feature a clearer distinction between a largely ceremonial head of state and a politically active head of government. Of these parliamentary systems, two are constitutional monarchies (the UK and the Netherlands) where the King appoints prime-ministers and ministers in the light of the composition of the lower chamber of parliament. Germany is a republic where parliamentary investiture precedes the appointment of a new head of government by the President. In all three parliamentary systems, as well as in France, parliament or the lower chamber thereof may oust an incumbent cabinet, but procedural requirements differ. In the Netherlands and the UK, votes of no-confidence may be expressed without procedural constraints and against any minister. In Germany and France, votes of no-confidence may be directed only against the head of government and thus the cabinet as a whole, and the procedure is stricter so as to discourage rash dismissal, and a similar procedure applies to the censure of the Commission by the European Parliament; in Germany, furthermore, votes of no-confidence against the Chancellor must be constructive, meaning that a successor must be elected for the motion to be valid. The heads of state in all five systems are not subject to no-confidence motions from parliament, but the presidents in the three republics studied (the US, France and Germany) may be removed from office in special impeachment procedures. An early dissolution of parliament or the lower chamber thereof by the President is not possible in the US; it is possible but only under certain conditions in Germany and France; it is a matter of political considerations in the Netherlands as the government effectively has discretion when to call new elections; in the UK, Parliament only dissolves itself based on statutory regulation, and the monarch is stripped of his traditional royal prerogative to call early elections.

1.9. Further Reading

M. Bovens, *The Quest for Responsibility: Accountability and Citizenship in Complex Organisations* (Cambridge: CUP 1998).
C. Harlow, *Accountability in the European Union* (Oxford: OUP 2002).

Ph. Kiiver, *The National Parliaments in the European Union – A Critical View on EU Constitution-Building* (The Hague/London/New York: Kluwer Law International 2006).

Ph. Kiiver, 'European Treaty Reform and the National Parliaments: Towards a New Assessment of Parliament-Friendly Treaty Provisions', in J. Wouters, L. Verhey & Ph. Kiiver (eds.), *European Constitutionalism Beyond Lisbon* (Antwerp/ Oxford: Intersentia, 2009).

Ph. Norton (ed.), *Parliaments and Governments in Western Europe* (London/ Portland: Frank Cass 1998).

K. Strøm, W. Müller & T. Bergman (eds.), *Delegation and Accountability in Parliamentary Democracies* (Oxford: OUP 2003).

L. Verhey, H. Broeksteeg & I. Van den Driessche (eds.), *Political Accountability in Europe: Which Way Forward?* (Groningen: Europa Law Publishing 2008).

2. The United States

The office of head of state and head of government in the United States is merged into the single office of the US President, who is assisted by a Vice-President. The President exercises highest federal executive power and represents the US internationally. The first US President was George Washington, a general of the American war of independence against Britain, who was elected in 1789. Originally the Congress, rather than the President, was seen as the crucial and dominant institution; that perception however changed over time. Certainly when seen from abroad, the US President has considerable might; on the domestic scene things tend to be different, however, as Congress still holds important prerogatives, most notably the power to actually make laws and to allocate money in the national budget.

2.1. The President and Vice-President

The US President is elected by an electoral college for a term of four years (Art. II (1) and 12th Amendment US Constitution). The term is renewable once (22nd Amendment to the US Constitution). Electors are elected State by State. Each State may have as many electors as it has Senators in the US Senate (always two) and congressmen in the US House of Representatives (at least one, but mostly more depending on population size, see also Chapter 4). The capital district of Washington, D.C., is not a State but may nevertheless have as many electors as it would be entitled to if it were a State, yet not more than the least populous State has, which is ultimately three (23rd Amendment to the US Constitution). Thus, there are in total 100 + 435 + 3 = 538 electors. The electors meet and vote in their own State; the results of their voting are then transmitted to the US capital. This way the electors vote by absolute majority of members for the President and by absolute majority of members for the Vice-President.

Chapter 5

> *The Original System*
>
> Originally, the presidential candidate with the second-highest number of votes was elected Vice-President. This proved problematic, as the new President might have to work together with his political opponent. A system of separate voting for both posts was quickly proposed and entered into force as the 12th Amendment in 1804, superseding the text of Article II of the Constitution. Now there are separate ballots for each of the two posts and electors can cast both votes for the presidential and vice-presidential candidate from the same ticket.

If after the counting of all incoming electoral votes no candidate has received an absolute majority for the office he is running for, then the House of Representatives votes for the President from among the three strongest contenders for that post; the Senate votes for the Vice-President from among the two strongest contenders for that post. The House members, exceptionally for that purpose, then vote as delegations from the States they are from, each delegation having one vote; both House and Senate act, in their respective votes, by absolute majority with elevated quorums of two-thirds of Senators and two-thirds of State delegations in the House, respectively. This parliamentary election as a back-up procedure to the electoral college might be considered a trace of a parliamentary system in the otherwise presidential US.

> *The Relevance of the Backup System*
>
> In a two-party system presidencies are occupied through alternating absolute majorities in the electoral college; the backup procedure becomes relevant in situations where a third-party candidate successfully enters the race and carries one or more States, which decreases the likelihood of any one candidate securing an absolute majority of electoral votes.

States are free to determine the nomination procedure for electors (primaries, party conventions, or fixed party lists), just like they determine the manner in which presidential candidates secure a nomination from their own political party. States are also free to determine the actual election mode for the election of 'their' electors; almost all of them employ a first-past-the-post system, however. This means that a ticket, which is a presidential candidate and his vice-presidential running mate together, wins all the electoral votes in the State if it receives a relative majority of votes cast for the corresponding electors in that State. Thus, if presidential candidate A together with his running mate for Vice-President wins 45% of popular support in a State, whereas candidate B and his running mate win 40%, then that State's body of electors will be composed entirely of electors who have pledged to support candidate A and his running mate. Only Maine and Nebraska have two of their electors elected State-wide and the rest per congressional district. It should be noted that ballot papers indicate the names of the presidential candidates, rather than the names of the electors, which to voters creates the impression of direct elections even though technically the choice is between different sets of electors.

> *Popular Vote versus Electoral Votes*
>
> What counts in US presidential elections is the number of electors supporting a candidate. Since electors are elected in the States, and the predominant method of electing electors in the States is the winner-takes-all system, candidates are interested in securing relative majorities in as many States as possible so as to gain an absolute majority of electoral votes. More precisely, they are interested in winning large States that are worth many electoral votes because large States have many House seats which translates into many electoral votes. Even more precisely, candidates have an interest in investing their campaign resources into large 'swing States', States which are not only worth many votes, but which are furthermore not dominated by one of the two large political parties, and where the majority can thus tilt either way. Campaigning in hostile States makes little sense if a relative majority there is unattainable and not many electoral votes are forfeited anyway; campaigning in friendly States makes little practical sense either, since the size of a majority in a State is irrelevant as long as it is a relative majority. The number of electoral votes per State is not directly proportional to population size: Rhode Island, with about one million inhabitants, is worth four votes; yet Michigan, which is ten times bigger, does not have forty votes but merely seventeen. As a result, it can be that a candidate wins more votes from voters nation-wide compared to his opponent, but that he nevertheless wins fewer electoral votes. In that case he has won the popular vote but lost the presidential race. Even if a candidate wins both the electoral and the popular vote, margins can differ. Barack Obama won the 2008 elections by a landslide in terms of electoral votes, but the victory was narrower in terms of the popular vote.

The President heads the federal executive branch, including not only the central administration but also federal executive agencies. He appoints a cabinet of ministers ('secretaries'), for which he however needs the advice and consent of the Senate; the same holds true for his nomination of Supreme Court justices and, where applicable, other federal judges (Art. II (2) US Constitution). Thus, the Senate holds hearings and must approve the President's nominees. The President may dismiss ministers on his own. The President is commander-in-chief of the armed forces (Art. II (2) US Constitution). His powers further include a veto in the legislative process, subject to an override by two-thirds majorities in both chambers of Congress (Art. I (7) US Constitution, see also Chapter 4).

The Vice-President supports the President in the carrying out of his duties; he is also the first to succeed him in case of a vacancy (20th and 25th Amendment to the US Constitution). The Vice-President is furthermore automatically the president of the Senate, wielding a tie-breaking vote (Art. I (3) US Constitution).

2.2. The President and Congress

The President and Vice-President are not accountable to Congress in the sense of a confidence rule, since they have an electoral mandate of their own. The executive does not rely on the confidence of Congress to stay in office. A change of majorities in the Senate or the House of Representatives in mid-term, while having political consequences for the support for bills and nominations desired by the government, will have no bearing on the continuation of the presidential term as such. The same applies to inferior executive officers. In 1986, the Supreme Court stressed this principle in the case *Bowsher* v. *Synar* (478 U.S. 714), where it assessed the constitutionality of a newly created post of 'comptroller general'. The comptroller general was charged with ensuring that budget deficits stay within the limits set by Congress; he could, according to the empowering statute, be dismissed by a joint resolution of the two chambers of Congress for broad reasons including 'inefficiency'. The US Supreme Court held:

> 'By placing the responsibility for execution of [budget control legislation] in the hands of an officer who is subject to removal only by itself, Congress in effect has retained control over the execution of the [legislation] and has intruded into the executive function. The Constitution does not permit such intrusion'.

The comptroller general was an officer charged with an executive task. Congress has no executive power and can therefore not delegate such power to one of its agents. Properly executive agents cannot be removed by a mere resolution, however. They are accountable to the President, who in turn is elected, via an electoral college, by the people.

Once in office, the President, Vice-President, ministers and other executive officers may be removed from office only in an impeachment procedure (Art. II (4) US Constitution). Impeachment is a quasi-criminal procedure for treason, bribery, or other high crime or misdemeanour. The House of Representatives can start an impeachment procedure (Art. I (2) US Constitution), approving 'articles of impeachment' containing charges; the Senate then tries the impeachment, as in conducting a court trial (Art. I (3) US Constitution). If the President is being tried, the Senate presidency shifts from the US Vice-President to the chief justice of the Supreme Court, in order to avoid loyalty conflicts. In any impeachment procedure a 'guilty' verdict requires a two-thirds majority of Senators present.

Whereas in the US the executive does not rely on parliamentary confidence, Congress can nevertheless exercise parliamentary oversight. This it can do via scrutiny of policies and public hearings, backed up by the congressional legislative power including the power of the purse – the power to allocate and withdraw funding for government departments or specific policies.

Iran-Contra

The Iran-Contra affair in the 1980s exemplified the supervisory role of Congress over executive action via the congressional legislative and budgetary power. Congress had stipulated that no weapons may be sold to Iran; it had also stipulated that Nicaragua's Contra guerrilla may not be supported. Subsequently, Ronald Reagan's executive administration, hoping to solve a hostage crisis by appeasing Iran, nevertheless went on to sell weapons to Iran; it then used the proceeds of that sale to finance the Contras. A political scandal ensued that resulted in resignations (though not Reagan's).

3. Germany

Germany features a President as head of state, and a Federal Chancellor as head of the government. The President is elected by an electoral college; the Chancellor is elected by the Bundestag and remains accountable to it. In 1949, Theodor Heuss was elected to become the first President under the Basic Law. Konrad Adenauer, who had presided over the Parliamentary Council which had adopted the Basic Law in the first place, was elected Chancellor.

3.1. The Federal President

The German head of state is the Federal President. He is elected for a once-renewable term of five years by the Federal Convention, a single-purpose electoral college (Art. 54 Basic Law). The Federal Convention comprises all members of the Bundestag plus an equal number of delegates who are elected via proportional representation by the parliaments of the sixteen States. The number of delegates per State parliament is calculated based on the States' share of the total German population, and the parliaments themselves also elect their delegates by proportional representation. A candidate requires the votes of an absolute majority of Convention members; if no candidate obtains such majority, a second ballot is held; if the second ballot was inconclusive as well because again no-one mustered an absolute majority, a third and final ballot is held wherein the candidate who obtains a relative majority wins (Art. 54 (6) Basic Law).

The President carries out largely ceremonial functions; internationally, the President has a representative function under diplomatic protocol, including the conclusion of international treaties (Art. 59 (1) Basic Law). Overall, the Basic Law does not provide for a strong presidency and thereby stands in marked and deliberate contrast to the Weimar Constitution. The indirect elections contribute to the weakening of the office, as a President cannot claim strong popular support in order to make discretionary choices.

On the domestic scene, the President formally appoints and dismisses the Federal Chancellor, and he nominates a candidate to be elected by the Bundestag in the first place (Art. 63 Basic Law); he appoints and dismisses federal ministers (Art. 64 Basic Law) and other functionaries (Art. 60 (1) Basic Law); he has the right to grant pardons (Art. 60 (2) Basic Law); he promulgates federal legislation (Art. 82 (1) Basic Law) and can dissolve the Bundestag to call early elections (Arts. 63 (4) and 68 (1) Basic Law). However, the exercise of these powers is severely conditioned in reality. When nominating a candidate for Chancellor, the President takes account of relative party strengths in the Bundestag and conventionally nominates the candidate of the largest party controlling, usually in a coalition with another party, an absolute majority of Bundestag seats. He must appoint any person elected Chancellor by absolute majority. The President has no political discretion in appointing ministers and other functionaries or in international affairs either; almost all of his decisions require the countersignature of government members to be valid in the first place (Art. 58 (1) Basic Law).

Two presidential powers stand out, however. First, while the President promulgates bills adopted in the federal legislative process, and while he may not veto legislation for political reasons, he may and in fact must refuse to sign legislation that in his view violates the Basic Law (see Chapter 4). Second, the President plays more than a merely ceremonial role when it comes to the dissolution of the Bundestag. He may dissolve the Bundestag only in two situations, namely if in the third round the Bundestag has still not elected a Chancellor by absolute majority (Art. 63 (4) Basic Law) or if the Chancellor requests early elections after having lost a confidence vote in the Bundestag (Art. 68 (1) Basic Law); however, in both situations the President does have a choice. After the third inconclusive round of Chancellor elections in the Bundestag the President may call early Bundestag elections, but he may also appoint the candidate who has obtained a relative majority of votes. Likewise, if the Chancellor requests early Bundestag elections after a failed confidence vote the President may comply, but he may equally refuse, keeping the Bundestag and the Chancellor in place. For a dissolution of the Bundestag in the first scenario, and for his decision to keep the Chancellor in office, the President does not need a countersignature (Art. 58 Basic Law). Overall, however, the President bears in mind the non-partisan dignity of his office, the indirect character of his election in the first place, and the supremacy of the Basic Law as interpreted by the Constitutional Court.

Personal Credibility

The 2011/2012 scandal involving President Christian Wulff, who in the end resigned – in a string of revelations, his contacts with businessmen during the time when he was still premier of Lower Saxony came to look inappropriate, as did his handling of the scandal itself – highlighted the fact that since the President does not wield any actual powers, he can rely only on his moral authority to exert influence. If the personal credibility of the incumbent is damaged, the Presidency itself can quickly become meaningless, even before actual criminal charges are brought against him.

Once in place, the President can be removed from office, yet only for having intentionally violated the Basic Law or another federal statute, in a procedure before the Federal Constitutional Court (Art. 61 Basic Law). Such an impeachment procedure can be initiated by the Bundestag or the Bundesrat, whereby one-quarter of Bundestag members respectively Bundesrat votes is necessary to table the initiative and qualified majorities are needed to actually start the procedure (two-thirds of Bundestag members respectively Bundesrat votes).

3.2. The Chancellor and his Government

The German federal government is headed by the Federal Chancellor. The term 'chancellor' (*Kanzler* in German) had been applied to national-level prime-ministers already under the Constitution of the North German Confederation of 1867. This was partly to stress that the Confederation respected the position of the prime-ministers of the individual member States, who were called *Ministerpräsident*, by choosing a deliberately different title. The term 'chancellor' thus entered into usage and was retained during the Empire of 1871 and under the Weimar Republic. Historically, the chancellor was a senior executive post in the Holy Roman Empire. In modern-day Germany, most State premiers are still called *Ministerpräsident*, which is also a generic term to describe prime-ministers of foreign countries, while the federal government leader is still called Chancellor.

The Federal Chancellor is elected by the Bundestag upon a proposal by the Federal President (Art. 63 Basic Law). The President's nominee requires the support of an absolute majority of Bundestag members, and he is afterwards appointed Chancellor by the Federal President. If the nominee does not receive an absolute majority, another voting round is held, whereby the Bundestag can elect a Chancellor itself, without any nomination of a candidate by the President; the winner is again the candidate who receives the votes of an absolute majority of Bundestag members. If no candidate musters an absolute majority at that stage, a third voting round is held, and the candidate receiving a relative majority wins. If that candidate also in fact wins an absolute majority in the Bundestag, the Federal President appoints him Chancellor; if he has a relative but not an absolute majority, the President can decide whether to appoint the relative-majority winner or to call for new Bundestag elections. It is permissible for the Chancellor or any other minister to remain a Bundestag member; in practice, most cabinet members are also parliamentarians.

Parliamentary Investiture

The 1949 Basic Law provides that the Chancellor is elected by the Bundestag; if an absolute majority is secured, the President may not refuse to appoint the person thus elected. This stands in contrast to the Weimar Constitution, where the President could choose and appoint a Chancellor himself. The reversal of the procedural order (first election, then appointment) reflects the general trimming of presidential powers under the Basic Law.

The federal government itself, also called cabinet, comprises the Federal Chancellor and the federal ministers (Art. 62 Basic Law). Once a Chancellor is appointed, the President appoints and dismisses federal ministers upon the Chancellor's proposal (Art. 64 (1) Basic Law). Ministers are responsible for their policy area; the Chancellor retains the power of giving overall policy guidelines (Art. 65 Basic Law). The function of commander-in-chief of the armed forces is exercised by the minister of defence in peacetime (Art. 65a Basic Law), but it shifts to the Chancellor if the country is in a state of defence against foreign aggression (Art. 115b Basic Law).

The federal government forms the highest authority of the German federal executive. As the head of the German government, the Federal Chancellor is a member of the European Council, a supreme organ of the European Union; ministers participate in the Union's Council of Ministers depending on the subject-matter to be discussed.

3.3. Ministerial Accountability

The Chancellor and his federal government are accountable to the Bundestag, meaning that they have to justify their actions before it and may face a sanction. The Chancellor owes his office to being elected by the Bundestag in the first place, and the Bundestag can censure the government if it has lost confidence in the Chancellor (Arts. 67 and 68 German Basic Law). The Bundestag may primarily extract information on government conduct via its right to summon ministers under Article 43 (1) of the Basic Law.

To avoid instability, the power of the Bundestag to censure the government is conditioned. The federal government can be brought down only by applying a constructive vote of no-confidence against the Chancellor. The Bundestag can oust a sitting Chancellor only by electing a new one with the votes of an absolute majority of Bundestag members (Art. 67 Basic Law). That is the same majority a Chancellor would need to be regularly elected in the first place. A cooling-off period of forty-eight hours must lapse between the introduction of the initiative and the vote itself. The President must appoint the new Chancellor thus elected. With the termination of the old Chancellor's term, the term of office of the other ministers ends as well (Art. 69 (2) Basic Law), and therefore the entire government falls with the Chancellor. No-confidence votes against individual ministers, constructive or otherwise, are not possible.

> *Stabilized Government*
>
> The limitation of the Bundestag's censure powers to constructive no-confidence votes means a stabilization of the government in office. First, while it may be easy to be against an incumbent Chancellor, it is harder for the opposition to agree on a better alternative; until a united and hostile absolute majority has formed, the Chancellor and his government can stay in power. Second, censure motions against individual ministers are not possible, whereas censure of the Chancellor would be a 'nuclear option'. Third, even when a Chancellor is ousted, a new one can immediately take over with a proven workable parliamentary majority; power vacuums, as seen during the Weimar Republic, are avoided.

Based on this basic relationship of accountability, the Bundestag is capable of exercising parliamentary oversight over the government's actions. This applies to domestic and ordinary foreign policies; it also applies to the government's conduct of European Union policies. The government is obliged to keep the Bundestag, but also the Bundesrat, informed about European developments in general and draft European legislation in particular (Art. 23 Basic Law). Bundestag and Bundesrat involvement in the European legislative process is relevant since European law is binding upon Germany and can take precedence over German law, without the two chambers being the formal lawmaker (see also Chapter 6). The government 'takes into account' Bundestag opinion on European legislative proposals. Involvement of the Bundesrat is relevant also for another reason: the government is not accountable to the Bundesrat, yet still it is to be avoided that States' powers and Germany's federal character are quietly hollowed out by European integration. In the most far-reaching scenario, therefore, if a European measure affects primarily the States' exclusive legislative competences in the field of schooling, culture or broadcasting, Germany's representation in the EU is taken over by a representative who is appointed by the Bundesrat (Art. 23 (6) Basic Law). That representative closely coordinates his actions with the federal government in order to ensure a coherent representation of Germany in Europe. In 2009 the Federal Constitutional Court has furthermore ruled that certain decisions introduced with the Treaty of Lisbon to expand EU powers without there being a formal Treaty amendment must also be approved by the German legislature before the government may agree to them in Brussels, and national legislation was changed accordingly before the Treaty entered into force.

3.4. *Confidence Question*

The reversal of the constructive vote of no-confidence, whereby the initiative lies with the Chancellor rather than the Bundestag, is the 'confidence question'. The Chancellor may, whenever he chooses, ask the Bundestag to affirm its confidence in him (Art. 68 Basic Law). If the confidence motion succeeds, receiving the support of an absolute majority of Bundestag members, the Chancellor can remain in office; if the motion fails, because less than an absolute Bundestag majority supports it, the Chancellor may either decide to stay in office or ask the President to dissolve the Bundestag and call for early elections. The President can then decide to do this within twenty-one days, unless the Bundestag has already elected a new Chancellor in the meantime.

The 'confidence question' that the Chancellor can ask the Bundestag is, in principle, intended as a means for the Chancellor to clear an impasse. If his Bundestag majority is apparently no longer loyal to him, but would not elect another Chancellor in his stead either, the Chancellor can clarify the situation by calling for an explicit vote. The Chancellor may also tie the confidence question to the passing of a specific bill or policy proposal: the majority then should either support the Chancellor and his project or risk early elections, with the possible consequence that government parties end up in the opposition. This is a political means to discipline the Chancellor's own rank-and-file.

The Chancellor may also seek to lose a confidence vote on purpose, asking his majority not to support the motion and to abstain. Since the Bundestag cannot dissolve itself, and the President can in this situation dissolve it only after a lost confidence vote, this is the Chancellor's only means to have early elections take place. New elections are to gain fresh legitimacy, resolve policy deadlocks, or to boost the government's majority in the Bundestag. It is the President's task to decide whether the Chancellor's assessment that he can no longer govern is justified, in which case he may go on and dissolve the Bundestag, or whether the Chancellor is plainly abusing the procedure for political gains, in which case he may and must refuse to call early elections. The Federal Constitutional Court has ruled twice on the legality of early elections: Helmut Kohl, who had won a constructive vote of no-confidence in 1982, immediately sought a consolidation of his majority through early elections; Gerhard Schröder sought to break out of political paralysis, after his party lost important regional elections, in the same way in 2005. Both Chancellors lost their confidence vote on purpose, and the President dissolved parliament in both cases. The Federal Constitutional Court accorded the Chancellor discretion to assess the political situation and to choose the means of resolving political crises; confidence questions with a view to allow for early elections are not per se unlawful. Thus, in its judgment of 25 August 2005 (2 BvE 4/05 and 2 BvE 7/05), the Court held:

> 'The confidence question aimed at a dissolution of the Bundestag is only constitutional if it complies not only with the formal requirements but also with the purpose of Article 68 Basic Law. The Basic Law, through Articles 63, 67 and 68, seeks a government capable of action. (...) The Federal Constitutional Court reviews the application of Article 68 Basic Law in accordance with its purpose only in a restricted manner as prescribed by the Constitution'.

Exercising judicial restraint, and noting that it comes last in a process involving the Chancellor, the Bundestag and the President, each having the means to stop the entire process, the Federal Constitutional Court therefore upheld the legality of the manoeuvre in both cases.

4. The United Kingdom

The UK is a monarchy, albeit a constitutional or parliamentary one. The head of state is the King, a hereditary office; the government is headed by a Prime-Minister who is formally appointed by the King but in practice the King always appoints the leader of the majority party in the House of Commons, at least if one party does have an absolute majority, which is usually, if not always, the case. Save for a brief republican period under Oliver Cromwell and his son as well as another interregnum after the expulsion of James II, both during the 17th century, the monarchical system of England, Britain and the United Kingdom has been uninterrupted for over eleven hundred years. The current Windsor dynasty descends from George I, who became the first King from the Protestant House of Hanover in 1714. 18th century statesman Robert Walpole is generally considered to be the first British Prime-Minister, as he exerted leadership over the other ministers in a setting of parliamentary government.

4.1. The King

The head of state of the United Kingdom is the King, which is a hereditary monarchical office. Into the 9th century, different kingdoms competed for hegemony in England; Wessex defeated the other kingdoms and established a line of Anglo-Saxon Kings of England. William the Conqueror became the first Anglo-Norman King of England in 1066; in 1714, the throne passed from the Stuart dynasty to the German House of Hanover as it became law that the monarch must be a Protestant. The Windsor dynasty is a continuation of the House of Hanover: it was renamed after Windsor castle during World War I so as to emphasize its patriotic link with the UK. The throne passes to the oldest legitimate child upon the death or abdication of a King, yet sons have priority over daughters. The King must still always be a Protestant and become the head of the Anglican Church (Act of Settlement 1701). Being, becoming, or marrying a Catholic permanently excludes potential successors from the order of succession. A reform process has been set in motion, however, to abolish male succession priority and the ban on marriage with Catholics. In late 2011 this reform intention was endorsed by the leaders of the 16 Commonwealth countries where the UK monarch is head of state. The implementation of this reform requires changes to the Act of Settlement as well as the Bill of Rights of 1689 and the Royal Marriages Act of 1772.

The King's powers are all but ceremonial in practice (see also Chapter 2). Notionally, the King reigns over the country himself, with the advice of his Privy Council, an advisory body; he makes legislation, giving his royal assent to statutes adopted by Parliament; and he adjudicates with the help of his royal courts. In reality, the King is stripped of discretionary power and is constrained by the supremacy of Parliament and the discretion of the Prime-Minister. The King and the Privy Council do not reign, instead government policy is conducted by the Prime-Minister and his cabinet of ministers; the judiciary is independent; by constitutional convention, the King gives royal assent to any and all bills that have passed Parliament, without any choice to refuse; under the Bill of Rights 1689 the King effectively cannot legislate without Parliament, and the courts accept the supremacy of statute over royal prerogative. As regards other decisions, such as the appointment of new peers to the Lords, the conclusion of treaties or the appointment of judges to the Supreme Court or Anglican bishops, the King acts with the 'advice' of the Prime-Minister. In reality this means that the King merely approves decisions that are in fact taken by the Prime-Minister.

Historically, the King was in a much stronger position compared with today, but already throughout the Middle Ages and the early modern period he relied on consultation with Parliament to govern effectively, not least due to the feudal system. Conflicts between the Stuarts and Parliament in the 17th century resulted first in a civil war, then in the abolition of the monarchy and, shortly after its restoration, in the assertion of parliamentary supremacy over the crown. The Hanover monarchs, who were installed by virtue of the Act of Settlement 1701, were much more restrained from the outset. 19th and 20th century monarchs from that dynasty effectively ceded their political prerogatives to their democratically legitimized Prime-Ministers and retained a symbolic role as embodying the unity and continuity of the state.

4.2. *The Prime-Minister and his Cabinet*

The Prime-Minister is effectively the head of the government in the UK (technically, it is the King's government). The office of the Prime-Minister is almost entirely conventional. It emerged in practice in the 18th century as one of the King's ministers would become the leading, or 'first' minister. Even today, statute only incidentally even mentions the Prime-Minister, such as when it regulates the salaries of different government officials. In reality, the Prime-Minister is the most prominent and dominant figure in UK politics.

The government is in principle formed by the political party that commands an absolute majority in the House of Commons. Coalitions or minority governments in a 'hung' Parliament, where no single party has an absolute majority, are an exception in the light of the electoral system that applies to the Commons (see Chapter 4). The King appoints the Prime-Minister, but by convention he always appoints the leader of the majority party in the Commons. The last royal appointee to be rejected in the Commons was the Duke of Wellington, who had to be quickly dismissed again by King William IV in the 1830s. If no party commands an absolute majority in the Commons, the King may appoint the previous Prime-Minister to attempt forming a minority cabinet or the person most likely to otherwise form a stable government.

Once installed, the Prime-Minister goes on to select fellow parliamentarians to become ministers and form the inner cabinet. The King formally appoints cabinet ministers with the Prime-Minister's advice, again without a choice but to agree with the Prime-Minister's nominations. Cabinet ministers must conventionally be members of Parliament, preferably of the House of Commons. Ministers recruited from outside Parliament may be granted a peerage so as to become a member of the Lords.

Cabinet ministers are responsible for a specific sector of government policy, and they are also 'secretaries of state' if they head a government department. Further junior ministerial posts are awarded below the level of secretaries of state. Members of the majority party in the Commons who are left without a ministerial or junior ministerial post remain as 'backbenchers', sitting in the back of the government's ranks.

> *The Parliament, the Government, the Cabinet and its Shadow*
>
> The majority party in the UK House of Commons is the government in a broad sense, seated to the right of the speaker. The main executive body is the cabinet, comprising the Prime-Minister and his cabinet ministers. Government parliamentarians holding cabinet posts are seated on the front bench; behind them are the 'backbenchers' with no ministerial posts. On the opposite side of the aisle, parliamentarians of the opposition are seated. Some senior opposition members specialize in subject-matters mirroring government departments; opposite to the cabinet there will thus be an informal 'shadow' cabinet, comprising 'shadow' ministers, making clear that the parliamentary opposition is ready to take over the government at any time.

The cabinet forms the highest executive authority in the UK. As it is formed from within Parliament and remains accountable to the plenary, it is sometimes described as an executive committee of the House of Commons. An important difference with an actual committee is, of course, that committees reflect, on a smaller scale, the composition of the plenary and the relative share of seats of political parties, whereas the government does not include the opposition. The Prime-Minister, while notionally a first among equal ministers, is the effective leader of the cabinet. As the head of the cabinet, the Prime-Minister is furthermore a member of the European Council, a supreme organ of the European Union; cabinet ministers participate in the Union's Council of Ministers depending on the subject-matter to be discussed.

4.3. Ministerial Accountability

The UK cabinet is accountable to the House of Commons. By convention, the Prime-Minister resigns if the House of Commons passes a vote of no-confidence against him; the same applies to individual cabinet ministers, who can be ousted by a Commons vote as well. There are no special procedural requirements for such censure votes. In reality, ministers resign voluntarily or are reshuffled after having become a liability.

> *Party Revolt*
>
> Cabinets do not usually fall after a no-confidence vote triggered by the opposition, but rather by internal power shifts within the government party. Margaret Thatcher lost office in 1990 after losing the backing of her own party. Transition of power from one Prime-Minister to another within the same party, whether peaceful or by revolt, does not necessarily require fresh elections, as long as the majority accepts the successor. Thus, Gordon Brown succeeded Tony Blair as Prime-Minister in 2007 with the continued support of his party which held a parliamentary majority, without any intervening general elections.

Based on this basic relationship of accountability, the House of Commons is capable of exercising parliamentary oversight over the government's actions. The Lords, although they cannot bring down the cabinet, possess sufficient political leverage to put the government under scrutiny as well. This applies to domestic and ordinary foreign government policies; it also applies to the cabinet's conduct of European Union policies. Parliamentary involvement in the European legislative process is relevant since European law is binding upon the UK and can take precedence over UK law, without Westminster Parliament being the formal lawmaker (see also Chapter 6). The main tool by which Parliament exercises some influence over the UK government at European lawmaking is the 'scrutiny reserve'. Based on parliamentary resolutions, and applicable to both Commons and Lords, UK ministers are in principle barred from giving their consent to European drafts until Parliament has completed its consideration of that draft.

> *Elective Dictatorship?*
>
> The person who is the leader of the majority party in the House of Commons will be appointed Prime-Minister. As Prime-Minister, he will wield a considerable amount of power. Advising the King, he can compose and reshuffle his cabinet and decide over royal appointments including peerages. In the past, he could even have the Commons dissolved at a moment he freely chose. Via internal party discipline, he can also lead the Commons majority. Whoever controls the majority party controls

the House of Commons; whoever controls the Commons controls Parliament; whoever controls Parliament can make statutes which the monarch will sign; and whoever is in control of statute-making is omnipotent in accordance with parliamentary sovereignty. At times, the Prime-Minister is therefore referred to as an elected dictator. We should, however, not underestimate the political constraints on a Prime-Minister: self-assured cabinet ministers; rebellious backbenchers and competing 'wings' within his own party; the party base; the opposition in the Commons and the House of Lords, which can expose government failures; the media; and external forces, not least European law. If the Prime-Minister does not head a single-party government, as is usual, but a coalition government such as the one that took office in 2010, his freedom to act is furthermore limited by the interests of the junior coalition partner.

The statutory maximum term for Parliament is five years. The Commons can extend the regular maximum term by statute, but such a statute must receive the approval of the Lords as well (Section 7 Parliament Act 1911), whereas in most other cases the Lords can be overridden. The polling day can be postponed beyond the five-year term by the Prime-Minister, but by no more than two months, and only if reasons are given and the draft order to that effect is approved by resolutions in both the Commons and the Lords (Section 1 Fixed-Term Parliaments Act 2011). Early elections *before* the end of the five-year term can be called only if the House of Commons passes a motion to that effect with a majority representing two-thirds of its total seats including vacant seats, or if a vote of no-confidence is not followed, within 14 days, by a vote of confidence in the government (Section 2 Fixed-Term Parliaments Act 2011).

5. France

The executive branch under the French Constitution of the Fifth Republic is two-headed. The head of the government in a narrow sense is the Prime-Minister (Art. 21 French Constitution), who is accountable to the French parliament. The President, in turn, is not only head of state, but also wields important executive powers of his own. Elected directly by the people, the President is not accountable to the French parliament in the sense of a confidence rule. Without a Prime-Minister, and with the directly elected President heading the government alone, France would be a fully presidential republic similar to the US; without its powerful and directly elected President, and with just the Prime-Minister heading the government, France would be a fully parliamentary system comparable to Germany. Since it has both, a President who is directly elected and not accountable to parliament in the sense of a confidence rule and a Prime-Minister who is not directly elected and who is accountable to parliament, both sharing executive powers, France is referred to as a semi-presidential system: half presidential, half parliamentary. Charles de Gaulle was the first President of the Fifth Republic, first elected through an electoral college in 1958 and in popular elections in 1965. The first prime-minister of the Fifth Republic was Michel Debré, who also played a major role in drafting the current Constitution.

5.1. The President

The President of the French Republic is elected directly via a run-off system. In order to get elected in the first round, a candidate must obtain an absolute majority of votes cast; if no candidate obtains an absolute majority, the two candidates with the most votes proceed to a second round. In the second round, plurality suffices in order to get elected (Art. 7 French Constitution).

Originally, the President was elected via an electoral college. President de Gaulle called and won a referendum to introduce direct election in 1962. The direct elections boosted the legitimacy and weight of the office, and marked the decisive step from a parliamentary to a semi-presidential system in France. The President is elected for a term of five years. The original term was seven years, yet a constitutional amendment in 2000 shortened the term; it now matches the term of the National Assembly, which lowers the likelihood of opposing political parties gaining control of the presidency and a parliamentary majority. Since the constitutional reform of 2008, a President may only serve two consecutive terms (Art. 6 French Constitution).

Once in office, the President may be removed from office when found incapacitated by the Constitutional Council (Art. 7 French Constitution). Furthermore, the President may be removed in an impeachment-type procedure for a 'breach of his duties manifestly incompatible with the exercise of his mandate' (Art. 68 French Constitution). The removal is decided on by a joint session of the two chambers of parliament sitting as the High Court. A removal requires the votes of a two-thirds majority of the members of the High Court.

As head of state the President represents France abroad and fulfils diplomatic functions (Art. 14 French Constitution), he concludes international treaties (Art. 52 French Constitution) although the significant ones require parliamentary ratification; he appoints functionaries (Art. 13 French Constitution) and grants individual pardons (Art. 17 French Constitution). His executive powers include the right to appoint a Prime-Minister as head of the government (Art. 8 French Constitution); the President presides over the council of ministers, which is the 'inner' government, when it meets (Art. 9 French Constitution); he is commander-in-chief of the armed forces (Art. 15 French Constitution) and he wields far-reaching emergency powers (Art. 16 French Constitution).

As regards legislation, while it is the Prime-Minister who introduces bills on behalf of the executive, the President is involved via the council of ministers and can also have influence over such initiatives depending on the political constellation. In the legislative process, although he has no veto power, the President may insist on one reconsideration of bills passed by parliament (Art. 10 French Constitution), and he can refer adopted bills for constitutional review by the Constitutional Council (Art. 61 French Constitution). Upon governmental or joint parliamentary proposal he may also refer listed categories of government bills for referendum (Art. 11 French Constitution); the 2008 reform also authorizes referendums upon the initiative of a parliamentary minority. The President may dissolve the National Assembly, though not more than once a year (Art. 12 French Constitution).

5.2. *The Prime-Minister and his Government*

The Prime-Minister, the other head of the French executive next to the President, is the head of the government proper. The Prime-Minister is appointed by the President (Art. 8 French Constitution), and he and his government are accountable to the parliament, in particular the National Assembly (Arts. 20, 49 and 50 French Constitution). The President removes the Prime-Minister from office if the Prime-Minister tenders the government's resignation (Art. 8 French Constitution); this he may do voluntarily of his own motion, or after having been defeated in the National Assembly (Art. 49 French Constitution).

> *Cohabitation*
>
> The French Prime-Minister, although appointed by the President, requires the confidence of the National Assembly. It may be that the President is forced to appoint a Prime-Minister who is of a political colour other than his own: since the President and the National Assembly are elected in separate elections, the party-political affiliation of the parliamentary majority and that of the head of state do not have to coincide. When President and Prime-Minister are thus of different political colours, a cohabitation situation arises: the two have to cooperate sharing their powers and to overcome their differences. They live together without being married, as it were, which is what cohabitation in fact means. Cohabitations are more likely if parliamentary elections are held in mid-term of the President's tenure, with voters expressing their dissatisfaction with the incumbent executive by voting the opposition into office, than when both elections take place at around the same time. Cohabitation tends to strengthen the position of the Prime-Minister with respect to the President, since the latter cannot exert internal party pressure upon the former. Since 2000, the likelihood of cohabitations is lowered as by way of constitutional amendment the President's term of office is shortened to five years, down from the previous seven years, to match the five-year term of the National Assembly. Voters are supposedly not likely to 'split the ticket' if both elections take place at around the same time, so any President can count on a friendly majority in the National Assembly, which gives him leeway in appointing a Prime-Minister of his liking. To illustrate the President's might in a non-cohabitation setting, legend has it that President De Gaulle required his Prime-Ministers to give him a signed but yet undated letter of resignation, which the President could then use as he might see fit, and that later Presidents continued the practice.

The government, headed by the Prime-Minister, is in charge of national policy-making (Art. 20 French Constitution). Since in France executive and foreign-policy powers are shared between Prime-Minister and President, both of them together may participate in the European Council, a supreme organ of the European Union; government ministers participate in the Union's Council of Ministers depending on the subject-matter to be discussed.

5.3. Ministerial Accountability

The French government is accountable to the National Assembly, though the President is not. The government members are appointed by the President; they do not require an explicit vote of confidence from the National Assembly in order to assume office. The Prime-Minister may present a policy programme or make a general policy statement and make this a matter of parliamentary confidence (Art. 49, first paragraph, French Constitution), but he does not have to. If he does ask for such a vote of confidence and the National Assembly rejects his programme or statement, he must tender the government's resignation.

Otherwise the government can be brought down by a motion of censure in which the National Assembly expresses its lack of confidence in the government (Art. 49, second paragraph, French Constitution). In line with the rationalization of parliament, censure votes are procedurally constrained. To introduce a censure motion it must be signed by at least one-tenth of the members of the National Assembly. Then, a cooling-off period of 48 hours must pass between the initiative and the vote. The motion itself is only passed if an absolute majority of members supports it. Only votes in favour are counted towards the absolute majority, which means that abstentions count as votes against the motion and for the government. Parliamentarians are restricted in the number of motions they may sign. The Prime-Minister and his government resign if successfully censured. The President may then appoint a new Prime-Minister or dissolve the National Assembly.

Government members may not at the same time be members of parliament (Art. 23 French Constitution). The seat of a parliamentarian who receives a ministerial appointment is taken over by his alternate: his running-mate who got elected on the same ticket to fill his seat in case of a vacancy. Since 2008, the French Constitution stresses that the replacement is temporary, so that former ministers may return to parliament and reassume their seat (Art. 25 French Constitution).

Based on the basic relationship of accountability, the National Assembly is capable of exercising parliamentary oversight over the actions of the Prime-Minister and the government. The practical possibilities are constrained in the light of the executive's dominance and the rules applying to the functioning of the parliament. The principle nevertheless applies to domestic and ordinary foreign government policies; it also applies to the government's conduct of European Union policies. Parliamentary involvement in the European legislative process is relevant since European law is binding upon France and can take precedence over French law, without the parliament being the formal lawmaker (see also Chapter 6). The two chambers of parliament are therefore to be kept informed about European developments and may pass resolutions on drafts (Art. 88-4 French Constitution); the government furthermore agrees in principle not to approve European drafts while parliament is still considering them.

Regarding domestic bills, to expedite the approval of the National Assembly to statutes, the Prime-Minister may make the passing of bills a matter of parliamentary confidence; the bill is then considered adopted unless the National Assembly introduces a censure motion within 24 hours and successfully censures the government (Art. 49, third paragraph, French Constitution). Since the constitutional reform of 2008, this procedure may only be applied to finance bills and social security financing bills, and otherwise to one bill per parliamentary session.

> *Blackmailing Parliament*
>
> Under Article 49 of the French Constitution, the Prime-Minister may make a bill a matter of confidence in his government as a whole; in Germany, under Article 68 of the Basic Law, the Chancellor can ask for parliamentary confidence in connection with the passing of a bill as well. The difference is that in Germany the bill is deemed rejected, and confidence is deemed denied, unless the Bundestag supports the bill; in France, however, the bill is deemed approved, and confidence is deemed confirmed, unless the National Assembly brings down the government. The French default is therefore in favour of the government.

The French Constitution stresses the homogeneity of the government as a collective body. Powers are assigned to the Prime-Minister or to the government as a whole, not to individual ministers. The government can also be censured only as a unit.

6. The Netherlands

The head of state of the Netherlands (the country in Europe) is the King, who is also head of state of the overarching Kingdom of the Netherlands (the Netherlands plus the three overseas countries in the Caribbean). The Dutch head of the cabinet is the Prime-Minister; the overseas countries in the Kingdom have prime-ministers of their own. As part of post-Napoleonic restoration, William I of Orange-Nassau became first 'Sovereign Prince' and then the first King of the Netherlands in 1815. The office of Prime-Minister became politically prominent after the constitutional reform of 1848, which allocated responsibility for government action with the ministers rather than with the monarch. The statesman Johan Rudolph Thorbecke, the main drafter of the reform, became Prime-Minister in 1849.

6.1. *The King*

The Dutch monarchy is hereditary. The royal dynasty of Orange-Nassau descends from King William I, Prince of Orange (Art. 24 Dutch Constitution). After the fall of the Napoleonic Empire, the Republic as it had lasted until 1795 was not restored. Instead, in 1813, William, who was the son of William V, a stadholder of Holland in the United Provinces before the French invasion, accepted sovereignty. The Constitution of 1814 referred to him as the 'Sovereign Prince', which was changed in 1815 to 'King'.

The Dutch King is also the head of state of the overarching Kingdom of the Netherlands as descending from Queen Juliana, the monarch at the time of the creation of the overarching Kingdom (Art. 1a Charter for the Kingdom of the Netherlands).

The rules of royal succession are laid down in the Dutch Constitution (Art. 25 Dutch Constitution; Art. 5 (1) Charter for the Kingdom). Upon the death of the

King, his oldest legitimate child, son or daughter, ascends the throne. Upon ascending the throne, a new King must take an oath on the Constitution (Art. 32 Dutch Constitution). A King may abdicate by unilateral declaration. In that case, the rule of royal succession is applied as it would be in the case of his death. A King is deemed to have automatically abdicated, and a potential heir is deemed to have waived his claim to the throne, if they marry without legislative approval. Approval for marriages in the royal house take the form of statute; the States-General meet in joint session to discuss and adopt a bill to that effect (Art. 28 Dutch Constitution).

Marriage without Approval

All three sons of Queen Beatrix of Orange-Nassau got married. Prince Willem Alexander and Prince Constantijn received statutory approval for their respective marriage, and they and their offspring were thus entitled to inherit the crown. For Prince Friso's marriage, however, the government did not even introduce a bill for a statute of approval, in the light of the controversial past of the Prince's bride. Having married without statutory approval, he and his offspring were excluded from the line of succession.

The Dutch 'government' (*regering*) strictly speaking comprises the King and his ministers (Art. 42 Dutch Constitution). The ministers without the King together form the council of ministers. The ministers plus the secretaries of state, a sort of junior ministers, together form the cabinet (*kabinet*). The council of ministers – and the cabinet as a whole – are headed by the Prime-Minister (Art. 45 Dutch Constitution).

The King is stipulated to be 'inviolable', which means he is above legal and political pressures; responsibility for government action is instead borne by the ministers, including the Prime-Minister (Art. 42 (2) Dutch Constitution), as well as secretaries of state (Art. 46 (2) Dutch Constitution). All royal decrees and the approval of legislation must be countersigned by cabinet members to take effect (Art. 47 Dutch Constitution). This means that the King does not exercise any personal constitutional function. Instead, he and his government members act jointly, whereby only the latter bear responsibility. 'Royal decrees' by which the King appoints ministers, dissolves parliament, or appoints provincial governors, are de facto government orders.

The fact that the King himself exercises no power autonomously however does not mean that, as a person, he is not involved in government policy. The Prime-Minister consults with the monarch weekly. In the process of cabinet formation, even though again only the cabinet bears responsibility, the King's personal preferences may play a role. The extent to which the monarch as a person actually influences government policy is not disclosed to the public, though. It is the Prime-Minister and his cabinet who explain and defend government policies in public in general, and before parliament in particular.

6.2. The Prime-Minister and his Cabinet

Virtually all rules governing ministerial accountability and the process of cabinet formation in the Netherlands are matters of constitutional custom. The Constitution itself merely provides that the cabinet members are appointed by royal decree (Art. 43 Dutch Constitution).

In practice, modern cabinet formation processes follow an established pattern. On the day that regular new Second Chamber elections are held, the cabinet tenders its resignation to the King, indicating that it is prepared to make room for a new cabinet to face a newly composed parliament. The cabinet then stays on as a caretaker cabinet or demissionary cabinet. Once parliamentary election results are established, the King considers a choice of new Prime-Minister. The applicable proportional representation system does not tend to yield any clear absolute majorities (see Chapter 4), which means that several parties together must form a coalition so as to rely on an absolute majority of seats. For that, in turn, several alternative combinations may be possible.

The King first obtains the advice from the vice-president of the Council of State (an advisory body, the King is notionally its chairman himself), the presidents of both Chambers of parliament, and the leaders of the party groups in the new Second Chamber. He then appoints one or more *informateurs*. The *informateur* is a mediator whose task it is to probe in informal talks which political parties are likely to form a stable coalition, and to report to the King about the available options. Based on the *informateur's* recommendations, the King then appoints a *formateur*, who is the envisaged Prime-Minister and whose task it is to actually form a cabinet.

If he has been successful, the *formateur* is then appointed by the King as Prime-Minister. A new Prime-Minister receives a new appointment; if he had already been the head of the previous cabinet, the King refuses his earlier resignation offer and keeps him in office. The appointment or re-appointment is signed by the King and, since it is a royal decree, it must be countersigned by the new Prime-Minister. The other members of the tentative cabinet are also appointed or re-appointed as ministers and secretaries of state, by the King's signature and the Prime-Minister's counter-signature.

Once appointed, the Prime-Minister goes on to issue a statement before the Second Chamber, giving account for his role as *formateur* and setting out policy priorities. He does not ask for a vote of approval, however. As long as he and his cabinet have not lost confidence in the Second Chamber, they remain in office.

6.3. Ministerial Accountability

The Dutch Constitution does not stipulate to whom ministers and secretaries of state are accountable. The prevailing understanding has in fact shifted in the course of the 19th century, namely from ministerial accountability to the King towards ministerial accountability to the parliament, in particular the Second Chamber, the directly elected lower house. As a result, the cabinet, once it is installed, must be able to rely on a workable supportive majority in the Second Chamber.

Under the original Constitution of 1815, the King bore responsibility for government policy himself. Ministers were considered the King's advisors. Pressure to allow for more democracy and popular participation however kept rising in most of post-restoration Europe. In the Netherlands, the middle of the 19th century saw a power struggle between parliament and the monarch, in which the latter ceded power to the former. In 1840, the countersign for royal decrees was introduced. Acts of the King thus required approval from ministers, depriving him of the capacity to act alone. For ministers, this meant that they were subject to criminal liability in case the King violated criminal law. The key moment in the development of a democratic constitutional order came with the constitutional amendment of 1848. Along with other democratic changes, such as direct elections to the Second Chamber, ministers were declared to be responsible for government policy. This formed the basis of political ministerial responsibility as it still exists to date (Art. 42 (2) Dutch Constitution). Gradually, the ministers asserted their power vis-à-vis the monarch and played a more independent role. In return for the reduction of the King's power, the right to dissolve parliament was introduced (Art. 64 (1) Dutch Constitution).

Still, while ministers had to defend government policy before parliament, since they were the ones responsible for it, it was not yet established that they also needed parliamentary confidence to stay in office. Strictly speaking, ministers remained accountable to the King, not to parliament, in the sense that ministers primarily needed the King's trust. This changed in a sequence of political follow-up incidents which expanded ministerial responsibility for *all* actions of the King, and which ultimately established the 'confidence rule' as it applies today: ministers who can no longer count on parliamentary confidence must resign, irrespective of whether they still enjoy the King's support or not. By extension, the King must appoint ministers who are acceptable to a parliamentary majority.

In 1853, Prime-Minister Thorbecke resigned over a dispute with King William III. In a period of social unrest – a confrontation between the Protestant majority and the Catholic Church – the King had rejected the Prime-Minister's advice on how to proceed. In a speech, the King sided with the Protestants instead of stressing the freedom of religion. The Prime-Minister refused to take responsibility for the King's acts and tendered his resignation. This first incident underlined that ministers bear responsibility for the King. A second incident, the so-called 'Mijer affair' of 1866, showed that ministers were responsible even in areas then considered to be royal prerogatives. Having just approved the budget of the minister for the colonies, Mijer, the parliament learned that the minister had been appointed to an overseas post. The parliamentarians had expected Mijer to implement the approved policies himself. They adopted a motion disapproving of the cabinet's behaviour in this matter. The government responded by dissolving parliament, which is considered to show how seriously it took the criticism. In 1867, finally, the 'Luxembourg affair' brought about the definitive confirmation of the parliamentary confidence rule. The government of William III, who at the time was also Grand-Duke of Luxembourg in personal union, agreed to guarantee the neutrality of Luxembourg. The Dutch Second Chamber criticized the cabinet, in particular the minister of foreign affairs, for harming Dutch interests while taking action with respect to a country with which the Dutch had in fact little connection. The Chamber rejected the budget of the ministry of foreign affairs. The cabinet tendered its resignation, but the King refused and instead dissolved the Chamber: the parliamentarians were said to have abused their budgetary powers. The new Second Chamber took issue again and adopted a motion stating that the previous dissolution of parliament had not been justified on any ground of national interest; also the next budget of the ministry of foreign affairs got rejected. Again the cabinet tendered its resignation. Yet this time the King did not dissolve parliament but accepted the resignation. The States-General, and the Second Chamber in particular, had asserted their rights vis-à-vis the government: the cabinet had to resign over a conflict with parliament.

The cabinet, and the 'inner' council of ministers, headed by the Prime-Minister, exercise executive power. Command of the armed forces is assumed by the government as a collective body (Art. 97 (2) Dutch Constitution). The Prime-Minister is strictly speaking a first among equal ministers; however, as he is for all practical purposes the head of the government, he is the one to participate in the European Council, a supreme organ of the European Union; cabinet ministers participate in the Union's Council of Ministers depending on the subject-matter to be discussed.

Based on the basic relationship of accountability, the Second Chamber is capable of exercising parliamentary oversight over the actions of the Prime-Minister and the cabinet. The First Chamber is more restricted in its real capabilities but wields political influence as well. Ministers must answer parliamentary questions under Article 68 of the Dutch Constitution. Ministerial accountability applies to domestic and ordinary foreign policies; it also applies to the cabinet's conduct of European Union policies. Parliamentary involvement in the European legislative process is relevant since European law is binding upon the Netherlands and can take precedence over Dutch law, without the Dutch legislature being the formal lawmaker (see also Chapter 6). The Second and First Chamber therefore monitor European developments; as regards certain European measures in the field of police and judicial cooperation in criminal matters, ministers may in principle only give their approval if such approval has been cleared by both Chambers.

6.4. *Motions of No-Confidence*

The established twin concept of ministerial responsibility and the parliamentary confidence rule remains in place to date. Ministers bear responsibility for their own actions and for the actions of their subordinates (individual ministerial responsibility) as well as for actions of the cabinet as a whole (collective ministerial responsibility). This means that ministers may be forced to resign individually; it is not accepted that ministers claim that they were personally against a cabinet decision.

The ultimate sanction against a cabinet is the parliamentary motion of no-confidence. Like most other aspects of ministerial accountability, this is not regulated in the Dutch Constitution itself. Thus, a motion of no-confidence is not bound to any formal conditions. It can be directed at the cabinet as a whole or at one or more individual ministers. In its form it remains a regular motion by which the Second Chamber expresses its opinion. It may be tabled by any member of the

Second Chamber and must be supported by a simple majority vote. What is essential is that the cabinet or individual ministers conclude that they have lost the confidence of the Second Chamber. A motion is merely one of the means by which to express such loss.

In reality, motions of no-confidence do not explicitly call for a minister's resignation. Instead, ministers resign over events which they *interpret* as a sign of a loss of parliamentary confidence. More usual means are therefore motions calling for policies which would deviate from a minister's policies so much that the minister cannot read the motion in any way other than as a no-confidence vote against him; the rejection of a minister's draft budget; or the adoption of an amendment to a bill which is deemed unacceptable to the cabinet or a minister. This also means that ministers retain a margin of freedom to interpret unfriendly motions. A minister may interpret a motion or amendment as criticizing only a particular policy, rather than him as a functionary. The size of the majority that carried the motion may also play a role in interpreting the gravity of the criticism. Again, a motion of no-confidence is any motion or other expression of parliamentary opinion that is interpreted by the cabinet or minister as signifying a loss of confidence.

What is usually decisive is the confidence that ministers enjoy, or do not enjoy, in the Second Chamber. The Second Chamber is directly elected and enjoys the political primacy over the First Chamber. It is disputed whether the confidence rule also applies to the First Chamber, as also here the rules are not codified. A minister in any event remains free to tie the continuation of his office to approval in the First Chamber, and to resign after a conflict with the First Chamber.

The consequence of a loss of parliamentary confidence, in one way or another, is that a minister must tender his resignation with the King. If the entire cabinet tenders its resignation, it is up to the King to decide whether to keep the cabinet in office as a minority cabinet, to have a new cabinet formed, or to call for early elections. Usually, the fall of a cabinet leads to the dissolution of the Second Chamber and therefore to early elections. Rather than as an anti-parliamentarian move, such dissolution of the Second Chamber is seen as a way to allow the citizens to judge on the preceding crisis and to cast a fresh democratic vote. Technically, though, a change of government does not require parliamentary elections if the successor government is supported or tolerated in office by the same parliament that had brought down the previous government.

6.5. *The Government of the Kingdom*

Government functions for the overarching Kingdom of the Netherlands are exercised by the Dutch King and the Kingdom Council of Ministers. The Kingdom Council of Ministers is the ordinary Dutch council of ministers, except that it includes the ministers plenipotentiary from the overseas countries as well (Art. 7 Charter for the Kingdom). The overseas ministers plenipotentiary are rather ambassadors than actual ministers, in that they do not act freely but represent, and are instructed by, the government of their home country. They may delay decision-making and seek consultation, but ultimately the Council may decide by majority

Chapter 5

(Art. 12 Charter for the Kingdom), meaning that the overseas representatives can be outvoted (see also Chapters 2 and 4).

Chapter 6

JUDICIAL REVIEW AND HUMAN RIGHTS

1. Overview

The term 'judicial review' means that a judge can examine a legal decision or norm, or another object of scrutiny, and check its compatibility with a higher norm. Thus, a judge may, depending on the system, test whether a regional law is in harmony or in conflict with a higher, national law. If the lower law provides rules that go against the provisions of the higher law, then the judge, if he has review power, may establish a conflict. Similarly, he may check whether an administrative decision by a public authority complies with the authorizing general legislation. He may further, again depending on the system, examine the validity of a national statute by setting it against the national constitution, an exercise called constitutional review of legislation. A crass but illustrative example would be the hypothetical review of the constitutionality of a criminal provision that prescribes the death penalty whereas the constitution bans the death penalty. In some systems, the judge may review the constitutionality of political parties. He may review the compatibility of national law with general principles of law, such as proportionality, or with an international treaty, such as the European Convention on Human Rights. Conversely, he may also, where applicable, check the compliance of treaties or acts of international organizations with the national constitution. Judicial review is thus a court's power to detect conflicts in law, and possibly to attach consequences to resolve the conflict.

Three subjects shall be discussed here in greater detail. First, constitutional review of legislation, pertaining to the constitutionality of statutes made by the central or national lawmaker; second, review of such legislation for treaty compliance, in particular for compliance with the European Convention on Human Rights where applicable; and review of legislation for compliance with the law of the European Union, including the reverse scenario of the review of the constitutionality of European law.

1.1. Constitutional Review of Legislation

There are few issues where the same doctrinal arguments can lead to such differing results across constitutional systems like the issue of constitutional review of legislation. While the right of judges to declare laws unconstitutional is perceived to be acceptable, normal and perhaps even natural in some systems, in other systems this right is fiercely contested. The two arguments typically brought forward to justify the right for judges to review the constitutionality of legislation are, first, that judicial review guarantees the supremacy of the constitution and, second, that judicial review provides a check on the lawmaker for the protection of minorities.

The first argument stresses that the constitution is the highest norm in a legal system, and that all other law derives from its authority. Thus, legislation should not be allowed to violate the constitution. Supporters of judicial review would argue that, consequently, judges should refuse to apply normal statutes if they violate the constitution. Having a constitution but no constitutional review powers for the courts would, in that view, be pointless, since the lawmaker could violate the constitution with impunity. Hans Kelsen, an Austrian scholar credited with designing the prototype of a continental European constitutional court in 1920, argued that laws derive their authority from their compliance with higher law, that non-compliant laws cannot be normative and that a constitution cannot be supreme unless it is enforced by judicial review of legislation. US Supreme Court chief justice Marshall had already stated that judicial review necessarily follows from the supremacy of the Constitution in the 1803 case of *Marbury* v. *Madison*.

However, one may equally argue that the constitution can very well be supreme, but that this supremacy does not mean that judges should be able to frustrate the will of the lawmaker. The lawmaker should simply take account of the constitution when passing statutes in the first place, and make the right choices himself, subject as he is to democratic oversight from the voters. The Netherlands subscribes to such 'optimist' school of thought, putting trust in democratically elected office-holders rather than in unelected judges. In France, historically immunity of legislation resulted from the sovereignty of the people whose representatives adopt laws, although France did introduce constitutional review in 2008 after all, and a Dutch proposal to allow the same had been adopted, also in 2008, in first reading. In the UK, the ban on judicial review of statutes results from the fact that statute already *is* the highest norm in the legal system.

The second argument holds that checks and balances are necessary to provide a counterweight against the majority of the day. Democracy is not the same as tyranny of the majority, it also includes the protection of minorities. In the rule of law, minorities can find such protection as even the majority is bound by law. At the same time, especially in the US, this very counter-majoritarian character of judicial review is often perceived as problematic, especially where judges are suspected of pursuing their own political agenda against the preferences of the elected institutions. More fundamentally, one may wonder what exactly makes majority-appointed judges more likely than legislative majorities to respect minorities.

There are more examples how it is possible to invoke the same principles and arrive at opposite conclusions regarding the justification of judicial review. Separation of powers, the notion that legislature and judiciary should be kept apart, can be construed as meaning that courts should apply the law, not criticize or second-guess it. This is the traditional French reading of such separation, namely the separation of the judiciary from the legislature. Yet separation of powers can also be taken to include the notion of checks and balances, so that it would appear healthy to have a judicial check on the lawmaker. Legal certainty would command that statutes, once in force, should stand until they are repealed, without courts casting doubt on their validity; citizens should however also be able to rely, with certainty, on their constitution, which should always triumph over conflicting legislation. One might say that judges should not be trusted, and not be given too much power, because they are, after all, not elected; one might equally argue that judges are trustworthy *because* they are not elected, and that they can have a more objective and professional view on constitutionality questions compared to political and majority-driven lawmakers. The rule of law can be seen as a principle which judges are qualified to enforce, as they are trained to interpret written law in practice. Conversely, one may argue that there cannot possibly be only one 'correct' or 'orthodox' meaning of constitutional provisions, and that there is no reason to assume that the interpretation given by judges is any better than the interpretation given by lawmakers. One might adopt a nuanced approach and distinguish between constitutional human rights norms, on the one hand, and procedural and competence norms such as those governing the scope of decentralization, on the other hand, but even then opposite conclusions are possible. It can be argued that judges should review statutes only against human rights norms while leaving questions of institutional competence allocation to the political branches, which is a choice underlying the Dutch initiative to introduce constitutional review; yet it can also be argued that judges should, to the contrary, only settle competence disputes without interfering with the actual content of statutory regulation, a choice originally underlying the creation of the French Constitutional Council and the *Staatsgerichtshof*, the German constitutional court under the Weimar Republic. And again, it can be argued that judges should have the power to engage in both types of review, as the modern German Constitutional Court does, or in neither, as the current Dutch Constitution insists. Even where broad powers of review exist, a case can be made that courts should be stricter in some areas, such as those relating to fundamental rights, and be more lenient and self-restrained in areas relating to economic policy choices or foreign affairs. A clear distinction between areas calling for either strict scrutiny or judicial restraint is not always possible, though.

1.2. *The Procedural Setting of Constitutional Review*

In those systems which do feature constitutional review of legislation, it is possible to classify different models under different headings. Systems differ most fundamentally in whether their constitutional review is:

- abstract or concrete;
- *ex ante* or *ex post*;
- centralized or decentralized.

Concrete review of legislation means the verification whether a law that is about to be applied in adversarial judicial proceedings is actually constitutional. It arises out of a concrete dispute between two parties before a court. In abstract review, a law is submitted to scrutiny outside the context of an actual application in a dispute; it is typically triggered by office-holders, such as the government. Ex ante review takes place before the law has entered into force, and strictly speaking it targets bills rather than existing legislation; ex post review subjects legislation in force to judicial scrutiny. In decentralized systems of review, any court may check the constitutionality of legislation; in centralized systems, a special constitutional court or quasi-judicial body exists to carry out this task exclusively.

Modern notions of constitutional review are rooted in a historical breakthrough within American constitutional law. In 1803, the US Supreme Court had held that the US Constitution had to prevail over ordinary legislation, and that it followed from their professional tasks that in the course of proceedings before them, judges should detect whether different applicable norms conflict with each other. As a result, all courts in the US have the power to verify whether legislation that they are about to apply is at all constitutional. This construction rules out abstract review or the review of bills in the form of advisory opinions or otherwise, because that would take place outside the context of an actual court case and would thus not fall within the professional tasks of the judiciary.

Germany, like many other states in Central, Southern and Eastern Europe, features a special constitutional court that carries out review functions. The system is called the continental, Austrian or Kelsenian model of judicial review. These systems allow courts to examine the constitutionality of statutes, but keep the power to invalidate these statutes centralized in one constitutional court set up specifically for that purpose. Review is therefore decentralized when arising from concrete cases, but the final decision on constitutionality is always centralized. In addition, Kelsenian systems typically allow constitutional courts to engage in abstract review of legislation upon request from enumerated state institutions.

France was long famous for having a system whereby laws could only be reviewed before they had entered into force. This task was carried out by the Constitutional Council. The Council was not strictly a court as it was not necessarily staffed by lawyers and did not hear individual cases, but was usually nevertheless considered to belong to the larger family of constitutional courts in Europe. Since the constitutional reform of 2008, France allows its two supreme courts to refer questions regarding the constitutionality of statutes to the Constitutional Council as well, which they in turn may receive from lower courts. Thus, in addition to its ex ante review in the abstract, France now also features concrete review ex post.

In the United Kingdom, constitutionality review of statutes would be difficult, since there is no central document that would codify the most fundamental rules governing the state to start with; furthermore, second-guessing Parliament would mean to violate one of the most important principles of the UK constitution itself, namely parliamentary sovereignty in the sense of legislative supremacy. Thus, Parliament and only Parliament can unmake a statute. The Netherlands explicitly prohibits its judges from questioning the constitutionality of statutes, although an amendment to allow review on enumerated grounds has been adopted in first reading in 2008.

What exactly is the consequence of a judicial decision stating that a statute is unconstitutional? Often terms are used interchangeably: the court invalidates the statute, quashes it, strikes it down, annuls it, declares it void, disapplies it, sets it aside, etc. Two principal effects should be distinguished, however. 'Disapplication', 'invalidation' or 'setting aside' means to leave the statute as it stands, but to refrain from applying it to a particular case. 'Annulment' or 'declaring void' carries further-reaching consequences. It means that the statute is struck out and ceases to exist, as it were. One might compare it to an annulled contract. The legal fiction should then strictly speaking even be that it in fact never has existed, although typically retroactive effects of the annulment of statutes are limited in order to preserve legal certainty. The German Constitutional Court can declare a statute void; the judgment itself then carries the rank of a repealing statute and is published as such. In the US, since all constitutionality review is decentralized and concrete, unconstitutionality means disapplication in concrete cases; however, once the US Supreme Court has found a statute in violation of the Constitution, a common-law precedent is established so that in the future all other courts will have to disapply the statute as well. One might say that in this case 'setting aside' and 'declaring void' boils down to the same thing, namely that the statute loses all practical effect. The legal construction nevertheless is different, since a void statute disappears whereas a statute that is set aside is technically still in force and might potentially even be 'revived' if either case-law or the Constitution is changed. A similar distinction is applied in proceedings before the Court of Justice of the European Union: if EU legislation, such as a directive, is contested in annulment proceedings for an alleged violation of the Treaties (Art. 263 TFEU), the legislation may indeed be annulled; if the unlawfulness of legislation is established incidentally in the course of a preliminary reference procedure (Art. 267 TFEU), it is merely invalidated in the sense of being disapplied.

In any case it should be remembered that while annulment or disapplication of legislation may be powerful tools for a court to wield, their actual use is highly exceptional. It is much more common for a court to resort to interpretation techniques which allow the disputed legislation to remain on the statute books and be applied as long as it is interpreted in such way that it does not conflict with higher law.

1.3. *Review of Treaty Law Compliance*

A subject often associated with judicial review as regards constitutionality is judicial review as regards compliance of statutes with international treaty provisions. After all, here again judges would test legislation for their compatibility with a higher norm; and yet again, the question arises whether treaty law really is 'higher' in rank, and what the consequence of that would be. International treaty provisions gain particular relevance when human rights are to be derived from them in a domestic setting. The European Convention on Human Rights, a multilateral human-rights instrument, is a case in point. The domestic effect that states give to treaty provisions essentially depends on whether they adhere to a monist or dualist model.

In a *monist* system, national statutes and provisions from treaties ratified by the state are treated as forming part of one and the same national legal order, hence the term monism. This allows individuals to invoke treaty provisions before a national court, in the same manner as they would invoke national law. If a conflict arises between national law and a treaty provision, the latter prevails. Under *dualism*, meanwhile, national law and treaties are treated as falling under two separate realms. Individuals can invoke national provisions only; in order to benefit from treaty provisions, they would have to wait until their lawmaker has transposed them into national law, in pursuance of the state's international obligations.

The case for embracing monism is straightforward. The argument would be that it is pointless to have treaties if citizens cannot rely on them before their national judge; and such reliance would be pointless if treaties would not also override conflicting national legislation. Monism may also signal to the outside world a system's willingness to open up to the international legal order, for example free trade regimes, by making its international commitments enforceable in its regular domestic courts. The case for dualism is not without merit, either. Under the private law concept of privity of contract, contracts are binding upon the parties thereto, not upon third parties; a treaty may be likened to a contract between the state and a foreign state making mutual promises, not between the state and its own citizens. To a dualist state, treaty enforcement should be a matter for international diplomacy and public international law, not domestic judicial action. Another argument against unconditional monism might be that it would allow treaties to undermine the national constitution via 'imported' law taking precedence over national law: constitutional review of treaties might be called for. Even where there is no conflict with the constitution, it may be noted that not all systems allow their national parliament to be involved in the ratification of treaties to an extent that would match their role in domestic lawmaking; thus, it may be argued that domestically enforceable rights and obligations should only be created in an ordinary legislative procedure for the adoption of domestic statutes, with full parliamentary involvement.

France and the Netherlands are monist systems, although both qualify the overriding effect of treaties somewhat. France makes the override subject to reciprocity in the other contracting states, the Netherlands limits overrides to treaty provisions that can confer individual rights. In both systems, treaty review may be seen as 'compensating' somewhat for the judges' current (the Netherlands) or historical (France) lack of constitutional review powers. The US is a qualified monist system: federal treaties override State law and earlier federal legislation, but their domestic effect can be undone by later federal legislation. The UK and Germany, meanwhile, are dualist: treaties can be relied upon only once they have been implemented into national law.

A challenge arises for dualist systems when it comes to giving domestic effect to human-rights treaties such as the European Convention on Human Rights. It may reasonably be argued, and even the lawmaker might agree, that human-rights commitments are only credible if they endure and override conflicting national legislation. Think, for example, of unintended human-rights breaches. Yet national legislation implementing international human-rights treaties in a dualist system is not necessarily superior in rank with respect to any other piece of national legislation. Thus, the *lex posterior* rule, and implied repeal in the UK (meaning that later law overrides earlier law) threaten to render earlier human-rights commitments obsolete. Both Germany and the UK therefore have found techniques how to circumnavigate the hierarchy dilemma, to take into account European human rights and still hold on to a dualist model with respect to treaties. The UK has incorporated the rights from the European Convention on Human Rights in a national statute, the Human Rights Act 1998, it compels judges to interpret national legislation in the light of these rights, and it allows higher judges to make known if they detect a violation by another statute (however judges are still not allowed to disapply the statute for that reason). German courts take Convention rights into account when interpreting the rights enshrined in the Basic Law; the fact that the Basic Law anyway contains a human-rights catalogue that goes far beyond the minimum guarantees in the Convention already makes the issue less pressing there.

1.4. *European Union Law*

For those states that are members of the European Union, the domestic effect of international treaties is no longer merely a question of monism or dualism. The European (Economic) Community, the historical core branch of socio-economic European integration since 1957 and the European Union's main predecessor organization, while still treaty-based, has been defined as a *sui generis* legal order: as one of its kind. The European Court of Justice (ECJ) has interpreted the law of the European Community as being capable of having 'direct effect' and 'supremacy' in the member states. With direct effect, individuals can invoke European law before national courts, without waiting for transposition; with supremacy, European law overrides all conflicting national provisions, no matter their rank. The novel thing, which distinguishes the historical Community and the present-day Union from any other international organization in the world, is that direct effect and supremacy is taken to apply irrespective of whether the member state in question happens to be monist or dualist. No matter what the approach to 'normal' treaties is, the ECJ ruled, Community law and today Union law possesses special qualities by virtue of its own special character. After all, the European common market goes far beyond any ordinary trade agreement; the treaties mention not only the member states but also their people; they create permanent institutions; and they give the ECJ jurisdiction in preliminary rulings precisely so as to ensure uniform application of European law. Thus, in its breakthrough decision of *Van Gend & Loos* v. *Nederlandse Administratie der Belastingen* (26/62, [1963] ECR 1), the ECJ held:

> 'The conclusion to be drawn from this is that the Community constitutes a new legal order of international law for the benefit of which the States have limited their sovereign rights, albeit within limited fields, and the subjects of which comprise not only Member States but also their nationals'.

Thus, the Community was not considered to be based on a 'normal' treaty at all, but on one in which the member states have decided to share their sovereignty for the effective pursuit of rather ambitious common goals. In the follow-up case to *Van Gend & Loos*, namely *Flaminio Costa* v. *ENEL* (6/64, [1964] ECR 585, 593), the ECJ furthermore made clear that European law with direct effect had supremacy over conflicting national law:

> 'The transfer by the States from their domestic legal system to the Community legal system of the rights and obligations arising under the [EEC] Treaty carries with it a permanent limitation of their sovereign rights, against which a subsequent unilateral act incompatible with the concept of the Community cannot prevail'.

Later case-law specified that Community law overrides all conflicting national law, whenever and in whatever form adopted. The role of national judges is crucial to the uniform application of Community law in the member states. Indeed, judges must set aside all conflicting national provisions. In *Administrazione delle Finanze dello Stato* v. *Simmenthal SpA* (106/77, [1978] ECR 629), the ECJ confirmed the *Van Gend & Loos* and *Costa* doctrines, and added:

> 'It follows from the foregoing that every national court must, in a case within its jurisdiction, apply Community law in its entirety and protect rights which the latter confers on individuals and must accordingly set aside any provision of national law which may conflict with it, whether prior or subsequent to the Community rule'.

National judges must invalidate all national provisions incompatible with Community law. They may, in turn, not invalidate secondary Community law, such as regulations and directives, on their own. As the ECJ held in *Firma Foto-Frost* v. *Hauptzollamt Lübeck-Ost* (314/85, [1987] ECR 4199):

> 'Since Article 177 [renumbered 267 TFEU] gives the [ECJ] exclusive jurisdiction to declare void an act of a Community institution, the coherence of the system requires that where the validity of a Community act is challenged before a national court the power to declare the act invalid must also be reserved to the Court of Justice'.

If in doubt about the validity, or simply the correct interpretation, of European Union law, both primary and secondary, national judges are free to halt proceedings and ask a preliminary question to the ECJ before resolving the case before them. Courts of last instance in principle even have to refer preliminary questions to the ECJ (Art. 267 TFEU).

Many national courts, in particular constitutional courts, disagree with such a far-reaching and unconditional interpretation of the effect of European law as maintained by the ECJ. In their view, while European Union law indeed should enjoy direct effect and supremacy, these features must be accommodated into national constitutional law, and thus cannot be unconditional. France, for example, accepts direct effect and supremacy of European law, but only by virtue of France's monism. Thus, treaty law does override ordinary legislation, but the French Constitution is above both. The constitutional courts of Italy and other member states also stress that there are certain core features of the domestic constitution which cannot be overridden by European law. Germany is famous for its case-law whereby a constant threat is in the air that the Federal Constitutional Court might strike down a piece of secondary EU legislation as being incompatible with the Basic Law.

In the Netherlands, direct effect and supremacy of European law poses no real conflict. Since the Netherlands is monist, and judges have no power of constitutional review anyway, which also extends to the review of the constitutionality of treaties, the Dutch courts have no problem in pragmatically accepting the ECJ's reasoning. In the UK, meanwhile, problems could not have been greater. Parliamentary sovereignty would seem incompatible with a system where, like the ECJ demands, a judge can set aside a national statute.

In reality, European law does possess the qualities that the ECJ has interpreted it to have. The French qualifications on European law supremacy are largely academic; the German Constitutional Court has indicated that constitutional review of European law would not be exercised, and instead be reserved only for grave cases: a deterioration of human rights standards, but also an unlawful expansion of EU powers without authorization from the member states. Even the UK has found a way to reconcile parliamentary sovereignty with European law supremacy: Parliament, by freely deciding to join the Community, must have wanted to accept the relevant ECJ doctrines as part of the deal itself. Indeed, the European Union context is the only case where a UK judge may disapply an Act of Parliament.

The European Union truly is a new legal order. It is just not unconditionally ECJ-driven. The complex interrelations between European and national law, and the 'dialogue', through the preliminary reference procedure, between European and national judges over fundamental doctrines, is part of the European order's uniqueness. And European Union law is not somewhere 'abroad': in one way or another it is an integral part of the member states' constitutions. No matter what the doctrinal embedding, it also affects the domestic relations between judge and lawmaker. After all, the judge has, or gains, 'European' review powers, while national legislation cannot stand if it violates European law.

1.5. Summary

Of the five systems under consideration, three (the US, France and Germany) allow courts or court-like institutions to review the constitutionality of legislation. In the US, review powers in concrete judicial disputes apply to all courts; in Germany the courts have to refer questions regarding the constitutionality of legislation to a central constitutional court, whereas in France they can do so via a reference to one of the two supreme courts which in turn can refer questions to the Constitutional Council. Abstract review of laws is possible in France (before promulgation) and in Germany (after promulgation), but impossible in the US. The constitutionality of legislation may not be questioned by judges in the UK or the Netherlands. The Netherlands does allow judges to check the compatibility between legislation and international treaty provisions, however; the same holds true for France and the US. The UK and Germany remain dualist with respect to treaty provisions. The latter however applies in a straightforward way only to international treaties other than those of the European Union: the case-law of the European Court of Justice regarding the direct effect and supremacy of EU law in the member states has transformed the EU into a sui generis legal order, and national approaches to embedding these doctrines into constitutional law reflect their uniqueness.

1.6. Further Reading

R. Blackburn & J. Polakiewicz (eds.) *Fundamental Rights in Europe: The European Convention on Human Rights and its Member States 1950-2000* (Oxford: OUP 2001).
M. Claes, *The National Courts' Mandate in the European Constitution* (Oxford: Hart 2006).
T. Koopmans, *Courts and Political Institutions: A Comparative View* (Cambridge: CUP 2003).
M. Rosenfeld, 'Constitutional adjudication in Europe and the United States: Paradoxes and Contrasts', 2 *International Journal of Constitutional Law* (2004), p. 633-668.
A. Stone Sweet, *Governing with Judges: Constitutional Politics in Europe* (Oxford: OUP 2000).
M. Troper, 'The logic of Justification of Judicial Review', 1 *International Journal of Constitutional Law* (2003), p. 99-121.

2. The United States

2.1. The Court System

There is no such thing as a uniform US court system. Instead, there are fifty-one court systems. Each of the fifty States has its own hierarchy of State courts, while next to these State courts there exists a parallel hierarchy of federal courts. The highest federal court is the US Supreme Court, which is provided for in the US Constitution; other federal courts – the district courts, courts of appeal and specialized federal courts – are set up by federal legislation (Art. III (1) US Constitution). Federal judges, including Supreme Court justices, are appointed by the President with the advice and consent of the Senate (Art. II (2) US Constitution). Supreme Court justices, as well as the judges of lower federal courts in the US proper are appointed for life ('during good behaviour', Art. III (1) US Constitution), and may be removed only by conviction upon impeachment by Congress (the Senate deciding upon an initiative of the House of Representatives). As to State courts, each State decides on its own what courts to set up and how they are to function, including the tenure and manner of appointment, or in fact popular election, of judges.

In principle, State courts are competent to hear disputes, whereas parties may bring an action before a federal court only in enumerated cases. These are cases where a 'federal question' involving the federal Constitution or federal legislation is at hand, including criminal cases launched for violations of federal law; cases where the US federation is either the defendant or the applicant; cases of maritime law; disputes between States; and cross-State border cases where the two parties are citizens of different States (Art. III (2) US Constitution), but the latter type of cases must concern a minimum money value fixed by federal legislation, otherwise State courts are exclusively competent. The US Supreme Court acts as a court of first instance in cases involving, in short, diplomats, and in cases brought by or against a State; it also hears appeals from lower federal courts (Art. III (2) US Constitution), although federal legislation has severely limited the Supreme Court's appellate jurisdiction. The most important jurisdiction that the Supreme Court assumes is discretionary review of cases. This is a common-law practice which is not spelt out in the Constitution, whereby the Court chooses to grant a permission, called writ of certiorari (colloquially abbreviated 'cert'), to parties who have petitioned the Court to present their case. Certiorari jurisdiction, where the Court freely chooses whether or not to hear a case upon a petition, is therefore distinct from appellate jurisdiction where parties are entitled to an appeal as of right. By granting writs of certiorari, the Supreme Court may consider cases from within both the State and the federal court hierarchies. The Court then picks the cases it finds worth considering, where the legal question is of importance or where different federal courts of appeal have developed conflicting case-law. The Supreme Court generally gives no reasons for rejecting petitions, though, and if a petition is rejected then the final State or lower federal court judgment remains binding.

2.2. *Constitutional Review*

All federal judges in the US may review the constitutionality of legislation, of both State and federal statutes, as well as of State and lower federal court decisions upholding legislation. If a constitutionality question arises in a dispute before a State court, or a question of constitutionality of a federal statute, the matter becomes a 'federal question' and can be taken to a federal court.

The US Constitution does not explicitly provide for any such review power for the courts itself, and the historical record of the Constitution's drafting process, regarding the intention of the drafters, is also inconclusive. The US Supreme Court, however, in the 1803 case *Marbury* v. *Madison* (5 U.S. 137), established that judicial review powers do flow logically from the Constitution. Several arguments were put forward to justify this conclusion. The Constitution is defined the highest law of the land, and judges, as well as the other functionaries, take an oath to uphold it (Art. VI US Constitution). The Constitution derives directly from the will of the people (Preamble to the US Constitution) through a solemn and rarely repeated act. The Constitution would lose all practical effect if Congress could violate or change it via simple legislation; the complicated amendment procedure (Art. V US Constitution), even the effort of writing constitutional rules down in the first place, would become pointless if simple statutes would do just as well. Furthermore, legislation is only possible thanks to the Constitution, and the conferral of power upon Congress. Statutes can only have authority if made in pursuance of the Constitution (Art. VI US Constitution), whereas a statute that violates the Constitution is clearly not made in pursuance of it. Rests the question whether judges should be the ones to verify the constitutionality of statutes, rather than Congress and the State lawmakers themselves. On this point, the Supreme Court held:

'It is emphatically the province and duty of the judicial department to say what the law is. Those who apply the rule to particular cases, must of necessity expound and interpret that rule. If two laws conflict with each other, the courts must decide on the operation of each. (...) If, then, the courts are to regard the constitution, and the constitution is superior to any ordinary act of the legislature, the constitution, and not such ordinary act, must govern the case to which they both apply'.

Thus, it is the judiciary's task to solve disputes between parties by applying the law. If in that context two applicable sources of law are in conflict with each other, the judge must resolve this conflict of norms before being able to solve his case. If a conflict arises between the Constitution and an ordinary statute, then the former is higher in rank and thus overrides the latter. Unconstitutional statutes must therefore not be applied to a case, but instead left aside. Since all judges in the country are engaged in the same activity, namely applying the law in order to resolve disputes, and since they all may be confronted with the same problem, namely a conflict between a lower norm and a higher norm, they must all adopt the same solution, namely setting aside unconstitutional legislation. Under the common-law doctrine of stare decisis, the binding rule of precedent, later and lower judges follow the case-law of earlier and higher judges. This means that ultimately, once the US Supreme Court has set legislation aside, all other courts, both State and federal, will follow this example. Thus, in effect the US Supreme Court has the last word on constitutionality questions. However being the highest federal court does not make it a special 'constitutional court': all federal courts in the US are constitutional courts, because they all have the same power of review.

Since judicial review of the constitutionality of legislation follows from the tasks of the judiciary, it should be noted that such review can only be exercised within the courts' delimited jurisdiction in actual 'cases and controversies' (Art. III (2) US Constitution). Review must be crucial for the resolution of real disputes. This excludes the review of the constitutionality of statutes in hypothetical, moot, or fabricated cases, as well as any kind of advisory opinions to Congress or a constitutionality assessment in the abstract.

The Background to Marbury

The US Supreme Court decision in *Marbury* v. *Madison* of 1803 can be seen against the backdrop of power politics. The applicant in this case, William Marbury, had been appointed, in a last-minute move, by the outgoing President John Adams to become a justice of the peace, a type of lower judge; all he needed was the commission, his appointment certificate, to be handed over by the secretary of state. The outgoing secretary of state however had failed to do so in time, and the new one, under the new President Thomas Jefferson who was hostile to his predecessor, deliberately refused to deliver the document. The applicant sued the new secretary of state, James Madison, seeking a 'writ of mandamus' as a judicial remedy to receive the document. In accordance with a federal legislative provision, the Judiciary Act, the competent court to ask for this remedy was the US Supreme Court acting as a court of first instance because the defendant was a US office-holder. The Supreme Court was presided over by chief justice John Marshall, who himself was another of the former

> President's appointees, and, somewhat embarrassingly, he was the very same former secretary of state who had failed to deliver the sought document to the applicant in the first place. Simply finding in favour of the applicant, the chief justice's political ally, would however have meant to deliver a judgment that the Supreme Court knew would be ignored; that would have damaged the Court's credibility. Instead, the Court ruled that, while the applicant was in principle entitled to receive the document on the merits, the statute that established the Court's jurisdiction in this case was in fact unconstitutional. Article III of the US Constitution provides an exhaustive list of cases that can be brought before the Supreme Court in first instance, and the present case did not fall under that list. Congress had unconstitutionally expanded the Court's first-instance jurisdiction. Declaring the jurisdiction-granting statute unconstitutional, the Court was able to note that the applicant was right; it could nevertheless avoid having to actually grant the requested remedy itself; and it set a ground-breaking precedent all at once. Thus, while the applicant lost his case (he had a case but had addressed the wrong court, or the right court but under an invalid statute), the Supreme Court, and the entire US federal judiciary, gained the power to set aside legislation.

Statutes declared unconstitutional lose part or all of their practical effect, since the invalidating court, and all courts below them, will refuse to apply them. Congress, as well as State legislatures in case a State law has been invalidated, may then choose to repeal these statutes formally and replace them with ones that do comply with the Constitution. In case of a fundamental issue, Congress or the State legislatures may also resort to an overriding measure: start a process of constitutional amendment, which is available even though it is extremely difficult to complete.

2.3. *International Treaties*

As regards international treaties, domestic effect depends on whether the treaty is self-executing or not. In general, treaties made by the US federal authority are qualified as being the supreme law of the land (Art. VI US Constitution). They therefore override State law. However, treaties are listed as 'supreme law' alongside federal legislation, with no hierarchical relation between the two. Thus, treaties override pre-existing legislation, but otherwise the *lex posterior* rule applies, meaning that statutes made later can override treaty provisions made earlier.

> *Legislation through Treaties*
>
> As international treaties can take precedence over statutes, the regular lawmaking procedure can be circumvented. Treaties are made by the President with the approval of a two-thirds majority in the Senate (Art. II (2) US Constitution). This gives these two institutions quasi-legislative power which they otherwise would not have: the President may adopt binding normative acts, and the Senate does not need to agree with the House of Representatives. The real extent of this phenomenon is limited since overriding effect is only granted to few treaty provisions, namely those considered self-executing, whereas all other treaties require transposition through

> national legislation. Still, the US Constitution is not the only constitution in the world which clearly did not foresee the domestic impact that internationalization would one day have.

3. Germany

3.1. The Court System

The German judicial system is characterized by a distinction of layers of lower courts at State level and, above them, supreme courts at the federal level. Courts fall into five categories of subject-matter jurisdiction: general jurisdiction (civil and criminal law), administrative law, social security law, labour law and tax law. The manner of appointment of lower judges is determined by the States where the courts are located. Atop of each of the five court hierarchies there is a federal court acting as court of last instance, next to a number of specialized federal courts. Ordinary federal judges are selected by the competent federal minister together with a judicial selections committee consisting of the competent State ministers and an equal number of members elected by the Bundestag (Art. 95 (2) Basic Law). What is usually referred to as the German 'supreme court' is the *Bundesgerichtshof*, the highest court of general jurisdiction dealing with civil and criminal cases.

Set up as another federal court, yet placed outside normal court hierarchies, is the Federal Constitutional Court, the *Bundesverfassungsgericht*. Its task is to uphold the German Basic Law as a specialized judicial body for constitutional matters. It is therefore not a 'supreme court' but rather a permanent constitutional organ alongside the parliament, the government, the Bundesrat and the Federal President. The Constitutional Court consists of sixteen members, half of whom are elected by the Bundestag and half by the Bundesrat (Art. 94 (1) Basic Law). Constitutional judges serve non-renewable terms of twelve years until the maximum age of 68 (§ 4 Federal Constitutional Court Act).

3.2. Constitutional Review

All ordinary German courts have the power to examine the constitutionality of statutes; however, they do not have the power to annul these statutes on their own. Instead, if an ordinary court concludes that a statute on the validity of which its decision in a dispute before it depends is unconstitutional, it must freeze proceedings and refer a preliminary question to the Federal Constitutional Court (Art. 100 (1) Basic Law). It is then up to the Constitutional Court to rule on the constitutionality question. This procedure is called concrete review, or concrete norm control, since it stems from an actual judicial dispute in a concrete case.

The Federal Constitutional Court is also competent to decide in a host of other situations, most of them listed in Article 93 of the Basic Law. This includes disputes between different organs or layers of public authority about the correct interpretation of the Basic Law concerning the scope of their competences. The Court is therefore competent to decide on substantive constitutional interpretation including the area of human rights as well as to settle inter-institutional disputes.

Two procedures listed in Article 93 of the Basic Law stand out: the constitutional complaint procedure and the procedure of abstract review. These are the other two procedures, next to concrete review, where the constitutionality of a federal statute can be of the issue.

In the constitutional complaint procedure, an individual can claim an infringement on enumerated constitutional rights by public authority (Art. 93 (1) (4a) Basic Law). The scope of constitutional complaints is broader than what can be reviewed via concrete review, since the Constitutional Court's jurisdiction is not limited to statutes but extends to any act of public authority, including court decisions; if statutes are contested, they do not have to be crucial to the resolution of a judicial dispute, like it is the case in concrete review, and individuals are furthermore not dependent on their judge's willingness to refer a question to the Constitutional Court. At the same time, access for individuals to the Court is restricted: applicants must in principle exhaust all ordinary judicial remedies before launching a case before the Constitutional Court (Art. 94 (2) Basic Law and § 90 (2) Federal Constitutional Court Act). Furthermore, as is further specified in case-law, applicants must demonstrate a direct and concrete injury as a result of the contested measure in order to be admissible in the first place.

In abstract review, meanwhile, the Constitutional Court can be seized by the federal government, a State government, or historically one-third and, since an amendment in 2009, one-quarter of Bundestag members, to rule on the constitutionality of a statute (Art. 93 (2) Basic Law). The abstractness of this procedure lies in the fact that it can be triggered at any time, without there being a concrete application of the statute in adversarial proceedings. Strictly speaking, in abstract review there is only an applicant but no defendant, although the Court in practice hears parties on both sides of the argument, for example a State government versus the federal government.

The Sensitivity of Judicial Review

That a judge might resolve disputes concerning the distribution of power in a federal system is, in the German case, nothing new: this was already the case during the Weimar Republic. It is even a defining feature of a federation that an independent arbiter may check compliance of sub-national with national law, or with the constitution, as far as the allocation of competences is concerned. The review of statutes for their substantive compliance with the constitution, including human rights, however, collides with the legitimacy of the democratic lawmaker – even in Germany, which otherwise seeks to establish many checks on political institutions. Therefore, the Basic Law confines this extraordinary judicial review power to a single and special court, the Constitutional Court. In fact, this power originally was even confined to only one chamber within that Court. The Court is made up of two chambers, or 'Senates', of eight judges each. Originally, one of them would hear the 'usual' cases on competence questions between organs of public authority, while the other one would hear cases concerning individual rights. It quickly became clear, though, that the latter was burdened with

> a heavy workload while the former had hardly any cases at all. Today, the two chambers both deal with individual rights, dividing the work between them by subject-matter.

The Federal Constitutional Court interprets legislation as far as possible in the light of the Basic Law. If constitution-friendly interpretation is not possible, the Constitutional Court may, in the course of abstract review, concrete review and constitutional complaint procedures, declare a statute unconstitutional and void (§§ 78, 82 and 95 (2) Federal Constitutional Court Act). The statute is then quashed and ceases to exist. Retroactive effects of such a decision (i.e. the legal fiction that the statute never existed) are however limited to criminal provisions, where retrials are made possible in case of a past conviction based on a statute that is later annulled (§§ 79, 82 and 95 (3) Federal Constitutional Court Act). In all other cases, there is no retroactive effect. The Court may include provisional measures which, just like the judgment itself, enjoy the rank of statutory law.

Stopping short of voidance, the Court has in its case-law also developed other techniques. Thus, the Court may declare a statute unconstitutional but not void, meaning that the statute will remain in force. Alternatively, it may declare a statute constitutional for now yet note that it will become unconstitutional in the near future. The latter two options are admonitory decisions, reprimanding the lawmaker and prompting him to change the statute bearing in mind the Court's guidelines.

> *Why not Quash the Law?*
>
> The German Constitutional Court resorts to annulment of legislation only in extreme cases, bearing in mind the democratic and federal legitimacy of the lawmaker and the interest of legal certainty. The Court prefers constitution-friendly interpretation. In case interpretation techniques do not help, it prefers admonitory decisions, telling the lawmaker to change the statute in question himself. There are practical reasons to leave an otherwise unconstitutional statute intact. At times, it is better to have a defective statute than no statute at all. An example is the electoral system, which was found unconstitutional in 2008 but which was left in force since the country cannot have *no* election system. Furthermore, a defect can be remedied in very different manners. For example, different solutions were available to correct the election system after 2008; another example is unlawful discrimination, which can be addressed by treating the disadvantaged group better, but also by treating the advantaged group worse, as long as both groups are treated equally. It is up to the lawmaker, not the judge, to make such political choices.

3.3. International Treaties and the ECHR

As far as the review of legislation for treaty compatibility is concerned, Germany is a dualist system. International treaty obligations must be met by transposing them into national law at the appropriate level, and treaties do not override legislation.

Principles of international law do (Art. 25 Basic Law), but this is not the same as treaties: one should rather think of *ius cogens* norms of public international law. Direct reliance on treaties as such before German courts is in principle not possible. The federal statute that transposes the European Convention on Human Rights (ECHR) into German law is formally no different from any other piece of federal legislation, enjoying equal rank with other statutes.

There are ways to nevertheless have treaties prevail domestically, however. The ECHR, to which Germany is a party, can be invoked indirectly. The German Basic Law itself contains an enforceable human-rights catalogue; the national judge and the Constitutional Court would then interpret these constitutional human rights in an ECHR-friendly manner, taking into account the case-law of the European Court of Human Rights in Strasbourg. Another way of indirect reliance is to see at least some ECHR rights as a codification of principles of international law, which do take precedence over national law. Yet another manner of indirect reliance is to invoke the ECHR as overriding *lex specialis* on human-rights guarantees where national law is broadly worded. Thus, the ECHR is integrated into the German legal order as a privileged source of law via techniques of legal interpretation. If ECHR protection is deemed to have failed within Germany, individuals may bring an action against the state before the European Court of Human Rights (see § 7).

3.4. European Union Law

The law of the European Union has, according to the European Court of Justice (ECJ), special characteristics as a new legal order. It is capable of having direct effect in the member states by virtue of its own nature, irrespective of whether the member states are monist or dualist, and supremacy over all national provisions. National judges must set aside all conflicting national provisions, including their constitutions, in favour of European Union law (see § 1.4). Such unconditional supremacy of European law collides with the approach of the German Constitutional Court, holding that European law may ultimately be invalidated if in conflict with the German Basic Law.

In 1974, deciding on a preliminary reference in *Internationale Handelsgesellschaft mbH v. Einfuhr- und Vorratstelle für Getreide und Futtermittel* (29 May 1974, BvL 52/71), in a decision better known as *Solange I*, the Constitutional Court noted that the European Economic Community did not yet offer democratic standards and fundamental-rights protection equivalent to German standards. It therefore held that German constitutional provisions would prevail over European law as long as (German: *Solange*) the Community did not remove hypothetical conflicts of norms. In 1986, then, the Court gave a more Europe-friendly ruling, stating that it would refrain from constitutional review of European law as long as the Community kept the human-rights standards that it had developed in the meantime. This ruling, on a constitutional complaint by *Wünsche Handelsgesellschaft* (22 October 1986, 2 BvR 197/83) became known as *Solange II*. Later, prompted by a constitutional complaint by *Brunner* to review the constitutionality of the Maastricht Treaty (12 October 1993, 2 BvR 2134, 2159/92), the Constitutional Court shifted its attention to the safeguarding of the borders of competences as conferred from Germany to the EU. In

Maastricht, as in its judgment on the constitutionality of the Treaty of Lisbon of 2009 (30 June 2009, 2 BvE 2/08; 2 BvE 5/08; 2 BvR 1010/08; 2 BvR 1022/08; 2 BvR 1259/08; 2 BvR 182/09) the Court restated that it reserves the right to review European Union law, recalling the paramount position of the constituent member states in the treaty-based Union. Especially as regards procedures whereby EU institutions can expand their competences without there being a proper Treaty ratification in all member states, it warned that it would invalidate EU decisions that are based on unlawfully arrogated powers. In the *Lisbon* judgment of 2009, it prescribed prior approval from the German legislature for each such dynamic expansion of powers as if it were a proper treaty amendment. But in spite of the dogmatic upheavals, and subject to the Court's warnings, German courts keep applying European law in everyday practice, giving it precedence over national provisions. If in doubt about the right interpretation of Union law that is relevant to the case before them, judges may, and in some cases must, refer a preliminary question to the ECJ.

The Court and Europe

When ruling on the constitutionality of German financial commitments to contribute to the European Union's stabilization mechanism for the euro area in 2011, the Federal Constitutional Court rejected a request for an injunction and held that the measure as such was constitutional, but insisted that each new commitment be approved by the Bundestag. Otherwise, the parliament's budgetary authority to decide on revenue and public spending, as an expression of a nation's right to exercise its political will, would be undermined (2 BvR 987/10). Subsequently, in 2012, the Court ruled that such decisions cannot be authorized by a mere committee on behalf of the plenary. Already in 2009 the Court had ruled in a quite similar way on the constitutionality of the Treaty of Lisbon: its ratification was allowed, but only provided that the German legislature would be fully involved in the approval of subsequent steps to change the EU Treaties via simplified procedures (2 BvE 2/08). In 1994 the Court had allowed armed military missions outside NATO territory as long as each deployment was authorized by the parliament (2 BvE 3/92); and this condition, as it noted in its Lisbon ruling, also applies to EU-led missions. The Court thus does not have to adopt a confrontational stance regarding the constitutionality of aspects of European integration: it may also insist upon respect for parliamentary prerogatives as a procedural safeguard. It should not be forgotten, after all, that Germany is not actually free to decide whether or not to participate in European integration: the Basic Law's preamble clearly declares such participation to be an objective of the constitutional order.

---

4. The United Kingdom

4.1. *The Court System*

The court system in the UK is divided into separate court systems for England and Wales, Scotland, and Northern Ireland. The English and Welsh court system is based on a hierarchy of county courts and magistrate courts at the lowest level; above that the High Court, with three divisions for different subject-matter jurisdictions and the Crown Court for criminal cases; and the Court of Appeal, with a criminal division. The highest court in the UK was traditionally the House of Lords. In accordance with the Constitutional Reform Act 2005, however, the Lords have lost their role as a court; the Law Lords who have been exercising the House's judicial functions have been transferred to a Supreme Court of the UK, which now is the highest UK judicial instance. Judges in England and Wales were traditionally appointed by the King upon the advice of the Lord Chancellor as both government member and head of the judiciary; the 2005 statute created an independent judicial appointments commission, and the Lord Chancellor is obliged to act based on this commission's recommendations.

4.2. *Constitutional Review*

Constitutional review of statutes by judges is not permitted in the UK in the light of the doctrine of parliamentary sovereignty in the sense of legislative supremacy. The King-in-Parliament is sovereign, meaning that the lawmaker can be bound by no-one, not even by itself, and that no-one except Parliament itself can undo the will of Parliament. Constitutional review would mean to hold Parliament to a higher norm. That is already problematic since the constitution is not codified in a single document to start with, and, more fundamentally, Acts of Parliament which have received royal assent already are the highest norm. Judges are bound by Parliament, they are not to second-guess legislation. Courts accept the supremacy of Parliament over judge-made law like they accept the supremacy of statute over royal prerogative. It should be noted that judicial interpretation of statutes may serve to protect certain principles of 'constitutional rank'. The implication would be that Parliament, when granting broad executive powers, is deemed not to wish to deviate from these principles, such as the presumption of innocence, by implied repeal, and would only deviate from them explicitly. The Human Rights Act 1998 in fact orders judges to apply human rights-friendly interpretation as far as possible, meaning unless Parliament explicitly deviates from protected rights. That last aspect is crucial: Parliament does remain free under domestic law to encroach upon fundamental rights if it so desires.

4.3. *International Treaties and the ECHR*

Parliamentary sovereignty in the UK extends to supremacy over domestic as well as foreign sources of law. The UK is a dualist system; individuals can rely on international treaties only in as far as such treaties have been transposed into national law. For a long time, therefore, individuals could not even invoke the rights contained in the European Convention on Human Rights (ECHR) before domestic courts.

The Human Rights Act (HRA) 1998 finally did transpose most of the ECHR into national law. Since its entry into force in 2000, individuals can rely on Convention rights as enumerated in the Human Rights Act (Section 1 HRA 1998). That does however not mean that judges can set aside Acts of Parliament, since that would again undermine legislative supremacy. Instead, judges are instructed to interpret legislation as far as possible in the light of the protected Convention rights (Section 3 HRA 1998). If a violation is apparent and cannot be remedied via interpretation, the court, from the High Court level upwards, may issue a 'declaration of incompatibility', drawing Parliament's attention to the perceived infringement (Section 4 HRA 1998). Before doing so, the court must notify the government so as to allow it to intervene in the proceedings and comment on the disputed statute. If it is issued, the declaration of incompatibility triggers a fast-track legislative procedure, enabling, once the case is concluded and appeal is no longer possible, the minister to insert amendments to the statute by way of an order (Section 10 HRA 1998). He then puts a draft order before both houses of Parliament, which then can approve it by a resolution; in cases of urgency, the minister may insert changes without parliamentary approval, but must then seek approval by resolution for a second order so as to keep the original change in force (Schedule 2 HRA 1998). This procedure of resolution-plus-order is far quicker than the usual process of passing formal bills to amend legislation in three readings and a committee stage. If there is no particular urgency, however, the formal legislative procedure, not the fast-track procedure, should be preferred. Either way, Parliament remains free to keep its legislation in place, even if a court has declared an incompatibility with Convention rights. After all, Parliament can refuse to accept the minister's draft order, and refuse to change the statute in an ordinary process, so that the statute can remain unamended.

The Statistics of Judicial Review

According to a 2011 report of the UK ministry of justice, between 2000 (when the Human Rights Act 1998 entered into force) and late 2011, 27 declarations of incompatibility have been issued, of which 19 became final and eight were overturned on appeal. Of the 19 that became final, 12 were due to be remedied by later primary legislation; two were subject to remedy by a remedial order under section 10 of the HRA; four related to provisions that had already been remedied by primary legislation at the time of the declaration, and one was still under consideration. This serves to illustrate that while mechanisms of judicial review and simplified legislative procedures are highly important, this importance should not be taken to imply frequent use.

The issuing court, meanwhile, must complete the proceedings before it and apply the statute in its original form. Courts below the High Court cannot issue declarations of incompatibility but may express their concerns in their judgment so that higher courts may take note on appeal. If ECHR protection is deemed to have failed within the UK, individuals may bring an action against the state before the European Court of Human Rights (see § 7).

4.4. *European Union Law*

The law of the European Union, while also based on a treaty, enjoys a special status in the UK. If UK judges would treat European Union law on par with ordinary treaty law, then non-transposed EU law would have no effect in UK courts, and, because of parliamentary sovereignty, would certainly not override any national statutes. The law of the European Union however has, according to the European Court of Justice (ECJ), special characteristics as a new legal order. It is capable of having direct effect in the member states by virtue of its own character, even in dualist states, and supremacy over all national provisions. National judges must set aside all conflicting national provisions, including their constitutions, in favour of Union law (see § 1.4).

The first open clash between European Community supremacy and the UK doctrine of parliamentary sovereignty came with the *Factortame* litigation. A fishing company sought interim relief to be able to speedily register its ships as UK vessels. UK legislation had limited the registration of fishing vessels to companies that were, essentially, domestic; this was to prevent foreign fishermen – Spaniards, in *Factortame's* case – from registering their vessels in the UK and then exploiting UK fishing quotas. While this was plainly in violation of Community law, being a discriminatory barrier to free movement, giving interim relief would have meant to ignore and set aside an Act of Parliament. The House of Lords, the highest court at the time, referred a preliminary question to the ECJ, asking whether legislation had to be set aside even against a national constitutional rule; the ECJ, repeating *Simmenthal*, confirmed that this was indeed what had to be done. The House of Lords went on to accept the ECJ's ruling (*Factortame Ltd.* v. *Secretary of State for Transport*, [1991] 1 AC 603). Parliamentary sovereignty was doctrinally preserved, however. It was noted that the UK joined the European Economic Community in 1973 by virtue of the European Communities Act 1972. If the Community Treaty was not explicit as regards direct effect and supremacy, the relevant ECJ case-law on this issue in any event predated the accession of the UK.

> 'Thus, whatever limitation of its sovereignty Parliament accepted when it enacted the European Communities Act 1972 was entirely voluntary. Under the terms of the 1972 Act it has always been clear that it was the duty of a United Kingdom court, when delivering final judgment, to override any rule of national law found to be in conflict with any directly enforceable rule of Community law'.

Parliament had itself accepted Community membership, and by the time that it did, the ECJ case-law on direct effect and supremacy had already been an established part of European law. Parliament knew what it was doing and, by implication, could, if it liked, repeal again the European Communities Act and have the UK withdraw from the Community. Thus, UK courts keep applying European Union law in everyday practice, giving it precedence over national provisions. If in doubt about the right interpretation of Union law that is relevant to the case before them, judges may, and in some cases must, refer a preliminary question to the ECJ.

5. France

5.1. The Court System

The most prominent characteristic of the French court system is the parallel hierarchy of ordinary courts for civil and criminal cases, on the one hand, and administrative courts, on the other hand. The administrative court hierarchy comprises administrative courts, administrative courts of appeal, and the judicial division of the Council of State as the final instance. The ordinary judiciary comprises an echelon of courts of first instance specializing in different subject-matter jurisdictions, and above that the courts of appeal and, finally, the Court of Cassation. Disputes as to which of the two jurisdictions is competent in a matter (imagine a tort claim against a public authority) are settled by the court of conflicts of jurisdiction, the *Tribunal des conflits*. Judges are appointed by the President in a procedure involving the competent section of the high council of the judiciary (Art. 65 French Constitution).

5.2. Constitutional Review

Constitutional review of statutes was originally prohibited in France. Judges were to apply the law, not second-guess its constitutionality. The constitutionality of statutes was ensured by the lawmaker, and reviewed before promulgation, where applicable, by the Constitutional Council (see for details Chapter 4). After promulgation, if the Constitutional Council had either cleared a bill as constitutional or had not been asked to rule on a bill, statutes were immune from judicial review.

The Constitutional Council comprises nine appointed members serving nine-year terms as well as former Presidents for life (Art. 56 French Constitution). Of the nine appointed members, three are appointed by the President of the Republic, three by the president of the National Assembly, and three by the president of the Senate, appointments taking place once every three years. Thus, three of the members are replaced once every three years, meaning that once every three years the President and the two chamber presidents get to appoint one new member each. Since the constitutional reform of 2008, the Constitution authorizes parliamentary committees from both chambers to participate in the President's appointments, and such an appointment can be vetoed if three-fifths of the added total votes cast by both committees are against the nomination (Arts. 13 and 56 French Constitution).

The constitutional reform of 2008 also introduced a new Article 61-1 to the French Constitution. The provision allows the Court of Cassation, the top court of general jurisdiction, and the Council of State, the highest administrative court, to refer questions on the constitutionality of statutes to the Constitutional Council if the constitutionality of a statute is challenged in court proceedings. The procedural details regarding these preliminary questions (*question prioritaire de constitutionnalité* in French) are regulated by organic statute no. 2009-1523 of 10 December 2009. Lower ordinary or administrative courts must refer a preliminary question to their respective supreme court if three conditions are fulfilled: the constitutionality of the contested statutory provision must be relevant to the proceedings; the statute may not already have been declared constitutional by the Constitutional Council at an earlier stage, unless there has been a change of circumstances; and the question must represent a necessary degree of seriousness. The Court of Cassation and the Council of State, respectively, check whether these conditions truly are fulfilled and refer the question to the Constitutional Council if they are. Article 61-1 speaks of the rights and freedoms which the Constitution guarantees as grounds for review; this refers to the body of constitutional law that, in the case-law of the Constitutional Council, refers not only to the provisions of the Constitution itself but also includes, via the Preamble, the Declaration of the Rights of Man and the Citizen of 1789. Statutes declared unconstitutional for violating such rights and freedoms are repealed (Art. 62 French Constitution).

To French constitutional law, all this is a remarkable novelty. In a comparative perspective, however, the reform places France in a larger family of European constitutional systems in the Kelsenian tradition which allow courts, or at least special constitutional courts, to review the constitutionality of legislation. The most notable procedural difference is the fact that in France preliminary references for concrete review are filtered through a supreme court and do not reach the constitutional adjudicator directly.

The new procedure for concrete *ex post* review does not replace but rather complements the pre-existing procedure of *ex ante* review. Thus, the Constitutional Council may still be asked to review the constitutionality of bills before promulgation.

5.3. *International Treaties and the ECHR*

As far as treaties are concerned, France is a monist system. Treaty law takes precedence over national statutes, both earlier and subsequent, under the condition of reciprocity (Art. 55 French Constitution). The European Convention on Human Rights (ECHR) can therefore be directly relied upon before all French courts. If a statute potentially violates both a constitutionally protected right and a Convention right, organic statute provides that a constitutionality question must be referred first, before the lower judge may consider treaty compliance. The procedural difference between the two review types is that while the resolution of constitutionality requires the formulation of a preliminary question to the relevant supreme court, with a view to a reference to the Constitutional Council, a breach of a treaty obligation can be established by lower judges themselves. If ECHR protection is deemed to have failed within France, individuals may bring an action against the state before the European Court of Human Rights (see § 7).

5.4. *European Union Law*

The law of the European Union has, according to the European Court of Justice, special characteristics as a new legal order. It is capable of having direct effect in the member states by virtue of its own character, irrespective of whether the member states are monist or dualist, and supremacy over all national provisions. National judges must set aside all conflicting national provisions, including their constitutions, in favour of European Union law.

Supremacy of European law over French statutes would be largely unproblematic since France is monist anyway. Thus, the Court of Cassation accepted the supremacy of Community law over statutes by virtue of France's monism clause (Art. 55 French Constitution) in its ruling in *Cafés Jacques Vabre* (23 May 1975, D. 1975 II 497). The Council of State, for the administrative courts, seems to have accepted Community supremacy over statutes on the same basis, in a procedure brought by *Raoul Georges Nicolo* (20 October 1989, RTDeur 1989, 771). It is the claimed supremacy over the Constitution that causes doctrinal concerns, however. Indeed, the Constitutional Council affirmed in its decision of 10 June 2004 (2004-496 DC) that European Union law does not prevail over the French Constitution. The transposition of European law into national law is a duty based on Article 88-1 of the French Constitution, which authorizes French EU membership, save for cases where the French Constitution expressly stands in the way of French compliance with European law. Such specific contrary constitutional provision may exist only in theory; yet in dogmatic terms the hierarchy of norms from the French point of view is clear: European law takes precedence over French statutes in as far as the French Constitution allows it to. Under this proviso, French courts keep applying European law in everyday practice, giving it precedence over national provisions. If in doubt about the right interpretation of Union law that is relevant to the case before them, judges may, and in some cases must, refer a preliminary question to the European Court of Justice.

6. The Netherlands

6.1. *The Court System*

The judicial system of the Netherlands as discussed here is the court system of the Netherlands in Europe; the overarching Kingdom of the Netherlands (the Netherlands proper plus the overseas countries) does not have any courts of its own, even though the governments of the overseas constituent countries may request the inclusion of an additional member to the Dutch Supreme Court for a particular case (Art. 23 (2) Charter for the Kingdom). The Dutch court system is based on a hierarchy of local courts, district courts, and courts of appeal, all of which deal with civil and criminal law cases; district courts are also competent in matters of administrative law. The highest court for civil and criminal matters is the Supreme Court, or *Hoge Raad*, acting as a court of cassation. As regards administrative law, three courts of last instance exist side by side, competent for different subject-matters: the administrative jurisprudence division of the Council of State, the Central Council of Appeals for social security and cases involving rules on civil servants, and a tribunal for commercial matters. Judges are appointed by royal decree for life but statute may (and does) fix a maximum age (Art. 117 Dutch Constitution).

6.2. Constitutional Review

While applying the law to judicial conflicts, Dutch judges are explicitly forbidden from checking the constitutionality of statutes (Art. 120 Dutch Constitution). This prohibition of constitutional review is also taken to include review with respect to the Charter for the Kingdom, the constitution of the overarching Kingdom of the Netherlands. The Dutch Supreme Court held this in its prominent ruling regarding the Harmonization Act (*Harmonisatiewetarrest*, 14 April 1989, AB 1989, 207). In the same ruling, it held that Article 120 equally prohibits judicial review of statutes against unwritten general principles of law, in that case legal certainty, even though it took the liberty of explicitly noting that the statute in question in fact did violate that principle. Such a finding may have as a result that the application of a statute in individual cases must not take place, unless the legislature had expressly considered the statute's potentially unfair effects during the legislative process and had discounted them, in which case the application must be carried out nevertheless; even when the application of a statute is deemed to violate general principles of law in circumstances which the legislature had *not* anticipated, this still does not affect the validity of the statute as such. Nor is the judiciary allowed to compel the legislature to enact legislation (*Waterpakt-arrest*, 21 March 2003, AB 2004, 39), not even in order to transpose an EU directive into national law. Article 120 is therefore more than a narrow exclusion of constitutional review of statutes and treaties: embedded in a system of strict separation of judicial and lawmaking tasks, the provision is a basis for a much broader immunity of the legislature as against the courts.

It is a recurring item on the Dutch constitutional reform agenda to either repeal Article 120 of the Constitution, and to allow constitutional review, or to insert exceptions so that judges may at least check the compatibility of statutes with constitutional human rights. In late 2008, an amendment that would allow for judicial review on human-rights grounds passed the two Chambers of parliament in first reading. A constitutional amendment also needs approval in a second reading, however, where two-thirds majorities are required. Right-of-centre parties remain opposed to such a reform, however, so a quick approval in second reading was never likely. It appears anyway that the need for such a change is not very pressing. Dutch monism with respect to treaties, most importantly the European Convention on Human Rights, already allows individuals to rely on human rights in another way. Self-executing treaty provisions override conflicting national legislation already, by virtue of the Dutch Constitution's Articles 93 and 94. Thus, what the Dutch judge lacks in constitutional review, at least as far as human rights are concerned, he largely makes up for via treaty review.

6.3. International Treaties and the ECHR

The Netherlands is a monist system with respect to international treaties; individuals can rely on provisions from treaties that are ratified by the Netherlands in court (Art. 93 Dutch Constitution), and when they do, treaty provisions override conflicting national statutes (Art. 94 Dutch Constitution). The only qualification is that not all treaty provisions can be relied upon, but only those that can 'bind anyone', meaning provisions that can be binding upon individuals because they are self-executing.

> *Gaps in the Prerogatives of Parliament*
>
> Several Dutch constitutional scholars have pointed out a gap in the systematic preservation of the prerogatives of parliament regarding the supremacy of treaties over statutes. It results from the fact that while all treaties override statutes, not all treaties actually require parliamentary ratification in the Netherlands. Notable exceptions under the Kingdom Statute on the Ratification and Publication of Treaties include treaties that are concluded for up to one year and which do not lead to significant government expenditure. The scholars suggest to limit the overriding effect of treaties only to those which have been approved by parliament.

The substantive rights enshrined in the European Convention on Human Rights all take precedence over national statutes. If protection of Convention rights is deemed to have failed within the Netherlands, individuals may bring an action against the state before the European Court of Human Rights (see § 7).

6.4. European Union Law

The law of the European Union has, according to the European Court of Justice (ECJ), special characteristics as a new legal order. It is capable of having direct effect in the member states by virtue of its own character, and supremacy over all national provisions. National judges must set aside all conflicting national provisions in favour of European law. *Van Gend & Loos*, the groundbreaking direct-effect judgment of the ECJ, was, incidentally, triggered by a preliminary reference from a Dutch court (see § 1.4). The national court had asked, in essence, whether the European treaty provision on free movement of goods was capable of binding 'anyone', conferring individual rights, in the sense of the Dutch monism clause. The ECJ's answer was, famously, that this provision indeed had direct effect, and that in fact this would even be the case if the member state in question were not monist. According to the ECJ, Community law even overrides national constitutions; within the Netherlands, monism is interpreted in a very far-reaching manner, so that treaties are indeed capable of overriding not just statutes but the Constitution, too. There is no constitutional court that might take issue, and a review of the constitutionality of treaties is banned by the same provision of the Constitution that bans constitutional review of statutes, namely Article 120. Essentially, European Union law is accepted in the Dutch legal order as unconditionally as the ECJ has stipulated. If in doubt about the right interpretation of Union law that is relevant to the case before them, judges may, and in some cases must, refer a preliminary question to the ECJ.

7. European Human Rights

Signed in 1950, the European Convention on Human Rights (ECHR) is a multilateral treaty committing the contracting states to human-rights obligations, from the prohibition of torture to the freedom of expression. The contracting states are the member states of the Council of Europe, an international organization that is devoted to promoting democracy, human rights and the rule of law. The Council of Europe started out with ten members in 1949; the UK, France and the Netherlands were among the founding members, (West) Germany joined in 1950. By now the organization comprises 47 states across Europe.

> *The Boundaries of Europe*
>
> The Council of Europe presently comprises 47 states; in fact, it comprises all states in Europe (including the microstates), with only three exceptions: the Vatican State, recently-independent Kosovo as well as Belarus (whose application is pending since 1993). The easternmost member states of the Council of Europe are Russia, Ukraine, Armenia, Georgia, Azerbaijan, Cyprus and Turkey.

What is special about the ECHR is that an international judicial mechanism is set up to enforce the rights and freedoms stipulated in the Convention: the Strasbourg-based European Court of Human Rights. The Strasbourg Court consists of 47 judges, one per contracting state; they are elected by the Parliamentary Assembly of the Council of Europe, a body comprising members of the national parliaments of the contracting states, from a government shortlist of three nominees each. Judges serve non-renewable terms of nine years until the maximum age of seventy (Arts. 19, 20, 22 and 23 ECHR). Until the entry into force of Protocol 14 in 2010 they served renewable six-year terms. The Court decides over the admissibility of complaints and adjudicates in cases of alleged ECHR violations.

What is special about the Strasbourg Court is that while it is an international court, not only member states or, as in the Inter-American Court of Human Rights, an international commission, but also individual applicants can bring cases before it. Thus, individuals can 'sue' a state that is party to the ECHR for violations of the human rights to which that state has committed itself. The ECHR, and the case-law of the Strasbourg Court, have already had a profound impact on domestic constitutional systems, from the requirements of impartiality and independence of national judges to voting rights and the immunity of politicians. More generally, Strasbourg places domestic relations between citizens and national public authority under human-rights scrutiny via added international judicial review in individual cases. The Court interprets the ECHR as a 'living document', keeping pace with societal developments, and is also in other areas ready to expand, or fix autonomously from the contracting states, the scope of ECHR concepts. For example, individuals have the right to a fair trial to decide on a 'criminal charge' against them (Art. 6 (1) ECHR), but states cannot escape responsibility simply by calling a procedure differently in national terms: the Strasbourg Court determines what falls under 'criminal charge' as an autonomous concept.

It may be argued that the Strasbourg Court resembles a pan-European constitutional court, at least as far as human rights are concerned, actively holding the contracting states to standards enshrined in a central document. No matter the activity in Strasbourg, however, the task of safeguarding human rights primarily remains with the contracting states themselves. It is up to the states to secure ECHR rights within their jurisdiction (Art. 1 ECHR), and to provide a remedy for possible infringements domestically (Art. 13 ECHR). While the Strasbourg Court has noted that being monist certainly helps, contracting states are not obliged to give the ECHR itself overriding domestic effect. Thus, there are no supremacy or direct-effect doctrines under the ECHR like they exist under the European Community. As the contracting states must keep up their human-rights levels themselves, the Strasbourg Court only steps in as a subsidiary mechanism, as a last resort if domestic human-rights protection is deemed to have failed. This approach is reflected in the central criteria that determine whether or not an individual is actually admissible before the Strasbourg Court or not. Before launching his case, the applicant must, among other things, first have exhausted all domestic remedies (Art. 35 (1) ECHR), meaning that he must have tried everything to seek a remedy domestically up until the last instance of appeal. He must then launch his case within six months of the final domestic decision in last instance. And he is only admissible in as far as he still is a 'victim' (Art. 34 ECHR), meaning that once he has received satisfaction for his alleged suffering from domestic authorities, he will no longer be heard in Strasbourg on the merits.

Since prior exhaustion of domestic remedies is an admissibility criterion for individual applicants, the European Court of Human Rights becomes relevant at the end of domestic proceedings. It does not, for example, answer preliminary questions. In that context, the Court might appear to be a kind of 'super appeal', a supreme European court of very last instance. Such an assessment would be misleading, however. The Strasbourg Court cannot overturn any national administrative or judicial decisions. It does not quash administrative orders, it does not invalidate any national statutes, it does not reverse a 'guilty' verdict against a convicted person nor find in favour of the losing party in a private law dispute. What it can do, however, is find that the respondent state as a whole, including its court system, has infringed upon, and has failed to safeguard, rights and freedoms that are protected under the ECHR. The remedy it can award to individuals in such case is 'just satisfaction' (Art. 41 ECHR). In light cases, the judgment itself that confirms that the applicant was right after all is satisfaction enough; in most cases, however, just satisfaction means compensation for pecuniary and non-pecuniary damage suffered as a consequence of the human-rights infringement: money, to be paid out to the applicant by the infringing respondent state. While the judgment itself pertains to the case at hand only, states may change their laws and practices if they wish to prevent the future cost and embarrassment of more judgments against them in similar situations.

8. The ECHR, the European Union and the National Constitutions

The member states of the EU have in common their commitment to the ECHR. This means that while not all ECHR contracting parties are at the same time EU members, all EU member states are also parties to the ECHR. Accession to the ECHR is in fact a membership criterion for candidate countries seeking EU membership; the Union's attachment to the ECHR is spelt out in Article 6 TEU. Two fundamental problems can arise from this situation, though.

The first problem is that the meaning of the ECHR is interpreted by the Strasbourg-based European Court of Human Rights, while European Union law is interpreted, ultimately, by the Luxembourg-based European Court of Justice. As long as case-law between the two Courts can diverge, it may be that member states breach the ECHR by correctly executing EU law, or risk violating EU law by adhering to the ECHR. Strictly speaking, the ECHR would not permit member states to escape their obligations simply by setting up international organizations like the EU; EU law as interpreted by the ECJ does not envisage any exceptions to its supremacy doctrine either, though. A classical example of diverging interpretations of one and the same human right is *Niemietz* v. *Germany* of 16 December 1992 (no. 13710/88), where the Strasbourg Court held that business premises could be considered part of the 'home' in the sense of the right to inviolability of the home and private life under Article 8 ECHR, whereas earlier the ECJ had ruled in *Hoechst AG* v. *Commission* (46/87 and 227/88, [1989] ECR 2859) that business premises were in fact not 'home'.

The second problem is that as long as the EU member states are parties to the ECHR but the EU itself is not, breaches of the ECHR can be caused by EU institutions, like the Commission, for which the EU cannot be challenged but for which it is also hard to blame the member states. Practical examples may include the Commission's failure to offer a hearing in competition law investigations, or the ECJ's not granting parties an opportunity to respond to the opinion of the Advocate-General, or its violating the reasonable time requirement under Article 6 ECHR by taking too long to process preliminary questions. Since neither of these actions or omissions are plausibly imputable to all member states jointly, let alone any one particular member state, the risk arises that no-one can be held accountable for breaches of the ECHR. In the case *Bosphorus Airways* v. *Ireland* of 30 June 2005 (no. 45036/98) over the grounding by Ireland of Yugoslav-owned airplanes pursuant to an EU measure implementing a UN sanction, the Strasbourg Court famously held that it would not subject EU law to ECHR review as long as the EU, overall, sticks to the human-rights levels that the ECJ had already developed. Thus, ECJ human-rights protection was declared to be equivalent to Strasbourg standards.

Indeed, the ECJ had developed an entire body of case-law incorporating human rights as 'general principles' of EU law, seeking inspiration in the constitutional traditions common to the member states and treaties to which they were all party, in particular the ECHR; Article 6 TEU, originally inserted with the 1992 Maastricht Treaty, is merely a codification of that judge-driven development. In addition, the EU adopted a Charter of Fundamental Rights of its own in 2000, which was accorded legally binding force through the Treaty of Lisbon in 2009. The

Charter refers to the ECHR and must be interpreted in the light of the Convention (Art. 52 (3) EU Charter of Fundamental Rights). However it may be argued that ultimately the only convincing resolution of the parallel existence of ECHR and EU human rights standards is the accession of the EU as a contracting party to the ECHR.

Originally, the EU could not accede to the ECHR, as the ECJ held that such a transformative step would require an explicit legal basis in the EU Treaties (ECJ Opinion 2/94, [1996] ECR I-1759). With the entry into force of the Treaty of Lisbon in 2009, however, accession was not only authorized but in fact mandated (Art. 6 (2) TEU); a matching provision allowing the EU to join has been inserted into the ECHR with the entry into force of its Protocol No. 14 (Art. 59 (2) ECHR). However, the actual accession did not take place instantly, since it still required arrangements specific to the EU to be found. One notable issue that required resolution was the fact that individual applications in Strasbourg still require the exhaustion of domestic remedies as an admissibility condition. Private parties may seek the annulment of EU measures directed at them before the ECJ, but otherwise the ECJ is not an appeal court: it can be reached via preliminary references as part of domestic proceedings. If national judges simply did not refer such a preliminary question, whereas alleged breaches of the ECHR resulted from EU law, the ECJ will not have had an opportunity to pronounce itself on whether EU law could have actually remedied the alleged breach itself. Another issue relates to the fact that breaches of the ECHR may result from action by a member state pursuant to EU obligations, so a system of the EU and its member state acting jointly as defendants ('co-respondents') in Strasbourg was proposed. After accession, the ECHR and the EU Charter may still co-exist; that, however, would not be much different from the already existing situation where ECHR contracting states have their own human rights catalogues in their own national constitutions. In fact, this reflects the desired situation: the ECHR represents minimum levels of human rights protection, and contracting parties, whether they be states or the EU, are encouraged to afford higher standards, and to enforce them on their own, so that individuals should not *have* to seek justice before the Strasbourg Court.

Annex 1

USEFUL LINKS

Legislative chambers

- www.house.gov
- www.senate.gov
- www.bundestag.de
- www.bundesrat.de
- www.parliament.uk
- www.assemblee-nationale.fr
- www.senat.fr
- www.tweedekamer.nl
- www.eerstekamer.nl

Case law

- www.supremecourtus.gov
- www.bverfg.de
- www.supremecourt.gov.uk
- www.conseil-constitutionnel.fr
- www.rechtspraak.nl
- curia.europa.eu
- www.echr.coe.int

Annex 2

EXERCISES AND MODEL EXAM QUESTIONS

The following section contains exercises that may serve as tests for self-study and as examples for possible exam questions in introductory courses on comparative constitutional law. All questions can be answered based on information contained in this book.

* * *

A number of US politicians have proposed that the smallest US State by population size, Wyoming, should have only one instead of two Senators in the US Senate. A number of German politicians have proposed that the smallest German State by population size, Bremen, should have only one instead of three votes in the German Bundesrat. Both Wyoming and Bremen firmly oppose this idea. How would the respective idea have to be implemented, and in which country would it be procedurally easier to implement the proposed change – considering both Wyoming's and Bremen's opposition?

* * *

In 2028, the President of the US, the French President and the British Prime Minister are all nearing the end of their second consecutive term in office. All three of them came into office regularly in the first place, not in any exceptional circumstances. All three of them would like to run for a third term. Assuming that the constitutional rules are the same as they are today: are they all allowed to serve a third term, is none of them allowed, or is only one or two of them allowed to serve and if so which one(s)?

* * *

What is the main difference between the French and the German system of referring preliminary questions on the constitutionality of statutes in force as it is laid down in the respective Constitution?

* * *

The United Kingdom has considered introducing an Alternative Vote system for electing the members of the House of Commons. Would it be constitutional for the Netherlands, France and Germany to adopt such a system for elections of their respective lower chambers?

* * *

After the German electoral system for the election of the Bundestag has been declared unconstitutional due to the negative vote value phenomenon, the political party groups in the Bundestag are now considering alternatives. The government coalition parties argue in favour of introducing a system as it currently applies to elections of the Dutch Second Chamber. The opposition retorts, however, that such a reform would require a constitutional amendment, and without the opposition's support the government would not be able to secure the required two-thirds majority in either chamber. Is the opposition right when it argues that the reform would require a constitutional amendment?

* * *

Do the constitutional systems of the Netherlands and Germany provide for parliamentary investiture when a new cabinet is to take office?

* * *

Which body comprises more members: the Federal Convention that elects the German President, or the Electoral College that elects the President of the US?

* * *

The new Dutch government has decided to sharpen penalties for immigrants committing crimes. A new Immigration Act has been introduced and adopted, which provides in Article 21 that immigrants shall be expelled from Dutch territory if they have committed a crime under Dutch law. M., a 17 year old Argentinean national, is convicted of theft and is due to be expelled to Argentina. He claims that he has lived in the Netherlands all his life, that all his family and friends live here, including his Dutch fiancée, that he does not speak any Spanish and has been to Argentina only briefly, and instead considers the Netherlands his home country. He claims that expulsion would violate his right to protection of his family life under Article 8 of the European Convention on Human Rights. Can M. rely on the ECHR considering that he is an Argentinean national, not a Dutch national? Can the Dutch judge declare Article 21 of the Dutch Immigration Act void if it violates Article 8 of the ECHR? Can the Dutch judge, in case he is not sure whether the ECHR is violated, refer a preliminary question to the European Court of Human Rights to resolve whether Article 21 of the Dutch Immigration Act violates Article 8 of the ECHR? Assume the above scenario takes place in the UK, and the individual in question is a French national. Can the UK judge declare Section 21 of the Immigration Act 2010 void if it violates Article 8 of the ECHR? Can the UK judge, in case he is not sure whether the ECHR is violated, refer a preliminary question to the European Court of Human Rights to resolve whether the Immigration Act violates Article 8 of the ECHR? If the individual claims that as an EU citizen he may rely on his free movement rights under the EU Treaty and may therefore stay in the UK, can the UK judge rule on that basis that he is not to be expelled to France even though the Immigration Act clearly says that he must be expelled?

* * *

The opposition parties in the Dutch Second Chamber are still furious about the new sharpened Immigration Act. In December a Dutch judge, in a case involving M., an Argentinean citizen, had declared that the statute violated human rights. The opposition now demands the resignation of the responsible ministers who had tabled the new Immigration Act. The ministers retort that (A) the Immigration Act had been signed by the Queen, and that (B) consequently any criticism should be directed at her, not them. Are these two statements correct as a matter of constitutional law?

* * *

In order to deal with the effects of the financial crisis and the impact of migration flows in the wake of the uprisings in the Arab world, the government leaders of the United Kingdom and the Netherlands decide that the term of the lower chamber of their respective parliament should be extended to seven years. This way the governments will not be distracted too much by election campaigns and will be able to function more efficiently. Several members of the UK House of Lords as well as of the Dutch First Chamber argue, however, that their respective chambers will not agree to such a move, which they perceive as undermining democracy. Can the Lords and the First Chamber, respectively, veto the reform?

* * *

The President of France can be impeached 'in case of a breach of his duties manifestly incompatible with the exercise of his mandate'. Considering the body that judges him, which system does the French presidential impeachment procedure resemble more: the German one or the one of the United States?

* * *

Does the presidential decision to dissolve the lower chamber of parliament need to be countersigned in Germany or in France?

* * *

'The First Chamber of the Netherlands is a federal senate since it represents the Dutch Provinces'. Discuss this proposition, also referring to relevant examples of other upper chambers discussed in this book.

* * *

The defendant in a libel suit in France asserts that the French statute on personal dignity that is invoked against him breaches his rights to freedom of expression as enshrined in the European Convention on Human Rights. His opponent, the applicant, argues that only French law applies before a French court, and that anyway, if the defendant loses his case, he can still appeal to the European Court of Human Rights and have the judgment annulled. Discuss the correctness of both arguments as raised by the applicant.

* * *

A French statute, Loi 2001-911, provides that in criminal proceedings for terrorist offences involving the killing of more than nine persons, the defendant is presumed guilty when charged by the prosecution service and must prove his innocence in court to be acquitted. This is an exception to the presumption of innocence that usually applies according to the Code of Criminal Procedure. A young man, N., has been charged with twenty-nine counts of murder in relation to the terrorist bombing of a train station in Lyon in August 2005. N.'s lawyer argues that Loi 2001-911 should not be applied because it violates Article 6 (2) of the ECHR. Can the criminal court in Lyon set aside the contested statute for that reason?

* * *

'The involvement of Parliament in the appointment of members of the Constitutional Council by the President of France is similar to the involvement of the Senate in the appointment of members of the federal Supreme Court by the President of the United States'. Discuss this proposition, providing reasons for your answers and citing relevant constitutional provisions.

* * *

Name two examples of how a state's membership of the European Union affects its domestic separation of powers and the relative strengths of the main national legislative, executive and judicial organs vis-à-vis each other.

Exercises and Model Exam Questions

* * *

Can the French Senate veto its own abolition? Can the German Bundesrat veto its own abolition?

* * *

Would it be constitutional for the French legislature to change the Constitution so as to introduce a system whereby the President gets elected via an electoral college, rather than via direct elections?

* * *

Would it be constitutional for a Dutch judge to examine whether the Treaty of Lisbon is compatible with Article 1 of the Dutch Constitution?

* * *

Would it be constitutional for the German legislature to change the Basic Law so as to replace the Bundesrat with a body modelled after the UK House of Lords?

* * *

The Latvian constitution provides that the head of state may propose a dissolution of parliament but that this must be confirmed in a referendum. To what extent is this arrangement comparable to the German situation?

* * *

Would you consider the French National Assembly election system to constitute a form of proportional representation?

* * *

'Neither Dutch nor French lower judges may annul unconstitutional statutes'. Discuss the truthfulness and accuracy of this proposition.

* * *

Assume the UK and the Netherlands wanted to introduce a republic and replace their monarchs with directly elected Presidents who would exercise exactly the same functions as the monarchs do today. Would the Netherlands and Britain then be considered presidential systems?

* * *

Does the election system for the UK House of Commons and the French National Assembly lead to the creation of overhang mandates like those in the German Bundestag?

* * *

Consult a world map. Can you name a republic which at the same time has a presidential system of government? Can you name a republic which at the same time is federal? Can you name a unitary state which is at the same time a republic? Can you name a republic which at the same time is a monarchy? Can you name a federation which at the same time has a presidential system of government? Can you name a federation which at the same time is a monarchy? Can you name a federation which at the same time is a unitary state? Can you name a state with a parliamentary system of government which at the same time is federal? Can you name a state with a parliamentary system of government which at the same time has a presidential system? Can you name a state with a parliamentary system of government which at the same time is a monarchy? Can you name a monarchy which is at the same time a unitary state?

Annex 3

GLOSSARY

Page references are included with respect to selected terms.

Absolutism	System where the powers of the monarch are unlimited. 5, 12, 16, 40, 66.
Abstract review	Examination of the validity of laws without there being an inter-party dispute. 112, 161-2, 167, 170, 173-4.
Assemblée Nationale	National Assembly, lower chamber of the French parliament.
Backbencher	Non-prominent member of parliament; parliamentarian without a government office. 145, 147.
Bicameralism	A legislature's division into two separate assemblies. 25, 41-2, 45-6, 50-2, 55-6, 69, 72, 78-9, 80-1, 84-5, 87, 89, 96-8, 104, 112, 114-5, 126-7.
Bill	Legislative proposal, draft law.
Bundesrat	Federal Council, representation of State governments in Germany.
Bundestag	Federal Diet, German parliament.
Cabinet	Collegiate body of government ministers.
Censure – see no-confidence, vote of –	
Certiorary, writ of –	Discretionary permission to be heard by a court. 169.
Checks and balances	Mutual interference between branches of government under separation of powers. 22-5, 29, 56, 88, 124, 128, 160-1.
Cohabitation	Situation where two leading office-holders, especially head of state and head of government in France, are of opposing political colours. 148-9.
Concrete review	Examination of the validity of laws in the course of an ongoing inter-party dispute. 112, 161-3, 167, 172-4, 181.
Congress	The US parliament.
Constituency	Group of people represented; (population of) an electoral district.

197

Constitutional court	Judicial body specialized in resolving constitutional disputes. 4, 7, 25, 34, 46, 50, 64, 73, 89, 91-2, 94, 111-2, 131, 139, 142-3, 160-3, 166-7, 170, 172-6, 181, 184, 186.
Constitutionalism	Doctrine stating that public power, including the monarchy, derives from, and is limited by, a constitution. 5, 40.
Constructive vote of no-confidence – see no-confidence, constructive vote of –	
Council of Europe	International organization devoted to democracy, human rights and rule of law. 185.
Council of the EU	EU institution comprising national ministers, also called Council of Ministers. 53, 122, 129, 140, 146, 149, 155.
Countersign	Confirmation of decisions of the head of state by a cabinet member. 23, 98, 116, 130, 132, 138-9, 152-4.
Decentralization	Passing power down to sub-national entities, typically administrative competences in a symmetrical way.
Devolution	Passing power down to sub-national entities, typically legislative competences in an asymmetrical way. 3, 8, 26, 37, 51-5, 64-7.
Direct effect (EU)	Principle giving individuals the right to rely on European Union law before a national court. 20, 40, 165-8, 175, 179, 181, 184.
Dualism	Treatment of international treaty provisions as separate from national law, with domestic effect only after implementation. 164-5, 167, 174, 175, 177, 179, 181.
Eerste Kamer	First Chamber, upper chamber of the Dutch parliament.
Electoral college	Body charged with electing an office-holder. 28, 34, 63, 106, 124, 131, 134-5, 137, 138, 147-8.
En-bloc voting	Multi-member delegations casting one uniform vote. 34, 135.
European Council	EU institution comprising national heads of state and government and the Commission president. 53, 122-3, 127, 140, 146, 149, 155.
European Court of Human Rights	Strasbourg-based international court established under the European Convention on Human Rights. 1, 7, 75, 175, 178, 181, 184, 185-8.
European Court of Justice	Luxembourg-based court of the the European Union.
European Union	Supranational organization for socio-economic and political cooperation and integration between its member states in defined policy areas. 1, 2, 6, 8, 15, 19, 20, 32, 34, 37, 39, 43, 46, 53-4, 65, 72, 79, 80-2, 95, 98, 102, 107, 115, 120, 122, 127-9, 140-1, 146, 149, 150, 155, 159, 163, 165-7, 175-6, 179, 181-2, 184, 187-8.
Executive	Branch of government charged with implementing and enforcing laws.

Annex 3

Federalism	A state's division into territorial sub-units with constitutionally enshrined powers. 6, 9, 15, 17- 19, 25-6, 27-8, 30-4, 43-4, 47-8, 49-55, 55-70, 71, 79, 82, 84-8, 93-7, 114, 142, 164, 168-9, 172.
First-past-the-post	Electoral system where a relative majority is needed to win. 76-8, 84, 86, 90-1, 99-100, 105, 135.
Formateur	Person charged with forming a cabinet. 153.
Gerrymandering	Manipulative drawing of electoral district borders for tactical advantage. 86.
Hereditary peers (UK)	Members of the House of Lords who pass on their seat to heirs. 100.
House of Commons	Lower chamber of the UK Parliament.
House of Lords	Upper chamber of the UK Parliament.
House of Representatives	Lower chamber of the US parliament.
Impeachment	Quasi-criminal procedure against office-holders. 21, 23, 56, 128, 131, 133, 137, 139, 148, 188.
Implied repeal	Later laws deviating from earlier laws automatically supersede the earlier laws. 65, 165, 177.
Informateur (NL)	Mediator charged with probing possible government coalitions. 153.
Initiative, power of –	The right to propose the adoption of a decision, notably the right to table bills. 29, 34, 37, 42, 46, 80, 83-4, 87, 95, 107, 115, 148.
Judicial activism	Practice of creative and expansive interpretation of law by courts.
Judicial restraint	Practice of narrow and literal interpretation of law by courts.
Judiciary	Branch of government charged with applying laws in case of disputes.
Law Lords (UK)	Members of the House of Lords exercising judicial functions. 24, 100-1, 177.
Legislature	Branch of government charged with making laws.
Lex posterior rule	Later laws override earlier laws.
Lex specialis rule	Special laws override general laws.
Lex superior rule	Higher laws override lower laws.
Life peers (UK)	Non-hereditary members of the House of Lords appointed for life. 100.
Literalism	Interpretation of a constitutional document in the light of the drafters' original intentions. 7.
Living constitution	Interpretation of a constitutional document in the light of societal changes. 7, 185.
Lords Spiritual (UK)	Clergymen with a seat in the House of Lords.
Lords Temporal (UK)	Members of the House of Lords other than clergymen.
Majority, absolute –	More than half the total number of votes or voters.

Majority, qualified –	Higher-than-usual majority, majority subject to additional requirements.
Majority, relative –	Largest number of votes received.
Majority, simple – see majority, relative –	
Mixed-member system	Electoral system combining different electoral systems. 62, 77, 89, 114.
Monarchy	Constitutional system where the head of state is a monarch.
Monarchy, absolute – see absolutism	
Monarchy, constitutional –	Monarchy with royal powers limited by a constitution.
Monarchy, parliamentary –	Monarchy with royal powers limited by a parliament.
Monism	Automatic incorporation of international treaty provisions as an enforceable part of national law with precedence over national laws. See also dualism.
No-confidence, constructive vote of –	No-confidence motion against an incumbent executive office-holder requiring the immediate election of a successor. 33, 125-7, 133, 141-2.
No-confidence, vote of –	Parliamentary motion expressing lack of trust in an executive or office-holder.
Originalists – see literalism	
Overhang mandates	Additional parliamentary seats created to accommodate an excess of electoral district winners in a mixed-member proportional system. 90-3, 114.
Parliamentary system	Constitutional system where the cabinet is accountable to the parliament in the sense of a confidence rule.
Plurality – see majority, relative –	
Pocket veto (US)	A President's neither signing nor vetoing a bill. 88.
Preamble	Declaratory introduction to a legal document. 16, 19, 23, 32, 110, 169, 176, 181.
Presentment	Referral of bills to the President for signature. 88.
Presidential system	Constitutional system where the head of the government has a separate mandate and is not accountable to the parliament in the sense of a confidence rule.
Prime-Minister	Head of the cabinet in a parliamentary system.
Promulgation	The signing of a bill into law by the head of state.
Proportional representation	Electoral system whereby the share of seats assigned corresponds to the share of the vote gained.
Purse, power of the –	The right to decide on the budget. 58, 137.
Quorum	Minimum number of present members required for a valid parliamentary vote. 80, 135.
Rationalized parliament	Parliament whose legislative and censure powers are restricted with a view to government efficiency. 42, 108.
Reading	Process of parliamentary consideration of a bill.

Republic	Constitutional system where the head of state is not a monarch.
Rest seats	Remainder of vacant seats after proportional seat distribution based on whole numbers. 113-4.
Royal assent	The monarch's approval of a bill. 12, 18, 36, 38, 81, 83-4, 101-4, 177.
Rule of law	Doctrine stating that the exercise of public authority is bound by legal norms. 5, 7, 12, 19, 24, 67, 160-1, 185.
Semi-presidential system	Constitutional system where the head of state, with his own mandate, and a prime-minister, who is accountable to parliament, share executive powers. 21-2, 26, 42, 123, 133, 147-8.
Sénat	Senate, upper chamber of the French parliament.
Senate	Upper chamber of US parliament.
Separation of powers	Distinction of public authority into different functions. 12, 22-4, 28, 42, 57, 87, 161, 183.
Session of parliament	Period when parliament is working, between recesses.
Speaker	Chairman of a parliamentary chamber.
Stare decisis	Common-law doctrine stating that courts must follow established case-law. 170.
Staten-Generaal	States-General, the Dutch parliament.
Supremacy (EU)	Principle stating that European Union law with direct effect overrides all conflicting national provisions. See also direct effect.
Tweede Kamer	Second Chamber, lower chamber of the Dutch parliament.
Unicameralism	A parliament's comprising a single assembly. 27, 32, 40, 45, 52, 55, 60, 78, 79, 102, 104, 127.
Unitarism	Non-federal state structure. 15, 25-6, 32, 37, 42, 44, 46, 49-55, 60, 61, 66-7, 68, 79, 82.
Veto power	The right to prevent the adoption of a decision. 6, 23, 29, 31, 34, 37, 51, 63, 80-1, 83-4, 87-8, 97-8, 101-4, 108-10, 115, 117, 136, 139, 148, 180.
Veto, absolute –	Veto that is final and not subject to an override.
Veto, suspensive –	Veto that can delay but not completely prevent the adoption of a decision.
Whip	Enforcer of party discipline in parliament. 73-4.

OVERVIEW OF CONSTITUTIONS COMPARED

	United States of America	United Kingdom	Federal Republic of Germany	French Republic	Kingdom of the Netherlands — Kingdom*	Kingdom of the Netherlands — NL (Europe)
State form	Republic	Constitutional monarchy	Republic	Republic	Constitutional monarchy	Constitutional monarchy
Form of government	Presidential	Parliamentary	Parliamentary	Semi-Presidential	↑	Parliamentary
State Structure	Federal	Unitary, with devolution	Federal	Decentralized unitary	Quasi-federal	Decentralized unitary
Head of State	President	King	Federal President	President of the Republic	King	King
Head of Government	President	Prime-Minister	Federal Chancellor	Prime Minister	Dutch PM (Europe)	Prime-Minister
Lower Chamber	House of Representatives	House of Commons	Bundestag	National Assembly	↑	Second Chamber
Upper Chamber	Senate	House of Lords	Bundesrat	Senate	↑	First Chamber
Parliamentary motion of censure against executive	No	Simple vote against PM or ministers in Commons	Constructive vote against Chancellor by qualified procedure in Bundestag	Censure vote against government by qualified procedure in Nat. Ass.	↑	Simple vote against PM or ministers in Second Chamber
(Residual) legislative power	States	(King in) Parliament	States	Government	Constituent countries	Government plus States-General

202

	United States of America	United Kingdom	Federal Republic of Germany	French Republic	Kingdom of the Netherlands Kingdom*	Kingdom of the Netherlands NL (Europe)
Legislative initiative	Senate, House (tax bills House only)	Government, Commons, Lords	Government, Bundestag, Bundesrat	PM, Nat. Ass., Senate	↑	Government, Second Chamber
Bicameralism: can upper chamber be overridden	No, House and Senate must concur	Yes, with exceptions	Yes, unless concurrence is required	Yes, with exceptions	↑	No, both Chambers must concur
Veto against bills by head of state	Yes, subject to override	By convention not	Yes, if bill unconstitutional	No	↑	No (King cannot act alone)
Concrete const. review of legislation	Yes, by all courts	No	Yes, via referral to Const. Court	Yes, via referral to Const. Council	–	No
Abstract constitutional review	No	No	Yes, by Const. Court	Review of bills by Const. Council	–	No
Constitutional human-rights catalogue	Yes	Various statutes	Yes	No, but reference in preamble	No	Yes
Effect of international treaties	Qualified monism	Dualism	Dualism	Monism	–	Monism
Supremacy of EC law over national law qualified	n/a	No, but UK may repeal EEC Act '72	Yes, by supremacy of Constitution	Yes, by supremacy of Constitution	–	No

* The overarching Kingdom of the Netherlands has no separate institutions; legislative and executive functions are carried out by (European) Dutch institutions acting by qualified procedures. The overseas countries each have their own constitution.

Annex 5

THE CONSTITUTION OF THE UNITED STATES

Constitution of the United States of America of 17 September 1787, with Amendments.[1]

Preamble
We the People of the United States, in Order to form a more perfect Union, establish Justice, insure domestic Tranquility, provide for the common defence, promote the general Welfare, and secure the Blessings of Liberty to ourselves and our Posterity, do ordain and establish this Constitution for the United States of America.

Article I.
Section 1. All legislative Powers herein granted shall be vested in a Congress of the United States, which shall consist of a Senate and House of Representatives.

Section 2. The House of Representatives shall be composed of Members chosen every second Year by the People of the several States, and the Electors in each State shall have the Qualifications requisite for Electors of the most numerous Branch of the State Legislature.

No Person shall be a Representative who shall not have attained to the Age of twenty five Years, and been seven Years a Citizen of the United States, and who shall not, when elected, be an Inhabitant of that State in which he shall be chosen.

Representatives and direct Taxes shall be apportioned among the several States which may be included within this Union, according to their respective Numbers, which shall be determined by adding to the whole Number of free Persons, including those bound to Service for a Term of Years, and excluding Indians not taxed, three fifths of all other Persons. The actual Enumeration shall be made within three Years after the first Meeting of the Congress of the United States, and within every subsequent Term of ten Years, in such Manner as they shall by Law direct. The Number of Representatives shall not exceed one for every thirty Thousand, but each State shall have at Least one Representative; and until such enumeration

---

[1] This text has also been published separately in: Ph. Kiiver & N. Kornet, eds., *The Maastricht Collection: Selected National, European and International Provisions from Public and Private Law*, Second Edition (Groningen: Europa Law Publishing, 2010). It has also been published in a smaller compilation covering only the area of constitutional law: Ph. Kiiver, ed., *Sources of Constitutional Law: Constitutions and Fundamental Legal Provisions from the United States, France, Germany, the Netherlands, the United Kingdom, the ECHR and the EU*, Second Edition (Groningen: Europa Law Publishing, 2010).

The Constitution of the United States

shall be made, the State of New Hampshire shall be entitled to chuse three, Massachusetts eight, Rhode-Island and Providence Plantations one, Connecticut five, New-York six, New Jersey four, Pennsylvania eight, Delaware one, Maryland six, Virginia ten, North Carolina five, South Carolina five, and Georgia three.

When vacancies happen in the Representation from any State, the Executive Authority thereof shall issue Writs of Election to fill such Vacancies.

The House of Representatives shall chuse their Speaker and other Officers; and shall have the sole Power of Impeachment.

Section 3. The Senate of the United States shall be composed of two Senators from each State, chosen by the Legislature thereof for six Years; and each Senator shall have one Vote.

Immediately after they shall be assembled in Consequence of the first Election, they shall be divided as equally as may be into three Classes. The Seats of the Senators of the first Class shall be vacated at the Expiration of the second Year, of the second Class at the Expiration of the fourth Year, and of the third Class at the Expiration of the sixth Year, so that one third may be chosen every second Year; and if Vacancies happen by Resignation, or otherwise, during the Recess of the Legislature of any State, the Executive thereof may make temporary Appointments until the next Meeting of the Legislature, which shall then fill such Vacancies.

No Person shall be a Senator who shall not have attained to the Age of thirty Years, and been nine Years a Citizen of the United States, and who shall not, when elected, be an Inhabitant of that State for which he shall be chosen.

The Vice President of the United States shall be President of the Senate, but shall have no Vote, unless they be equally divided.

The Senate shall chuse their other Officers, and also a President pro tempore, in the Absence of the Vice President, or when he shall exercise the Office of President of the United States.

The Senate shall have the sole Power to try all Impeachments. When sitting for that Purpose, they shall be on Oath or Affirmation. When the President of the United States is tried, the Chief Justice shall preside: And no Person shall be convicted without the Concurrence of two thirds of the Members present.

Judgment in Cases of Impeachment shall not extend further than to removal from Office, and disqualification to hold and enjoy any Office of honor, Trust or Profit under the United States: but the Party convicted shall nevertheless be liable and subject to Indictment, Trial, Judgment and Punishment, according to Law.

Section 4. The Times, Places and Manner of holding Elections for Senators and Representatives, shall be prescribed in each State by the Legislature thereof; but the Congress may at any time by Law make or alter such Regulations, except as to the Places of chusing Senators.

The Congress shall assemble at least once in every Year, and such Meeting shall be on the first Monday in December, unless they shall by Law appoint a different Day.

Section 5. Each House shall be the Judge of the Elections, Returns and Qualifications of its own Members, and a Majority of each shall constitute a Quorum to do Business; but a smaller Number may adjourn from day to day, and may be authorized to compel the Attendance of absent Members, in such Manner, and under such Penalties as each House may provide.

Each House may determine the Rules of its Proceedings, punish its Members for disorderly Behaviour, and, with the Concurrence of two thirds, expel a Member.

Each House shall keep a Journal of its Proceedings, and from time to time publish the same, excepting such Parts as may in their Judgment require Secrecy; and the Yeas and Nays of the Members of either House on any question shall, at the Desire of one fifth of those Present, be entered on the Journal.

Neither House, during the Session of Congress, shall, without the Consent of the other, adjourn for more than three days, nor to any other Place than that in which the two Houses shall be sitting.

Section 6. The Senators and Representatives shall receive a Compensation for their Services, to be ascertained by Law, and paid out of the Treasury of the United States. They shall in all Cases, except Treason, Felony and Breach of the Peace, be privileged from Arrest during their Attendance at the Session of their respective Houses, and in going to and returning from the same; and for any Speech or Debate in either House, they shall not be questioned in any other Place.

No Senator or Representative shall, during the Time for which he was elected, be appointed to any civil Office under the Authority of the United States, which shall have been created, or the Emoluments whereof shall have been encreased during such time; and no Person holding any Office under the United States, shall be a Member of either House during his Continuance in Office.

Section 7. All Bills for raising Revenue shall originate in the House of Representatives; but the Senate may propose or concur with Amendments as on other Bills.

Every Bill which shall have passed the House of Representatives and the Senate, shall, before it become a Law, be presented to the President of the United States: If he approve he shall sign it, but if not he shall return it, with his Objections to that House in which it shall have originated, who shall enter the Objections at large on their Journal, and proceed to reconsider it. If after such Reconsideration two thirds of that House shall agree to pass the Bill, it shall be sent, together with the Objections, to the other House, by which it shall likewise be reconsidered, and if approved by two thirds of that House, it shall become a Law. But in all such Cases the Votes of both Houses shall be determined by yeas and Nays, and the Names of the Persons voting for and against the Bill shall be entered on the Journal of each House respectively. If any Bill shall not be returned by the President within ten Days (Sundays excepted) after it shall have been presented to him, the Same shall be a Law, in like Manner as if he had signed it, unless the Congress by their Adjournment prevent its Return, in which Case it shall not be a Law.

Every Order, Resolution, or Vote to which the Concurrence of the Senate and House of Representatives may be necessary (except on a question of Adjournment) shall be presented to the President of the United States; and before the Same shall take Effect, shall be approved by him, or being disapproved by him, shall be repassed by two thirds of the Senate and House of Representatives, according to the Rules and Limitations prescribed in the Case of a Bill.

Section 8. The Congress shall have Power To lay and collect Taxes, Duties, Imposts and Excises, to pay the Debts and provide for the common Defence and general Welfare of the United States; but all Duties, Imposts and Excises shall be uniform throughout the United States;

To borrow Money on the credit of the United States;

To regulate Commerce with foreign Nations, and among the several States, and with the Indian Tribes;

To establish an uniform Rule of Naturalization, and uniform Laws on the subject of Bankruptcies throughout the United States;

To coin Money, regulate the Value thereof, and of foreign Coin, and fix the Standard of Weights and Measures;

To provide for the Punishment of counterfeiting the Securities and current Coin of the United States;

To establish Post Offices and post Roads;

To promote the Progress of Science and useful Arts, by securing for limited Times to Authors and Inventors the exclusive Right to their respective Writings and Discoveries;

To constitute Tribunals inferior to the supreme Court;

To define and punish Piracies and Felonies committed on the high Seas, and Offences against the Law of Nations;

To declare War, grant Letters of Marque and Reprisal, and make Rules concerning Captures on Land and Water;

To raise and support Armies, but no Appropriation of Money to that Use shall be for a longer Term than two Years;

To provide and maintain a Navy;

To make Rules for the Government and Regulation of the land and naval Forces;

To provide for calling forth the Militia to execute the Laws of the Union, suppress Insurrections and repel Invasions;

To provide for organizing, arming, and disciplining, the Militia, and for governing such Part of them as may be employed in the Service of the United States, reserving to the States respectively, the Appointment of the Officers, and the Authority of training the Militia according to the discipline prescribed by Congress;

To exercise exclusive Legislation in all Cases whatsoever, over such District (not exceeding ten Miles square) as may, by Cession of particular States, and the Acceptance of Congress, become the Seat of the Government of the United States, and to exercise like Authority over all Places purchased by the Consent of the Legislature of the State in which the Same shall be, for the Erection of Forts, Magazines, Arsenals, dock-Yards, and other needful Buildings;--And

To make all Laws which shall be necessary and proper for carrying into Execution the foregoing Powers, and all other Powers vested by this Constitution in the Government of the United States, or in any Department or Officer thereof.

Section 9. The Migration or Importation of such Persons as any of the States now existing shall think proper to admit, shall not be prohibited by the Congress prior to the Year one thousand eight hundred and eight, but a Tax or duty may be imposed on such Importation, not exceeding ten dollars for each Person.

The Privilege of the Writ of Habeas Corpus shall not be suspended, unless when in Cases of Rebellion or Invasion the public Safety may require it.

No Bill of Attainder or ex post facto Law shall be passed.

No Capitation, or other direct, Tax shall be laid, unless in Proportion to the Census or enumeration herein before directed to be taken.

No Tax or Duty shall be laid on Articles exported from any State.

No Preference shall be given by any Regulation of Commerce or Revenue to the Ports of one State over those of another; nor shall Vessels bound to, or from, one State, be obliged to enter, clear, or pay Duties in another.

No Money shall be drawn from the Treasury, but in Consequence of Appropriations made by Law; and a regular Statement and Account of the Receipts and Expenditures of all public Money shall be published from time to time.

No Title of Nobility shall be granted by the United States: And no Person holding any Office of Profit or Trust under them, shall, without the Consent of the Congress, accept of any present, Emolument, Office, or Title, of any kind whatever, from any King, Prince, or foreign State.

Section 10. No State shall enter into any Treaty, Alliance, or Confederation; grant Letters of Marque and Reprisal; coin Money; emit Bills of Credit; make any Thing but gold and silver Coin a Tender in Payment of Debts; pass any Bill of Attainder, ex post facto Law, or Law impairing the Obligation of Contracts, or grant any Title of Nobility.

No State shall, without the Consent of the Congress, lay any Imposts or Duties on Imports or Exports, except what may be absolutely necessary for executing it's inspection Laws: and the net Produce of all Duties and Imposts, laid by any State on Imports or Exports, shall be for the Use of the Treasury of the United States; and all such Laws shall be subject to the Revision and Controul of the Congress.

No State shall, without the Consent of Congress, lay any Duty of Tonnage, keep Troops, or Ships of War in time of Peace, enter into any Agreement or Compact with another State, or with a foreign Power, or engage in War, unless actually invaded, or in such imminent Danger as will not admit of delay.

Article II.
Section 1. The executive Power shall be vested in a President of the United States of America. He shall hold his Office during the Term of four Years, and, together with the Vice President, chosen for the same Term, be elected, as follows:

Each State shall appoint, in such Manner as the Legislature thereof may direct, a Number of Electors, equal to the whole Number of Senators and Representatives to which the State may be entitled in the Congress: but no Senator or Representative, or Person holding an Office of Trust or Profit under the United States, shall be appointed an Elector.

The Electors shall meet in their respective States, and vote by Ballot for two Persons, of whom one at least shall not be an Inhabitant of the same State with themselves. And they shall make a List of all the Persons voted for, and of the Number of Votes for each; which List they shall sign and certify, and transmit sealed to the Seat of the Government of the United States, directed to the President of the Senate. The President of the Senate shall, in the Presence of the Senate and House of Representatives, open all the Certificates, and the Votes shall then be counted. The Person having the greatest Number of Votes shall be the President, if such Number be a Majority of the whole Number of Electors appointed; and if there be more than one who have such Majority, and have an equal Number of Votes, then the House of Representatives shall immediately chuse by Ballot one of them for President; and if no Person have a Majority, then from the five highest on the List the said House shall in like Manner chuse the President. But in chusing the President, the Votes shall be taken by States, the Representation from each State having one Vote; A quorum for this purpose shall consist of a Member or Members from two thirds of the States, and a Majority of all the States shall be necessary to a Choice. In every Case, after the Choice of the President, the Person having the greatest Number of Votes of the Electors shall be the Vice President. But if there should remain two or more who have equal Votes, the Senate shall chuse from them by Ballot the Vice President.

The Congress may determine the Time of chusing the Electors, and the Day on which they shall give their Votes; which Day shall be the same throughout the United States.

No Person except a natural born Citizen, or a Citizen of the United States, at the time of the Adoption of this Constitution, shall be eligible to the Office of President; neither shall any Person be eligible to that Office who shall not have attained to the Age of thirty five Years, and been fourteen Years a Resident within the United States.

In Case of the Removal of the President from Office, or of his Death, Resignation, or Inability to discharge the Powers and Duties of the said Office, the Same shall devolve on the Vice President, and the Congress may by Law provide for the Case of Removal, Death, Resignation or Inability, both of the President and Vice President, declaring what Officer shall then act as President, and such Officer shall act accordingly, until the Disability be removed, or a President shall be elected.

The President shall, at stated Times, receive for his Services, a Compensation, which shall neither be increased nor diminished during the Period for which he shall have been elected, and he shall not receive within that Period any other Emolument from the United States, or any of them.

Before he enter on the Execution of his Office, he shall take the following Oath or Affirmation:--"I do solemnly swear (or affirm) that I will faithfully execute the Office of President of the United States, and will to the best of my Ability, preserve, protect and defend the Constitution of the United States."

Section 2. The President shall be Commander in Chief of the Army and Navy of the United States, and of the Militia of the several States, when called into the actual Service of the United States; he may require the Opinion, in writing, of the principal Officer in each of the executive Departments, upon any Subject relating to the Duties of their respective Offices, and he shall have Power to grant Reprieves and Pardons for Offences against the United States, except in Cases of Impeachment.

He shall have Power, by and with the Advice and Consent of the Senate, to make Treaties, provided two thirds of the Senators present concur; and he shall nominate, and by and with the Advice and Consent of the Senate, shall appoint Ambassadors, other public Ministers and Consuls, Judges of the supreme Court, and all other Officers of the United States, whose Appointments are not herein otherwise provided for, and which shall be established by Law: but the Congress may by Law vest the Appointment of such inferior Officers, as they think proper, in the President alone, in the Courts of Law, or in the Heads of Departments.

The President shall have Power to fill up all Vacancies that may happen during the Recess of the Senate, by granting Commissions which shall expire at the End of their next Session.

Section 3. He shall from time to time give to the Congress Information of the State of the Union, and recommend to their Consideration such Measures as he shall judge necessary and expedient; he may, on extraordinary Occasions, convene both Houses, or either of them, and in Case of Disagreement between them, with Respect to the Time of Adjournment, he may adjourn them to such Time as he shall think proper; he shall receive Ambassadors and other public Ministers; he shall take Care that the Laws be faithfully executed, and shall Commission all the Officers of the United States.

Section 4. The President, Vice President and all civil Officers of the United States, shall be removed from Office on Impeachment for, and Conviction of, Treason, Bribery, or other high Crimes and Misdemeanors.

Article III.
Section 1. The judicial Power of the United States shall be vested in one supreme Court, and in such inferior Courts as the Congress may from time to time ordain and establish. The Judges, both of the supreme and inferior Courts, shall hold their Offices during good Behaviour, and shall, at stated Times, receive for their Services a Compensation, which shall not be diminished during their Continuance in Office.

Section 2. The judicial Power shall extend to all Cases, in Law and Equity, arising under this Constitution, the Laws of the United States, and Treaties made, or which shall be made, under their Authority;--to all Cases affecting Ambassadors, other public Ministers and Consuls;--to all Cases of admiralty and maritime Jurisdiction;--to Controversies to which the United States shall be a Party;--to Controversies between two or more States;-- between a State and Citizens of another State;--between Citizens of different States;--between Citizens of the same State claiming Lands under Grants of different States, and between a State, or the Citizens thereof, and foreign States, Citizens or Subjects.

In all Cases affecting Ambassadors, other public Ministers and Consuls, and those in which a State shall be Party, the supreme Court shall have original Jurisdiction. In all the other Cases before mentioned, the supreme Court shall have appellate Jurisdiction, both as to Law and Fact, with such Exceptions, and under such Regulations as the Congress shall make.

The Trial of all Crimes, except in Cases of Impeachment, shall be by Jury; and such Trial shall be held in the State where the said Crimes shall have been committed; but when not committed within any State, the Trial shall be at such Place or Places as the Congress may by Law have directed.

Section 3. Treason against the United States, shall consist only in levying War against them, or in adhering to their Enemies, giving them Aid and Comfort. No Person shall be convicted of Treason unless on the Testimony of two Witnesses to the same overt Act, or on Confession in open Court.

The Congress shall have Power to declare the Punishment of Treason, but no Attainder of Treason shall work Corruption of Blood, or Forfeiture except during the Life of the Person attainted.

Article IV.
Section 1. Full Faith and Credit shall be given in each State to the public Acts, Records, and judicial Proceedings of every other State. And the Congress may by general Laws prescribe the Manner in which such Acts, Records and Proceedings shall be proved, and the Effect thereof.

Section 2. The Citizens of each State shall be entitled to all Privileges and Immunities of Citizens in the several States.

A Person charged in any State with Treason, Felony, or other Crime, who shall flee from Justice, and be found in another State, shall on Demand of the executive Authority of the State from which he fled, be delivered up, to be removed to the State having Jurisdiction of the Crime.

No Person held to Service or Labour in one State, under the Laws thereof, escaping into another, shall, in Consequence of any Law or Regulation therein, be discharged from such

Service or Labour, but shall be delivered up on Claim of the Party to whom such Service or Labour may be due.

Section 3. New States may be admitted by the Congress into this Union; but no new State shall be formed or erected within the Jurisdiction of any other State; nor any State be formed by the Junction of two or more States, or Parts of States, without the Consent of the Legislatures of the States concerned as well as of the Congress.

The Congress shall have Power to dispose of and make all needful Rules and Regulations respecting the Territory or other Property belonging to the United States; and nothing in this Constitution shall be so construed as to Prejudice any Claims of the United States, or of any particular State.

Section 4. The United States shall guarantee to every State in this Union a Republican Form of Government, and shall protect each of them against Invasion; and on Application of the Legislature, or of the Executive (when the Legislature cannot be convened), against domestic Violence.

Article V.
The Congress, whenever two thirds of both Houses shall deem it necessary, shall propose Amendments to this Constitution, or, on the Application of the Legislatures of two thirds of the several States, shall call a Convention for proposing Amendments, which, in either Case, shall be valid to all Intents and Purposes, as Part of this Constitution, when ratified by the Legislatures of three fourths of the several States, or by Conventions in three fourths thereof, as the one or the other Mode of Ratification may be proposed by the Congress; Provided that no Amendment which may be made prior to the Year One thousand eight hundred and eight shall in any Manner affect the first and fourth Clauses in the Ninth Section of the first Article; and that no State, without its Consent, shall be deprived of its equal Suffrage in the Senate.

Article VI.
All Debts contracted and Engagements entered into, before the Adoption of this Constitution, shall be as valid against the United States under this Constitution, as under the Confederation.

This Constitution, and the Laws of the United States which shall be made in Pursuance thereof; and all Treaties made, or which shall be made, under the Authority of the United States, shall be the supreme Law of the Land; and the Judges in every State shall be bound thereby, any Thing in the Constitution or Laws of any State to the Contrary notwithstanding.

The Senators and Representatives before mentioned, and the Members of the several State Legislatures, and all executive and judicial Officers, both of the United States and of the several States, shall be bound by Oath or Affirmation, to support this Constitution; but no religious Test shall ever be required as a Qualification to any Office or public Trust under the United States.

Article VII.
The Ratification of the Conventions of nine States, shall be sufficient for the Establishment of this Constitution between the States so ratifying the Same.

[The remainder of Article 7 is omitted.]

Amendments to the US Constitution

[The preamble to the Bill of Rights is omitted.]

Amendment I. Congress shall make no law respecting an establishment of religion, or prohibiting the free exercise thereof; or abridging the freedom of speech, or of the press; or the right of the people peaceably to assemble, and to petition the Government for a redress of grievances.

Amendment II. A well regulated Militia, being necessary to the security of a free State, the right of the people to keep and bear Arms, shall not be infringed.

Amendment III. No Soldier shall, in time of peace be quartered in any house, without the consent of the Owner, nor in time of war, but in a manner to be prescribed by law.

Amendment IV. The right of the people to be secure in their persons, houses, papers, and effects, against unreasonable searches and seizures, shall not be violated, and no Warrants shall issue, but upon probable cause, supported by Oath or affirmation, and particularly describing the place to be searched, and the persons or things to be seized.

Amendment V. No person shall be held to answer for a capital, or otherwise infamous crime, unless on a presentment or indictment of a Grand Jury, except in cases arising in the land or naval forces, or in the Militia, when in actual service in time of War or public danger; nor shall any person be subject for the same offence to be twice put in jeopardy of life or limb; nor shall be compelled in any criminal case to be a witness against himself, nor be deprived of life, liberty, or property, without due process of law; nor shall private property be taken for public use, without just compensation.

Amendment VI. In all criminal prosecutions, the accused shall enjoy the right to a speedy and public trial, by an impartial jury of the State and district wherein the crime shall have been committed, which district shall have been previously ascertained by law, and to be informed of the nature and cause of the accusation; to be confronted with the witnesses against him; to have compulsory process for obtaining witnesses in his favor, and to have the Assistance of Counsel for his defence.

Amendment VII. In Suits at common law, where the value in controversy shall exceed twenty dollars, the right of trial by jury shall be preserved, and no fact tried by a jury, shall be otherwise re-examined in any Court of the United States, than according to the rules of the common law.

Amendment VIII. Excessive bail shall not be required, nor excessive fines imposed, nor cruel and unusual punishments inflicted.

Amendment IX. The enumeration in the Constitution, of certain rights, shall not be construed to deny or disparage others retained by the people.

Amendment X. The powers not delegated to the United States by the Constitution, nor prohibited by it to the States, are reserved to the States respectively, or to the people.

Amendment XI. The Judicial power of the United States shall not be construed to extend to any suit in law or equity, commenced or prosecuted against one of the United States by Citizens of another State, or by Citizens or Subjects of any Foreign State.

Amendment XII. The Electors shall meet in their respective states and vote by ballot for President and Vice-President, one of whom, at least, shall not be an inhabitant of the same state with themselves; they shall name in their ballots the person voted for as President, and in distinct ballots the person voted for as Vice-President, and they shall make distinct lists of all persons voted for as President, and of all persons voted for as Vice-President, and of the number of votes for each, which lists they shall sign and certify, and transmit sealed to the seat of the government of the United States, directed to the President of the Senate; -- the President of the Senate shall, in the presence of the Senate and House of Representatives, open all the certificates and the votes shall then be counted; -- The person having the greatest number of votes for President, shall be the President, if such number be a majority of the whole number of Electors appointed; and if no person have such majority, then from the persons having the highest numbers not exceeding three on the list of those voted for as President, the House of Representatives shall choose immediately, by ballot, the President. But in choosing the President, the votes shall be taken by states, the representation from each state having one vote; a quorum for this purpose shall consist of a member or members from two-thirds of the states, and a majority of all the states shall be necessary to a choice. And if the House of Representatives shall not choose a President whenever the right of choice shall devolve upon them, before the fourth day of March next following, then the Vice-President shall act as President, as in case of the death or other constitutional disability of the President. The person having the greatest number of votes as Vice-President, shall be the Vice-President, if such number be a majority of the whole number of Electors appointed, and if no person have a majority, then from the two highest numbers on the list, the Senate shall choose the Vice-President; a quorum for the purpose shall consist of two-thirds of the whole number of Senators, and a majority of the whole number shall be necessary to a choice. But no person constitutionally ineligible to the office of President shall be eligible to that of Vice-President of the United States.

Amendment XIII. Section 1. Neither slavery nor involuntary servitude, except as a punishment for crime whereof the party shall have been duly convicted, shall exist within the United States, or any place subject to their jurisdiction.

Section 2. Congress shall have power to enforce this article by appropriate legislation.

Amendment XIV. Section 1. All persons born or naturalized in the United States, and subject to the jurisdiction thereof, are citizens of the United States and of the State wherein they reside. No State shall make or enforce any law which shall abridge the privileges or immunities of citizens of the United States; nor shall any State deprive any person of life, liberty, or property, without due process of law; nor deny to any person within its jurisdiction the equal protection of the laws.

Section 2. Representatives shall be apportioned among the several States according to their respective numbers, counting the whole number of persons in each State, excluding Indians not taxed. But when the right to vote at any election for the choice of electors for President and Vice-President of the United States, Representatives in Congress, the Executive and Judicial officers of a State, or the members of the Legislature thereof, is denied to any of the male inhabitants of such State, being twenty-one years of age, and citizens of the United States, or in any way abridged, except for participation in rebellion, or other crime, the basis of representation therein shall be reduced in the proportion which the number of such male citizens shall bear to the whole number of male citizens twenty-one years of age in such State.

Section 3. No person shall be a Senator or Representative in Congress, or elector of President and Vice-President, or hold any office, civil or military, under the United States, or under any State, who, having previously taken an oath, as a member of Congress, or as an officer of the

United States, or as a member of any State legislature, or as an executive or judicial officer of any State, to support the Constitution of the United States, shall have engaged in insurrection or rebellion against the same, or given aid or comfort to the enemies thereof. But Congress may by a vote of two-thirds of each House, remove such disability.

Section 4. The validity of the public debt of the United States, authorized by law, including debts incurred for payment of pensions and bounties for services in suppressing insurrection or rebellion, shall not be questioned. But neither the United States nor any State shall assume or pay any debt or obligation incurred in aid of insurrection or rebellion against the United States, or any claim for the loss or emancipation of any slave; but all such debts, obligations and claims shall be held illegal and void.

Section 5. The Congress shall have the power to enforce, by appropriate legislation, the provisions of this article.

Amendment XV. Section 1. The right of citizens of the United States to vote shall not be denied or abridged by the United States or by any State on account of race, color, or previous condition of servitude--

Section 2. The Congress shall have the power to enforce this article by appropriate legislation.

Amendment XVI. The Congress shall have power to lay and collect taxes on incomes, from whatever source derived, without apportionment among the several States, and without regard to any census or enumeration.

Amendment XVII. The Senate of the United States shall be composed of two Senators from each State, elected by the people thereof, for six years; and each Senator shall have one vote. The electors in each State shall have the qualifications requisite for electors of the most numerous branch of the State legislatures.

When vacancies happen in the representation of any State in the Senate, the executive authority of such State shall issue writs of election to fill such vacancies: Provided, That the legislature of any State may empower the executive thereof to make temporary appointments until the people fill the vacancies by election as the legislature may direct.

This amendment shall not be so construed as to affect the election or term of any Senator chosen before it becomes valid as part of the Constitution.

Amendment XVIII. Section 1. After one year from the ratification of this article the manufacture, sale, or transportation of intoxicating liquors within, the importation thereof into, or the exportation thereof from the United States and all territory subject to the jurisdiction thereof for beverage purposes is hereby prohibited.

Section 2. The Congress and the several States shall have concurrent power to enforce this article by appropriate legislation.

Section 3. This article shall be inoperative unless it shall have been ratified as an amendment to the Constitution by the legislatures of the several States, as provided in the Constitution, within seven years from the date of the submission hereof to the States by the Congress.

Amendment XIX. The right of citizens of the United States to vote shall not be denied or abridged by the United States or by any State on account of sex.

Congress shall have power to enforce this article by appropriate legislation.

Amendment XX. Section 1. The terms of the President and the Vice President shall end at noon on the 20th day of January, and the terms of Senators and Representatives at noon on the 3d day of January, of the years in which such terms would have ended if this article had not been ratified; and the terms of their successors shall then begin.

Section 2. The Congress shall assemble at least once in every year, and such meeting shall begin at noon on the 3d day of January, unless they shall by law appoint a different day.

Section 3. If, at the time fixed for the beginning of the term of the President, the President elect shall have died, the Vice President elect shall become President. If a President shall not have been chosen before the time fixed for the beginning of his term, or if the President elect shall have failed to qualify, then the Vice President elect shall act as President until a President shall have qualified; and the Congress may by law provide for the case wherein neither a President elect nor a Vice President shall have qualified, declaring who shall then act as President, or the manner in which one who is to act shall be selected, and such person shall act accordingly until a President or Vice President shall have qualified.

Section 4. The Congress may by law provide for the case of the death of any of the persons from whom the House of Representatives may choose a President whenever the right of choice shall have devolved upon them, and for the case of the death of any of the persons from whom the Senate may choose a Vice President whenever the right of choice shall have devolved upon them.

Section 5. Sections 1 and 2 shall take effect on the 15th day of October following the ratification of this article.

Section 6. This article shall be inoperative unless it shall have been ratified as an amendment to the Constitution by the legislatures of three-fourths of the several States within seven years from the date of its submission.

Amendment XXI. Section 1. The eighteenth article of amendment to the Constitution of the United States is hereby repealed.

Section 2. The transportation or importation into any State, Territory, or Possession of the United States for delivery or use therein of intoxicating liquors, in violation of the laws thereof, is hereby prohibited.

Section 3. This article shall be inoperative unless it shall have been ratified as an amendment to the Constitution by conventions in the several States, as provided in the Constitution, within seven years from the date of the submission hereof to the States by the Congress.

Amendment XXII. Section 1. No person shall be elected to the office of the President more than twice, and no person who has held the office of President, or acted as President, for more than two years of a term to which some other person was elected President shall be elected to the office of President more than once. But this Article shall not apply to any person holding the office of President when this Article was proposed by Congress, and shall not prevent any person who may be holding the office of President, or acting as President, during the term within which this Article becomes operative from holding the office of President or acting as President during the remainder of such term.

Section 2. This article shall be inoperative unless it shall have been ratified as an amendment to the Constitution by the legislatures of three-fourths of the several States within seven years from the date of its submission to the States by the Congress.

Amendment XXIII. Section 1. The District constituting the seat of Government of the United States shall appoint in such manner as Congress may direct:

A number of electors of President and Vice President equal to the whole number of Senators and Representatives in Congress to which the District would be entitled if it were a State, but in no event more than the least populous State; they shall be in addition to those appointed by the States, but they shall be considered, for the purposes of the election of President and Vice President, to be electors appointed by a State; and they shall meet in the District and perform such duties as provided by the twelfth article of amendment.

Section 2. The Congress shall have power to enforce this article by appropriate legislation.

Amendment XXIV. Section 1. The right of citizens of the United States to vote in any primary or other election for President or Vice President, for electors for President or Vice President, or for Senator or Representative in Congress, shall not be denied or abridged by the United States or any State by reason of failure to pay poll tax or other tax.

Section 2. The Congress shall have power to enforce this article by appropriate legislation.

Amendment XXV. Section 1. In case of the removal of the President from office or of his death or resignation, the Vice President shall become President.

Section 2. Whenever there is a vacancy in the office of the Vice President, the President shall nominate a Vice President who shall take office upon confirmation by a majority vote of both Houses of Congress.

Section 3. Whenever the President transmits to the President pro tempore of the Senate and the Speaker of the House of Representatives his written declaration that he is unable to discharge the powers and duties of his office, and until he transmits to them a written declaration to the contrary, such powers and duties shall be discharged by the Vice President as Acting President.

Section 4. Whenever the Vice President and a majority of either the principal officers of the executive departments or of such other body as Congress may by law provide, transmit to the President pro tempore of the Senate and the Speaker of the House of Representatives their written declaration that the President is unable to discharge the powers and duties of his office, the Vice President shall immediately assume the powers and duties of the office as Acting President.

Thereafter, when the President transmits to the President pro tempore of the Senate and the Speaker of the House of Representatives his written declaration that no inability exists, he shall resume the powers and duties of his office unless the Vice President and a majority of either the principal officers of the executive department or of such other body as Congress may by law provide, transmit within four days to the President pro tempore of the Senate and the Speaker of the House of Representatives their written declaration that the President is unable to discharge the powers and duties of his office. Thereupon Congress shall decide the issue, assembling within forty-eight hours for that purpose if not in session. If the Congress, within twenty-one days after receipt of the latter written declaration, or, if Congress is not in session, within twenty-one days after Congress is required to assemble, determines by two-thirds vote of both Houses that the President is unable to discharge the powers and duties of his office, the Vice President shall continue to discharge the same as Acting President; otherwise, the President shall resume the powers and duties of his office.

Amendment XXVI. Section 1. The right of citizens of the United States, who are eighteen years of age or older, to vote shall not be denied or abridged by the United States or by any State on account of age.

Section 2. The Congress shall have power to enforce this article by appropriate legislation.

Amendment XXVII. No law, varying the compensation for the services of the Senators and Representatives, shall take effect, until an election of representatives shall have intervened.

Annex 6

THE FRENCH CONSTITUTION

Constitution (of the Fifth Republic) [Constitution (de la Ve République)] of 4 October 1958 as last amended by constitutional statute 2008-724 of 23 July 2008.[1]

Preamble

The French people solemnly proclaim their attachment to human rights and the principles of national sovereignty as they are defined by the Declaration of 1789, confirmed and complemented by the Preamble to the Constitution of 1946, as well as to the rights and obligations as defined in the Charter on the Environment of 2004. By virtue of these principles and that of the self-determination of peoples, the Republic offers to the overseas territories that express the will to adhere to them, new institutions founded on the common ideal of liberty, equality and fraternity and conceived with a view to their democratic development.

Article 1. France is an indivisible, secular, democratic and social Republic. It ensures the equality of all citizens before the law, without distinction of origin, race or religion. It respects all beliefs. Its organization is decentralized.
Statute promotes equal access of women and men to elected offices and electoral functions as well as to professional and social positions.

Title I. On sovereignty

Article 2. The language of the Republic is French.
The national emblem is the tricolour flag of blue, white, red.
The national anthem is the Marseillaise.
The motto of the Republic is Liberty, Equality, Fraternity.
Its principle is: government of the people, by the people and for the people.

---

[1] Translation by Ph. Kiiver, S. Hardt & G. Kristoferitsch. This text has also been published separately in: Ph. Kiiver & N. Kornet, eds., *The Maastricht Collection: Selected National, European and International Provisions from Public and Private Law*, Second Edition (Groningen: Europa Law Publishing, 2010). It has also been published in a smaller compilation covering only the area of constitutional law: Ph. Kiiver, ed., *Sources of Constitutional Law: Constitutions and Fundamental Legal Provisions from the United States, France, Germany, the Netherlands, the United Kingdom, the ECHR and the EU*, Second Edition (Groningen: Europa Law Publishing, 2010).

Article 3. National sovereignty belongs to the people, who exercise it through their representatives and by means of referendum.

No part of the population nor any individual may arrogate the exercise thereof.

Suffrage may be direct or indirect in accordance with the condition of the Constitution. It is always universal, equal and secret.

All French nationals of the age of majority and of both sexes, who enjoy their civil and political rights, have the right to vote, under the conditions provided by statute.

Article 4. Political parties and groups contribute to the expression of suffrage. They establish themselves and carry out their activity freely. They must respect the principles of national sovereignty and of democracy.

They contribute to the giving effect to the principle enshrined in the second paragraph of Article 1 under the conditions provided by statute.

Statute guarantees pluralist expressions of opinions and the fair participation of political parties and groups in the democratic life of the Nation.

Title II. The President of the Republic

Article 5. The President of the Republic sees that the Constitution is respected. He ensures, by his arbitration, the proper functioning of the public authorities as well as the continuity of the State.

He is the guarantor of national independence, territorial integrity and observance of treaties.

Article 6. The President of the Republic is elected for five years by direct universal suffrage.

No-one may serve more than two consecutive terms.

The details of the implementation of this Article are determined by an organic statute.

Article 7. The President of the Republic is elected by the absolute majority of votes cast. If this is not obtained in the first round of elections, a second round is held on the fourteenth day thereafter. Only the two candidates may run who, after the withdrawal of candidates with more votes where applicable, find themselves having obtained the largest number of votes in the first round.

The elections are opened by a call of the Government.

The election of a new President takes place at least twenty days and, at most, thirty-five days before the expiry of the powers of the incumbent President.

In case of a vacancy of the Presidency of the Republic for whatever reason, or in case the President is prevented from exercising his functions as declared by the Constitutional Council [Conseil Constitutionnel] by absolute majority of its members upon request by the Government, the functions of the President of the Republic, with the exception of those provided by Articles 11 and 12 below, are provisionally exercised by the president of the Senate and, if he in turn is prevented from exercising his functions, by the Government.

In case of a vacancy or when the prevention from the exercise of functions is declared definitive by the Constitutional Council, a vote for an election of a new President takes place, except in cases of force majeure established by the Constitutional Council, at least twenty days and at most thirty-five days after the opening of the vacancy or the declaration of the definitive character of the prevention.

If within seven days prior to the deadline for the filing of candidacies, one of the persons who has publicly announced his decision to be a candidate less than thirty days before that date, dies or finds himself prevented from running, the Constitutional Council may decide to postpone the elections.

If before the first round one of the candidates dies or finds himself prevented from running, the Constitutional Council declares the postponement of the elections.

In the case of death or prevention of one of the two candidates with the largest number of votes in the first round before any withdrawals, the Constitutional Council declares that the election procedure must start entirely anew; the same applies in the case of death or prevention of one of the two remaining candidates for the second round.

In all cases, the Constitutional Council is seized under the conditions prescribed by the second paragraph of Article 61 below or under those provided for the running as a candidate by the organic statute stipulated by Article 6 above.

The Constitutional Council may extend the periods provided by the third and fifth paragraph as long as the vote does not take place any later than thirty-five days after the date of the decision of the Constitutional Council. If the application of the provisions of the present paragraph has as an effect that elections are postponed to a date after the expiry of the powers of the incumbent President, he remains in office until the proclamation of his successor.

Neither Articles 49 and 50 nor Article 89 of the Constitution may be applied during a vacancy of the Presidency of the Republic or during the period between the declaration of the definitive character of the prevention of the President of the Republic from exercising his functions and the election of his successor.

Article 8. The President of the Republic appoints the Prime Minister. He terminates the functions of the Prime Minister when the latter tenders the resignation of the Government.

On the proposal of the Prime Minister, he appoints the other members of the Government and terminates their functions.

Article 9. The President of the Republic presides over the Council of Ministers.

Article 10. The President of the Republic promulgates statutes within fifteen days following the transmission to the Government of the statute finally adopted.

He may, before the expiry of this period, ask Parliament to deliberate anew on the statute or certain provisions of it. Such new deliberation may not be refused.

Article 11. The President of the Republic, on proposal of the Government during sessions or on joint proposal of the two chambers, which are published in the Official Journal [Journal Officiel], may submit to a referendum any government bill [projet de loi] regarding the organization of public authorities, reforms relating to the economic, social or environmental policy of the nation and the public services which contribute to it, or proposing the authorization of the ratification of a treaty which, while not being contrary to the Constitution, would have an effect on the functioning of the institutions.

Where a referendum is organized on the proposal of the Government, it makes a declaration before each chamber, which is followed by a debate.

A referendum regarding a subject mentioned in the first paragraph may be organized on the initiative of one-fifth of the members of Parliament, supported by one-tenth of the voters registered in the electoral lists. Such initiative takes the form of a private member's bill and may not have as its subject the repeal of a statutory provision promulgated less than one year earlier.

The conditions of its submission and those under which the Constitutional Council controls the compliance with the provisions of the preceding paragraph are established by an organic statute.

If the private member's bill has not been considered by the two chambers within a period determined by organic statute, the President of the Republic submits it to referendum.

Where the private member's bill has not been adopted by the French people, no new proposal for referendum regarding the same subject may be submitted before the expiry of a period of two years following the date of the vote.

Where a referendum has resulted in the adoption of a government bill or private member's bill, the President of the Republic promulgates the statute within fifteen days following the proclamation of the results of the referendum.

Article 12. The President of the Republic may, after consultations with the Prime Minister and the presidents of the chambers, declare the dissolution of the National Assembly.

General elections take place at least twenty days and at the latest forty days after the dissolution.

The National Assembly reconvenes by operation of law on the second Thursday following its election. If this convention takes place outside the period envisaged for an ordinary session, a session is opened by operation of law for a period of fifteen days.

No new dissolution may take place during the year following these elections.

Article 13. The President of the Republic signs ordinances [ordonnances] and decrees [décrets] debated in the Council of Ministers.

He appoints civil servants and military personnel of the State.

The members of the Council of State [conseillers d'État], the grand chancellor of the Legion of Honour, the ambassadors and special envoys, the magistrates of the Court of Auditors [Cour des Comptes], the prefects, the representatives of the State in overseas entities governed by Article 74 and in New Caledonia, generals, the rectors of the academies and the directors of the central administration are appointed in the Council of Ministers.

An organic statute determines the other posts to be filled in the Council of Ministers as well as the conditions under which the power of the President of the Republic to make appointments may be delegated by him to be exercised in his name.

An organic statute determines the posts or functions, other than those mentioned in the third paragraph, for which, by reason of their importance to the guarantee of rights and freedoms or the economic and social life of the Nation, the power of appointment of the President of the Republic is exercised on public advice by the competent permanent committee of each chamber. The President of the Republic may not proceed with an appointment where the added negative votes in each committee represent at least three-fifths of votes cast in the two committees. Statute determines the competent permanent committees for the posts or functions concerned.

Article 14. The President of the Republic accredits ambassadors and special envoys to foreign states; foreign ambassadors and special envoys are accredited before him.

Article 15. The President of the Republic is the commander-in-chief of the armies. He presides over the supreme councils and committees of National Defence.

Article 16. Where the institutions of the Republic, the independence of the Nation, the integrity of its territory or the execution of its international commitments is jeopardized in a serious and immediate manner and the regular functioning of the constitutional public authorities is interrupted, the President of the Republic takes measures as the circumstances demand, after official consultation with the Prime Minister, the presidents of the chambers as well as the Constitutional Council.

He informs the Nation in an address.

These measures must be inspired by the will to ensure the constitutional public authorities, in the shortest of periods, of the means to accomplish their mission. The Constitutional Council is consulted regarding their subject.

The Parliament convenes by operation of law.

The National Assembly may not be dissolved during the exercise of exceptional powers.

After thirty days of exercise of exceptional powers, the Constitutional Council may be seized by the president of the National Assembly, the president of the Senate, sixty deputies or sixty senators, with a view to examining whether the conditions provided in the first paragraph remain met. It decides within the shortest of periods by a public advice. It commences such examination by operation of law and decides under the same conditions after a period of sixty days of exercise of exceptional powers and at any further moment after that period.

Article 17. The President of the Republic has the right to grant pardons in individual cases.

Article 18. The President of the Republic communicates with the two chambers of the Parliament by addresses which he orders to be read out and which are not followed by any debate.
He may speak before Parliament assembled for that purpose in Congress. His statement may, in his absence, be followed by a debate which may not be the object of any vote.
Outside sessions, the parliamentary chambers convene especially for that purpose.

Article 19. The acts of the President of the Republic other than those stipulated in Articles 8 (first paragraph), 11, 12, 16, 18, 54, 56 and 61 are countersigned by the Prime Minister and, where appropriate, the competent ministers.

Title III. The Government

Article 20. The Government determines and conducts the policy of the Nation.
It has at its disposal the administration and the armed forces.
It is responsible before the Parliament under the conditions and following the procedures stipulated in Articles 49 and 50.

Article 21. The Prime Minister directs the actions of the Government. He is responsible for the National Defence. He ensures the execution of statutes. Save for the provisions of Article 13, he exercises the power of regulation [pouvoir réglementaire] and appoints civilian and military personnel.
He may delegate some of his powers to the ministers.
He substitutes, where appropriate, the President of the Republic in the presidency over the councils and committees stipulated in Article 15.
He may, by way of exception, substitute him in the presidency over a Council of Ministers by virtue of an express delegation and for a fixed agenda.

Article 22. The acts of the Prime Minister are countersigned, where appropriate, by the ministers who are charged with the execution thereof.

Article 23. The functions of a member of the Government are incompatible with the exercise of any parliamentary mandate, any function of professional representation at national level and any public employment or any professional activity.
An organic statute determines the conditions under which a replacement of the holders of such mandates, functions or employments is provided for.
The replacement of members of the Parliament takes place in accordance with the provisions of Article 25.

Title IV. The Parliament

Article 24. The Parliament adopts statutes [loi]. It controls the action of the government. It evaluates public policies.
It comprises the National Assembly [Assemblée Nationale] and the Senate [Sénat].
The deputies of the National Assembly, whose number may not exceed five hundred seventy-seven, are elected by direct suffrage.
The Senate, the number of whose members may not exceed three hundred forty-eight, is elected by indirect suffrage. It ensures the representation of the territorial entities of the Republic.
The French established outside France are represented in the National Assembly and in the Senate.

Article 25. An organic statute determines the length of the powers of each chamber, the number of its members, their remuneration, the conditions of eligibility, the regime regarding disqualification and incompatibilities.

It equally determines the conditions under which the persons are elected who are called upon to ensure, in case of a vacancy of a seat, the replacement of deputies or senators until new general or partial elections of the chamber to which they belonged or their temporary replacement in case of the acceptance by them of governmental functions.

An independent commission, the composition and rules of organization and functioning of which are determined by statute, pronounces itself in a public advice on government proposals for texts and private member's bills for statutes delimiting the districts for the election of deputies or modifying the distribution of seats of deputies or senators.

Article 26. No member of Parliament may be prosecuted, investigated, arrested, detained or tried based on the opinions or votes expressed by him in the exercise of his functions.

No member of Parliament may be subject to an arrest or any other measure of a criminal or correctional nature depriving him of or restricting his liberty, except with the authorization of the Bureau of the chamber to which he belongs. Such authorization is not required in case of a crime or misdemeanour in flagrante or in case of a final conviction.

The detention, the measures depriving of or restricting liberty or the prosecution of a member of Parliament are suspended for the period of the session if the chamber to which he belongs so demands.

The affected chamber convenes by operation of law for supplementary meetings in order to allow, where appropriate, the application of the preceding paragraph.

Article 27. Any binding mandate is void. The right to vote of the members of Parliament is personal. An organic statute may authorize, by way of exception, the delegation of a vote. In such case, no-one may receive the delegation of more than one mandate.

Article 28. The Parliament convenes by operation of law in an ordinary session [session ordinaire] which starts on the first working day of October and ends on the last working day of June.

The number of meeting days [jours de séance] which each chamber may hold during an ordinary session may not exceed one hundred and twenty. The meeting weeks are determined by each chamber.

The Prime Minister, after consultations with the president of the chamber concerned, or the majority of the members of each chamber may decide on holding additional meeting days.

The meeting days and hours are determined by the rules of procedure [règlement] of each chamber.

Article 29. The Parliament convenes in an extraordinary session upon the demand of the Prime Minister or of the majority of the members composing the National Assembly, under a fixed agenda.

Where the extraordinary session is held upon the demand of the members of the National Assembly, a decree of closure intervenes as soon as the Parliament has exhausted the agenda for which it has been convened and, at the latest, twelve days from its convention.

Only the Prime Minister may demand a new session before the expiry of the month that follows the decree of closure.

Article 30. Outside the cases where the Parliament convenes by operation of law, the extraordinary sessions are opened and closed by decree from the President of the Republic.

Article 31. The members of the Government have access to the two chambers. They are heard when they so demand.

They may be assisted by Government agents [commissaires].

Article 32. The president of the National Assembly is elected for the legislative term. The president of the Senate is elected after each partial elections.

Article 33. The meetings of the two chambers are public. The complete minutes of the debates are published in the Official Journal [Journal officiel].
Each chamber may meet in closed committee upon the demand of the Prime Minister or of a tenth of its members.

Title V. The relations between Parliament and the Government

Article 34. Statute determines the rules regarding:
• the civil rights and fundamental guarantees granted to citizens for the exercise of the civil liberties; the freedom, pluralism and independence of the media; the duties imposed on the person and property of citizens by the National Defence;
• the nationality, the status and capacity of persons, the matrimonial regime, inheritance and gifts;
• the determination of crimes and misdemeanours as well as the penalties applicable to them; criminal procedure; amnesty; the establishment of new court systems and the status of magistrates;
• the basis, rate and method of collection of taxes and charges of any nature; the regime for the issuing of currency.

Statute equally determines the rules regarding:
• the electoral system for the parliamentary chambers and local assemblies and the
representative bodies for the French established outside France as well as the conditions for
the exercise of elected offices and electoral functions for members of the deliberative
assemblies of the territorial entities;
• the establishment of categories of public bodies;
• the fundamental guarantees granted to civil servants and members of the armed forces of the State;
• the nationalization of enterprises and the transfer of property of enterprises from the public to the private sector.

Statute determines the fundamental principles:
• of the general organization of the National Defence;
• of the self-administration of territorial entities, their competences and their revenue;
• of education;
• of the preservation of the environment;
• of the property system, real rights and civil and commercial obligations;
• of labour law, trade union law and social security law.

Financial statutes [lois de finances] determine the revenue and the expenditure of the State subject to the conditions and with the reservations provided for by an organic statute.
Social security financing statutes determine the general conditions of their financial equilibrium and, taking into account anticipated revenue, set expenditure objectives subject to the conditions and with the reservations provided for by an organic statute.
Programming statutes [lois des programmation] determine the objectives of the action of the State.
The multiannual directions for public finances are defined by programming statutes. They are in line with the objective of a balance of accounts of the public administration.
The provisions of the present Article may be specified and completed by an organic statute.

Article 34-1. The chambers may pass resolutions under the conditions set by an organic statute [loi organique].

Bills for resolutions of which the Government considers that their adoption or rejection would become a matter of its responsibility or that they contain injunctions against it are inadmissible and may not be included in the agenda.

Article 35. A declaration of war is authorized by Parliament.
The Government informs Parliament of its decision to have the Armed Forces intervene abroad, at the latest three days after the start of the intervention. It specifies the objectives pursued. This information may lead to a debate which is not followed by any vote.
Where the length of the intervention exceeds four months, the Government submits its extension to Parliament for authorization. It may ask the National Assembly to decide in final instance.
If Parliament is not in session after four months have expired, it decides at the opening of the following session.

Article 36. A state of siege is decreed in the Council of Ministers.
Its extension beyond twelve days may only be authorized by Parliament.

Article 37. Matters other than those falling under the scope of statute [loi] are of regulatory nature [réglementaire].
Texts of statutory form enacted with regard to these matters may be modified by decree issued after an opinion by the Council of State [Conseil d'État]. Of these texts, those enacted after the entry into force of the present Constitution may not be modified by decree except if the Constitutional Council [Conseil Constitutionnel] has declared that they are of a regulatory nature pursuant to the foregoing paragraph.

Article 37-1. Statute and regulation may contain, for a limited purpose and time, provisions of an experimental nature.

Article 38. The Government may, in order to implement its programme, request Parliament to authorize, for a limited period of time, the taking of measures by ordinances [ordonnances] which normally fall under the scope of statute.
Ordinances are issued in the Council of Ministers after an opinion by the Council of State. They enter into force upon their publication but become ineffective if the government bill for their ratification is not submitted to Parliament before the date set by the enabling statute. They may only be ratified in an explicit manner.
Upon the expiry of the period of time referred to in the first paragraph of the present Article, ordinances may not be modified except by statute in matters within the scope of statute.

Article 39. The right of initiative for statutes rests both with the Prime Minister and the members of Parliament.
Government bills [projets de loi] are discussed in the Council of Ministers after an opinion by the Council of State and submitted to the bureau of one of the two chambers. Government bills for financial statutes and social security financing statutes are submitted to the National Assembly first. Without prejudice to the first paragraph of Article 44, government bills having as their primary object the organization of the territorial entities are submitted to the Senate first.
The presentation of government bills [projets de loi] submitted to the National Assembly or the Senate meets the conditions set by an organic statute [loi organique].
Government bills may not be included in the agenda if the conference of the presidents of the first chamber seized declares that the rules set by the organic statute have been disregarded. In case of disagreement between the conference of presidents and the Government, the president of the chamber concerned or the Prime Minister may refer the matter to the Constitutional Council which decides within eight days.

Under the conditions stipulated by statute, the president of a chamber may submit to the Council of State [Conseil d'État] a private member's bill submitted by one of the members of that chamber, before its examination in a committee, for its opinion, unless that member objects.

Article 40. Private member's bills [propositions] and amendments formulated by members of Parliament are not admissible if their adoption would have as a consequence either a diminution of public revenue or the creation or aggravation of public expenditure.

Article 41. If it appears, during the legislative process, that a private member's bill or amendment is not a matter of statute or is contrary to a delegation granted by virtue of Article 38, the Government or the president of the chamber seized may oppose it as inadmissible.

In case of disagreement between the Government and the president of the chamber concerned, the Constitutional Council, at the request of either party, rules within a period of eight days.

Article 42. Debate on government bills [projets] and private member's bills [propositions de loi] in the meeting takes place on the basis of the text adopted by the committee seized by application of Article 43 or, by default, the text referred to the chamber.

However, the debate in the meeting on government bills for constitutional amendment statutes [projets de révision constitutionnelle], financial statutes [projets de loi de finances] and social security financing statutes [projets de loi de financement de la sécurité sociale] takes place, in the first reading in front of the first chamber seized, on the basis of the text presented by the Government and, in the other readings, the text transmitted by the other chamber.

The debate in the meeting, in the first reading, of a government bill or a private member's bill may only take place before the first chamber seized after the expiry of a period of six weeks after its submission. It may only take place before the second chamber seized after the expiry of a period of four weeks from the moment of its transmission.

The previous paragraph does not apply if the accelerated procedure has been initiated under the conditions stipulated in Article 45. Nor does it apply to government bills for financial statutes, social security financing statutes and to government bills relating to a state of crisis [états de crise].

Article 43. Government and private member's bills are sent for examination to one of the permanent committees, the number of which is limited to eight in each chamber.

Upon the demand of the Government or the chamber seized, government or private member's bills are sent for examination to a committee set up especially for that purpose.

Article 44. Members of Parliament and the Government have the right of amendment. This right is exercised in the meeting or in a committee under the conditions prescribed in the rules of procedure of the chambers, within the framework determined by an organic statute.

After the opening of the debate, the Government may object to the consideration of any amendment which has not previously been submitted to a committee.

If the Government so demands, the chamber seized decides by a single vote on the whole or part of the debated text, containing only the amendments proposed or accepted by the Government.

Article 45. Every government or private member's bill is considered successively in the two chambers of Parliament with a view to the adoption of an identical text. Without prejudice to the application of Articles 40 and 41, any amendment that has a link, even an indirect one, with the text submitted or transmitted is admissible in the first reading.

Where, as a result of a disagreement between the two chambers, a government or private member's bill could not be adopted after two readings by each chamber or, if the Government has decided to apply the accelerated procedure without the conference of presidents being jointly opposed, after one reading by each of them, the Prime Minister or, for a private member's bill, the presidents of the two chambers acting jointly, have the right to convene a joint committee, composed of an equal number of members of each chamber, charged with the task to propose a text on the provisions still under debate.

The text drafted by the joint committee may be submitted by the Government to the two chambers for adoption. No amendment is admissible except with the consent of the Government.

If the joint committee does not succeed in agreeing on a common text or if this text is not adopted under the conditions provided for by the foregoing paragraph, the Government may, after a new reading by the National Assembly and by the Senate, request the National Assembly to adopt a definitive decision. In that case, the National Assembly may reconsider either the text drafted by the joint committee or the last text adopted by itself, modified, where appropriate, by one or more amendments adopted by the Senate.

Article 46. Statutes which the Constitution defines as organic statutes [lois organiques] are adopted and amended under the following conditions.

The government or private member's bill may not be subjected to deliberation and to a vote of the chambers in the first reading until the expiry of the period fixed in the third paragraph of Article 42. However, if the accelerated procedure has been applied under the conditions stipulated in Article 45, the government or private member's bill may not be subjected to deliberation in the first chamber seized until the expiry of a period of fifteen days after its submission.

The procedure of Article 45 applies. However, failing agreement between the two chambers, the text may be adopted by the National Assembly in final reading only by an absolute majority of its members.

Organic statutes relating to the Senate must be adopted in the same terms by the two chambers.

Organic statutes may not be promulgated until the Constitutional Council has declared their conformity with the Constitution.

Article 47. Parliament adopts government bills for financial statutes under the conditions provided by an organic statute.

If the National Assembly has not reached a decision in the first reading within a period of forty days after the submission of a government bill, the Government seizes the Senate which must reach a decision within a period of fifteen days. Thereafter the procedure of Article 45 is applied.

If Parliament has not reached a decision within a period of seventy days, the provisions of the government bill may be enacted by ordinance.

If a financial statute setting revenues and expenditure for a financial year has not been submitted in time for promulgation before the beginning of that financial year, the Government requests from Parliament, as a matter of urgency, the authorization to collect taxes and make available by decree the funds needed for measures already adopted. The time limits set by the present Article are suspended when Parliament is not in session.

Article 47-1. Parliament adopts government bills for social security financing statutes under the conditions provided by an organic statute. If the National Assembly has not reached a decision in the first reading within a period of twenty days after the submission of a government bill, the Government seizes the Senate which must reach a decision within a period of fifteen days. Thereafter the procedure of Article 45 is applied. If Parliament has not reached a decision within a period of fifty days, the provisions of the government bill may be put into effect by ordinance.

The time limits set by the present Article are suspended when Parliament is not in session and, with respect to each chamber, during the weeks during which it has decided not to meet in conformity with the second paragraph of Article 28.

Article 47-2. The Court of Auditors [Cour des Comptes] assists the Parliament with the control of the action of the Government. It assists the Parliament and the Government with the control of the execution of financial statutes and the implementation of social security financing statutes as well as with the assessment of public policies. With its public reports, it contributes to the informing of the citizens.

The accounts of the public administration are regular and sincere. They provide a picture that faithfully shows the results of their management, their assets and their financial situation.

Article 48. Without prejudice to the application of the last three paragraphs of Article 28, the agenda is fixed by each chamber.

Two weeks of meetings out of four are reserved with priority, in the order that the Government has fixed, for the examination of texts and for debates which it requests to be included in the agenda.

Furthermore, the examination of government bills for financial statutes, social security financing statutes and, subject to the provisions of the following paragraph, texts transmitted by the other chamber at least six weeks earlier, government bills relating to a state of crisis and requests for authorization envisaged by Article 35, is, upon request of the Government, included in the agenda with priority.

One week of meetings out of four is reserved, with priority and in the order fixed by each assembly, for the control of the action of the Government and for the assessment of public policies.

One day of meeting per month is reserved for an agenda determined by each chamber upon the initiative of opposition groups of the chamber concerned, as well as of minority groups.

At least one meeting per week, including during extraordinary sessions provided for in Article 29, is reserved, with priority, for questions of members of Parliament and answers by the Government.

Article 49. The Prime Minister, after deliberation by the Council of Ministers, ties the responsibility of the Government before the National Assembly to the Government's programme or possibly a general policy statement.

The National Assembly invokes the responsibility of the Government by a vote on a motion of censure. Such a motion is only admissible if it is signed by at least one tenth of the members of the National Assembly. The vote may not take place until forty-eight hours have elapsed after the tabling. Solely votes in favour of the motion of censure are counted, which may only be adopted by a majority of the members composing the Assembly. Except in the case stipulated by the paragraph hereunder, a deputy may not be a signatory to more than three motions of censure during one ordinary session and to more than one during one extraordinary session.

The Prime Minister may, after deliberation by the Council of Ministers, make a matter of the responsibility of the Government before the National Assembly the adoption of a government bill for a financial statute or a social security financing statute. In that event, the government bill is considered adopted unless a motion of censure, tabled within the twenty-four hours that follow, is adopted under the conditions provided for by the foregoing paragraph. The Prime Minister may furthermore resort to this procedure for one other government bill or one private member's bill per session.

The Prime Minister has the option to request from the Senate the approval of a general policy statement.

Article 50. When the National Assembly adopts a motion of censure or when it disapproves the programme or a general policy statement of the Government, the Prime Minister must tender the resignation of the Government to the President of the Republic.

Article 50-1. Before one of the chambers the Government may, on its own initiative or at the request of a parliamentary group in the sense of Article 51-1, make a statement on a specified subject that is followed by a debate and that may, if it so decides, be the object of a vote without making it a matter of its responsibility.

Article 51. The closure of an ordinary session or of extraordinary sessions is postponed by operation of law in order to allow, where applicable, the application of Article 49. For that same purpose, supplementary meetings are held by operation of law.

Article 51-1. The rules of procedure of each chamber determine the rights of parliamentary groups constituted within it. It recognizes the rights specific to opposition groups of the chamber concerned as well as to minority groups.

Article 51-2. For the exercise of the controlling and evaluation tasks defined in the first paragraph of Article 24, commissions of inquiry may be created within each chamber in order to gather information under the conditions stipulated by statute.
Statute determines their rules of organization and functioning. The conditions of their establishment are determined by the rules of procedure of each chamber.

Title VI. On international treaties and agreements

Article 52. The President of the Republic negotiates and ratifies treaties [traités].
He is informed of any negotiation for the conclusion of an international agreement [accord international] not subject to ratification.

Article 53. Peace treaties, treaties on trade, treaties or agreements relating to international organization, those which affect the finances of the State, those which modify provisions of statutory nature, those which relate to the status of persons, those which entail the cession, exchange or acquisition of territory, may only be ratified or approved by statute.
They do not take effect until they have been ratified or approved.
No cession, no exchange, no acquisition of territory is valid without the consent of the population concerned.

Article 53-1. The Republic may conclude, with European States bound by commitments identical to its own in matters of asylum and the protection of human rights and fundamental freedoms, agreements determining their respective competences for the consideration of requests for asylum submitted to them.
However, even if, pursuant to these agreements, a request does not fall under its competences, the authorities of the Republic always have the right to grant asylum to any foreigner persecuted for his action in pursuit of freedom or who seeks protection by France for another reason.

Article 53-2. The Republic may recognize the jurisdiction of the International Criminal Court under the conditions provided by the treaty signed on 18 July 1998.

Article 54. If the Constitutional Council, seized by the President of the Republic, by the Prime Minister, by the president of one of the chambers or by sixty deputies or sixty senators, has declared that an international commitment contains a clause contrary to the Constitution, the authorization to ratify or approve the international commitment in question may only be given after amendment of the Constitution.

Article 55. Treaties or agreements duly ratified or approved have, upon their publication, authority superior to that of statutes, subject, with respect to each agreement or treaty, to their application by the other party.

Title VII. The Constitutional Council

Article 56. The Constitutional Council [Conseil Constitutionnel] comprises nine members whose mandate lasts nine years and is not renewable. One third of the Constitutional Council is renewed every three years. Three of the members are appointed by the President of the Republic, three by the president of the National Assembly, three by the president of the Senate. The procedure stipulated in the last paragraph of Article 13 is applicable to these appointments. The appointments made by the president of each chamber are submitted for an opinion only to the competent permanent committee of the relevant chamber.

In addition to the nine members provided for above, former Presidents of the Republic are by operation of law members of the Constitutional Council for life.

The president is appointed by the President of the Republic. He has the decisive vote in case of a tie.

Article 57. The office of a member of the Constitutional Council is incompatible with that of a minister or a member of Parliament. Other incompatibilities are established by an organic statute.

Article 58. The Constitutional Council ensures the proper conduct of the election of the President of the Republic.

It examines complaints and proclaims the result of the election.

Article 59. The Constitutional Council rules, in case of a challenge, on the proper conduct of the election of deputies and senators.

Article 60. The Constitutional Council ensures the proper conduct of referendums as provided for by Articles 11 and 89 and by Title XV. It proclaims the results thereof.

Article 61. Organic statutes, prior to their promulgation, private member's bills mentioned in Article 11 before they have been submitted to referendum, and the rules of procedure of the parliamentary chambers, before coming into force, must be submitted to the Constitutional Council which rules on their conformity with the Constitution.

For the same purpose, statutes may be referred to the Constitutional Council, before their promulgation, by the President of the Republic, the Prime Minister, the president of the National Assembly, the president of the Senate or sixty deputies or sixty senators.

In the cases provided for by the two foregoing paragraphs, the Constitutional Council must rule within a period of one month. However, at the request of the Government, in cases of urgency, this period is reduced to eight days.

In the same cases, referral to the Constitutional Council suspends the time period for promulgation.

Article 61-1. When, in the course of proceedings before a court, it is submitted that a statutory provision jeopardizes the rights and freedoms which the Constitution guarantees, the Constitutional Council may be seized on that question by reference from the Council of State or the Court of Cassation which decide within a determined period.

An organic statute determines the conditions for the application of the present Article.

Article 62. A provision declared unconstitutional on the basis of Article 61 may neither be promulgated nor implemented.

A provision declared unconstitutional on the basis of Article 61-1 is repealed from the moment of the publication of the decision of the Constitutional Council or a later date established in that decision. The Constitutional Council determines the conditions and limits within which the effects that the provision has created may be called into question.

The decisions of the Constitutional Council are not open to any appeal. They are binding on public authority and on all administrative and judicial authorities.

Article 63. An organic statute determines the organization and functioning of the Constitutional Council, the procedure followed before it and, in particular, the time limits for submitting complaints to it.

Title VIII. On the judicial authority

Article 64. The President of the Republic is the guarantor of the independence of the judicial authority.
He is assisted by the High Council of the Judiciary [Conseil Supérieur de la Magistrature].
An organic statute contains the rules governing magistrates.
Judges [magistrats du siège] are irremovable.

Article 65. The High Council of the Judiciary comprises a section competent with regard to judges [magistrats du siège] and one competent with regard to public prosecutors [magistrats du parquet].
The section competent with regard to judges is presided over by the first president of the Court of Cassation [Cour de cassation]. It comprises furthermore five judges and one public prosecutor, one member of the Council of State nominated by the Council of State [Conseil d'État], one advocate [avocat] as well as six distinguished persons who are not members of either Parliament or the judiciary or the administration. The President of the Republic, the president of the National Assembly and the president of the Senate each appoint two distinguished persons. The procedure stipulated in the last paragraph of Article 13 is applicable to the appointment of distinguished persons. The appointments made by the president of each chamber of Parliament are submitted for an opinion only to the competent permanent committee of the relevant chamber.
The section competent with regard to public prosecutors is presided over by the procurator-general at the Court of Cassation. It comprises furthermore five public prosecutors and one judge, as well as the member of the Council of State, the advocate and the six distinguished persons mentioned in the second paragraph.
The section of the High Council of the Judiciary competent with regard to judges submits proposals for the appointments of judges at the Court of Cassation, for those of the first president of a court of appeals [cour d'appel] and for those of the president of a district court [tribunal de grande instance]. The other judges are appointed upon its assent.
The section of the High Council of the Judiciary competent with regard to public prosecutors gives its opinion on appointments that affect public prosecutors.
The section of the High Council of the Judiciary competent with regard to judges rules as a disciplinary council for judges. It then comprises besides the members envisaged in the second paragraph the judge who is a member of the section competent with regard to public prosecutors.
The section of the High Council of the Judiciary competent with regard to public prosecutors gives its opinion on those disciplinary sanctions that affect them. It then comprises besides the members envisaged in the third paragraph, the public prosecutor who is a member of the section competent with regard to judges.
The High Council of the Judiciary meets in plenary composition in order to answer requests for an opinion made by the President of the Republic in application of Article 64. It gives, in the same composition, its opinion on questions regarding the ethics of magistrates as well as on any question regarding the functioning of the justice system on which it is seized by the minister of justice. The plenary composition comprises three of the five judges mentioned in the second paragraph, three of the five public prosecutors mentioned in the third paragraph as well as the member of the Council of State, the advocate and the six distinguished persons mentioned in the second paragraph. It is presided over by the first president of the Court of Cassation who may be substituted by the procurator-general at that Court.

Except in disciplinary matters the minister of justice may participate in the meetings of the sections of the High Council of the Judiciary.
The High Council of the Judiciary may be seized by a person undergoing a trial under the conditions determined by organic statute.
An organic statute determines the conditions for the application of the present Article.

Article 66. No-one may be detained arbitrarily.
The judicial authority, guardian of individual liberty, ensures the observance of this principle under the conditions provided by statute.

Article 66-1. No-one may be sentenced to the death penalty.

Title IX. The High Court

Article 67. The President of the Republic is not liable for any acts committed in this capacity, subject to the provisions of the Articles 53-2 and 68.
He may not, during his mandate and before no French court or administrative authority, be required to testify, nor be the object of a court action, investigatory action, instruction or prosecution. Any period of prescription or foreclosure is suspended.
All actions and proceedings thus barred may be resumed or brought against him upon expiry of a period of one month after the end of his office.

Article 68. The President of the Republic may only be removed from office in case of a breach of his duties manifestly incompatible with the exercise of his mandate. The removal is proclaimed by Parliament sitting as the High Court [Haute Cour].
The proposal to convene the High Court adopted by one of the chambers of Parliament is immediately transmitted to the other, which reaches its decision within fifteen days.
The High Court is chaired by the president of the National Assembly. It rules within a period of one month, by secret ballot, on the removal from office. Its decision is of immediate effect.
The decisions taken in the application of the present Article are taken by two thirds of the members composing the chamber concerned or the High Court. Any delegation of votes is prohibited. Only the votes in favour of the proposal to convene the High Court or of the removal from office are counted.
An organic statute determines the conditions for the application of the present Article.

Title X. On the criminal liability of members of the government

Article 68-1. The members of the government are liable for acts committed in the exercise of their office and qualified as crimes [crime] or misdemeanours [délit] at the time they were committed.
They are tried by the Court of Justice of the Republic [Cour de justice de la République].
The Court of Justice of the Republic is bound by such definition of crimes and misdemeanours as well as by such determination of penalties as follows from statute.

Article 68-2. The Court of Justice of the Republic consists of fifteen judges: twelve parliamentarians elected from among their ranks and in equal number by the National Assembly and by the Senate after each general or partial election of these chambers, and three judges at the Court of Cassation, one of whom presides over the Court of Justice of the Republic.
Any person who claims to be a victim of a crime or misdemeanour committed by a member of the government in the exercise of his office may file a complaint with a petitions committee.
This committee orders either the closure of the procedure or its transmission to the procurator-general at the Court of Cassation for the seizing of the Court of Justice of the Republic.
The procurator-general at the Court of Cassation may also upon his own motion seize the Court of Justice of the Republic upon the assent of the petitions committee.

An organic statute determines the conditions for the application of the present Article.

Article 68-3. The provisions of the present Title are applicable to acts committed before its entry into force.

Title XI. The Economic, Social and Environmental Council

Article 69. The Economic, Social and Environmental Council [Conseil économique, social et environnemental], seized by the Government, gives its opinion on government bills, draft ordinances or draft decrees as well as on private member's bills which are submitted to it.
A member of the Economic, Social and Environmental Council may be appointed by it to present to the parliamentary chambers the opinion of the Council on the government or private member's bills which have been submitted to it.
The Economic, Social and Environmental Council may be seized by way of petition under the conditions determined by organic statute. After examination of the petition, it notifies the Government and Parliament of the follow-up actions that it proposes to take.

Article 70. The Economic, Social and Environmental Council may be consulted by the Government and Parliament on any problem of an economic, social or environmental nature. The Government may equally consult it on government bills for programming statutes defining the multiannual directions for public finances. Any plan or any government bill for a programming statute of an economic, social or environmental nature is submitted to it for its opinion.

Article 71. The composition of the Economic and Social and Environmental Council, the number of whose members may not exceed two hundred and thirty-three, and its rules of procedure are determined by an organic statute.

Title XI bis. The Defender of Rights

Article 71-1. The Defender of Rights guards the respect of rights and liberties by the administrations of the State, the territorial entities, public bodies, as well as by any body charged with a public service task, or with respect to which an organic statute confers competences on him.
He may be seized, under the conditions stipulated by an organic statute, by any person who considers himself harmed by the functioning of a public service or a body envisaged in the first paragraph. He may consider a matter on his own initiative.
An organic statute specifies the competences and the terms of intervention of the Defender of Rights. It determines the conditions under which he may be assisted by a collegiate body in the exercise of some of his competences.
The Defender of Rights is appointed by the President of the Republic for a non-renewable term of six years after application of the procedure stipulated in the last paragraph of Article 13. His functions are incompatible with those of a member of Government and of a member of Parliament. Other incompatibilities are determined by organic statute.
The Defender of Rights gives account of his activity to the President of the Republic and to Parliament.

Title XII. The territorial entities

Article 72. The territorial entities [collectivités territoriales] of the Republic are the municipalities [communes], the departments [départements], the regions [régions], the special-status entities and the overseas entities governed by Article 74. Any other territorial entity is created by statute, where appropriate in place of one or more entities referred to in the present paragraph.

Territorial entities are charged with taking decisions on the entirety of competences that can best be exercised at their level.

Under the conditions provided by statute, the entities administer themselves freely through elected councils and possess regulatory powers [réglementaire] for the exercise of their competences.

Under the conditions provided by organic statute, provided that the essential conditions for the exercise of a public liberty or a constitutionally guaranteed right is not affected, territorial entities or associations thereof may, where such is provided by statute or regulation, as the case may be, derogate on an experimental basis for limited purpose and duration from statutory or regulatory provisions governing the exercise of their competences.

No territorial entity may exercise tutelage over another. However, where the exercise of a competence requires the co-operation of several territorial entities, statute may authorize one of them or one of their associations to organize the modalities of their joint action.

In the territorial entities of the Republic, the representative of the State, representing each of the members of the Government, is responsible for the national interests, administrative supervision and the observance of statutes.

Article 72-1. Statute determines the conditions under which voters in each territorial entity may, by exercising the right of petition, request that a question relevant to its competence be included in the agenda of the deliberative assembly of that entity.

Under the conditions determined by organic statute, government bills for deliberation or acts relevant to the competence of a territorial entity may, on its initiative, by means of referendum, be submitted to the decision of the voters of that entity.

When it is envisaged that a territorial entity be created or provided with a special status or its organization be modified, it may be decided by statute to consult the voters registered in the concerned entities. The modification of the borders of territorial entities may equally give rise to a consultation of the voters under the conditions provided by statute.

Article 72-2. Territorial entities enjoy resources of which they may dispose freely under the conditions determined by statute.

They may receive all or a part of the revenue from taxes of any nature. Statute may authorize them to specify the basis and rate thereof within the limits it determines.

Fiscal revenue and other own resources of the territorial entities represent, for each category of entities, a decisive share of the entirety of their resources. Organic statute determines the conditions under which this rule is given effect.

Any transfer of competences between the State and the territorial entities is accompanied by an allocation of resources equivalent to what had been dedicated to the exercise of those competences. Any creation or extension of competences having as a consequence an increase in expenditures of territorial entities is accompanied by resources determined by statute.

Statute provides for equalization mechanisms designed to promote equality between territorial entities.

Article 72-3. The Republic recognizes, within the French people, the overseas populations in a common ideal of liberty, equality and fraternity.

Guadeloupe, Guiana, Martinique, Réunion, Mayotte, Saint-Barthélemy, Saint-Martin, Saint-Pierre-and-Miquelon, the Islands of Wallis and Futuna and French Polynesia are governed by Article 73 for departments and overseas regions and for territorial entities created by application of the last paragraph of Article 73, and by Article 74 for the other entities.

The status of New Caledonia is governed by Title XIII.

Statute determines the legislative regime and the special organization of the French Southern and Antarctic Territories and of Clipperton.

Article 72-4. No change, regarding the whole or a part of one of the entities mentioned in the second paragraph of Article 72-3, of one towards the other of the regimes provided for by Articles 73 and 74, takes place unless the consent of the voters of the entity or the part of the entity concerned has been obtained beforehand under the conditions provided by the following paragraph. This change of regime is decided on by organic statute.
The President of the Republic, on a proposal of the Government during sessions or on joint proposal of the two chambers, which are published in the Official Journal [Journal officiel], may decide to consult the voters of a territorial entity situated overseas on a question relating to its organization, to its competences or to its legislative regime. Where this consultation concerns a change stipulated in the foregoing paragraph and is organized on proposal of the Government, it makes a statement before each chamber, which is followed by a debate.

Article 73. In the overseas departments and regions, statutes and regulations are applicable by operation of law. They may be the object of adaptations in view of the particular characteristics and constraints of these entities.
These adaptations may be decided by the entities on matters where they exercise their competences and if they were enabled to do so, as the case may be, by statute or by regulation.
By derogation from the first paragraph and in order to take account of their specificities, entities governed by the present Article may be enabled, as the case may be by statute or by regulation, to themselves determine the rules applicable on their territory in a limited number of matters that can fall under the scope of statute or regulation.
These rules may not concern nationality, civil rights, guarantees of civil liberties, the status and capacity of persons, the organization of justice system, criminal law, criminal procedure, foreign policy, defence, public security and order, currency, credit and exchange, as well as electoral law. This enumeration may be specified and completed by organic statute.
The provisions stipulated in the two preceding paragraphs are not applicable to the department and to the region of Réunion.
The enabling provided for in the second and third paragraph is decided, upon request of the entity concerned, subject to the conditions and with the reservations provided by an organic statute. They may not be carried out where the essential conditions for the exercise of a public liberty or a constitutionally guaranteed right is at issue.
The creation by statute of an entity substituting an overseas department and region or the establishment of a single deliberative assembly for those two entities may not take place unless the consent of the voters registered in the territory of these entities has been obtained according to the procedure provided in the second paragraph of Article 72-4.

Article 74. The overseas entities governed by the present Article have a status that takes account of their particular interests within the Republic.
This status is defined by organic statute, adopted after an opinion of the deliberative assembly, which determines:
- the conditions under which statutes and regulations are applicable there;
- the competences of this entity; subject to those already exercised by it, the transfer of competences by the State may not concern the matters enumerated in the fourth paragraph of Article 73, specified and complemented, as the case may be, by organic statute;
- the rules on the organization and functioning of the institutions of the entity and the electoral regime of its deliberative assembly;
- the conditions under which its institutions are consulted on government bills and private member's bills and drafts of ordinances or decrees containing provisions that are specific to the entity as well as to the ratification or approval of international commitments concluded in matters relevant to its competence.
The organic statute may equally determine, for those entities that are provided with autonomy, the conditions under which:

- the Council of State exercises specific judicial review over certain categories of acts of the deliberative assembly effected on the basis of competences that it exercises within the scope of statute;
- the deliberative assembly may amend a statute promulgated after the entry into force of the status of the entity, where the Constitutional Council, seized in particular by the authorities of that entity, has established that the statute has intervened in the scope of competence of that entity;
- measures justified by local needs may be taken by the entity in favour of its population, in matters of access to employment, the right of establishment for the exercise of a professional activity or the protection of land property;
- the entity may participate, under the control of the State, in the exercise of the competences it retains, respecting the guarantees granted to the entire national territory for the exercise of public liberties.

The other modalities of the organization specific to the entities subject to the present Article are determined and amended by statute after consultation of their deliberative assembly.

Article 74-1. In the overseas entities envisaged by Article 74 and in New Caledonia, the Government may, by ordinance, in the matters that remain in the competence of the State, extend, with the necessary adaptations, the provisions of statutory nature in force in Metropolitan France or adapt the provisions of statutory nature in force to the specific organization of the entity concerned, provided that the statute did not explicitly exclude, for the provisions in question, recourse to this procedure.

The ordinances are issued in the Council of Ministers after an opinion of the deliberative assembly concerned and the Council of State. They enter into force upon their publication. They become ineffective in the absence of ratification by Parliament within a period of eighteen months after that publication.

Article 75. The citizens of the Republic who do not have ordinary civil status, only envisaged in Article 34, retain their personal status as long as they have not renounced it.

Article 75-1. Regional languages belong to the heritage of France.

Title XIII. Transitional provisions regarding New Caledonia

Article 76. The population of New Caledonia is called upon to pronounce itself before the 31 December 1998 on the provisions of the agreement signed at Nouméa on 5 May 1998 and published on 27 May 1998 in the Official Journal of the French Republic.

Admitted to participate in the vote are the persons who fulfil the conditions determined in Article 2 of statute no. 88-1028 of 9 November 1988.

The measures necessary for the organization of the vote are taken by decree in consultation with the Council of State [Conseil d'Etat] after having been discussed in the council of ministers.

Article 77. After adoption of the agreement by the vote provided in Article 76, an organic statute, passed after an opinion of the deliberative assembly of New Caledonia, determines, in order to ensure the development of New Caledonia respecting the directions defined by that agreement and in accordance with the terms necessary in order to give it effect:
- the competences of the State that will be transferred definitively to the institutions of New Caledonia, the time scale and the modalities of the transfer, as well as the allocation of the expenditures resulting therefrom;
- the rules of the organization and functioning of the institutions of New Caledonia and in particular the conditions under which certain categories of acts of the deliberative assembly of New Caledonia may be submitted for review to the Constitutional Council [Conseil Constitutionnel] before publication;

- the rules relating to citizenship, to the electoral regime, to employment and to the customary civil status;
- the conditions and time limits within which the population concerned in New Caledonia will be led to pronounce themselves on the attainment of full sovereignty.

The other measures necessary for giving effect of the agreement mentioned in Article 76 are defined by statute.

For the definition of the electoral body called upon to elect the members of the deliberative assemblies of New Caledonia and its provinces, the list to which the agreement mentioned in Article 76 and in Article 188 and 189 of the organic statute no. 99-209 of 19 March 1999 relating to New Caledonia refer is the list drawn up in the course of the vote provided for in Article 76 and including the persons not admitted to participate in it.

Title XIV. On the French-speaking World and on Association Agreements

Article 87. The Republic takes part in the development of solidarity and cooperation between the States and peoples which have the French language in common.

Title XV. On the European Union

Article 88-1. The Republic participates in the European Union, constituted by States that have freely chosen to exercise certain of their powers conjointly by virtue of the Treaty on European Union and the Treaty on the Functioning of the European Union as they result from the Treaty signed at Lisbon on 13 December 2007.

Article 88-2. Statute determines the rules regarding the European arrest warrant by application of the acts taken by the institutions of the European Union.

Article 88-3. Subject to reciprocity and in accordance with the terms laid down by the Treaty on European Union signed on 7 February 1992, the right to vote and to stand in municipal elections may be granted only to citizens of the Union residing in France. These citizens may neither exercise the office of mayor or deputy mayor, nor participate in the designation of senatorial electors and in the election of senators. An organic statute adopted in identical terms by both chambers determines the conditions under which the present Article is applied.

Article 88-4. The Government submits to the National Assembly and to the Senate, when they have been transmitted to the Council of the European Union, drafts of or proposals for acts of the European Communities and of the European Union.

In accordance with the terms set by the rules of procedure of each chamber, European resolutions may be adopted, also outside sessions where appropriate, on the drafts and proposals mentioned in the first paragraph, as well as on any document emanating from an institution of the European Union.

Within each parliamentary chamber a committee responsible for European affairs is established.

Article 88-5. Any government bill authorizing the ratification of a Treaty regarding the accession of a State to the European Union and to the European Communities is submitted to referendum by the President of the Republic.

However, by a vote on a motion adopted in identical terms by each assembly by a majority of three fifths, Parliament may authorize the adoption of the government bill in accordance with the procedure stipulated in the third paragraph of Article 89.

[Note: This Article does not apply to accessions made following an intergovernmental conference whose convocation was decided by the European Council before 1 July 2004.]

Article 88-6. The National Assembly or the Senate may adopt a reasoned opinion on the compliance of a draft European legislative act with the principle of subsidiarity. The opinion is addressed by the president of the chamber concerned to the presidents of the European Parliament, of the Council and of the European Commission. The Government is informed of this.

Each chamber may bring an action before the Court of Justice of the European Union against a European legislative act for a violation of the principle of subsidiarity. The action is transmitted to the Court of Justice of the European Union by the Government.

To that end, resolutions may be adopted, also outside sessions where appropriate, in accordance with the terms on initiative and debate set by the rules of procedure of each chamber. Upon request of sixty deputies or of sixty senators, the action is brought by operation of law.

Article 88-7. By adoption of a motion passed in identical terms by the National Assembly and the Senate, Parliament may oppose an amendment of the rules for the adoption of acts of the European Union in the cases envisaged, under the simplified treaty revision procedure or judicial cooperation in civil matters, by the Treaty on European Union and the Treaty on the Functioning of the European Union as they result from the Treaty signed at Lisbon on 13 December 2007.

Title XVI. On amendments

Article 89. The right of initiative for a revision of the Constitution lies concurrently with the President of the Republic, upon a proposal by the Prime Minister, and with the members of Parliament.

A government or private member's bill for a revision must be examined under the conditions of the fixed periods determined in the third paragraph of Article 42 and adopted by both chambers in identical terms. The revision is final after having been approved by referendum.

However, a government bill for a revision is not submitted to referendum where the President of the Republic decides to submit it to Parliament convened in Congress [Congrès]; in that case, the government bill for revision is not approved unless it is adopted by a majority of three fifths of the votes cast. The bureau of the Congress is that of the National Assembly.

No procedure of revision may be initiated or continued where the integrity of the territory is jeopardized.

The republican form of Government may not be the object of a revision.

Title XVII. (Repealed).

Annex 7

FRENCH DECLARATION OF THE RIGHTS OF MAN

Declaration of the Rights of Man and the Citizen [Déclaration des Droits de l'homme et du Citoyen] of 26 August 1789.[1]

The Representatives of the French People, organized in a National Assembly, considering that ignorance, neglect or contempt of the rights of man are the only causes of the public misfortunes and of Governments' corruption, have decided to expose, in a solemn Declaration, the natural, inalienable and sacred rights of man, so that this Declaration, constantly present to all members of the social body, continually reminds them of their rights and their duties; so that the acts of the legislative power and those of the executive power may be compared at any time with the aim of every political institution, and that they would be more respected; so that the grievances of citizens, founded henceforth on simple and incontestable principles, result in the preservation of the Constitution and in the happiness of all.
Therefore the National Assembly recognizes and proclaims, in the presence and under the auspices of the Supreme Being, the following rights of man and of the citizen:

First Article. Men are born and remain free and equal in rights. Social distinctions may be based only on the common good.

Article II. The aim of every political association is the conservation of the natural and imprescriptible rights of man. These rights are liberty, property, safety and resistance to oppression.

Article III. The principle of all Sovereignty resides essentially in the Nation. No body, no individual may exercise any authority that does not expressly emanate from it.

Article IV. Liberty consists of being able to do everything that does not harm anybody else: thus the exercise of the natural rights of every man has no boundaries except those that ensure to other Members of the Society the enjoyment of those same rights. Those boundaries may be defined only by Law.

---

[1] Translation by I. Wieczorek. This text has also been published separately in: Ph. Kiiver & N. Kornet, eds., *The Maastricht Collection: Selected National, European and International Provisions from Public and Private Law*, Second Edition (Groningen: Europa Law Publishing, 2010). It has also been published in a smaller compilation covering only the area of constitutional law: Ph. Kiiver, ed., *Sources of Constitutional Law: Constitutions and Fundamental Legal Provisions from the United States, France, Germany, the Netherlands, the United Kingdom, the ECHR and the EU*, Second Edition (Groningen: Europa Law Publishing, 2010).

Article V. The Law does not have the right to forbid any action except those that are harmful to society. Nothing which is not forbidden by the Law may be barred, and no-one may be forced to do what it does not dictate.

Article VI. The Law is the expression of the general will. All Citizens have the right to contribute personally, or through their Representatives, to its formation. It must be the same for everybody, whether it protects or punishes. All citizens, being equal before it, are equally eligible to all public dignities, positions and employments, according to their capacities, without any distinction other than those of their virtues and their talents.

Article VII. No man may be accused, arrested or detained except in the cases determined by Law and in the forms that it has prescribed. Those who solicit, send, execute or let execute arbitrary orders must be punished; however every Citizen summoned or arrested pursuant to the Law must obey immediately: he makes himself guilty with his resistance.

Article VIII. The Law must establish only strictly and evidently necessary penalties, and no-one may be punished except pursuant to a Law established and promulgated prior to the crime, and lawfully applied.

Article IX. Every man being presumed innocent until he has been declared guilty, if it is deemed indispensable to arrest him, any harshness which is not necessary for the securing of his person must be severely repressed by Law.

Article X. No-one may be disquieted because of his opinions, even religious, provided that their manifestation does not disturb the public order established by Law.

Article XI. The free communication of thoughts and of opinions is one of the most precious rights of Man; every Citizen may therefore speak, write, print freely, save answering for the abuse of this freedom in the cases determined by the Law.

Article XII. The guarantee of the rights of Man and the Citizen requires a public force: such force is therefore established for the advantage of all and not for the specific utility of those who have been entrusted with it.

Article XIII. For the maintenance of the public force, and for the expenses of the administration, a common contribution is indispensable. It must be equally distributed among the citizens according to their means.

Article XIV. All Citizens have the right to ascertain, personally or through their Representatives, the necessity of the public contribution, to freely consent to it, to monitor its use and to determine its proportion, base, collection and duration.

Article XV. Society has the right to call every public Agent to account for the administration.

Article XVI. Any society in which the guarantee of Rights is not ensured and the separation of Powers is not determined, has no Constitution.

Article XVII. Property being an inviolable and sacred right, no-one may be deprived of it, except when public necessity, lawfully assessed, evidently requires it, and under the condition of a just and prior indemnity.

Annex 8

THE GERMAN BASIC LAW

Basic Law for the Federal Republic of Germany [Grundgesetz für die Bundesrepublik Deutschland] of 23 May 1949 as last amended by federal statute of 29 July 2009 (BGBl. I p. 2248) and incorporating the amendments resulting from the federal statute of 8 October 2008 (BGBl. I p. 1926) which entered into force together with the Treaty of Lisbon on 1 December 2009.[1]

Preamble

Conscious of its responsibility before God and man, inspired by the will to serve world peace as an equal partner in a united Europe, the German people, by virtue of its constituent power, has adopted for itself this Basic Law. Germans in the States of Baden-Württemberg, Bavaria, Berlin, Brandenburg, Bremen, Hamburg, Hesse, Mecklenburg-Western Pomerania, Lower Saxony, North Rhine-Westphalia, Rhineland-Palatinate, Saarland, Saxony, Saxony-Anhalt, Schleswig-Holstein and Thuringia have achieved the unity and freedom of Germany in free self-determination. This Basic Law thus applies to the entire German people.

I. The fundamental rights

Article 1. (1) Human dignity is inviolable. To respect and protect it is the duty of all state authority.
(2) The German people therefore acknowledges inviolable and inalienable human rights as the basis of every community of people, of peace and of justice in the world.
(3) The following fundamental rights bind the legislature, the executive and the judiciary as directly applicable law.

Article 2. (1) Everyone has the right to the free development of his personality, as far as he does not infringe on the rights of others and does not violate the constitutional order or the law of morality.

---

[1] Translation by Ph. Kiiver, G. Kristoferitsch & G. Rotering. This text has also been published separately in: Ph. Kiiver & N. Kornet, eds., *The Maastricht Collection: Selected National, European and International Provisions from Public and Private Law*, Second Edition (Groningen: Europa Law Publishing, 2010). It has also been published in a smaller compilation covering only the area of constitutional law: Ph. Kiiver, ed., *Sources of Constitutional Law: Constitutions and Fundamental Legal Provisions from the United States, France, Germany, the Netherlands, the United Kingdom, the ECHR and the EU*, Second Edition (Groningen: Europa Law Publishing, 2010).

(2) Everyone has the right to life and physical integrity. The freedom of the person is inviolable. These rights may be interfered with only pursuant to a statute.

Article 3. (1) All people are equal before the law.
(2) Men and women have equal rights. The state promotes the actual implementation of equal rights for women and men and takes measures to remove existing disadvantages.
(3) No-one may be disadvantaged or preferred because of his sex, his descent, his race, his language, his homeland and origin, his faith, his religious or political views. No-one may be disadvantaged because of his disability.

Article 4. (1) The freedom of faith, of conscience, and the freedom to manifest one's religious and world-view conviction, are inviolable.
(2) The undisturbed exercise of religion is ensured.
(3) No-one may be forced against his conscience into armed military service. Details are regulated by a federal statute.

Article 5. (1) Everyone has the right to freely express and disseminate his opinion in speech, writing and picture and to inform himself without interference from generally accessible sources. The freedom of the press and the freedom of reporting through radio and film are ensured. Censorship does not take place.
(2) These rights find their limits in the regulations of general statutes, in statutory provisions for the protection of the youth and in the right to personal honour.
(3) Art and science, research and teaching are free. The freedom of teaching does not release from the loyalty to the constitution.

Article 6. (1) Marriage and family are placed under the special protection of the state order.
(2) The care and upbringing of children are the natural right of the parents and are an obligation that is primarily theirs. The community of the state watches over their performance.
(3) Children may be separated from the family pursuant to a statute against the will of their custodians only when the custodians fail or when the children are in danger of becoming victims of neglect for other reasons.
(4) Every mother is entitled to the protection and care of the community.
(5) Legislation is to provide children born outside wedlock with conditions for their physical and mental development and their position in society equal to those of children born within wedlock.

Article 7. (1) The entire school system is placed under the supervision of the state.
(2) Custodians have the right to decide over the participation of their child in religion classes.
(3) Religion classes are a regular course at public schools with the exception of non-denominational schools. Without prejudice to the state right of supervision, religious classes are taught in accordance with the principles of the religious communities. No teacher may be obliged against his will to teach religion classes.
(4) The right to establish private schools is ensured. Private schools as a substitute for public schools require the approval of the state and are subject to State legislation. Approval is to be granted when private schools are not inferior to state schools in their teaching aims and facilities as well as the scientific training of their teaching staff, and when a segregation of pupils according to the economic standing of the parents is not promoted. Approval is to be denied when the economic and legal position of the teaching staff is insufficiently secured.
(5) A private primary-cum-secondary school is only to be allowed if the curriculum administration recognizes a special educational interest or, upon custodians' request, if it is to be established as a community school, a denominational school or as a school based on a particular world view and a public primary-cum-secondary school of that kind is lacking in the municipality.
(6) Nursery schools remain abolished.

Article 8. (1) All Germans have the right to assemble peacefully and unarmed without notification or permission.
(2) Regarding gatherings outdoors, this right may be limited by or pursuant to a statute.

Article 9. (1) All Germans have the right to form clubs and societies.
(2) Associations whose purposes or activities run counter to criminal law or which are aimed against the constitutional order or the idea of understanding between nations are prohibited.
(3) The right to form associations for the promotion of working and economic conditions is ensured for everyone and for all professions. Agreements that limit or seek to hinder this right are void, measures taken with a view thereto are illegal. Measures in the sense of Articles 12a, 35 (2) and (3), Article 87a (4) and Article 91 may not be directed against industrial dispute action that is taken for the protection and promotion of working and economic conditions by associations in the meaning of the first sentence.

Article 10. (1) The privacy of correspondence as well as the privacy of mail and telecommunications are inviolable.
(2) Limitations may be ordered only pursuant to a statute. If the limitation serves the protection of the liberal-democratic fundamental order or of the integrity or security of the Federation or a State, then statute may provide that it not be notified to those affected and that recourse to the courts be replaced by review by organs and auxiliary organs appointed by the parliament.

Article 11. (1) All Germans enjoy freedom of movement on the entire territory of the Federation.
(2) This right may be limited only by or pursuant to a statute and only for those cases where sufficient means to support life are lacking and where this would result in a special burden on the community or where it is necessary for the aversion of a danger to the integrity or the liberal democratic fundamental order of the Federation or a State, for the countering of an epidemic threat, natural disasters or very serious accidents, for the protection of the youth from neglect or for the prevention of criminal acts.

Article 12. (1) All Germans have the right to freely choose their profession, place of work and of their training. The exercise of a profession may be regulated by or pursuant to a statute.
(2) No-one may be forced to perform a particular work, except within the framework of a regular general public service obligation that is the same for everyone.
(3) Forced labour is permissible only in the context of a court-ordered deprivation of freedom.

Article 12a. (1) Men from the age of eighteen onwards can be obliged to serve in the armed forces, the Federal Border Guard [Bundesgrenzschutz] or in a civil defence organization.
(2) He who refuses armed military service on conscientious grounds may be obliged to serve in an alternative service. The length of the alternative service may not exceed the length of the military service. Details are regulated by a statute which may not compromise the freedom of conscientious decision and which must also provide for an alternative service option which is not connected with the units of the armed forces and the Federal Border Guard.
(3) Persons liable to conscription who have not been drafted in accordance with paragraphs 1 or 2 may in a state of defence, by or pursuant to a statute, be committed to an employment for civilian services for defence purposes including the protection of the civilian population; commitment to public employment is only permissible for the exercise of police tasks or such sovereign tasks of public administration that can be fulfilled only within a public employment. Employments in the meaning of the first sentence may be established with the armed forces, in the context of their supply, as well as in the public administration; commitment to employment in the context of the supply of the civilian population is permissible only to secure its basic needs or to maintain its safety.

(4) If in a state of defence the demand for civilian services in the civilian medical and health system as well as in the stationary military hospital system cannot be met on a voluntary basis, women from the age of eighteen until the age of fifty-five may be drafted to such services by or pursuant to a statute. They may in no event be drafted to armed service.
(5) For the time period before the state of defence, obligations under paragraph 3 may only be established within the guidelines of Article 80a (1). For the preparation to services according to paragraph 3 for which special knowledge or skills are required, by or pursuant to a statute the participation in training courses may be made mandatory. In that respect, the first sentence does not apply.
(6) If in a state of defence the demand for workers in the contexts stipulated in paragraph 3, second sentence, cannot be met on a voluntary basis, the freedom of Germans to give up a profession or a place of work may be limited, in order to meet this demand, by or pursuant to a statute. Prior to the beginning of a state of defence, paragraph 5, first sentence, applies mutatis mutandis.

Article 13. (1) The home is inviolable.
(2) Searches may be ordered only by a judge or, in case of an imminent threat, also by other organs provided for by statutes, and may be conducted only in the form stipulated there.
(3) When certain facts support the suspicion that someone has committed a certain very serious crime defined individually by statute, then, for the prosecution of this act, on the basis of a court order, technical means for the acoustic surveillance of homes in which the suspect is presumably staying may be used, if the investigation of the case by other means would be disproportionately burdensome or futile. The measure is to be of a limited duration. The order is to be given by a body staffed with three judges. In case of an imminent threat, it may also be given by a single judge.
(4) To avert acute threats to public safety, especially a threat to the public or to life, technical means for the surveillance of homes may be used only on the basis of a court order. In case of an imminent threat, the measure may also be ordered by another instance stipulated by statute; a court decision must afterwards be obtained without delay.
(5) If technical means are exclusively meant for the protection of persons operating in a home, the measure may be ordered by an instance stipulated by statute. Any other use of the information thus obtained is permissible only for the purpose of criminal prosecution or the aversion of dangers and only if the lawfulness of the measure has been established by a court; in case of an imminent threat, a court decision must afterwards be obtained without delay.
(6) The Federal Government informs the Bundestag annually about the use that has been made of technical means under paragraph 3, under paragraph 4 within the competence of the Federation, and under paragraph 5 in as far as it requires judicial review. A body elected by the Bundestag exercises parliamentary control on the basis of this report. The States ensure an equivalent parliamentary control.
(7) Interferences and limitations may otherwise be effected only for the aversion of a threat to the public or to the life of individual persons, pursuant to a statute also for the prevention of acute threats to public safety and order, especially to address a shortage of housing space, to combat epidemic threats or to protect endangered adolescents.

Article 14. (1) Property and the right of inheritance are ensured. The content and limits thereof are defined by statutes.
(2) Property entails obligations. Its use should also serve the public good.
(3) An expropriation is only permissible for the public good. It may be effected only by or pursuant to a statute which regulates the kind and extent of compensation. The compensation is to be established by justly weighing the interests of the community and of those involved. Recourse to the ordinary courts is open in case of a dispute regarding the amount of the compensation.

Article 15. Land, natural resources and means of production may, for the purpose of socialization, by a statute which regulates the kind and extent of compensation, be transferred into public ownership or into other forms of collective concern. As regards the compensation, Article 14 (3), third and fourth sentence, applies mutatis mutandis.

Article 16. (1) German citizenship may not be withdrawn. A loss of citizenship may occur only pursuant to a statute and, if against the will of the person affected, only when the person affected does not become stateless as a result.
(2) No German may be extradited to a foreign state. By statute a different regime may be established concerning extraditions to a member state of the European Union or an international tribunal, as long as principles of the rule of law are secured.

Article 16a. (1) Those politically persecuted enjoy the right to asylum.
(2) He who arrives from a member state of the European Communities or from another third country where the application of the Convention relating to the status of refugees and the Convention for the protection of human rights and fundamental freedoms is ensured, cannot rely on paragraph 1. The states outside the European Communities to which the conditions of the first sentence apply are designated by a statute which requires the consent of the Bundesrat. In cases stipulated by the first sentence, measures for the termination of a stay may be taken irrespectively of any court actions filed against them.
(3) By a statute which requires the consent of the Bundesrat, states may be designated where, based on the state of the law, the application of the law and the general political circumstances, it appears certain that neither political persecution nor inhuman or degrading punishment or treatment takes place. It is presumed that an alien from such a state is not being persecuted as long as he does not provide facts which support the conclusion that he is being politically persecuted contrary to this presumption.
(4) The execution of measures for the termination of a stay are, in the cases of paragraph 3 and in other cases that are manifestly ill-founded or are presumed manifestly ill-founded, suspended by a court only when serious doubts exist as to the lawfulness of the measure; the scope of review may be limited and belated submissions be disregarded. Details are to be regulated by statute.
(5) Paragraphs 1 to 4 do not bar any international treaties of member states of the European Communities among themselves and with third countries which, while respecting the obligations under the Convention relating to the status of refugees and the Convention for the protection of human rights and fundamental freedoms, the application of which must be ensured in the contracting states, provide for rules on jurisdiction for the review of applications for asylum, including the mutual recognition of decisions regarding asylum.

Article 17. Everyone has the right, individually or together with others in a group, to address in writing the competent authorities and parliament with petitions or complaints.

Article 17a. (1) Statutes regarding military and alternative service may provide that for members of the armed forces and the alternative service, for the duration of the military or alternative service, the fundamental right to freely express and disseminate one's opinion in speech, writing and picture (Article 5 (1), first sentence, first clause), the fundamental right of freedom of assembly (Article 8) and the right of petition (Article 17) in as far as it grants the right to submit petitions or complaints together with others in a group, be limited.
(2) Statutes which serve the purpose of defence, including the protection of the civilian population, may provide that the fundamental rights of free movement (Article 11) and the inviolability of the home (Article 13) be limited.

Article 18. He who abuses the freedom of expression, in particular the freedom of the press (Article 5 (1)), the freedom of teaching (Article 5 (3)), the freedom of assembly (Article 8), the freedom of association (Article 9), the privacy of the correspondence, the mail and telecommunications (Article 10), property (Article 14) or the right to asylum (Article 16a) in order to fight against the liberal democratic fundamental order, forfeits these fundamental rights. The forfeiture and its scope are established by the Federal Constitutional Court [Bundesverfassungsgericht].

Article 19. (1) In as far as a fundamental right may be limited by or pursuant to a statute in accordance with this Basic Law, such statute must be of a general nature and may not merely apply to an individual case. In addition, the statute must state the fundamental right and the Article concerned.
(2) In no event may a fundamental right be compromised in its essence.
(3) The fundamental rights also cover domestic legal persons, in as far as they are applicable in the light of their nature.
(4) If someone's rights are violated by public authority, he has recourse to the courts. In as far as no other jurisdiction applies, recourse may be had to the ordinary courts. Article 10 (2), second sentence, remains unaffected by this.

II. The Federation and the States

Article 20. (1) The Federal Republic of Germany is a democratic and social federal state.
(2) All state authority derives from the people. It is exercised by the people through elections and votes and through specific organs of the legislature, of executive power and the judiciary.
(3) The legislature is bound by the constitutional order, the executive power and the judiciary by law and justice.
(4) All Germans have the right to resist any person seeking to abolish this order, if no other remedy is available.

Article 20a. The state protects, also under its responsibility for future generations, the natural foundations of life and the animals, within the framework of the constitutional order through legislation and within the guidelines of law and justice through executive power and the judiciary.

Article 21. (1) Political parties contribute to the political will-formation of the people. Their establishment is free. Their internal order must correspond to democratic principles. They must render account about the origin and use of their means as well as about their assets in public.
(2) Political parties which, based on their aims or the conduct of their followers, are committed to jeopardizing or eliminating the liberal democratic fundamental order or to threatening the integrity of the Federal Republic of Germany, are unconstitutional. The Federal Constitutional Court [Bundesverfassungsgericht] rules on the question of unconstitutionality.
(3) Details are regulated by federal statutes.

Article 22. (1) The capital of the Federal Republic of Germany is Berlin. The representation of the state as a whole in the capital is a matter for the Federation. Details are regulated by statute.
(2) The federal flag is black-red-gold.

Article 23. (1) With a view to achieving a united Europe, the Federal Republic of Germany participates in the development of the European Union which is committed to democratic, rule-of-law, social, and federal principles and to the principle of subsidiarity, and which guarantees a level of protection of fundamental rights essentially comparable to that afforded by this Basic Law. To this end the Federation may, by a statute with the consent of the Bundesrat, transfer sovereign powers. For the establishment of the European Union, as well as for changes to its treaty foundations and comparable regulations that amend or supplement this Basic Law in its content, or that make such amendments or supplements possible, Article 79 (2) and (3) applies.

(1a) The Bundestag and the Bundesrat have the right to bring an action before the Court of Justice of the European Union if a legislative act of the European Union infringes upon the principle of subsidiarity. The Bundestag is obliged to do so on application by a quarter of its members. A statute which requires the consent of the Bundesrat may, with respect to the exercise of the rights accorded to the Bundestag and the Bundesrat in the treaty framework of the European Union, make deviations from the first sentence of Article 42 (2), first sentence, and Article 52 (3), first sentence.

(2) The Bundestag and, through the Bundesrat, the States, participate in matters concerning the European Union. The Federal Government must inform the Bundestag and the Bundesrat comprehensively and at the earliest possible time.

(3) The Federal Government provides the Bundestag with an opportunity to state its opinion prior to its participation in legislative acts of the European Union. The Federal Government takes into account the statements of opinion of the Bundestag during negotiations. Details are regulated by a statute.

(4) The Bundesrat is to be included in the will-formation of the Federation in as far as it would have had to participate in an equivalent domestic measure or in as far as the States would have been competent domestically.

(5) In as far as, in an area of exclusive competence of the Federation, interests of the States are affected, or in as far as the Federation has otherwise legislative competence, the Federal Government takes into account the statements of opinion of the Bundesrat. If primarily legislative competences of the States, the organization of their authorities or their administrative procedures are affected, the opinion of the Bundesrat must to that extent be given greatest consideration during the will-formation of the Federation; the responsibility of the Federation for the state as a whole must in that context be upheld. In matters that may result in an increase in spending or a decrease in revenue for the Federation, the consent of the Federal Government is required.

(6) If primarily exclusive legislative competences of the States in the areas of schooling, culture or broadcasting are affected, the exercise of the rights that the Federal Republic of Germany has as a member state of the European Union is transferred from the Federation to a representative of the States appointed by the Bundesrat. The exercise of these rights is carried out with the participation of and in coordination with the Federal Government; the responsibility of the Federation for the state as a whole must in that context be upheld.

(7) Details regarding paragraphs 4 to 6 are regulated by a statute that requires the consent of the Bundesrat.

Article 24. (1) The Federation may, by statute, transfer sovereign powers to international organizations.

(1a) In as far as the States are competent for the exercise of state power and the fulfilment of state tasks, they may, with the consent of the Federal Government, transfer sovereign powers to cross-border neighbourhood institutions.

(2) The Federation may, for the preservation of peace, enter into a system of mutual collective security; it will in that context agree to limitations of its sovereign powers which bring about and secure a peaceful and permanent order in Europe and between the nations of the world.

(3) For the settlement of international disputes, the Federation will accede to agreements regarding general, comprehensive and mandatory international arbitration.

Article 25. The general rules of international law are an integral part of federal law. They take precedence over statutes and directly create rights and obligations for the inhabitants of the territory of the Federation.

Article 26. (1) Acts that are capable of and are committed with the intent to disturb the peaceful coexistence of nations, in particular prepare the conduct of a war of aggression, are unconstitutional. They are to be made punishable offences.
(2) Weapons designed for warfare may be produced, transported and brought into circulation only with the consent of the Federal Government. Details are regulated by a federal statute.

Article 27. All German merchant vessels form a uniform merchant fleet.

Article 28. (1) The constitutional order in the States must comply with the principles of a republican, democratic and social state based on the rule of law in the meaning of this Basic Law. In the States, rural counties [Kreise] and municipalities [Gemeinden], the people must have a representative body that is formed in general, direct, free, equal and secret-ballot elections. At elections within rural counties and municipalities, persons with the citizenship of a member state of the European Community, within the guidelines of the law of the European Community, also have the right to vote and may be elected. In municipalities, a municipal assembly may take the place of an elected body.
(2) Municipalities must have the secured right to regulate all affairs of the local community, within the framework of statutes, on their own responsibility. Also associations of municipalities [Gemeindeverbände] have, within the framework of their statutory function, within the guidelines of statutes, the right to self-government. The securing of self-government also includes the foundations of financial autonomy; part of these foundations is a source of revenue related to economic strength to which municipalities with the right to set tax rates are entitled.
(3) The Federation ensures that the constitutional order of the States complies with fundamental rights and the provisions of paragraphs 1 and 2.

Article 29. (1) The territory of the Federation may be restructured so as to ensure that the States, in the light of their size and capacity, are able to effectively fulfil the tasks vested in them. Account is to be taken of regional attachment, historical and cultural connections, economic opportunity, as well as the requirements of regional planning and zoning.
(2) Measures for the restructuring of the territory of the Federation are effected by a federal statute which requires approval in a referendum [Volksentscheid]. The affected States are to be heard.
(3) The referendum takes place in those States from the territory or from parts of the territory of which a new or a redrawn State is to be formed (affected States). The object of the referendum is the question whether the affected States should continue to exist as before or whether the new or redrawn State should be formed. A referendum in favour of a new or redrawn State is established when majorities vote in favour of the change both within its future territory and within the territories or parts of territories of an affected State whose State affiliation is to be changed. It is not established when a majority within the territory of one of the affected States rejects the change; such rejection is however ineffective if in a part of a territory whose affiliation with the affected State is to be changed, a two-thirds majority votes in favour of the change, except when within the territory of the affected State as a whole a two-thirds majority rejects the change.
(4) If within a contiguous, separated residential and economic area whose parts lie in several States and which has at least one million inhabitants, one-tenth of the population entitled to vote for the Bundestag there demands by popular initiative [Volksbegehren] that for this area a single State affiliation be created, then within two years a federal statute is either to determine whether the State affiliation will be changed in accordance with paragraph 2 or that a consultative referendum [Volksbefragung] will be held in the affected States.
(5) The consultative referendum is aimed at establishing whether a change of State affiliation to be proposed by the statute finds approval. The statute may subject different, yet not more than two proposals to the consultative referendum. If a majority votes in favour of a proposed change of State affiliation, then within two years a federal statute is to determine whether the

State affiliation will be changed in accordance with paragraph 2. If a proposal subjected to a consultative referendum receives an approval corresponding with the provisions of paragraph 3, third and fourth sentence, then within two years after the consultative referendum a federal statute regarding the creation of the proposed State is to be adopted, which does no longer require approval by referendum.

(6) A majority in a referendum and in a consultative referendum is the majority of the votes cast, if that includes at least one quarter of the population entitled to vote for the Bundestag. As for the rest, details regarding the referendum, the popular initiative and the consultative referendum are regulated by a federal statute; this statute may also provide that popular initiatives may not be repeated within a time period of five years.

(7) Further changes to the territorial shape of the States may be effected by inter-State agreements [Staatsverträge] between the affected States or by a federal statute with the consent of the Bundesrat, if the territory whose State affiliation is to be changed has no more than 50,000 inhabitants. Details are regulated by a federal statute which requires the consent of the Bundesrat and the approval of the majority of the members of the Bundestag. It must provide for a hearing of the affected municipalities and rural counties.

(8) The States may regulate a restructuring of their territory or parts of their territory, in deviation from the provisions of paragraphs 2 to 7, by inter-State agreement. The affected municipalities and rural counties are to be heard. The inter-State agreement requires approval by referendum in each participating State. If the inter-State agreement concerns parts of the territories of States, the approval may be confined to referendums in these parts of the territories; the fifth sentence, second clause, does not apply. In a referendum the majority of votes cast decides if it includes at least one quarter of the population entitled to vote for the Bundestag; details are regulated by a statute. The inter-State agreement requires the consent of the Bundestag.

Article 30. The exercise of state power and the fulfilment of state tasks is a matter for the States, in as far as this Basic Law does not stipulate or permit otherwise.

Article 31. Federal law prevails over State law.

Article 32. (1) The conduct of relations with foreign states is a matter for the Federation.
(2) Before the conclusion of a treaty which affects the special circumstances of a State, that State is to be heard.
(3) In as far as the States have legislative competence, they may conclude treaties with foreign states with the consent of the Federal Government.

Article 33. (1) Every German has the same citizenship rights and obligations in all States.
(2) Every German has, in view of his aptitude, ability and professional performance, equal access to every public office.
(3) The enjoyment of civil and political rights, the admission to public offices as well as the rights acquired in public service are independent of religious conviction. No-one may be subject to disadvantage due to his adherence or non-adherence to a conviction or world view.
(4) The exercise of sovereign powers as a permanent task is, as a rule, to be transferred to members of the public service who are in a public-law relation of service and loyalty.
(5) The law on the public service is to be regulated and developed further, taking into account the traditional principles of the professional civil service.

Article 34. If someone violates his official duties with respect to a third person in the exercise of a public office entrusted to him, then liability lies in principle with the state or with the entity in the service of which he is. In case of intent or gross negligence, individual liability for indemnity is reserved. For the right to damages and indemnity, recourse to the ordinary courts may not be excluded.

Article 35. (1) All authorities of the Federation and the States provide to each other legal and inter-administrative assistance.

(2) In order to maintain or restore public safety or order, a State may in cases of special significance request forces and facilities of the Federal Border Guard to support its police, if the police could, without such support, not fulfil a task at all or only with great difficulty. For relief in case of a natural disaster or a very serious accident, a State may request police forces of other States, forces and facilities of other administrations as well as the Federal Border Guard and the armed forces.

(3) If the natural disaster or the accident threatens the territory of more than one State, the Federal Government may, in as far as that is necessary for effective relief, give the State governments the order to make police forces available to other States, and use units of the Federal Border Guard and the armed forces to support the police forces. Measures of the Federal Government under the first sentence must at any time be lifted upon request of the Bundesrat, otherwise without delay after the removal of the threat.

Article 36. (1) In the supreme federal authorities, civil servants from all States must be employed in appropriate proportions. Persons employed in the other federal authorities should, as a rule, be drawn from the State in which they serve.

(2) Statutes regarding the military must also take into account the division of the Federation into States and their special regional attachments.

Article 37. (1) If a State does not fulfil its federal duties according to the Basic Law or another federal statute, the Federal Government may, with the consent of the Bundesrat, take the necessary measures to compel that State to fulfil its duties by way of federal enforcement [Bundeszwang].

(2) For the execution of federal enforcement, the Federal Government or its representative has the right to give instructions to all States and their authorities.

III. The Bundestag

Article 38. (1) The members of the German Bundestag are elected in general, direct, free, equal and secret-ballot elections. They are the representatives of the whole people, not bound by orders or instructions, and responsible only to their conscience.

(2) He who has attained the age of eighteen years has the right to vote; he who has reached the age at which majority begins, has the right to be elected.

(3) Details are regulated by a federal statute.

Article 39. (1) The Bundestag is elected, subject to the following provisions, for four years. Its term ends with the convention of a new Bundestag. New elections take place at the earliest forty-six, at the latest forty-eight months after the beginning of a term. In the case of a dissolution of the Bundestag, new elections take place within sixty days.

(2) The Bundestag convenes, at the latest, on the thirtieth day after elections.

(3) The Bundestag determines the end and the beginning of its sessions. The president of the Bundestag may convene it earlier. He is obliged to do so if one-third of the members, the Federal President or the Federal Chancellor so demand.

Article 40. (1) The Bundestag elects its president, his deputy and the secretaries. It adopts its rules of procedure.

(2) The president exercises proprietary and police powers in the Bundestag building. Without his permission, no search or seizure may take place on the premises of the Bundestag.

Article 41. (1) Review of elections is a matter for the Bundestag. It also decides whether a member of the Bundestag has lost his membership.

(2) Complaints against the decision of the Bundestag are admissible before the Federal Constitutional Court.

(3) Details are regulated by a federal statute.

Article 42. (1) The Bundestag deliberates in public. Upon the request of one-tenth of its members or upon request of the Federal Government, the public may be excluded by a two-thirds majority. The decision on the request takes place in a non-public session.
(2) A decision of the Bundestag requires a majority of the votes cast, in as far as this Basic Law does not provide otherwise. For the elections to be carried out by the Bundestag, the rules of procedure may allow for exceptions.
(3) Truthful reports about the public sessions of the Bundestag and its committees do not give rise to any liability.

Article 43. (1) The Bundestag and its committees may demand the presence of any member of the Federal Government.
(2) The members of the Bundesrat and the Federal Government as well as their representatives have access to all sessions of the Bundestag and its committees. They have the right to be heard at all times.

Article 44. (1) The Bundestag has the right and, upon request of one quarter of its members the obligation, to establish an investigative committee [Untersuchungsausschuss] which gathers the necessary evidence in public deliberation. The public may be excluded.
(2) The rules regarding criminal procedure are applicable mutatis mutandis to the gathering of evidence. The privacy of the correspondence, mail and telecommunications remains unaffected.
(3) Courts and administrative authorities are obliged to provide legal and inter-administrative assistance.
(4) The decisions of investigative committees are outside the scope of judicial assessment. In the consideration and qualification of the facts subject to the investigation, the courts are free.

Article 45. The Bundestag establishes a committee for the affairs of the European Union. It may authorize it to exercise the rights of the Bundestag under Article 23 with respect to the Federal Government. It may also authorize it to exercise the rights that have been accorded to the Bundestag in the treaty framework of the European Union.

Article 45a. (1) The Bundestag establishes a committee for foreign affairs and a committee for defence.
(2) The committee for defence also has the rights of an investigative committee. Upon the request of one quarter of its members it has the obligation to make a matter the subject of an investigation.
(3) Article 44 (1) does not apply to the area of defence.

Article 45b. For the protection of fundamental rights and as an auxiliary organ of the Bundestag in the exercise of parliamentary control, a commissioner for the armed forces [Wehrbeauftragter] is appointed. Details are regulated by a federal statute.

Article 45c. (1) The Bundestag establishes a petitions committee which has as its task the consideration of petitions and complaints addressed to the Bundestag under Article 17.
(2) The competences of the committee for the consideration of complaints are regulated by a federal statute.

Article 45d. (1) The Bundestag establishes a body to control the intelligence activities of the Federation.
(2) Details are regulated by a federal statute.

Article 46. (1) A member of the Bundestag may at no time be prosecuted by judicial or disciplinary means or be in any other way held liable outside the Bundestag because of his voting or because of a statement which he made in the Bundestag or in one of its committees. This does not apply to defamatory insults.

(2) A member of the Bundestag may be held liable or arrested because of a punishable act only with the permission of the Bundestag, unless he is arrested as he committed the act or on the following day.

(3) Permission of the Bundestag is furthermore required for any other limitation of the personal freedom of a member of the Bundestag or for the commencement of a procedure against a member of the Bundestag under Article 18.

(4) Any criminal procedure and any procedure under Article 18 against a member of the Bundestag, any detention and any other limitation of his personal freedom must be suspended upon demand of the Bundestag.

Article 47. The members of the Bundestag have the right to refuse to testify regarding persons who have confided information to them in their capacity as members of the Bundestag or to whom they have in that capacity confided information, as well as regarding the information itself. In as far as this right to refuse to testify applies, the seizure of written documents is not permissible.

Article 48. (1) He who runs as a candidate for a seat in the Bundestag has a right to the leave necessary for the preparation of his election.

(2) No-one may be hindered from assuming and exercising the office of a member of the Bundestag. A dismissal or discharge from employment on this ground is not permissible.

(3) The members of the Bundestag have the right to an appropriate allowance that secures their independence. They have the right to the free use of all state-run means of transport. Details are regulated by a federal statute.

Article 49. (Repealed).

IV. The Bundesrat

Article 50. Through the Bundesrat, the States participate in the legislation and administration of the Federation and in matters concerning the European Union.

Article 51. (1) The Bundesrat consists of members of the State governments, which appoint and recall them. They may be represented by other members of their governments.

(2) Each State has at least three votes; States with more than two million inhabitants have four, States with more than six million inhabitants five, States with more than seven million inhabitants six votes.

(3) Each State may send as many members as it has votes. The votes of each State may be cast only as a unit and only by members present or their alternates.

Article 52. (1) The Bundesrat elects its president for one year.

(2) The president convenes the Bundesrat. He must convene it if the representatives of at least two States or the Federal Government so demand.

(3) The Bundesrat takes its decisions with at least a majority of its votes. It adopts its rules of procedure. It deliberates in public. The public may be excluded.

(3a) For matters concerning the European Union, the Bundesrat may establish a European affairs chamber whose decisions are considered decisions of the Bundesrat; the number of votes of the States to be cast as a unit is determined by Article 51 (2).

(4) In the committees of the Bundesrat, other members or representatives of the governments of the States may be members.

Article 53. The members of the Federal Government have the right and, upon demand, the duty to participate in the deliberations of the Bundesrat and its committees. They have the right to be heard at all times. The Bundesrat is to be kept informed by the Federal Government about the conduct of affairs.

IVa. The Joint Committee

Article 53a. Two-thirds of the members of the Joint Committee [Gemeinsamer Ausschuss] comprise members of the Bundestag and one-third members of the Bundesrat. The members of the Bundestag are appointed by the Bundestag according to the relative strength of the political party groups; they may not be members of the Federal Government. Each State is represented by a member of the Bundesrat appointed by it; these members are not bound by any instructions. The establishment of the Joint Committee and its procedures are regulated by rules of procedure which are to be adopted by the Bundestag and which require the consent of the Bundesrat.
(2) The Federal Government must inform the Joint Committee about its planning for the state of defence. The rights of the Bundestag and its committees under Article 43 (1) are not affected.

V. The Federal President

Article 54. (1) The Federal President is elected without debate by the Federal Convention [Bundesversammlung].
Any German may be elected who is entitled to vote for the Bundestag and who has attained the age of forty.
(2) The term of office of the Federal President is five years. A subsequent re-election is permissible only once.
(3) The Federal Convention consists of the members of the Bundestag and an equal number of members who are elected by the parliaments of the States on the basis of proportional representation.
(4) The Federal Convention convenes, at the latest, thirty days before the expiry of the term of office of the Federal President, and in case of an early termination thirty days after that moment at the latest. It is convened by the president of the Bundestag.
(5) After the expiry of a term, the period under paragraph 4, first sentence, begins with the first convention of the Bundestag.
(6) He who has received the votes of a majority of the members of the Federal Convention is elected. If after two ballots such majority is not obtained by any candidate, then he who receives the most votes in a further ballot is elected.
(7) Details are regulated by a federal statute.

Article 55. (1) The Federal President may not be a member of the Federal Government or of a legislative body of the Federation or of a State.
(2) The Federal President may not exercise any other remunerated office, he may pursue no trade or profession and may not be a member of either the board or the supervisory board of a profit-oriented company.

Article 56. The Federal President, when assuming office, takes the following oath before the assembled members of the Bundestag and the Bundesrat:
"I swear that I shall dedicate my strength to the well-being of the German people, promote its welfare, protect it from harm, uphold and defend the Basic Law and the legislation of the Federation, fulfil my duties conscientiously, and do justice to all. So help me God."
The oath may also be taken without the religious assertion.

Article 57. The powers of the Federal President, in case he is prevented from exercising his functions or in case of an early termination of his term, are exercised by the president of the Bundesrat.

Article 58. Instructions and orders of the Federal President require for their validity the countersignature by the Federal Chancellor or the competent federal minister. This does not apply to the appointment and dismissal of the Federal Chancellor, the dissolution of the Bundestag under Article 63 and the request under Article 69 (3).

Article 59. (1) The Federal President represents the Federation under international law. He concludes, in the name of the Federation, treaties with foreign states. He accredits and receives envoys.
(2) Treaties which regulate the political relations of the Federation, or which refer to objects of federal legislation, require the consent or participation of the organs competent for such federal legislation in the form of a federal statute. For administrative agreements, the regulations regarding the federal administration apply mutatis mutandis.

Article 59a. (Repealed).

Article 60. (1) The Federal President appoints and dismisses federal judges, federal civil servants, officers and non-commissioned officers, as far as statutory regulations do not provide otherwise.
(2) He exercises, in individual cases, the right of pardon for the Federation.
(3) He may transfer these competences to other authorities.
(4) Paragraphs 2 to 4 of Article 46 apply to the Federal President mutatis mutandis.

Article 61. (1) The Bundestag or the Bundesrat may impeach the Federal President for an intentional violation of the Basic Law or another federal statute before the Federal Constitutional Court. The motion to impeach must be tabled by at least a quarter of the members of the Bundestag or a quarter of the votes of the Bundesrat. The decision to impeach requires a majority of two-thirds of the members of the Bundestag or two-thirds of the votes of the Bundesrat. The prosecution is conducted by a representative of the impeaching organ.
(2) If the Federal Constitutional Court establishes that the Federal President is guilty of having committed an intentional violation of the Basic Law or another federal statute, it may declare that he is removed from office. By interim order after impeachment it may rule that he is prevented from exercising his functions.

VI. The Federal Government

Article 62. The Federal Government consists of the Federal Chancellor [Bundeskanzler] and the federal ministers.

Article 63. (1) The Federal Chancellor is elected, on the proposal of the Federal President, by the Bundestag without debate.
(2) He who receives the votes of a majority of the members of the Bundestag is elected. The person elected is to be appointed by the Federal President.
(3) If the nominee is not elected, the Bundestag may within fourteen days after the ballot, by the votes of more than half of its members, elect a Federal Chancellor.
(4) If no election is successful within this period, a new ballot takes place without delay, in which he who receives the most votes is elected. If the person elected receives the votes of a majority of the members of the Bundestag, the Federal President must appoint him within seven days after the election. If the person elected does not receive such a majority, then within seven days the Federal President must either appoint him or dissolve the Bundestag.

Article 64. (1) The federal ministers are appointed and dismissed by the Federal President on the proposal of the Federal Chancellor.
(2) The Federal Chancellor and the federal ministers, when assuming office, take the oath as stipulated in Article 56 before the Bundestag.

Article 65. The Federal Chancellor determines the guidelines of policy and bears responsibility for that. Within these guidelines, each federal minister directs his portfolio autonomously and on his own responsibility. The Federal Government rules in case of disagreements between federal ministers. The Federal Chancellor directs its affairs according to rules of procedure as adopted by the Federal Government and approved by the Federal President.

Article 65a. (1) The federal minister of defence has the command over the armed forces.
(2) (Repealed).

Article 66. The Federal Chancellor and the federal ministers may not exercise any other remunerated office, they may pursue no trade or profession and may not be a member of either the board or, without consent of the Bundestag, the supervisory board of a profit-oriented company.

Article 67. (1) The Bundestag may express its lack of confidence in the Federal Chancellor only by electing a successor by the vote of a majority of its members and by requesting the Federal President to dismiss the Federal Chancellor. The Federal President must comply with the request and appoint the person elected.
(2) Forty-eight hours must pass between the motion and the election.

Article 68. (1) If a motion of the Federal Chancellor for a vote of confidence is not supported by the majority of the members of the Bundestag, the Federal President may, on the proposal of the Federal Chancellor, dissolve the Bundestag within twenty-one days. The right of dissolution lapses as soon as the Bundestag elects another Federal Chancellor by the vote of a majority of its members.
(2) Forty-eight hours must pass between the motion and the vote.

Article 69. (1) The Federal Chancellor appoints a federal minister as his deputy.
(2) The office of the Federal Chancellor ends in any event with the convention of a new Bundestag, the office of a federal minister ends also with any other termination of the office of the Federal Chancellor.
(3) On the request of the Federal President, the Federal Chancellor is obliged, and on the request of the Federal Chancellor or the Federal President a federal minister is obliged to continue the affairs until the appointment of a successor.

VII. The legislation of the Federation

Article 70. (1) The States have the right to legislate in as far as this Basic Law does not confer legislative power on the Federation.
(2) The delimitation of competences between the Federation and the States is guided by the provisions of this Basic Law regarding exclusive and concurrent legislation.

Article 71. In the area of exclusive legislative power of the Federation, the States have power to legislate only when and in as far as they are expressly authorized to do so by a federal statute.

Article 72. (1) In the area of concurrent legislative power, the States have power to legislate so long as and to the extent that the Federation has not exercised its legislative power through a statute.
(2) The Federation has legislative power in the areas of Article 74 (1) no. 4, 7, 11, 13, 15, 19a, 20, 22, 25 and 26 when and to the extent that the bringing about of equivalent living standards throughout the territory of the Federation or the upholding of legal or economic unity in the interest of the state as a whole require a federal statutory regulation.
(3) If the Federation has made use of its legislative competence, the States may by statute adopt regulations that deviate therefrom regarding:

1. hunting (except the law on hunting permits);
2. nature conservation and landscape management (except the general principles of nature conservation, the law on the protection of species or maritime nature conservation);
3. the distribution of land;
4. regional planning;
5. water resources (except regulations on substances and facilities);
6. admissions to higher education and higher education diplomas.

Federal statutes in these areas enter into force at the earliest six months after their publication, in as far as nothing is provided otherwise with the consent of the Bundesrat. In the areas of the first sentence, in the relation between federal law and State law the later statute prevails.

(4) A federal statute may determine that a federal statutory regulation a need for which in the sense of paragraph 2 no longer exists, may be replaced by State law.

Article 73. (1) The Federation has exclusive legislative power regarding:
1. foreign relations as well as defence including the protection of the civilian population;
2. citizenship in the Federation;
3. free movement, the passport regime, population registers and identity documents, immigration, emigration and extradition;
4. currency, the money and coinage regime, measures and weights as well as the determination of the time;
5. the unity of the customs and trade area, trade and navigation agreements, the free movement of goods and the movement of goods and capital with foreign states including customs and border protection;
5a. the protection of German cultural assets from transfers abroad;
6. air traffic;
6a. rail traffic which falls entirely or predominantly under the ownership of the Federation (the railways of the Federation), the construction, maintenance and operation of tracks of the railways of the Federation as well as the levying of charges for the use of these tracks;
7. post and telecommunications;
8. legal relations of persons in the service of the Federation and of directly federal entities of public law;
9. intellectual property, copyright and publishing law;
9a. the protection from the dangers of international terrorism by the Federal Criminal Investigations Police Office [Bundeskriminalpolizeiamt] in cases where a danger transcending State borders is at hand, where the jurisdiction of a State police authority is not apparent or where a supreme State authority requests a takeover of jurisdiction;
10. the cooperation between the Federation and the States
a. regarding criminal police investigation,
b. for the protection of the liberal democratic fundamental order, the integrity and security of the Federation or a State (domestic intelligence [Verfassungsschutz]) and
c. for the protection against attempts within the territory of the Federation which jeopardize, through the use of force or preparatory acts with such aim, the external interests of the Federal Republic of Germany,
as well as the establishment of a Federal Criminal Investigations Police Office and the international fight against crime;
11. statistics for federal purposes;
12. the law on weapons and explosives;
13. care for those disabled in war and surviving dependants of war dead, and support for former prisoners of war;
14. the production and use of nuclear energy for peaceful purposes, the establishment and operation of facilities serving these purposes, the protection against dangers arising from the release of nuclear energy or from ionizing radiation, and the disposal of radioactive material.

(2) Statutes under paragraph 1 no. 9a require the consent of the Bundesrat.

Article 74. (1) Concurrent legislative power extends to the following areas:
1. private law, criminal law, the court system, judicial procedure (except the law on the execution of detentions pending criminal investigation), the advocacy, the notary and legal advice system;
2. the civil status registry;
3. the law on associations;
4. the law on the sojourn and establishment of aliens;
5. (repealed);
6. the affairs of refugees and expellees;
7. public welfare (except the law on homes);
8. (repealed);
9. war damages and reparations;
10. war graves and the graves of other victims of war and victims of tyranny;
11. commercial law (mining, industry, energy, crafts, trade, commerce, banking and stock exchange, private insurance) except the law on the closing times for shops, on bars and restaurants, on gambling halls, on acting performance by persons, fairs, exhibitions and markets;
12. labour law including the organization of enterprises, work safety and job agency services, as well as social security including unemployment insurance;
13. the regulation of education allowances and the promotion of scientific research;
14. the law on expropriation in as far as it is relevant in the areas of Articles 73 and 74;
15. the transfer of land, natural resources and means of production into public ownership or other forms of collective concern;
16. the prevention of abuses of economically powerful positions;
17. the promotion of agricultural and forestry production (except the law on rearrangements of terrain), the securing of food supply, the import and export of agricultural and forestry products, high-seas and coastal fisheries and coastal protection;
18. the transfer of urban real estate, land law (except the law on contributions for land development) and the law on housing allowances, the law on old debt relief, the law on homebuilding premiums, the law on homebuilding for miners and miner settlement law;
19. measures against human and animal diseases that are dangerous to the public or communicable, the admission to medical and other healing professions and the healing services, as well as the law on the pharmacy system, medicines, medical products, cures, narcotics and poisons;
19a. the securing of the economic viability of hospitals and the regulation of hospital charges;
20. the law on food including the animals used for the production thereof, the law on recreational consumables, on commodities for use and on feed, as well as the safety in the trade in agricultural and forestry seeds and seedlings, the protection of plants against diseases and pests as well as animal protection;
21. high-seas and coastal shipping as well as naval signalling, inland navigation, meteorological services, shipping routes and inland waterways serving general traffic;
22. road traffic, motor transport, the construction and maintenance of country roads for long-distance traffic, as well as the levying and distribution of fees or charges for the use of public roads by vehicle;
23. railways, which are not railways of the Federation, with the exception of mountain railways;
24. waste management, air pollution control and noise abatement (except protection from behaviour-related noise);
25. state liability;

26. the medically assisted creation of human life, the analysis and artificial modification of genetic information as well as regulations concerning transplantation of organs, tissues and cells;
27. the rights and obligations deriving from the status of civil servants of States, municipalities and other public-law entities as well as judges in the States except careers, salary and support;
28. hunting;
29. nature conservation and landscape management;
30. the distribution of land;
31. regional planning;
32. water resources;
33. admissions to higher education and higher education diplomas.
(2) Statutes under paragraph 1 no. 25 and 27 require the consent of the Bundesrat.

Articles 74a and 75. (Repealed).

Article 76. (1) Bills are introduced in the Bundestag by the Federal Government, from the floor of the Bundestag, or by the Bundesrat.
(2) Bills of the Federal Government must first be transmitted to the Bundesrat. The Bundesrat is entitled to give a reaction to such bills within six weeks. If it demands for important reasons, especially with regard to the size of a bill, an extension of the period, then the period is nine weeks. The Federal Government may transmit a bill, which it has by way of exception, when transmitting it to the Bundesrat, qualified as particularly urgent, to the Bundestag after three weeks or, if the Bundesrat has made a demand pursuant to the third sentence, after six weeks, even when it has not yet received the reaction of the Bundesrat; it must in that case transmit the reaction of the Bundesrat to the Bundestag without delay. In the case of bills for an amendment of this Basic Law and for the transfer of sovereign powers pursuant to Article 23 or Article 24, the period for a reaction is nine weeks; the fourth sentence does not apply.
(3) Bills of the Bundesrat must be transmitted to the Bundestag by the Federal Government within six weeks. The Federal Government, when transmitting them, is to give a statement of its opinion. If it demands for important reasons, especially with regard to the size of a bill, an extension of the period, the period is nine weeks. If the Bundesrat has by way of exception qualified a bill as particularly urgent, the period is three weeks or, if the Federal Government has made a demand pursuant to the third sentence, six weeks. In the case of bills for an amendment of this Basic Law and for the transfer of sovereign powers pursuant to Article 23 or Article 24, the period is nine weeks; the fourth sentence does not apply. The Bundestag must deliberate and decide on the bills within a reasonable time.

Article 77. (1) Federal statutes are adopted by the Bundestag. They must, after their adoption, be transmitted to the Bundesrat by the president of the Bundestag without delay.
(2) The Bundesrat may, within three weeks after receiving an adopted bill, demand that a committee for the joint consideration of bills, composed of members of the Bundestag and of the Bundesrat, be convened. The composition and procedure of this committee is regulated by rules of procedure which are adopted by the Bundestag and which require the consent of the Bundesrat. The members of the Bundesrat sent to this committee are not bound by instructions. If a statute requires the consent of the Bundesrat, then also the Bundestag and the Federal Government may demand a convention. If the committee proposes an amendment to the adopted bill, the Bundestag must decide again.
(2a) In as far as a statute requires the consent of the Bundesrat, the Bundesrat, if a demand under paragraph 2, first sentence, is not made or the conciliation procedure is concluded without any proposals for an amendment to the adopted bill, must decide on its consent within a reasonable time.

(3) In as far as a statute does not require the consent of the Bundesrat, the Bundesrat, once the procedure under paragraph 2 is completed, may within two weeks object to a statute adopted by the Bundestag. The period for objection starts, in the case under paragraph 2, last sentence, with the receipt of the new decision adopted by the Bundestag, and in all other cases with the receipt of the statement of the chairman of the committee stipulated under paragraph 2 that the procedure before the committee has been concluded.
(4) If the objection is adopted by the majority of the votes of the Bundesrat, it may be rejected by a decision of the majority of the members of the Bundestag. If the Bundesrat has adopted the objection by a majority of at least two-thirds of its votes, then its rejection by the Bundestag requires a two-thirds majority, including at least a majority of the members of the Bundestag.

Article 78. A statute adopted by the Bundestag is successfully completed if the Bundesrat consents to it, or does not make a demand pursuant to Article 77 (2), or does not enter an objection within the period stipulated in Article 77 (3) or withdraws such objection, or if the objection is overridden by the Bundestag.

Article 79. (1) The Basic Law may be amended only by a statute which expressly amends or supplements its text. In the case of international treaties which have as their object a peace settlement, the preparation of a peace settlement or the phasing out of an occupation regime, or which are intended to serve the defence of the Federal Republic, a clarification that the provisions of the Basic Law do not preclude the conclusion and entry into force of such treaties requires only a supplement to the text of the Basic Law which is confined to such clarification.
(2) Any such statute requires the approval by two-thirds of the members of the Bundestag and two-thirds of the votes of the Bundesrat.
(3) Any amendment to this Basic Law affecting the division of the Federation into States, the participation of the States in principle in the legislative process, or the principles laid down in Articles 1 and 20, is inadmissible.

Article 80. (1) By statute, the Federal Government, a federal minister or the State governments may be authorized to adopt ordinances [Rechtsverordnungen]. In that case, the content, purpose and scope of the given authorization must be determined in the statute. The legal basis must be stated in the ordinance. If by statute it is provided that an authorization may be delegated further, then such authorization of a delegation requires an ordinance.
(2) The consent of the Bundesrat is required, save for federal statutory regulations providing otherwise, for ordinances of the Federal Government or a federal minister regarding the principles and charges for the use of the facilities of the post and telecommunications system, regarding the principles of the levying of charges for the use of the facilities of the railways of the Federation, regarding the construction and operation of railways, as well as ordinances based on federal statutes which require the consent of the Bundesrat or which are executed by the States on behalf of the Federation or as their own affairs.
(3) The Bundesrat may transmit to the Federal Government proposals for the adoption of ordinances which require its consent.
(4) In as far as State governments are authorized to adopt ordinances by federal statute or pursuant to federal statutes, the States are also competent to regulate by statute.

Article 80a. (1) If this Basic Law or a federal statute regarding defence including the protection of the civilian population provides that regulations may be applied only within the guidelines of this Article, then such application except in a state of defence is only permissible when the Bundestag has declared the beginning of a state of tension [Spannungsfall] or when it has approved such application explicitly. The declaration of a state of tension and the special approval in the cases of Article 12a (5), first sentence, and (6), second sentence, require a majority of two-thirds of votes cast.

(2) Measures pursuant to regulations under paragraph 1 must be lifted when the Bundestag so demands.

(3) By deviation from paragraph 1, the application of such regulations is permissible also on the basis and within the guidelines of a decision that is taken by an international body in the framework of an alliance treaty with the consent of the Federal Government. Measures under this paragraph must be lifted when the Bundestag by the majority of its members so demands.

Article 81. (1) If in the case of Article 68 the Bundestag is not dissolved, the Federal President may, upon request of the Federal Government with the consent of the Bundesrat, declare a legislative emergency [Gesetzgebungsnotstand] for a bill if the Bundestag rejects it although the Federal Government has qualified it as urgent. The same applies when a bill has been rejected although the Federal Chancellor had linked it to a motion under Article 68.

(2) If the Bundestag rejects the bill after the declaration of a legislative emergency again or if it adopts it in a version qualified as unacceptable by the Federal Government, then the statute is deemed adopted if the Bundesrat consents to it. The same applies when the bill has not been adopted by the Bundestag within four weeks after the new introduction.

(3) During the term of office of a Federal Chancellor, also any other bill rejected by the Bundestag may be adopted within a period of six months following the first declaration of a legislative emergency under paragraphs 1 and 2. After the period has lapsed, during the term of office of that same Federal Chancellor another declaration of a legislative emergency is not permissible.

(4) The Basic Law may be neither amended nor wholly or partly suspended or rendered inapplicable by a statute that has been adopted under paragraph 2.

Article 82. (1) Statutes completed in accordance with the provisions of this Basic Law are, after counter-signature, certified by the Federal President and published in the Federal Law Gazette [Bundesgesetzblatt]. Ordinances are certified by the organ which adopts them and are, save for other statutory regulations, published in the Federal Law Gazette.

(2) All statutes and all ordinances are to determine the day of entry into force. If such a provision is lacking, they enter into force on the fourteenth day after the end of the day when the Federal Law Gazette has been published.

VIII. The execution of federal statutes and the federal administration

Article 83. The States execute federal statutes as their own affairs in as far as this Basic Law does not otherwise provide or permit.

Article 84. (1) Where the States execute federal statutes as their own affairs, they regulate the establishment of authorities and the administrative procedure. Where federal statutes provide otherwise, the States may make adopt regulations in deviation therefrom. Where a State has adopted a deviating regulation pursuant to the second sentence, subsequent federal regulations regarding the establishment of authorities and the administrative procedure relating to this enter into force in that State at the earliest six months after their publication, in as far as nothing is provided otherwise with the consent of the Bundesrat. Article 72 (3) third sentence applies mutatis mutandis. In exceptional cases the Federation may, because of a special need for uniform federal regulation, regulate the administrative procedure without a possibility of deviation for the States. Such statutes require the consent of the Bundesrat. A federal statute may not delegate tasks to municipalities and associations of municipalities.

(2) The Federal Government may, with the consent of the Bundesrat, issue general administrative regulations.

(3) The Federal Government exercises supervision to ensure that the States execute federal statutes in accordance with applicable law. The Federal Government may, for this purpose, send agents to the highest State authorities, with their consent or, if such consent is refused, with the consent of the Bundesrat, also to subordinate authorities.

(4) Should shortcomings which the Federal Government has established in the execution of federal statutes in the States not be corrected, the Bundesrat decides, at the request of the Federal Government or the State concerned, whether the State has violated the law. The decision of the Bundesrat may be challenged before the Federal Constitutional Court.

(5) The Federal Government may, by federal statute which requires the consent of the Bundesrat, be granted authorization, for the execution of federal statutes, to issue individual instructions in particular cases. They are, unless the Federal Government considers the matter urgent, to be addressed to the highest States authorities.

Article 85. (1) Where the States execute federal statutes on behalf of the Federation, the establishment of the authorities remains the concern of the States, unless federal statutes with the consent of the Bundesrat provide otherwise. A federal statute may not delegate tasks to municipalities and associations of municipalities.

(2) The Federal Government may, with the consent of the Bundesrat, issue general administrative regulations. It may regulate the uniform training of civil servants and employees. The heads of intermediate authorities are to be appointed with its approval.

(3) The State authorities are subordinate to the instructions of the competent highest federal authorities. The instructions are, unless the Federal Government considers the matter urgent, to be addressed to the highest State authorities. Execution of the instructions is to be ensured by the highest State authorities.

(4) Federal supervision extends to the lawfulness and expediency of execution. The Federal Government may, for this purpose, require reporting and submission of files and send agents to all authorities.

Article 86. Where the Federation executes statutes by direct federal administration or by directly federal entities or institutions of public law, the Federal Government issues, to the extent that a statute does not provide details, the general administrative regulations. It regulates, unless statute provides otherwise, the establishment of the authorities.

Article 87. (1) The Foreign Service [Auswärtiger Dienst], the Federal Revenue Administration [Bundesfinanzverwaltung] and, pursuant to Article 89, the administration of the federal waterways and navigation are managed by direct federal administration with a dedicated administrative substructure. By federal statute federal border guard authorities [Bundesgrenzschutzbehörden], and central offices for police information and communications, for the criminal police and for the collection of documents for the purposes of domestic intelligence [Verfassungsschutz] and of protection against endeavours on federal territory which, through the use of force or preparatory acts thereto endanger the foreign interests of the Federal Republic of Germany, may be established.

(2) Social insurance institutions whose competence extends beyond the territory of one State are managed as directly federal entities of public law. Social insurance institutions whose competence extends beyond the territory of one State but not more than three States are managed in deviation from the first sentence as directly State entities of public law if the supervising State is determined by the States involved.

(3) In addition, for matters on which the Federation is competent to legislate, independent higher federal authorities as well as new directly federal entities and institutions of public law may be established by federal statute. Where new tasks arise for the Federation in matters on which it has the power to legislate, then in cases of urgent need federal authorities at the intermediate and lower levels may be established with the consent of the Bundesrat and of the majority of the members of the Bundestag.

Article 87a. (1) The Federation establishes armed forces for the purpose of defence. Their numerical strength and the general outline of their organization must follow from the budget.
(2) Except for defence, the armed forces may only be deployed to the extent explicitly permitted by this Basic Law.
(3) The armed forces have, in a state of defence and in a state of tension [Spannungsfall], the competence to protect civilian objects and to perform tasks of traffic control to the extent that this is required for the accomplishment of their defence mission. Furthermore, during a state of defence or a state of tension the armed forces may also be assigned to protect civilian objects so as to support police measures; in such case the armed forces cooperate with the competent authorities.
(4) In order to avert an imminent danger to the existence or liberal democratic fundamental order of the Federation or of a State, the Federal Government may, if the conditions of Article 91 (2) are fulfilled and the police forces as well as the Federal Border Guard [Bundesgrenzschutz] are not sufficient, deploy the armed forces to support the police and the Federal Border Guard in protecting civilian objects and in fighting organized and militarily armed insurgents. The deployment of the armed forces is to be discontinued if the Bundestag or the Bundesrat so demands.

Article 87b. (1) The Federal Armed Forces Administration [Bundeswehrverwaltung] is managed by direct federal administration with a dedicated administrative substructure. It performs tasks of personnel management and tasks to cover the immediate material requirements of the armed forces. Tasks related to the maintenance of injured persons or construction work may only be delegated to the Federal Armed Forces Administration by federal statute which requires the consent of the Bundesrat. The consent of the Bundesrat is furthermore required for statutes to the extent that they authorize the Federal Armed Forces Administration to interfere with the rights of third parties; this does not apply to statutes in the area of personnel management.
(2) In addition, federal statutes concerning defence, including recruitment for military service and the protection of the civilian population may, with the consent of the Bundesrat, provide that they be executed, wholly or in part, by direct federal administration with a dedicated administrative substructure or by the States on behalf of the Federation. Where such statutes are executed by the States on behalf of the Federation, they may, with the consent of the Bundesrat, provide that the powers appertaining to the Federation and the competent supreme federal authorities pursuant to Article 85 are delegated wholly or in part to higher federal authorities; in such case it may be provided that these authorities do not require the consent of the Bundesrat in issuing general administrative regulations pursuant to Article 85 (2) first sentence.

Article 87c. Statutes that are enacted pursuant to Article 73 (1) no. 14, may, with the consent of the Bundesrat, provide that they be executed by the States on behalf of the Federation.

Article 87d. (1) The air traffic administration is managed by federal administration. Tasks related to air traffic control may also be executed by foreign air traffic organizations that are authorized pursuant to European Community law. Details are regulated by a federal statute.
(2) A federal statute requiring the consent of the Bundesrat may delegate tasks relating to air traffic administration to the States as commissioned administration [Auftragsverwaltung].

Article 87e. (1) The railway transport administration for railways of the Federation is managed by direct federal administration. By federal statute tasks relating to the railway transport administration may be delegated to the States as their own affairs.
(2) The Federation discharges tasks relating to the railway transport administration extending beyond the area of the railways of the Federation that are delegated to it by federal statute.

(3) Railways of the Federation are managed as commercial enterprises established under private law. These are owned by the Federation, to the extent that the activities of the commercial enterprise comprise the construction, maintenance and the operation of railroads. The transfer of federal shares in these commercial enterprises under to the second sentence is effected pursuant to a statute; the majority of the shares remains with the Federation. Details are regulated by a federal statute.

(4) The Federation ensures that account be taken of the benefit of the general public, especially the transportation needs, in developing and maintaining the federal railroad network of the railways of the Federation as well as in their transportation services on that railroad network, to the extent that they do not concern local passenger rail services. Details are regulated by a federal statute.

(5) Statutes enacted pursuant to paragraphs 1 to 4 require the consent of the Bundesrat. The consent of the Bundesrat is furthermore required for statutes which regulate the dissolution, merger and splitting-up of railway enterprises of the Federation, the transfer of railway tracks of the railways of the Federation to third parties as well as the abandonment of railroad tracks of railways of the Federation or which affect local passenger rail services.

Article 87f. (1) Within the guidelines of a federal statute requiring the consent of the Bundesrat, the Federation ensures area-wide adequate and sufficient services in the area of post and telecommunications.

(2) Services within the meaning of paragraph 1 are provided as private commercial activities by the enterprises that emerged from the special asset German Federal Post Office [Deutsche Bundespost] and by other private providers. Sovereign tasks in the area of post and telecommunications are performed by direct federal administration.

(3) Without prejudice to paragraph 2 second sentence, the Federation, in the form of a directly federal institution of public law, performs particular tasks with respect to the enterprises that emerged from the special asset German Federal Post Office within the guidelines of a federal statute.

Article 88. The Federation establishes a currency bank and bank of issue as the Federal Bank [Bundesbank]. Its tasks and powers may, within the framework of the European Union, be transferred to the European Central Bank, which is independent and committed to the primary goal of securing price stability.

Article 89. (1) The Federation is the owner of the former Reich waterways.

(2) The Federation manages the federal waterways through its own authorities. It performs the state tasks of inland navigation extending beyond the area of a single State and the tasks of maritime navigation which are assigned to it by statute. It may assign the management of federal waterways, to the extent that they lie within the territory of one State, upon request to that State as commissioned administration. If a waterway touches the territory of several States, the Federation may commission the State which is designated by the States concerned.

(3) In the administration, development and new construction of waterways, the requirements of land and water management are to be observed in agreement with the States.

Article 90. (1) The Federation is the owner of the former Reich motorways [Reichsautobahnen] and Reich roads.

(2) The States or the self-governing entities competent under State law manage the federal motorways [Bundesautobahnen] and other federal roads for long-distance traffic on behalf of the Federation.

(3) Upon the request by a State, the Federation may place federal motorways and other federal roads for long-distance traffic, to the extent that they lie within the territory of that State, under direct federal administration.

Article 91. (1) In order to avert an imminent danger to the existence or the liberal democratic fundamental order of the Federation or of a State, a State may request the services of the police forces of other States as well as forces and institutions of other administrations and of the Federal Border Guard [Bundesgrenzschutz].
(2) If the State where such danger is imminent is not itself prepared or able to combat the danger, the Federal Government may place the police in that State and police forces of other States under its own authority and deploy units of the Federal Border Guard. The order is to be lifted after the removal of the danger and, otherwise, at any time upon the demand of the Bundesrat. Where the danger extends to the territory of more than one State, the Federal Government may, to the extent that this is necessary for the effective combating, issue instructions to the State governments; the first and second sentence remain unaffected.

VIIIa. Joint tasks

Article 91a. (1) The Federation participates in the fulfilment of the tasks of the States in the following areas, if these tasks are important for the whole and the participation of the Federation is necessary for the improvement of living standards (joint tasks):
1. improvement of regional economic structure,
2. improvement of agricultural structure and coastal protection.
(2) By federal statute with the consent of the Bundesrat, joint tasks as well as the details of coordination are determined.
(3) The Federation bears in the cases of paragraph 1 no. 1 half of the costs in each State. In the cases of paragraph 1 no. 2, the Federation bears at least half; the contribution must be fixed uniformly for all States. Details are regulated by statute. The making available of funds remains a matter for the adoption of the budgets of the Federation and the States.

Article 91b. (1) The Federation and the States may, on the basis of agreements in cases of importance that transcends regions, cooperate in the promotion of:
1. establishments and projects of scientific research outside the universities;
2. projects of science and research at universities;
3. research facilities at universities including large machines.
Agreements under the first sentence, no. 2, require the consent of all States.
(2) The Federation and the States may cooperate on the basis of agreements for the assessment of the effectiveness of the educational system in international comparison and on reports and recommendations in that matter.
(3) The allocation of the financial burden is regulated in the agreement.

Article 91c. (1) The Federation and the States may cooperate in the planning, establishment and operation of the information systems needed for the fulfilment of their tasks.
(2) The Federation and the States may on the basis of agreements establish the standards and security requirements necessary for the communication between their information systems. Agreements concerning the principles of the cooperation pursuant to the first sentence may provide for individual tasks, circumscribed with regard to their content and extent, that details enter into force for the Federation and the States with the consent of a qualified majority to be determined by the agreement. They require the consent of the Bundestag and the parliaments of the participating States; the right to terminate these agreements may not be excluded. The agreements also regulate the bearing of burdens.
(3) The States may furthermore agree on the joint operation of information systems and the establishment of dedicated institutions.
(4) The Federation establishes a connecting network in order to connect the information systems of the Federation and of the States. The details regarding the establishment and the operation of the connecting network are regulated by federal statute which requires the consent of the Bundesrat.

Article 91d. The Federation and the States may, in order to determine and promote the performance of their administrations, conduct comparative studies and publish the results.

IX. The judiciary

Article 92. Judicial power is vested in the judges; it is exercised by the Federal Constitutional Court, by the federal courts provided for in this Basic Law, and by the courts of the States.

Article 93. (1) The Federal Constitutional Court [Bundesverfassungsgericht] rules:
1. on the interpretation of this Basic Law in the event of disputes concerning the extent of the rights and duties of a supreme federal body or of other parties vested with rights of their own by this Basic Law or by the rules of procedure of a supreme federal body;
2. in the event of disagreements or doubts regarding the formal or substantive compatibility of federal law or State law with this Basic Law, or the compatibility of State law with other federal law, on application of the Federal Government, a State government or one-quarter of the members of the Bundestag;
2a. in the event of disagreements whether a statute complies with the conditions under Article 72 (2) on application of the Bundesrat, a State government or the parliament of a State;
3. in the event of disagreements regarding the rights and duties of the Federation and the States, especially as regards the execution of federal law by the States and the performance of federal supervision;
4. in other public-law disputes between the Federation and the States, between different States, or within one State, in as far as another recourse is not available;
4a. on constitutional complaints, which may be filed by any person with the allegation that one of his fundamental rights or one of his rights contained in Article 20 (4), 33, 38, 101, 103 and 104 has been violated by public authority;
4b. on constitutional complaints of municipalities or associations of municipalities based on a violation of the right to self-government pursuant to Article 28 by a statute, or by State legislation yet only in as far as no complaint may be filed with the State constitutional court;
5. in the other cases provided by this Basic Law.
(2) The Federal Constitutional Court furthermore rules on the application of the Bundesrat, a State government or the parliament of a State whether in the case of Article 72 (4) the need for a federal statutory regulation under Article 72 (2) no longer exists or whether in the cases of Article 125a (2), first sentence, federal law could no longer be adopted. The finding that the need has ceased to exist or that federal law could no longer be adopted replaces a federal statute under Article 72 (4) or Article 125a (2), second sentence. An application under the first sentence is admissible only when a bill under Article 72 (4) or Article 125a (2), second sentence, has been rejected in the Bundestag or is not deliberated and decided upon within one year or when such bill has been rejected in the Bundesrat.
(3) The Federal Constitutional Court furthermore becomes active in the other cases assigned by federal statute.

Article 94. (1) The Federal Constitutional Court is composed of federal judges and other members. Half of the members of the Federal Constitutional Court are elected by the Bundestag and half by the Bundesrat. They may not be members of the Bundestag, the Bundesrat, the Federal Government or equivalent bodies of a State.
(2) A federal statute regulates its organization and its procedures and determines in which cases its decisions have statutory force. It may make the prior exhaustion of judicial remedies a precondition for constitutional complaints and stipulate a special admissibility procedure.

Article 95. (1) For the areas of general, administrative, tax, labour and social-security jurisdiction, the Federation establishes as supreme courts the Federal Supreme Court [Bundesgerichtshof], the Federal Administrative Court, the Federal Tax Court, the Federal Labour Court and the Federal Social-Security Court.

(2) The appointment of judges at these courts is decided by the federal minister competent for the respective subject-matter together with a judicial nomination committee [Richterwahlausschuss] which is composed of the ministers from the States competent for the respective subject-matter and an equal number of members who are elected by the Bundestag.
(3) For the upholding of the unity of jurisprudence, a Joint Chamber of the courts stipulated in paragraph 1 must be established. Details are regulated by a federal statute.

Article 96. (1) The Federation may establish a federal court for intellectual property law.
(2) The Federation may establish courts of military criminal justice for the armed forces as federal courts. They may exercise criminal law jurisdiction only in a state of defence as well as over members of the armed forces who are deployed abroad or are serving on board of warships. Details are regulated by a federal statute. These courts fall within the competence of the Federal minister of justice. Their salaried judges must possess the qualifications to be a judge.
(3) The supreme court for the courts stipulated in paragraphs 1 and 2 is the Federal Supreme Court.
(4) The Federation may, for persons in a public-law service relation to it, establish federal courts to decide in disciplinary and complaint procedures.
(5) For criminal procedures in the following areas, a federal statute with the consent of the Bundesrat may provide that State courts are to exercise the jurisdiction of the Federation:
1. genocide;
2. crimes against humanity under international criminal law;
3. war crimes;
4. other acts that are capable of and are committed with the intent to disturb the peaceful coexistence of nations (Article 26 (1));
5. protection of the state.

Article 97. (1) Judges are independent and are subject only to the law.
(2) Judges who are salaried and appointed permanently may be dismissed or suspended in their function permanently or temporarily or be transferred to another post or made to retire before the expiry of their term against their will only by virtue of a judicial decision and only for reasons and in the form provided by statutes. Legislation may determine age limits upon the reaching of which judges appointed for life retire. In the context of changes to the organization of courts or their districts, judges may be transferred to another court or removed from office, yet only while preserving their full salary.

Article 98. (1) The legal position of federal judges is to be regulated by a special federal statute.
(2) If a federal judge violates, in the exercise of his office or outside, the principles of the Basic Law or the constitutional order of a State, then the Federal Constitutional Court may order by a two-thirds majority upon request of the Bundestag that the judge be transferred to a different post or be made to retire. In case of an intentional violation, dismissal may be ordered.
(3) The legal position of judges in the States is to be regulated by special State statutes, in as far as Article 74 (1) no. 27 does not provide otherwise.
(4) The States may provide that the State minister of justice decides together with a judicial nomination committee over the appointment of judges in the States.
(5) The States may, as regards State judges, provide for a regulation corresponding to paragraph 2. State constitutional law in force remains unaffected. The Federal Constitutional Court may decide over the prosecution of a judge.

Article 99. By State statute, the Federal Constitutional Court may be assigned the jurisdiction to decide in constitutional disputes within one State, and the supreme courts stipulated in

Article 95 (1) may be assigned last-instance jurisdiction to decide in cases where the application of State law is of the issue.

Article 100. (1) If a court concludes that a statute on the validity of which its decision depends is unconstitutional, then the proceedings are to be stayed, and, where a violation of the constitution of a State is of the issue, a decision is to be obtained from the State court which is competent for constitutional disputes, or, when a violation of this Basic Law is of the issue, a decision from the Federal Constitutional Court is to be obtained. The same applies where a violation of this Basic Law by State law or an incompatibility between State statute and a federal statute is of the issue.
(2) If in a judicial dispute it is doubtful whether a rule of international law is part of federal law and whether it directly creates rights and obligations for individuals (Article 25), then the court must obtain a decision from the Federal Constitutional Court.
(3) If the constitutional court of a State wishes to deviate from a decision of the Federal Constitutional Court or the constitutional court of another State in the interpretation of the Basic Law, then the constitutional court must obtain a decision from the Federal Constitutional Court.

Article 101. (1) Extraordinary tribunals are inadmissible. No-one may be deprived of his right to a lawful judge.
(2) Courts for special subject-areas may be established only by statute.

Article 102. The death penalty is abolished.

Article 103. (1) Before a court, everyone has the right to a hearing in accordance with the law.
(2) An act may be punished only when the liability to punishment was determined by statute before the act was committed.
(3) No-one may be punished several times on the basis of general criminal statutes for the same act.

Article 104. (1) The freedom of a person may be limited only pursuant to a formal statute and only in accordance with the form prescribed therein. Detained persons may not be abused either psychologically or physically.
(2) The permissibility and continuation of a deprivation of freedom is decided only by a judge. In all cases of a deprivation of freedom that are not based on a court order, a judicial decision must be obtained without delay. The police may, based on their own powers, detain no-one any longer than until the end of the day following the arrest. Details must be regulated statutorily.
(3) Everyone provisionally detained based on the suspicion of a criminal act must, at the latest on the day following the arrest, be brought before a judge who must inform him of the reasons for the arrest, question him, and give him an opportunity to object. The judge must without delay either issue a written arrest warrant stating the reasons, or order a release.
(4) A relative [Angehöriger] of the detainee or a person of his trust must be notified without delay of any judicial decision regarding the order or continuation of a deprivation of freedom.

X. The finances system

Article 104a. (1) The Federation and the States bear the costs resulting from the exercise of their tasks separately to the extent that this Basic Law does not provide otherwise.
(2) Where the States act on behalf of the Federation, the Federation bears the costs resulting therefrom.
(3) Federal statutes that confer pecuniary benefits and are executed by the States may provide that the pecuniary benefits are borne wholly or in part by the Federation. Where the statute provides that the Federation bears half of the costs or more, it is executed on behalf of the Federation.

(4) Federal statutes that establish obligations for the States to provide pecuniary benefits, benefits in kind with pecuniary value, or comparable services with respect to third parties and that are executed by the States as their own affairs or pursuant to paragraph 3, second sentence, on behalf of the Federation, require the consent of the Bundesrat, if the costs resulting therefrom are to be borne by the States.

(5) The Federation and the States bear the administrative costs arising for their administrative authorities and are liable to each other for ensuring a proper administration. Details are regulated by a federal statute which requires the consent of the Bundesrat.

(6) The Federation and the States bear the burdens of a violation of supranational or international-law obligations of Germany according to the domestic distribution of responsibilities and tasks. In cases of financial corrections of the European Union affecting several States, the Federation and the States bear these burdens at a ratio of 15 to 85. In such case the collectivity of the States bears 35 percent of the total burdens in mutual solidarity pursuant to a general key; 50 percent are borne by the States that caused the burdens, proportionate to the amount of the funds received. Details are regulated by a federal statute which requires the consent of the Bundesrat.

Article 104b. (1) The Federation may, to the extent that this Basic Law confers legislative competences upon it, grant financial aids to the States for particularly significant investments of the States and municipalities (associations of municipalities) that are required to
1. avert a disturbance of the macro-economic equilibrium or to
2. equalize diverging economic strengths in the federal territory or to
3. stimulate economic growth.

In deviation from the first sentence, the Federation may, in cases of natural disasters or exceptional emergencies that are beyond the state's control and substantially compromise the state financial situation, grant financial aids even without legislative competences.

(2) Details, particularly the kinds of investments to be supported, are regulated by federal statute which requires the consent of the Bundesrat, or pursuant to the Federal Budget Act [Bundeshaushaltsgesetz] by administrative agreement. The funds are to be granted for a limited time period and to be reviewed at regular intervals with respect to their use. The financial aids are to be administered with annual sums decreasing over time.

(3) The Bundestag, the Federal Government and the Bundesrat are, upon request, to be informed about the execution of the measures and the improvements achieved.

Article 105. (1) The Federation has exclusive legislative power regarding customs duties and fiscal monopolies.

(2) The Federation has concurrent legislative power regarding other taxes where it is entitled, wholly or in part, to the revenue generated by these taxes, or where the conditions of Article 72 (2) are met.

(2a) The States have competence to legislate regarding local consumption and expenditure taxes for as long as and to the extent that they are not equivalent to taxes regulated by federal statute. They have competence to determine the tax rate of the real estate acquisition tax.

(3) Federal statutes regarding taxes whose revenue flows wholly or in part to the States or the municipalities (associations of municipalities) require the consent of the Bundesrat.

Article 106. (1) The Federation is entitled to the yield of fiscal monopolies and to the revenue from the following taxes:
1. customs duties;
2. consumption taxes, to the extent that they are not due to the States pursuant to paragraph 2 or jointly to the Federation and the States pursuant to paragraph 3 or to the municipalities pursuant to paragraph 6;
3. the road freight transportation tax, the motor vehicle tax and other traffic taxes related to motorized transportation;

4. capital transactions taxes, the insurance tax and the exchange tax;
5. one-time levies on property and compensation levies raised for the implementation of the equalization of burdens;
6. the supplementary levy on the income tax and corporation tax;
7. levies within the framework of the European Communities.
(2) The States are entitled to the revenue from the following taxes:
1. the property tax;
2. the inheritance tax;
3. the traffic taxes to the extent that they are not due to the Federation pursuant to paragraph 1 or jointly to the Federation and the States pursuant to paragraph 3;
4. the beer tax;
5. the levies of casinos.
(3) The revenue from the income tax, the corporation tax and the turnover tax is due to the Federation and the States jointly (joint taxes) to the extent that pursuant to paragraph 5 the revenue from the income tax and pursuant to paragraph 5a the revenue from the turnover tax is not allocated with the municipalities. The revenue from the income tax and the corporation tax is shared equally between the Federation and the States. The respective shares of the Federation and the States in the revenue from the turnover tax are determined by a federal statute that requires the consent of the Bundesrat. This determination is to be based on the following principles:
1. Within the framework of current revenues, the Federation and the States have an equal claim to recover their necessary expenditures. The extent of these expenditures is to be determined with regard to multi-annual financial planning.
2. The coverage requirements of the Federation and the States are to be coordinated in such way that a fair balance is achieved, an excessive burden on the taxpayers is avoided, and uniformity of living standards throughout the federal territory is maintained.
In addition, in the determination of the respective shares of the Federation and the States in the revenue from the turnover tax, losses in tax revenue incurred by the States from 1 January 1996 because of the consideration of children in income tax law are also to be taken into account. Details are regulated by the federal statute enacted pursuant to the third sentence.
(4) The respective shares of the Federation and the States in the turnover tax is to be determined anew when the ratio between revenue and expenditure of the Federation and the States develops in a substantially different manner; losses of revenue that are additionally taken into account under paragraph 3, fifth sentence, in determining the respective shares in the turnover tax remain disregarded in that context. Where additional tasks are assigned to or revenue is withdrawn from the States by federal statute, then the additional burden may be compensated by federal grants pursuant to a federal statute which requires the consent of the Bundesrat, if it is limited to a short time period. In the statute, the principles for calculating these grants and for their distribution among the States are to be established.
(5) The municipalities receive a share in the revenue of the income tax that is to be passed on by the States to their municipalities on the basis of the income tax payments of their inhabitants. Details are regulated by a federal statute which requires the consent of the Bundesrat. It may provide that municipalities may establish rate factors [Hebesatz] for the municipalities' share.
(5a) The municipalities receive a share in the revenue of the turnover tax from 1 January 1998. It is passed on by the States on the basis of a geographical and economic key. Details are regulated by a federal statute requiring the consent of the Bundesrat.
(6) The revenue from the real property tax and the trade tax is due to the municipalities; revenue from local consumption and expenditure taxes is due to the municipalities or, in accordance with State legislation, to the associations of municipalities. Municipalities are to be granted the right to establish rate factors for the real property tax and the trade tax within the framework of the statutes. Where there are no municipalities in a State, revenue from the real

property tax and the trade tax as well as revenue from local consumption and expenditure taxes is due to the State. The Federation and the States may, by virtue of an apportionment, share in the revenue from the trade tax. Details regarding the apportionment are regulated by a federal statute which requires the consent of the Bundesrat. In accordance with State legislation, the real property tax and the trade tax as well as the municipalities' share of the revenue from the income tax and turnover tax may be taken as a calculation basis for determining apportionments.

(7) From the State' share of the total revenue from joint taxes, a percentage to be determined by State legislation flows to the municipalities and associations of municipalities collectively. For the rest, State legislation determines whether and to what extent revenues from State taxes are due to municipalities (associations of municipalities).

(8) Where the Federation arranges for special facilities in individual States or municipalities (associations of municipalities) which directly result in an increase of expenditure or a loss of revenue (special burdens) for these States or municipalities (associations of municipalities), the Federation grants the necessary compensation where and to the extent that States or municipalities (associations of municipalities) cannot reasonably be expected to bear the special burdens. Compensations from third parties and financial benefits arising for the States or municipalities (associations of municipalities) from the facilities are to be taken into account in granting the compensation.

(9) Revenues and expenditures of municipalities (associations of municipalities) are considered to be States revenues and expenditures for the purposes of this Article.

Article 106a. The States are entitled, from 1 January 1996, to a sum from the tax revenue of the Federation for local public transport. Details are regulated by a federal statute which requires the consent of the Bundesrat. The sum pursuant to the first sentence is not taken into account in the assessment of financial strength pursuant to Article 107 (2).

Article 106b. The States are entitled from 1 July 2009 to a sum from the tax revenue of the Federation in consequence of the transfer of the motor vehicle tax to the Federation. Details are regulated by a federal statute which requires the consent of the Bundesrat.

Article 107. (1) The revenue from State taxes and the States' share of revenue from the income tax and the corporation tax belongs to the individual States to the extent that the taxes are collected by tax authorities within their territories (local revenue). A federal statute which requires the consent of the Bundesrat is to make more detailed provisions for the corporation tax and the wage tax regarding the delimitation as well as the manner and scope of the disaggregation of the local revenue. The statute may also make provision for the delimitation and disaggregation of local revenue from other taxes. The States' share of revenue from the turnover tax belongs to the individual States in accordance with their population numbers; for a part, but not for more than a quarter of that States' share, a federal statute which requires the consent of the Bundesrat may provide for supplementary shares for those States whose revenue per capita from State taxes, from the income tax and the corporation tax and pursuant to Article 106b is below the average of the States; for the real estate acquisition tax, the tax capacity is to be taken into account.

(2) It is to be ensured by statute that the diverging financial strengths of the States is appropriately equalized; at this the financial strength and financial requirements of municipalities (associations of municipalities) are to be taken into account. The conditions governing equalization claims of States entitled to equalization payments as well equalization duties of States obliged to provide equalization payments as well as the criteria for determining the amounts of equalization payments are to be specified in the statute. It may also provide that the Federation provides grants from its own funds to financially weak States in order to complement the coverage of their general financial requirements (supplementary grants).

Article 108. (1) Customs duties, fiscal monopolies, consumption taxes regulated by federal legislation including the import turnover tax, as well as the motor vehicle tax and other traffic taxes related to motorized transportation from 1 July 2009 onwards and charges within the framework of the European Communities are administered by federal tax authorities. The organization of these authorities is regulated by a federal statute. Where intermediate authorities are established, their heads are appointed in consultation with the State governments.
(2) The remaining taxes are administered by State tax authorities. The organization of these authorities and the uniform training of their civil servants may be regulated by a federal statute which requires the consent of the Bundesrat. Where intermediate authorities are established, their heads are appointed in agreement with the Federal Government.
(3) Where State tax authorities administer taxes which flow wholly or in part to the Federation, they act on behalf of the Federation. Article 85 (3) and (4) applies with the proviso that the Federal Government is substituted by the Minister of Finance.
(4) A federal statute which requires the consent of the Bundesrat may provide for a collaboration in the administration of taxes between federal and State tax authorities as well as in the case of taxes under Paragraph 1 for administration by State tax authorities or in the case of other taxes for their administration by federal tax authorities if and to the extent that the execution of tax laws will thereby be substantially facilitated or improved. For the taxes flowing exclusively to the municipalities (associations of municipalities), the administration that State tax authorities are entitled to may be delegated by the States to the municipalities (associations of municipalities) wholly or in part.
(5) The procedures to be applied by federal tax authorities are regulated by a federal statute. The procedures to be applied by State tax authorities, or, as provided by the second sentence of paragraph 4, by municipalities (associations of municipalities) may be regulated by a federal statute which requires the consent of the Bundesrat.
(6) Financial jurisdiction is uniformly regulated by a federal statute.
(7) The Federal Government may issue general administrative rules, which require the consent of the Bundesrat to the extent that the administration is incumbent upon State tax authorities or municipalities (associations of municipalities).

Article 109. (1) The Federation and the States are autonomous and independent from one another in their budget management.
(2) The Federation and the States jointly fulfil the responsibilities of the Federal Republic of Germany arising from legal acts of the European Community on the basis of Article 104 of the Treaty establishing the European Community for compliance with budgetary discipline and, within this framework, take due account of the requirements of the macro-economic equilibrium.
(3) The budgets of the Federation and the States are in principle to be balanced without revenue from credits. The Federation and the States may provide regulations regarding the consideration that is symmetrical for the upturn and downturn of the effects of an economic development that is deviating from the normal situation as well as an exception for natural disasters or exceptional emergencies that are beyond the state's control and that substantially compromise the state financial situation. For the exception, a corresponding redemption regulation is to be provided. Further details for the budget of the Federation are regulated by Article 115 with the proviso that the first sentence is complied with if the revenue from credits does not exceed 0.35 percent in proportion to the nominal gross domestic product. Details for the budgets of the States are regulated by them within the framework of their constitutional competences with the proviso that the first sentence is only complied with if no revenue from credits is admitted.
(4) By federal statute which requires the consent of the Bundesrat, common principles applying to the budgetary law, to budget management in line with cyclical economic requirements and to multi-annual financial planning may be established for the Federation and the States.

(5) Sanctions imposed by the European Community in relation to the provisions of Article 104 of the Treaty establishing the European Community for compliance with budgetary discipline are borne by the Federation and the States in a ratio of 65 to 35. The collectivity of the States bears 35 percent of the burdens allocated with the States in mutual solidarity and in proportion to their population; 65 percent of the burdens allocated with to the States is borne by the States in accordance with their share of causation. Details are regulated by a federal statute which requires the consent of the Bundesrat.

Article 109a. In order to avoid budgetary emergencies, a federal statute which requires the consent of the Bundesrat regulates
1. the continuous supervision of the budget management of the Federation and the States by a common panel (stability council [Stabilitätsrat]),
2. the requirements and the procedures for determining an imminent budgetary emergency,
3. the principles for establishing and executing restructuring programmes to avoid budgetary emergencies.
The decisions of the stability council and the underlying documentation of the deliberations are to be published.

Article 110. (1) All revenues and expenditures of the Federation are to be included in the budget; for federal enterprises and special assets only allocations or withdrawals need to be included. The budget is to be balanced for revenues and expenditures.
(2) The budget is established for one or more fiscal years divided by years, in a budget statute before the beginning of the first fiscal year. Parts of the budget may apply to different periods of time, divided by fiscal years.
(3) Bills pursuant to the first sentence of paragraph 2 as well as bills to amend the budget statute and the budget are to be submitted to the Bundesrat simultaneously with their transmission to the Bundestag; the Bundesrat is entitled to give a reaction on the bills within six weeks or, in the case of amendment bills, within three weeks.
(4) The budget statute may only contain provisions relating to revenues and expenditures of the Federation and to the period for which the budget statute is enacted. The budget statute may prescribe that its provisions expire only upon publication of the next budget statute or, in the event of an authorization pursuant to Article 115, at a later date.

Article 111. (1) If, by the end of a fiscal year, the budget for the following year has not been established by a statute, the Federal Government is authorized, until its entry into force, to make all expenditures that are necessary
a. to maintain statutory institutions and to carry out statutory measures,
b. to fulfil the legal obligations of the Federation,
c. to continue constructions, acquisitions and other services, or to continue to grant benefits for these purposes, to the extent that amounts have already been approved in the budget of a previous year.
(2) To the extent that revenues not based upon specific statutes from taxes, charges or other sources or the operational capital reserves do not cover the expenditures referred to in paragraph 1, the Federal Government may mobilize the funds necessary for sustaining operational management up to a maximum of one quarter of the total amount of the previous budget by way of a credit.

Article 112. Expenditures in excess of or outside the budgetary planning require the consent of the Minister of Finance. It may only be granted in the case of an unforeseen and irrefutable necessity. Details may be regulated by a federal statute.

Article 113. (1) Statutes which increase the expenditures of the budget proposed by the Federal Government or which comprise or will bring about in the future new expenditures require the consent of the Federal Government. The same applies to statutes that comprise or

will bring about in the future decreases in revenue. The Federal Government may demand that the Bundestag suspend its decision-making on these statutes. In such case the Federal Government is to transmit a statement to the Bundestag within six weeks.
(2) The Federal Government may, within four weeks after the Bundestag has adopted this statute, demand that it make a decision again.
(3) Where the statute has become effective pursuant to Article 78, the Federal Government may withhold its consent only within six weeks and only after having initiated the procedure provided for in the third and fourth sentence of paragraph 1 or in paragraph 2. Upon the expiry of that period, consent is deemed to have been given.

Article 114. (1) The Minister of Finance is to render annually to the Bundestag and to the Bundesrat an account of all revenues and expenditures as well as of assets and debts during the following fiscal year, for the relief of the Federal Government.
(2) The Federal Court of Audit [Bundesrechnungshof] whose members enjoy judicial independence audits the account as well as the economic efficiency and regularity of the budget and operational management. It is to report annually directly to the Bundestag and to the Bundesrat in addition to the Federal Government. In all other respects, the competences of the Federal Court of Audit are regulated by federal statute.

Article 115. (1) The raising of credit and the assumption of co-signing of obligations, of guarantees or of other commitments which may lead to expenditures in future fiscal years require authorization to a quantified or quantifiable amount by a federal statute.
(2) Revenues and expenditures are in principle to be balanced without revenues from credits. This principle is complied with if the revenues from credits do not exceed 0.35 percent in proportion to the nominal gross domestic product. In addition, for an economic development that is deviating from the normal situation, the effects on the budget are to be considered symmetrically for the upturn and the downturn. Deviations in the effective raising of credit from the credit maximum permissible pursuant to the first through third sentences are registered on a control account; burdens that exceed the threshold of 1.5 percent in proportion to the nominal gross domestic product are to be reduced in line with the economic development. Details, especially the correction of revenues and expenditures for financial transactions and the procedure for calculating the maximum limit of the annual net borrowing taking into account the economic developments on the basis of a procedure for economic development correction as well as the control and the offsetting of deviations in the effective raising of credit from the maximum limit, are regulated by a federal statute. In the case of natural disasters or exceptional emergencies that are beyond the state's control and that substantially compromise the state financial situation, these maximum credit limits may be exceeded on the basis of a decision of the majority of the members of the Bundestag. The decision is to be connected with a redemption plan. The redemption of the credits raised pursuant to the sixth sentence is to take place within an adequate timeframe.

Xa. State of defence

Article 115a. (1) The finding that the territory of the Federation is being attacked by force of arms or that there is an imminent threat of such an attack (state of defence) is pronounced by the Bundestag with the consent of the Bundesrat. The finding is pronounced on request of the Federal Government and requires a majority of two-thirds of votes cast, including at least the majority of the members of the Bundestag.
(2) If the situation imperatively requires immediate action and insurmountable impediments prevent the timely convention of the Bundestag or if it does not have capacity to take decisions, then the Joint Committee pronounces the finding with a majority of two-thirds of votes cast, including a majority if its members.

(3) The finding is published by the Federal President in accordance with Article 82 in the Federal Law Gazette. If this cannot be done in time, the publication takes place in another manner; it must later be effected in the Federal Law Gazette as soon as the circumstances permit.
(4) If the territory of the Federation is being attacked by force of arms and the competent federal organs are incapable of immediately pronouncing a finding under paragraph 1, first sentence, such finding is deemed pronounced and published as from the time when the attack started. The Federal President specifies that time as soon as the circumstances permit.
(5) If the finding of a state of defence has been published and the territory of the Federation is being attacked by force of arms, the Federal President may, with the consent of the Bundestag, make declarations under international law regarding the existence of a state of defence. Under the conditions of paragraph 2, the position of the Bundestag is assumed by the Joint Committee.

Article 115b. With the publication of the state of defence, the command over the armed forces passes to the Federal Chancellor.

Article 115c. (1) The Federation has the right of concurrent legislation for the state of defence also in the matters that fall within the legislative power of the States. These statutes require the consent of the Bundesrat.
(2) To the extent that the circumstances during the state of defence so require, for the state of defence a statute may
1. in case of expropriations in deviation from Article 14 (3) second sentence, regulate the compensation provisionally,
2. regarding deprivations of freedom, provide for a time limit deviating from Article 104 (2) third sentence and (3) first sentence, at most however one of four days, for the case that a judge could not act within the time limit applied in normal times.
(3) To the extent that it is necessary for the aversion of a present or immediately threatening attack, for the state of defence by federal statute with the consent of the Bundesrat the administration and the finances system of the Federation and the States may be regulated in deviation from the sections VIII, VIIIa and X, in which case the viability of the States, municipalities and associations of municipalities, especially in a financial perspective, is to be respected.
(4) Federal statutes in the sense of Paragraph 1 and 2 no. 1 may for the purpose of the preparation of their execution already be applied before the beginning of the state of defence.

Article 115d. (1) Regarding legislation of the Federation in a state of defence, the provisions of Paragraphs 2 and 3 apply in deviation from Article 76 (2), Article 77 (1) second sentence and (2) to (4), Article 78 and Article 82 (1).
(2) Bills of the Federal Government which it has qualified as urgent are to be transmitted to the Bundesrat at the same time as their submission to the Bundestag. The Bundestag and the Bundesrat immediately deliberate on these bills jointly. In as far as the consent of the Bundesrat is required for a statute, the majority of its votes are required for the adoption of the statute. Details are regulated by rules of procedure which are adopted by the Bundestag and which require the consent of the Bundesrat.
(3) For the publication of statutes, Article 115a (3) second sentence applies mutatis mutandis.

Article 115e. (1) If the Joint Committee declares in a state of defence with a majority of two thirds of the votes cast, at least with the majority of its members, that an insurmountable impediments prevent the timely convention of the Bundestag or that it does not have capacity to take decisions, the Joint Committee has the position of Bundestag and Bundesrat and exercises their rights unitarily.

(2) By statute of the Joint Committee the Basic Law may neither be amended nor wholly or partly suspended or rendered inapplicable. The Joint Committee is not entitled to adopt statutes under Article 23 (1) second sentence, Article 24 (1) or Article 29.

Article 115f. (1) The Federal Government may, in a state of defence, in as far as the circumstances so require,
1. use the Federal Border Guard throughout the entire territory of the Federation;
2. give orders, besides to the federal administration, also to the State governments and, if it considers it to be urgent, to the State authorities and transfer this power to members of the State governments to be determined by it.
(2) The Bundestag, the Bundesrat and the Joint Committee are to be informed of the measures taken under Paragraph 1 immediately.

Article 115g. The constitutional position and the fulfilment of the constitutional tasks of the Federal Constitutional Court and its judges may not be jeopardized. The statute regarding the Federal Constitutional Court may be amended by a statute of the Joint Committee only to the extent that this is also in the opinion of the Federal Constitutional Court required in order to maintain the capacity of the Court to function. Until the adoption of such a statute the Federal Constitutional Court may take the measures necessary for maintaining the capacity of the Court to function. The Federal Constitutional Court takes decisions under the second and third sentence by majority of the judges present.

Article 115h. (1) Electoral terms of the Bundestag or the parliaments of the States expiring during a state of defence end six months after the termination of the state of defence. The term of the Federal President expiring during a state of defence as well as the exercise of his powers in case of early termination of his term by the president of the Bundesrat end nine months after the termination of the state of defence. The term of a member of the Federal Constitutional Court expiring during a state of defence ends six months after the termination of the state of defence.
(2) Where a new election of a Federal Chancellor by the Joint Committee becomes necessary, it elects a new Federal Chancellor by a majority of its members; the Federal President submits a proposal to the Joint Committee. The Joint Committee may express its lack of confidence in the Federal Chancellor only by electing a successor by the vote of two-thirds of its members.
(3) For the duration of the state of defence, a dissolution of the Bundestag is excluded.

Article 115i. (1) If the competent federal organs are incapable of taking the measures necessary for the aversion of the danger and the situation imperatively requires an immediate autonomous action in certain parts of the territory of the Federation, the State governments or authorities or representatives appointed by them are authorized to take measures in the sense of Article 115f (1) in matters within their competence.
(2) Measures under Paragraph 1 may at any time be repealed by the Federal Government, in relation to State authorities and subordinated federal authorities also by the prime ministers of the States.

Article 115k. (1) For the duration of their applicability, statutes under Articles 115c, 115e and 115g and ordinances that are adopted pursuant such statutes render conflicting law inapplicable. This does not apply to earlier law that has been adopted pursuant to Articles 115c, 115e and 115g.
(2) Statutes that the Joint Committee has adopted and ordinances that were adopted pursuant to such statutes expire at the latest six months after the termination of the state of defence.
(3) Statutes that contain rules deviating from Articles 91a, 91b, 104a, 106 and 107 apply at the latest until the end of the second fiscal year following the termination of the state of defence. They may, after the termination of the state of defence, be amended by federal statute with the consent of the Bundesrat, in order to lead over to the regime under sections VIIIa and X.

Article 115l. (1) The Bundestag may at any time with the consent of the Bundesrat repeal statutes of the Joint Committee. The Bundesrat may demand that the Bundestag decide on this matter. Other measures taken for the aversion of the danger by the Joint Committee or the Federal Government are to be lifted when the Bundestag and the Bundesrat so decide.

(2) The Bundestag may at any time with the consent of the Bundesrat, by a decision which is to be published by the Federal President, declare the state of defence terminated. The Bundesrat may demand that the Bundestag decide on this matter. The state of defence is to be declared terminated immediately when the conditions for its declaration are no longer present.

(3) The conclusion of peace is decided by federal statute.

XI. Transitional and final provisions

Article 116. (1) German within the meaning of this Basic Law is, subject to other statutory provisions, he who has the German citizenship or who, as a refugee or expellee of German ethnicity or as his spouse or descendant found admittance to the territory of the German Reich as it existed on 31 December 1937.

(2) Former German citizens, who, between 30 January 1933 and 8 May 1945, had their citizenship revoked for political, racial or religious reasons, and their descendants, are, on application, to be renaturalized. They are considered as not denaturalized if they, after 8 May 1945, took up residence in Germany and have not expressed a contrary intention.

Article 117. (1) Law contrary to Article 3 (2) remains in force until its adaptation to that provision of the Basic Law, but not for longer than until 31 March 1953.

(2) Statutes which limit the right to freedom of movement due to the current shortage of living space remain in force until their repeal by federal statute.

Article 118. The reorganization in the territories comprising the States of Baden, Württemberg-Baden and Württemberg-Hohenzollern may be effected, in derogation from the provisions of Article 29, by agreement between the States concerned. If no agreement is reached, the reorganization will be regulated by federal statute which must provide for a consultative referendum.

Article 118a. The reorganization in the territory comprising the States of Berlin and Brandenburg may be effected, in derogation from the provisions of Article 29, by agreement, with the participation of their eligible voters, between the States concerned..

Article 119. In matters relating to refugees and expellees, in particular as regards their distribution among the States, the federal government, until the adoption of a settlement by federal statute, may, with the consent of the Bundesrat, issue ordinances having the force of statute. For special cases, the federal government may be authorized to issue individual instructions. These instructions are, unless in case of an imminent danger, to be addressed to the highest States authorities.

Article 120. (1) The Federation bears the expenses for occupation costs and other internal and external burdens resulting from the war, in accordance with the more detailed federal statutes. To the extent that these burdens resulting from the war have been regulated by federal statutes by 1 October 1969, the Federation and the States bear such expenses in the proportion established by such federal statutes. To the extent that expenditures for burdens resulting from the war which neither have been nor are regulated by federal statutes have been assumed by 1 October 1965 by the States, municipalities (associations of municipalities) or other agencies performing functions of the States or municipalities, the Federation is not obliged to assume expenditures of this nature even after that date. The Federation bears the supplementary contributions towards the expenses of social security, including unemployment insurance and unemployment assistance. The distribution of burdens resulting from the

war between the Federation and the States regulated by this paragraph does not affect the statutory regulation of compensation claims for effects of the war.
(2) Revenues pass to the Federation at the same time as it takes over the expenditures.

Article 120a. (1) The statutes concerning the implementation of the equalization of burdens may, with the consent of the Bundesrat, stipulate that in the field of equalization payments they will be executed partly by the Federation and partly by the States on behalf of the Federation and that the powers appertaining to the federal government and the competent highest federal authorities pursuant to Article 85 are delegated to the Federal Equalization of Burdens Office [Bundesausgleichsamt]. The Federal Equalization of Burdens Office does not require the consent of the Bundesrat in the exercise of these competences; its instructions are, except in cases of urgency, to be directed to the highest States authorities (State equalization of burdens offices).
(2) Article 87 (3), second sentence, remains unaffected.

Article 121. A majority of the members of the Bundestag and the Federal Convention within the meaning of this Basic Law is the majority of their statutory number.

Article 122. (1) From the convention of the Bundestag onwards, statutes are exclusively enacted by the legislative bodies recognized by this Basic Law.
(2) Legislative bodies and entities participating in the legislative process in an advisory capacity whose competence expires pursuant to paragraph 1 are dissolved from that moment.

Article 123. (1) Law predating the convention of the Bundestag remains in force to the extent that it does not conflict with the Basic Law.
(2) Treaties concluded by the German Reich, which pursuant to this Basic Law concern matters falling within the competence of State legislation, if under general principles of law they are and continue to be valid, remain in force, subject to all rights and objections of the parties, until new treaties are concluded by the authorities competent pursuant to this Basic Law or until their termination is otherwise effected by virtue of provisions contained in them.

Article 124. Law concerning matters falling within the exclusive legislative competence of the Federation becomes federal law within its scope of application.

Article 125. Law concerning matters falling within concurrent legislative powers of the Federation becomes federal law within its scope of application,
1. insofar as it applies uniformly within one or more occupation zones,
2. insofar as it is law by which after 8 May 1945 former Reich law has been amended.

Article 125a. (1) Law which has been enacted as federal law, but due to the amendment of Article 74 (1), the insertion of Article 84 (1) seventh sentence, Article 85 (1) second sentence or Article 105 (2a) second sentence or due to the repeal of Articles 74a, 75 or 98 (3) second sentence could no longer be enacted as federal law remains in force as federal law. It may be replaced by State law.
(2) Law which has been enacted pursuant to Article 72 (2) in the version applicable until 15 November 1994, but which due to the amendment of Article 72 (2) could no longer be enacted as federal law, remains in force as federal law. By federal statute it may be stipulated that it may be replaced by State law.
(3) Law which has been enacted as State law but due to the amendment of Article 73 could no longer be enacted as State law remains in force as State law. It may be replaced by federal law.

Article 125b. (1) Law which has been enacted pursuant to Article 75 in the version applicable until 1 September 2006 and which also after this date could be enacted as federal law, remains in force. Competences and obligations of the States to legislate remain in place in that respect. With respect to the areas mentioned in Article 72 (3) first sentence, the States may adopt

regulations in deviation from this law; in the areas of Article 72 (3) first sentence, nos. 2, 5 and 6 however only when and to the extent that the Federation has exercised its legislative powers after 1 September 2006, in the cases of numbers 2 and 5 from 1 January 2010 at the latest, in the case of number 6 from 1 August 2008 at the latest.
(2) The States may adopt regulations in deviation from federal legal provisions that have been enacted pursuant to Article 84 (1) in the version applicable until 1 September 2006, they may adopt regulations in deviation from regulations regarding administrative procedure until 31 December 2008 however only if after 1 September 2006 regulations regarding administrative procedure have been amended in the relevant federal statute.

Article 125c. (1) Law which has been enacted pursuant to Article 91a (2) in conjunction with paragraph 1 no. 1 in the version applicable until 1 September 2006 remains in force until 31 December 2006.
(2) The legal provisions in the areas of municipal traffic financing and promotion of social housing created pursuant to Article 104a (4) in the version applicable until 1 September 2006 remain in force until 31 December 2006. The legal provisions created for special programmes pursuant to § 6 (1) of the Municipal Traffic Financing Act [Gemeindeverkehrsfinanzierungsgesetz] in the area of municipal traffic financing as well as the other legal provisions created pursuant to Article 104a (4) in the version applicable until 1 September 2006 remain in force until 31 December 2019, unless a prior date is or will be set for expiry.

Article 126. Disagreements about the continuance of law as federal law are resolved by the Federal Constitutional Court.

Article 127. The federal government may, with the consent of the governments of the States concerned, within one year after the promulgation of this Basic Law, enact law of the Bizone administration [Vereinigtes Wirtschaftsgebiet], to the extent that it remains in force as federal law under Article 124 or 125, in the States of Baden, Greater Berlin, Rhineland-Palatinate and Württemberg-Hohenzollern..

Article 128. To the extent that law remaining in force provides for powers to issue instructions within the meaning of Article 84 (5), they remain in force until statutory regulation provides otherwise.

Article 129. (1) To the extent that legal provisions that remain in force as federal law contain an authorization to enact ordinances or general administrative regulations or to issue administrative acts, it passes to the authorities henceforth competent in the subject matter. In cases of doubt, the federal government decides in agreement with the Bundesrat; the decision is to be published.
(2) To the extent that legal provisions that remain in force as State law contain such an authorization, it is exercised by the authorities competent under State law.
(3) To the extent that legal provisions within the meaning of paragraphs 1 and 2 authorize their amendment or supplementation or the enactment of legal provisions in the place of statutes, such authorization is expired.
(4) The provisions of paragraphs 1 and 2 apply mutatis mutandis where legal provisions refer to provisions no longer in force or to institutions no longer existent.

Article 130. (1) Administrative bodies and other institutions serving the public administration or the administration of justice that are not based on State law or agreements between States as well as the administration of the South West German Railways and the administrative board for postal and telecommunications services for the French occupation zone are subordinate to the federal government. The latter regulates with the consent of the Bundesrat their transfer, dissolution or liquidation.

(2) The supreme disciplinary superior of the members of these administrations and institutions is the competent federal minister.
(3) Institutions and entities under public law not directly subordinate to a State and not based on agreements between the States are under the supervision of the competent supreme federal authority.

Article 131. The legal relationships of persons including refugees and expellees who on 8 May 1945 were employed in the public service, who have left it for reasons related to other than to civil servant or labour agreement law and who have not yet been employed or not in a position corresponding to their former one, are to be regulated by federal statute. The same applies mutatis mutandis to persons including refugees and expellees who on 8 May 1945 were entitled to support and who for reasons related to other than to civil servant or labour agreement law no longer receive support or equivalent support. Until the entry into force of the federal statute, no legal entitlements may be claimed save for other regulations under State law.

Article 132. (1) Civil servants and judges who, on the moment of the entry into force of this Basic Law, are appointed for life, may within six months after the first convention of the Bundestag be retired, suspended or transferred to an office with a lower salary if they lack the personal or professional aptitude required for their office. This provision applies mutatis mutandis to employees with a non-terminable employment. In the case of employees whose employment can be terminated, periods of notice exceeding those set by labour agreement may be terminated within the same time period.
(2) This provision does not apply to members of the public service who are not affected by the provisions regarding the "Liberation from National Socialism and Militarism" or who are recognized victims of National Socialism, unless an important personal ground obtains.
(3) Those affected may have recourse to the courts pursuant to Article 19 (4).
(4) Details are regulated by an ordinance of the federal government which requires the consent of the Bundesrat.

Article 133. The Federation succeeds to the rights and obligations of the Bizone administration [Vereinigtes Wirtschaftsgebiet].

Article 134. (1) The assets of the Reich in principle become federal assets.
(2) To the extent that they were, pursuant to their originally intended use, to be used principally for administrative tasks which pursuant to this Basic Law are not administrative tasks of the Federation, they are to be transferred free of charge to the authorities now competent and, to the extent that they, pursuant to their current and not merely temporary use, serve for administrative tasks that pursuant to this Basic Law are now to be performed by the States, they are to be transferred to the States. The Federation may also transfer other assets to the States.
(3) Assets that were placed at the disposal of the Reich free of charge by States and municipalities (associations of municipalities) become assets of the States and municipalities (associations of municipalities) again, to the extent that the Federation does not require them for its own administrative tasks.
(4) Details are regulated by a federal statute which requires the consent of the Bundesrat.

Article 135. (1) If after 8 May 1945 and before the entry into force of this Basic Law the affiliation of a territory to a State has changed, then the State to which the territory now belongs is entitled to the assets of the State to which it previously belonged that are located in that territory.
(2) The assets of no longer existing States and other entities and institutions under public law, to the extent that, pursuant to their originally intended use, they were to be used principally for administrative tasks or, pursuant to their current and not merely temporary use, serve

principally administrative tasks, pass to the State or entity or institution under public law that now performs these tasks.

(3) Land property of no longer existing States including appurtenances pass to the State within which it is located to the extent that it is not already included among the assets within the meaning of paragraph 1.

(4) To the extent that an overriding interest of the Federation or the particular interest of a territory so requires, arrangements deviating from the provisions of paragraphs 1 to 3 of this Article may be adopted by federal statute.

(5) In all other respects, the succession and disposition of assets, to the extent that it has not been resolved by 1 January 1952 by agreement between the States or entities or institutions under public law concerned, is regulated by a federal statute which requires the consent of the Bundesrat.

(6) Holdings of the former State of Prussia in private-law enterprises pass to the Federation. Details are regulated by a federal statute which may also deviate from this provision.

(7) To the extent that assets which would fall to a State or entity or institution under public law pursuant to paragraphs 1 to 3 had been used by the beneficiary by a State statute, pursuant to a State statute or in any other manner at the entry into force of this Basic Law, the transfer of assets is considered to have taken place before the use.

Article 135a. (1) By federal legislation reserved pursuant to Article 134 (4) and Article 135 (5) it may be provided that the following do not have to be fulfilled or do not have to be fulfilled in full:

1. liabilities of the Reich as well as liabilities of the former State of Prussia and other no longer existing entities and institutions under public law,

2. liabilities of the Federation or other entities or institutions under public law which are related to the passing of assets pursuant to Article 89, 90, 134 and 135 and liabilities of these legal bodies that are based on measures taken by the legal bodies designated under subparagraph 1,

3. liabilities of the States and municipalities (associations of municipalities) which have arisen from measures which these legal bodies have taken before 1 August 1945 in order to implement orders of the occupying powers or to remedy a state of emergency resulting from the war within the framework of the administrative tasks incumbent upon or delegated by the Reich.

(2) Paragraph 1 applies mutatis mutandis to liabilities of the German Democratic Republic or its legal bodies as well as to liabilities of the Federation or other entities or institutions under public law which are related to the passing of assets of the German Democratic Republic to the Federation, States and municipalities, and to liabilities arising from measures of the German Democratic Republic or its legal bodies.

Article 136. (1) The Bundesrat convenes for the first time on the day of the first convention of the Bundestag.

(2) Until the election of the first Federal President, his competences are exercised by the president of the Bundesrat. He does not have the right to dissolve the Bundestag.

Article 137. (1) The right of civil servants, employees in the public service, professional soldiers, temporary volunteer soldiers and judges to run in elections in the Federation, in the States and the municipalities may be restricted by statute.

(2) The electoral law to be adopted by the Parliamentary Council [Parlamentarischer Rat] applies to the election of the first Bundestag, the first Federal Convention and the first Federal President of the Federal Republic.

(3) The competence of the Federal Constitutional Court pursuant to Article 42 (2) is, until its establishment, exercised by the German High Court for the Bizone [Deutsches Obergericht für

das Vereinigte Wirtschaftsgebiet] which decides in accordance with its own rules of procedure.

Article 138. Changes to the constitutions of the profession of notary public as it now exists in the States of Baden, Bavaria, Württemberg-Baden and Württemberg-Hohenzollern require the consent of the governments of these States.

Article 139. The legal provisions enacted for the "Liberation of the German People from National Socialism and Militarism" [Befreiung des deutschen Volkes vom Nationalsozialismus und Militarismus] are not affected by the provisions of this Basic Law.

Article 140. The provisions of Articles 136, 137, 138, 139 and 141 of the German Constitution of 11 August 1919 are part of this Basic Law.

Article 141. Article 7 (3) first sentence does not apply in any State where State law providing otherwise was in force on 1 January 1949.

Article 142. Notwithstanding the provision of Article 31, provisions of State constitutions remain in force to the extent that they guarantee fundamental rights in conformity with Articles 1 to 18 of this Basic Law.

Article 142a. (Repealed).

Article 143. (1) Law in the territory specified in Article 3 of the Unification Treaty [Einigungsvertrag] may deviate from the provisions of this Basic Law at the latest until 31 December 1992, to the extent and so long as, due to the differing circumstances, a complete adaptation to the order of the Basic Law cannot be achieved yet. Deviations may not violate Article 19 (2) and must be compatible with the principles stipulated in Article 79 (3).
(2) Deviations from Titles II, VIII, VIIIa, IX, X and XI are permissible at the latest until 31 December 1995.
(3) Notwithstanding paragraphs 1 and 2, Article 41 of the Unification Treaty and provisions for its implementation remain in force to the extent that they provide that interference with property in the territory specified in Article 3 of that Treaty cannot be reversed.

Article 143a. (1) The Federation has exclusive legislative competence in all matters arising from the transformation of the federal railways administered by the Federation into commercial enterprises. Article 87e (5) applies mutatis mutandis. Civil servants of the federal railways may be assigned by statute, without prejudice to their legal status or the responsibility of the employer, to provide services for railways of the Federation organized under private law.
(2) The Federation executes statutes enacted pursuant to paragraph 1.
(3) The performance of the tasks relating to local public railway transport of the former federal railways is the responsibility of the Federation until 31 December 1995. The same applies to the corresponding tasks of the Rail Transport Administration [Eisenbahnverkehrsverwaltung]. Details are regulated by a federal statute that requires the consent of the Bundesrat.

Article 143b. (1) The special assets of the German Federal Post Office [Deutsche Bundespost] is transformed into private-law enterprises pursuant to a federal statute. The Federation has exclusive legislative competence in all matters arising herefrom.
(2) The exclusive rights of the Federation existing before the transformation may be conferred by a federal statute for a transitional period on the enterprises that succeed the postal service of the German Federal Post Office [Deutsche Bundespost Postdienst] and the telecommunications service of the German Federal Post Office [Deutsche Bundespost Telekom]. The majority interest in the enterprise that succeeds the postal service of the German Federal Post Office

may be surrendered by the Federation at the earliest five years after the entry into force of the statute. To do so requires a federal statute with the consent of the Bundesrat.

(3) The federal civil servants employed by the German Federal Post Office are employed by the private enterprises without prejudice to their legal status and the responsibility of their employer. The enterprises exercise employer's authority. Details are regulated by a federal statute.

Article 143c. (1) The States are entitled from 1 January 2007 until 31 December 2019 to receive amounts out of the federal budget annually for the discontinuation of the Federation's share in financing due to the abolition of the joint tasks of upgrading and constructing universities including university hospitals and educational guidance and due to the abolition of financial aid for the improvement of the traffic situation of the municipalities and for social housing subsidies. Until 31 December 2013, these amounts are calculated on the basis of the average financing shares of the Federation in the 2000 to 2008 frame of reference.

(2) The amounts are, until 31 December 2013, distributed among the States as follows:
1. as annual fixed amounts whose height is calculated on the basis of the average share of each State over the time period of 2000 to 2003;
2. for a specific purpose of the responsibilities under the previous mixed financing.

(3) The Federation and the States review until the end of 2013 to what extent the financing means the States have been assigned under paragraph 1 are still suitable and necessary for the performance of the States' tasks. From 1 January 2014 onwards, the purpose-bound appropriation designated in paragraph 2 (2) of the financing means assigned pursuant to paragraph 1 will lapse; the investment-related appropriation of the median volume remains valid. The agreements from the Second Solidarity Agreement [Solidarpakt II] remain unaffected.

(4) Details are regulated by a federal statute that requires the consent of the Bundesrat.

Article 143d. (1) Articles 109 and 115 in the version applicable until 31 July 2009 are to be applied for the last time to the 2010 fiscal year. Articles 109 and 115 in the version applicable as from 1 August 2009 are to be applied for the first time to the 2011 fiscal year; credit authorizations existing on 31 December 2010 for special assets [Sondervermögen] already established remain unaffected. The States may, in the period from 1 January 2011 to 31 December 2019, deviate from the target of Article 109 (3) in accordance with the applicable provisions of State law. The States' budgets are to be shaped in such way that in the 2020 fiscal year the target under Article 109 (3) fifth sentence is met. The Federation may, in the time period from 1 January 2011 to 31 December 2015 deviate from the target of Article 115 (2) second sentence. The reduction of the existing deficit shall begin in the 2011 fiscal year. The annual budgets are to be shaped in such way that in the 2016 fiscal year the target under Article 115 (2) second sentence is met; details are regulated by a federal statute.

(2) As an aid for compliance with the target under Article 109 (3) from 1 January 2020 onwards, the States of Berlin, Bremen, Saarland, Saxony-Anhalt and Schleswig-Holstein may be granted a total of 800 million Euros in consolidation aids per year out of the federal budget for the time period of 2011 to 2019. Thereof, 300 million Euros are allotted to Bremen, 260 million Euros to Saarland, and 80 million Euros each to Berlin, Saxony-Anhalt and Schleswig-Holstein. The aids are provided on the basis of an administrative agreement pursuant to a federal statute with the consent of the Bundesrat. The granting of aids presupposes a complete clearing of the financing deficits by the end of 2020. Details, in particular the annual stages of reduction of the financing deficit, the supervision of the reduction of the financing deficits by the Stability Council [Stabilitätsrat] as well as consequences in case of non-compliance with the stages of reduction are regulated by a federal statute with the consent of the Bundesrat and an administrative agreement. A simultaneous granting of consolidation aids and stabilization aids due to an extreme budgetary emergency is excluded.

(3) The financing burden resulting from the granting of consolidation aids is distributed in equal parts between the Federation and the States, in the case of the latter from their share of the turnover tax. Details are regulated by a federal statute with the consent of the Bundesrat.

Article 144. (1) This Basic Law requires ratification by the representative assemblies in two thirds of the States in which it is to apply initially.
(2) To the extent that the application of this Basic Law is subject to restrictions in one of the States listed in Article 23 or in a part of these States, that State or that part of the State has the right to send representatives to the Bundestag pursuant to Article 38 and to the Bundesrat pursuant to Article 50.

Article 145. (1) The Parliamentary Council [Parlamentarischer Rat], with the participation of the representatives of Greater Berlin, declares the adoption of this Basic Law in public session, promulgates and publishes it.
(2) This Basic Law enters into force at the end of the day on which it is published.
(3) It is to be published in the Federal Law Gazette [Bundesgesetzblatt].

Article 146. This Basic Law, which since the completion of the unity and freedom of Germany applies to the entire German people, shall cease to apply on the day on which a constitution enters into force which has been freely adopted by the German people.

Annex 9

THE CHARTER FOR THE KINGDOM OF THE NETHERLANDS

Charter for the Kingdom of the Netherlands [Statuut voor het Koninkrijk der Nederlanden] of 28 October 1954 as last amended by Kingdom Statute of 7 September 2010 (*Stb.* 333).[1]

Preamble

The Netherlands, Aruba, Curacao and Saint Martin,

noting that the Netherlands, Suriname and the Netherlands Antilles in 1954 have declared by free will to accept a new legal order in the Kingdom of the Netherlands, in which they conduct their own interests autonomously and pursue their common interests on a basis of equality and accord each other assistance, and have resolved in mutual consultation to adopt the Charter for the Kingdom;

noting that the connection with Surinam under the Charter has come to an end as per 25 November 1975 by virtue of an amendment of the Charter by Kingdom Statute of 22 November 1975, *Stb.* 617, PbNA 233;

noting that Aruba has declared by free will to accept this legal order as a country as per 1 January 1986 for a period of ten years and as per 1 January 1996 for an indefinite period;

considering that Curacao and Saint Martin have both declared by free will to accept this legal order as countries;

have resolved in mutual consultation to adopt the Charter for the Kingdom as follows.

---

[1] Translation by Ph. Kiiver. This text has also been published separately in: Ph. Kiiver & N. Kornet, eds., *The Maastricht Collection: Selected National, European and International Provisions from Public and Private Law*, Second Edition (Groningen: Europa Law Publishing, 2010). It has also been published in a smaller compilation covering only the area of constitutional law: Ph. Kiiver, ed., *Sources of Constitutional Law: Constitutions and Fundamental Legal Provisions from the United States, France, Germany, the Netherlands, the United Kingdom, the ECHR and the EU*, Second Edition (Groningen: Europa Law Publishing, 2010). In both cases the updates resulting from the 2010 reform, as they are included here, will be incorporated in the respective third edition.

§ 1. General provisions

Article 1. (1) The Kingdom comprises the countries of the Netherlands, Aruba, Curacao and Saint Martin.
(2) Bonaire, Saint Eustatius and Saba each form part of the state order of the Netherlands. For these islands regulations may be adopted and other specific measures may be taken on account of the economic and social circumstances, the large distance from the European part of the Netherlands, their island character, small territory and population size, geographical circumstances, the climate and other factors by which these islands significantly differ from the European part of the Netherlands.

Article 1a. The crown of the Kingdom is held by inheritance by Her Majesty Queen Juliana, Princess of Orange-Nassau, and, by succession, by her lawful successors.

Article 2. (1) The King heads the government of the Kingdom and of each of the countries. He is inviolable, the ministers are responsible.
(2) The King is represented in Aruba, Curacao and Saint Martin by the Governor [Gouverneur]. The competences, duties and responsibility of the Governor as representative of the government of the Kingdom are regulated by Kingdom Statute [rijkswet] or, where applicable, by Kingdom Ordinance [algemene maatregel van rijksbestuur].
(3) Kingdom Statute regulates that which relates to the appointment and the dismissal of the Governor. The appointment and the dismissal are effected by the King as head of the Kingdom.

Article 3. (1) Notwithstanding what is provided elsewhere in the Charter, matters for the Kingdom are:
a. the maintenance of the independence and the defence of the Kingdom;
b. foreign relations;
c. Dutch citizenship;
d. the regulation of chivalric orders as well as the flag and the coat of arms of the Kingdom;
e. the regulation of the nationality of vessels and the laying down of conditions regarding the safety and navigation of seagoing vessels which fly the flag of the Kingdom, except sailing vessels;
f. oversight over the general rules regarding the admission and expulsion of Dutch citizens;
g. the laying down of general conditions for the admission and expulsion of aliens;
h. extradition.
(2) Other matters may in mutual consultation be declared to be matters for the Kingdom. In that context, Article 55 applies mutatis mutandis.

Article 4. (1) Royal authority is exercised in matters for the Kingdom by the King as head of the Kingdom.
(2) Legislative authority is exercised in matters for the Kingdom by the legislator of the Kingdom. In cases of bills for Kingdom Statutes, consideration takes place with due regard to Articles 15 to 21.

Article 5. (1) The monarchy and the succession to the throne, the organs of the Kingdom referred to in the Charter, the exercise of royal and legislative authority in matters for the Kingdom are regulated, in as far as that is not provided for by the Charter, by the Constitution [Grondwet] for the Kingdom.
(2) The Constitution respects the provisions of the Charter.
(3) To a proposal for an amendment of the Constitution containing provisions regarding matters for the Kingdom, as well as to bills stating that there is reason to consider such a proposal, Articles 15 to 20 apply.

§ 2. The conduct of matters for the Kingdom

Article 6. (1) The matters for the Kingdom are conducted in cooperation between the Netherlands, Aruba, Curacao and Saint Martin in accordance with the following provisions.
(2) During the conduct of these matters, organs of the countries are involved where possible.

Article 7. The council of ministers of the Kingdom is composed of the ministers appointed by the King and the Minister Plenipotentiary [Gevolmachtigde Minister] appointed by the government of Aruba, Curacao and Saint Martin, respectively.

Article 8. (1) The Ministers Plenipotentiary act on behalf of the governments of their country, which appoint and dismiss them. They must be Dutch citizens.
(2) The government of the country involved determines who replaces the Minister Plenipotentiary in case of his being hindered or absent. That which is provided in this Charter regarding the Minister Plenipotentiary applies mutatis mutandis with respect to his substitute.

Article 9. (1) The Minister Plenipotentiary, before assuming his office, takes an oath or makes a promise of allegiance to the King and the Charter before the Governor. The formula for the oath or promise is established by Kingdom Ordinance.
(2) When in the Netherlands, the Minister Plenipotentiary takes the oath or makes the promise before the King.

Article 10. (1) The Minister Plenipotentiary participates in the deliberations in the meetings of the council of ministers and of the permanent bodies and special commissions of the council regarding matters for the Kingdom which affect the country in question.
(2) The governments of Aruba, Curacao and Saint Martin each have the right – if a certain subject-matter calls for such action – to also let a minister with an advisory vote participate next to the Minister Plenipotentiary in the deliberations stipulated in the preceding paragraph.

Article 11. (1) Proposals for an amendment of the Constitution containing provisions regarding matters for the Kingdom affect Aruba, Curacao and Saint Martin.
(2) As regards defence, it is assumed that the defence of the territory of Aruba, Curacao or Saint Martin, as well as agreements or understandings regarding an area that belongs to their sphere of interests, affect Aruba, Curacao and Saint Martin, respectively.
(3) As regards foreign affairs, it is assumed that foreign affairs where the interests of Aruba, Curacao or Saint Martin are involved, or where the conduct thereof can have serious consequences for these interests, affect Aruba, Curacao and Saint Martin, respectively.
(4) The determination of the contribution to the costs referred to in Article 35 affects Aruba, Curacao and Saint Martin, respectively.
(5) Proposals for naturalization are only considered to affect Aruba, Curacao and Saint Martin if persons are concerned who reside in the country in question.
(6) The governments of Aruba, Curacao and Saint Martin may state which matters for the Kingdom other than those stipulated in the first to fourth paragraph affect their country.

Article 12. (1) If the Minister Plenipotentiary of Aruba, Curacao or Saint Martin, indicating his reasons based on which he expects serious detriment to his country, has declared that his country should not be bound by a proposed instrument containing generally binding regulations, such instrument may not be adopted in a way that it applies in the country in question, unless this would be incompatible with the ties of the country within the Kingdom.
(2) If the Minister Plenipotentiary of Aruba, Curacao or Saint Martin has serious objections to the initial opinion of the council of ministers regarding the requirement of binding nature as stipulated in the first paragraph, or regarding any other matter in the consideration of which he has participated, then upon his request deliberations are continued, if necessary with due regard to a time limit to be determined by the council of ministers.

(3) The deliberations referred to above are conducted between the prime-minister, two ministers, the Minister Plenipotentiary and a minister or special plenipotentiary to be nominated by the government involved.
(4) If several Ministers Plenipotentiary wish to participate in continued deliberations, then these deliberations are conducted between these Ministers Plenipotentiary, an equal number of ministers and the prime-minister. The second paragraph of Article 10 applies mutatis mutandis.
(5) The council of ministers decides in accordance with the result of the continued deliberations. If the opportunity for continued deliberations has not been seized within the specified time limit, then the council of ministers takes its decision.

Article 12a. By Kingdom Statute provisions are adopted for the treatment of such disputes as stipulated by Kingdom Statute between the Kingdom and the countries.

Article 13. (1) There is a Council of State of the Kingdom [Raad van State van het Koninkrijk].
(2) If the government of Aruba, Curacao or Saint Martin makes known such wish, the King appoints a member to the Council of State for Aruba, Curacao and Saint Martin, respectively, whose appointment is effected in agreement with the government of the country involved. His dismissal is effected after consultation with that government.
(3) The members of the Council of State for Aruba, Curacao and Saint Martin participate in the activities of the Council of State in case the Council or a division of the Council is heard regarding bills for Kingdom Statutes and Kingdom Ordinances which shall apply in Aruba, Curacao and Saint Martin, respectively, or regarding other matters which, in accordance with Article 11, affect Aruba, Curacao and Saint Martin, respectively.
(4) By Kingdom Ordinance, regulations may be adopted with respect to the mentioned members of the Council of State that deviate from the provisions of the Council of State Act [Wet op de Raad van State].

Article 14. (1) Regulations regarding matters for the Kingdom – in as far as the relevant matter is not regulated in the Constitution and save for international regulations and that which is provided in the third paragraph – are established by Kingdom Statute [rijkswet] or, in cases where that is applicable, by Kingdom Ordinance [algemene maatregel van rijksbestuur]. The Kingdom Statute or the Kingdom Ordinance may charge other organs with, or leave to other organs, the establishment of more detailed regulations. The charging of or leaving to the countries is effected with respect to the legislator or the government of the countries.
(2) If the regulation is not reserved for Kingdom Statute, it may be effected by Kingdom Ordinance.
(3) Regulations regarding matters for the Kingdom which do not apply in Aruba, Curacao or Saint Martin are established by statute [wet] or ordinance [algemene maatregel van bestuur].
(4) The naturalization of persons resident in Aruba, Curacao or Saint Martin is effected by or pursuant to Kingdom Statute.

Article 15. (1) The King transmits a bill for a Kingdom Statute, simultaneously with its introduction in the States-General, to the representative bodies of Aruba, Curacao and Saint Martin.
(2) In case of a proposal for a bill for a Kingdom Statute emanating from the States-General, the transmission of the bill by the Second Chamber [Tweede Kamer] is effected immediately after it has been introduced in the Chamber.
(3) The Minister Plenipotentiary of Aruba, Curacao or Saint Martin has the right to propose to the Second Chamber to make a proposal for a bill for a Kingdom Statute.

Article 16. The representative body of the country where the regulation shall apply has the right to scrutinize it before the public consideration of the bill in the Second Chamber and, if necessary within a time period determined for that purpose, to issue a written report on it.

Article 17. (1) The Minister Plenipotentiary of the country where the regulation shall apply is offered the opportunity to attend the oral consideration of the bill for a Kingdom Statute in the Chambers of the States-General and to provide such information to the Chambers as he considers appropriate.
(2) The representative body of the country where the regulation shall apply may decide, for the consideration of a specific matter in the States-General, to delegate one or more special delegates who also have the right to attend the oral consideration and to provide information in that context.
(3) The Ministers Plenipotentiary and the special delegates are not liable to judicial prosecution for that which they have said in the meeting of the Chambers of the States-General or which they have submitted to them in writing.
(4) The Ministers Plenipotentiary and the special delegates have the right, during the consideration in the Second Chamber, to propose amendments to the bill.

Article 18. (1) The Minister Plenipotentiary of the country where the regulation shall apply is given the opportunity, before the final vote on a bill for a Kingdom Statute in the Chambers of the States-General, to give a statement regarding that bill. If the Minister Plenipotentiary declares his opposition to the bill, he may also request the Chamber to postpone the vote until the following meeting. If the Second Chamber, after the Minister Plenipotentiary has declared his opposition to the bill, adopts it with a majority smaller than three-fifths of the number of votes cast, the consideration is suspended and further deliberations regarding the bill take place in the council of ministers.
(2) If special delegates are attending the meeting of the Chambers, the right stipulated in the first paragraph also applies to the delegate nominated by the representative body for that purpose.

Article 19. Articles 17 and 18 apply mutatis mutandis to the consideration in the joint session of the States-General.

Article 20. By Kingdom Statute, further regulations may be established regarding that which is provided in Articles 15 to 19.

Article 21. If, after concluded deliberations with the Ministers Plenipotentiary of Aruba, Curacao and Saint Martin, in case of war or in other special cases where action must be taken swiftly, it is impossible in the opinion of the King to wait for the result of the scrutiny stipulated in Article 16, the provision of that Article may be deviated from.

Article 22. (1) The government of the Kingdom ensures the publication of Kingdom Statutes and Kingdom Ordinances. It is effected where the regulation shall apply in the official journal. The governments of the countries provide the necessary assistance in that context.
(2) They enter into force on the moment to be stipulated by or pursuant to these regulations.
(3) The enactment formula of Kingdom Statutes and of Kingdom Ordinances states that the provisions of the Charter for the Kingdom have been respected.

Article 23. (1) The jurisdiction of the Supreme Court of the Netherlands [Hoge Raad der Nederlanden] as regards disputes in Aruba, Curacao and Saint Martin, as well as on Bonaire, Saint Eustatius and Saba, is regulated by Kingdom Statute.
(2) If the government of Aruba, Curacao or Saint Martin so requests, by that Kingdom Statute the possibility is opened for a member, an extraordinary member or an advisory member to be added to the Court.

Article 24. (1) Agreements with foreign states and with international organizations which affect Aruba, Curacao or Saint Martin are submitted, simultaneously with the submission to the States-General, to the representative body of Aruba, Curacao and Saint Martin, respectively.
(2) In case the agreement is submitted to the States-General for tacit approval, the Minister Plenipotentiary may, within the period set for the Chambers of the States-General for that purpose, express the wish that the agreement be submitted to explicit approval by the States-General.
(3) The preceding paragraphs apply mutatis mutandis with respect to the termination of international agreements, the first paragraph applies with the provision that the intention of termination is notified to the representative body of Aruba, Curacao and Saint Martin, respectively.

Article 25. (1) The King does not commit Aruba, Curacao or Saint Martin to international economic and financial agreements if the government of the country, indicating the reasons based on which it expects serious detriment from the commitment to the country, has declared that the country should not be committed.
(2) The King does not terminate international economic and financial agreements as regards Aruba, Curacao or Saint Martin if the government of the country, indicating the reasons based on which it expects serious detriment from the termination to the country, has declared that for the country a termination should not take place. Termination may nevertheless be effected if it is incompatible with the provisions of the agreement that the country be excluded from the termination.

Article 26. If the government of Aruba, Curacao or Saint Martin expresses the wish that an international economic or financial agreement should be concluded which is to apply exclusively to the country involved, the government of the Kingdom shall cooperate with a view to such an agreement unless this would be incompatible with the ties of the country within the Kingdom.

Article 27. (1) Aruba, Curacao and Saint Martin are involved as early as possible in the preparation of agreements with foreign states which affect them in accordance with Article 11. They are also involved in the execution of agreements which affect them thus and which are binding upon them.
(2) The Netherlands, Aruba, Curacao and Saint Martin adopt a mutual provision on the cooperation between the countries regarding the adoption of regulations or other measures which are necessary for the execution of agreements with foreign states.
(3) If the interests of the Kingdom are affected by the continued absence of regulations or other measures which are necessary for the execution of an agreement with foreign states in one of the countries, whereas the agreement can be approved for that country only when the regulations or other measures are ready, a Kingdom Ordinance, or if necessary a Kingdom Statute may provide in which manner that agreement shall be executed.
(4) If the regulations or other measures for the execution of the agreement in question are adopted by the country, the Kingdom Ordinance or the Kingdom Statute will be repealed.

Article 28. On the basis of international agreements concluded by the Kingdom, Aruba, Curacao and Saint Martin may, if such wish exists, join international organizations as members.

Article 29. (1) The acquisition or guarantee of a credit outside the Kingdom in the name of or at the expense of one of the countries takes place in agreement with the government of the Kingdom.
(2) The council of ministers agrees with the acquisition or guarantee of such credit unless this would be contrary to the interests of the Kingdom.

Article 30. (1) Aruba, Curacao and Saint Martin provide the armed forces that are present in their territory with help and assistance which they require in the fulfillment of their task.
(2) By country statute, rules are established to ensure that the armed forces of the Kingdom in Aruba, Curacao and Saint Martin can fulfill their task.

Article 31. (1) Persons who are resident in Aruba, Curacao and Saint Martin may be obliged to serve in the armed forces or in civilian service only by country statute.
(2) It is reserved to the Regulation of State [Staatsregeling] to determine that servicemen serving in the armed forces may be deployed abroad without their consent only pursuant to country statute.

Article 32. In the armed forces for the defence of Aruba, Curacao and Saint Martin as far as possible persons shall be included who are resident in these countries.

Article 33. (1) For the purposes of defence, the confiscation of property and use of goods, the limitation of property and usage rights, the requisition of services and quartering is effected only under observance of general rules to be laid down by Kingdom Statute which also contain provisions regarding compensation.
(2) In that Kingdom Statute, further regulation is assigned where possible to country institutions.

Article 34. (1) The King may, for the maintenance of external or internal security, in case of war or threat of war or where a threat to or disruption of internal order and peace can lead to a substantial infringement on the interests of the Kingdom, declare each part of the territory in state of war or in state of siege.
(2) By or pursuant to Kingdom Statute the manner is determined in which such declaration is effected and the consequences are regulated.
(3) In this regulation is may be provided that and in which manner competences of bodies of civilian authority regarding public order and policing pass wholly or partly to other bodies of civilian authority or to military authority and that the civilian authorities in that latter case are subordinate to military authorities. Regarding the passing of competences, consultation with the government of the affected country takes place where possible. In that regulation it may be deviated from provisions regarding the freedom of the press, the right of association and assembly as well as the inviolability of the home and the respect for correspondence.
(4) For the territory declared in state of siege, in case of war in a manner determined by Kingdom Statute, military penal law and military penal jurisdiction may be wholly or partly declared applicable to everyone.

Article 35. (1) Aruba, Curacao and Saint Martin share, in accordance with their economic strength, the costs connected to the maintenance of the independence and defence of the Kingdom as well as the costs connected to the maintenance of other affairs of the Kingdom to the extent that this benefits Aruba, Curacao and Saint Martin respectively.
(2) The share for Aruba, Curacao and Saint Martin, respectively, stipulated in the first paragraph, is determined by the council of ministers for one fiscal year or for several consecutive fiscal years. Article 12 applies mutatis mutandis, with the exception that decisions are taken by unanimity.
(3) Where the determination stipulated in the second paragraph does not take place in time, pending that, for the duration of at most one fiscal year, the share determined in accordance with that paragraph for the previous fiscal year applies.
(4) The preceding paragraphs do not apply to measures for which special arrangements have been established.

§ 3. Mutual assistance, consultation and cooperation

Article 36. The Netherlands, Aruba, Curacao and Saint Martin provide to each other aid and assistance.

Article 36a. (Repealed).

Article 37. (1) The Netherlands, Aruba, Curacao and Saint Martin shall conduct as much consultation as possible regarding all matters where the interests of two or more of the countries are affected. For that purpose, special representatives may be appointed and common institutions may be established.
(2) As matters in the meaning of this Article are considered, among other things:
a. the promotion of cultural and social ties between the countries;
b. the promotion of effective economic, financial and monetary relations between the countries;
c. questions regarding the coinage and monetary system, banking and foreign-currency policy;
d. the promotion of economic resilience through mutual aid and assistance by the countries;
e. the exercise of professions and businesses by Dutch citizens in the countries;
f. matters regarding aviation, including the policy on unregulated air transportation;
g. matters regarding shipping;
h. cooperation in the field of telegraphy, telephony and radio communications.

Article 38. (1) The Netherlands, Aruba, Curacao and Saint Martin may establish regulations between each other.
(2) In mutual consultation it may be provided that such regulations and the change thereof are established by Kingdom Statute or Kingdom Ordinance.
(3) Regarding matters of private law and criminal law of an inter-regional or international nature, regulations may be established by Kingdom Statute if agreement over such regulations exists between the governments of the countries involved.
(4) The matter of the relocation of the seat of legal persons is regulated by Kingdom Statute. On this regulation, agreement between the governments of the countries is required.

Article 38a. The countries may, through mutual regulations, adopt provisions for the treatment of disputes between them. The second paragraph of Article 38 applies.

Article 39. (1) Private and commercial law, civil procedure, criminal law, criminal procedure, copyright law, industrial property, the office of the notary, as well as provisions regarding measures and weights are regulated as far as possible in an equivalent manner in the Netherlands, Aruba, Curacao and Saint Martin.
(2) A proposal for a far-reaching change in the existing legislation on this matter is not introduced in the representative body – or taken into consideration by the representative body – before the governments in the other countries have been given the opportunity to express their views in that matter.

Article 40. Judgments given by the judge in the Netherlands, Aruba, Curacao or Saint Martin, and orders issued by him, as well as engrossments of authentic acts issued there, may be executed in the entire Kingdom with due regard to the legal provisions of the country where the execution takes place.

§ 4. The constitutional system of the countries

Article 41. (1) The Netherlands, Aruba, Curacao and Saint Martin conduct their own affairs autonomously.
(2) The matters for the Kingdom are among the subjects of concern for the countries.

Article 42. (1) In the Kingdom, the constitutional system of the Netherlands is regulated in the Constitution [Grondwet], the one of Aruba, Curacao and Saint Martin in the Regulation of State [Staatsregeling] of Aruba, of Curacao and of Saint Martin.
(2) The Regulations of State of Aruba, of Curacao and of Saint Martin are established by country statute [landsverordening]. Each proposal for an amendment of the Regulation of State indicates clearly the proposed amendment. The representative body may not adopt the bill for such a country statute unless by two-thirds of votes cast.

Article 43. (1) Each of the countries ensures the realization of the fundamental human rights and freedoms, legal certainty and proper administration.
(2) The guarantee of these rights, freedoms, legal certainty and proper administration is a matter for the Kingdom.

Article 44. (1) A country statute for an amendment of the Regulation of State regarding:
a. the Articles relating to the fundamental human rights and freedoms;
b. the provisions relating to the competences of the Governor;
c. the Articles relating to the competences of the representative bodies of the countries;
d. the Articles relating to the judiciary,
is transmitted to the government of the Kingdom. It does not enter into force until after the government of the Kingdom has expressed its consent herein.
(2) A bill for a country statute regarding the preceding provisions is not presented to the representative body, nor taken into consideration by that body by way of a private member's initiative, until the opinion of the government of the Kingdom is obtained.

Article 45. Amendments to the Constitution [Grondwet] regarding:
a. the Articles relating to the fundamental human rights and freedoms;
b. the provisions relating to the competences of the government;
c. the Articles relating to the competences of the representative body;
d. the Articles relating to the judiciary,
are – notwithstanding the provisions of Article 5 – considered to affect Aruba, Curacao and Saint Martin in the meaning of Article 10.

Article 46. (1) The representative bodies are elected by the residents of the country involved who are Dutch citizens, who have reached an age to be determined by the countries, which may not be higher than 25 years. Each voter only casts one vote. The elections are free and secret. If a necessity thereto appears, the countries may establish restrictions. Every Dutch citizen may run in elections, with the provision that the countries may establish a requirement of residence and an age limit.
(2) The countries may confer the right to elect representative bodies to Dutch citizens who are not residents of the country involved, as well as the right to elect representative bodies and the right to run in elections to residents of the country involved who are not Dutch citizens, in any case provided that in that context at least the requirements for residents who are also Dutch citizens are observed.

Article 47. (1) The ministers and the members of the representative body in the countries, before assuming their office, take an oath or make a promise of allegiance to the King and the Charter.
(2) The ministers and the members of the representative body in Aruba, Curacao and Saint Martin take the oath or make the promise before the representative of the King.

Article 48. The countries respect the provisions of the Charter in their legislation and administration.

Article 49. By Kingdom Statute, regulations may be established regarding the binding effect of legislative measures which are incompatible with the Charter, an international regulation, a Kingdom Statute or a Kingdom Ordinance.

Article 50. (1) Legislative and administrative measures in Aruba, Curacao and Saint Martin which are incompatible with the Charter, an international regulation, a Kingdom Statute or a Kingdom Ordinance, or with interests the promotion or safeguarding of which is a matter for the Kingdom, may be suspended or annulled by the King as the head of the Kingdom by way of reasoned decree. The proposal for an annulment is issued by the council of ministers.
(2) For the Netherlands, this matter is regulated, where necessary, in the Constitution.

Article 51. (1) If an organ in Aruba, Curacao or Saint Martin does not, or does insufficiently perform what it must perform pursuant to the Charter, an international regulation, a Kingdom Statute or a Kingdom Ordinance, then a Kingdom Ordinance, while stating the legal grounds and reasons on which it is based, may determine in which manner this shall be performed.
(2) For the Netherlands, this matter is regulated, where necessary, in the Constitution.

Article 52. Country statute may confer competences with respect to country affairs, with the approval of the King, to the King as head of the Kingdom and to the Governor as an organ of the Kingdom.

Article 53. If Aruba, Curacao or Saint Martin express such wish, the independent supervision of the spending of funds in accordance with the budget of Aruba, Curacao and Saint Martin, respectively, is exercised by the General Chamber of Audit [Algemene Rekenkamer]. In that case, regulations are established after consultation with the Chamber of Audit by Kingdom Statute regarding the cooperation between the Chamber of Audit and the country involved. Thereafter, the government of the country may, upon a proposal from the representative body, appoint someone who is given the opportunity to participate in the deliberations on all matters of the country involved.

§ 5. Transitional and final provisions

Article 54. (1) In case of an amendment of the Constitution [Grondwet], Article 1, second paragraph, will be declared repealed at the moment that the position of Bonaire, Saint Eustatius and Saba within the state order of the Netherlands is provided for by the Constitution.
(2) This Article is repealed if, in accordance with the previous paragraph, Article 1, first paragraph, is declared repealed.

Article 55. (1) Amendments to this Charter are effected by Kingdom Statute.
(2) A proposal for an amendment adopted by the States-General is not approved by the King until it has been accepted by Aruba, Curacao and Saint Martin. Such acceptance is effected by country statute. Such country statute is not adopted until it has been approved by the Parliaments [Staten] in two readings. If the bill is adopted in the first reading by two-thirds of the votes cast, the adoption is effective immediately. The second reading takes place within one month after the bill has been adopted in first reading.
(3) If and in as far as a proposal for an amendment of the Charter deviates from the Constitution [Grondwet], the proposal is considered in such manner as the Constitution prescribes for proposals for an amendment of the Constitution, with the exception that both Chambers may adopt the proposed amendment in second reading by an absolute majority of votes cast.

Article 56. Authorities, binding statutes, decrees and decisions existing on the moment of the entry into force of the Charter remain in place until they are replaced by others under observance of this Charter. To the extent that the Charter itself regulates any matter differently, the regulation by the Charter applies.

Article 57. Statutes and ordinances which applied in the Netherlands Antilles have the status of Kingdom Statute or Kingdom Ordinance, respectively, with the exception that, to the extent that they may pursuant to the Charter be amended by country statute, they have the status of country statute.

Article 57a. Existing Kingdom Statutes, statutes, country statutes, Kingdom Ordinances, ordinances and other regulations which are incompatible with an amendment of the Charter remain in force until a provision for this is adopted in accordance with the Charter.

Article 58. (1) Aruba may declare by country statute that it wishes to terminate the legal order laid down by the Charter regarding Aruba.
(2) The proposal for such country statute is accompanied, when tabled, by an outline of a future constitution including at least provisions regarding fundamental rights, government, representative body, legislation and administration, judiciary and amendment of the constitution.
(3) Parliament may only adopt the proposal by a majority of two thirds of the votes of the sitting members.

Article 59. (1) Within six months after the Parliament of Aruba has adopted the proposal stipulated in Article 58 a referendum regulated by country statute is held whereby those entitled to vote may voice their opinion on the adopted proposal.
(2) The adopted proposal is adopted as country statute only if in the referendum a majority of those entitled to vote has voted in favour of the proposal.

Article 60. (1) After the adoption of the country statute in accordance with Articles 58 and 59 and the approval of the future constitution by the Parliament of Aruba by a majority of two thirds of the votes of the sitting members, by royal decree the moment of the termination of the legal order laid down by the Charter regarding Aruba is established in accordance with the wishes of the government of Aruba.
(2) That moment lies at the latest one month after the date of the adoption of the constitution. That adoption takes place at the latest one year after the date of the referendum stipulated in Article 59.

[Articles 60a to 60c are omitted.]

Article 61. The Charter enters into force on the moment of its ceremonial declaration, after it has been affirmed by the King.
Before the affirmation takes place, the Charter requires, for the Netherlands, approval in a manner provided by the Constitution; for Suriname and the Netherlands Antilles by a decision of the representative body.
This decision is taken by two thirds of votes cast. If such majority is not obtained, the Parliament is dissolved and it is decided by the new Parliament by an absolute majority of votes cast.

Article 62. (Repealed).

Annex 10

THE DUTCH CONSTITUTION

Constitution for the Kingdom of the Netherlands [Grondwet voor het Koninkrijk der Nederlanden] of 24 August 1815 as last amended by statute of 16 March 2006 (*Stb.* 170).[1]

Chapter 1. Fundamental rights

Article 1. All persons in the Netherlands are treated equally in equal circumstances. Discrimination on the grounds of religion, belief, political opinion, race, sex or any other ground is not permissible.

Article 2. (1) Statute regulates who is a Dutch citizen.
(2) Statute regulates the admission and expulsion of aliens.
(3) Extradition may only be effected pursuant to a treaty. Further regulations regarding extradition are provided by statute.
(4) Everyone has the right to leave the country, save for cases provided by statute.

Article 3. All Dutch citizens are eligible for appointment in the public service on an equal footing.

Article 4. Every Dutch citizen has the equal right to elect the members of general representative bodies as well as to be elected member of these bodies, save for limitations and exceptions provided by statute.

Article 5. Everyone has the right to submit petitions in writing to the competent authorities.

Article 6. (1) Everyone has the right to freely express his religion or belief, individually or in community with others, save for everybody's responsibility according to law.
(2) Statute may, regarding the exercise of this right outside of buildings and closed locations, provide for regulations for the protection of health, in the interest of traffic and for the combat against and prevention of disorder.

---

[1] Translation by Ph. Kiiver. This text has also been published separately in: Ph. Kiiver & N. Kornet, eds., *The Maastricht Collection: Selected National, European and International Provisions from Public and Private Law*, Second Edition (Groningen: Europa Law Publishing, 2010). It has also been published in a smaller compilation covering only the area of constitutional law: Ph. Kiiver, ed., *Sources of Constitutional Law: Constitutions and Fundamental Legal Provisions from the United States, France, Germany, the Netherlands, the United Kingdom, the ECHR and the EU*, Second Edition (Groningen: Europa Law Publishing, 2010).

Article 7. (1) No-one requires prior permission in order to publish thoughts or feelings via the press, save for everybody's responsibility according to law.
(2) Statute provides for regulations regarding radio and television. There is no supervision in advance of the content of a radio or television broadcast.
(3) For the publication of thoughts or feelings via means other than the ones stipulated in the preceding paragraphs, no-one requires prior permission regarding the content thereof, save for everybody's responsibility according to law. Statute may regulate the rendering of displays accessible to persons younger than sixteen years of age for the protection of good morals.
(4) The preceding paragraphs do not apply to commercial advertisement.

Article 8. The right of association is recognized. By statute this right may be limited in the interest of the public order.

Article 9. (1) The right of assembly and demonstration is recognized, save for everybody's responsibility according to law.
(2) Statute may provide for regulations for the protection of health, in the interest of traffic and for the combat against and prevention of disorder.

Article 10. (1) Everyone has, save for limitations to be provided by or pursuant to statute, the right to respect for his private life.
(2) Statute provides for regulations for the protection of private life in the context of the recording and transmission of personal data.
(3) Statute provides for regulations regarding the entitlements of persons to insight into the data recorded on them and into the use made thereof, as well as to a correction of such data.

Article 11. Everyone has, save for limitations to be provided by or pursuant to statute, the right to inviolability of his body.

Article 12. (1) The entry into a home without consent of the occupant is permissible only in cases provided by or pursuant to statute, by those who are designated to that end by or pursuant to statute.
(2) An entry in accordance with the preceding paragraph requires prior identification and notification of the purpose of the entry, save for exceptions provided by statute.
(3) A written report on the entry is delivered to the occupant as soon as possible. If the entry has been effected in the interest of national security or of criminal prosecution, the delivery of the report may be postponed in accordance with regulations to be provided by statute. In cases to be provided by statute, the delivery may be omitted if the interest of national security is permanently incompatible with such delivery.

Article 13. (1) The privacy of the correspondence is inviolable except, in cases provided by statute, by order of a judge.
(2) The privacy of telephone and telegraph communications is inviolable except, in cases provided by statute, by or with the authorization of those designated to that end by statute.

Article 14. (1) Expropriation may be effected only in the general interest and for a previously guaranteed compensation, all of which in accordance with regulations to be provided by or pursuant to statute.
(2) Compensation need not be guaranteed beforehand if in a case of emergency immediate expropriation is called for.
(3) In cases provided by or pursuant to statute there is a right to compensation or partial compensation if, in the general interest, by competent authorities property is being destroyed or made unusable or the exercise of ownership rights is being limited.

Article 15. (1) Save for cases provided by or pursuant to statute, no-one may be deprived of his freedom.
(2) He who is deprived of his freedom on a basis other than upon court order may request his release to a judge. In that case he is heard by the judge within a period to be provided by statute. The judge orders immediate release if he considers the deprivation of freedom unlawful.
(3) The trial of him who is deprived of his freedom with a view thereto, takes place within reasonable time.
(4) He who is lawfully deprived of his freedom may be limited in the exercise of his fundamental rights in as far as such exercise is not compatible with the deprivation of freedom.

Article 16. No act is punishable except by virtue of a prior statutory criminal provision.

Article 17. No-one may against his will be barred from access to the judge that statute accords him.

Article 18. (1) Everyone may be aided in court and in administrative appeal.
(2) Statute provides for regulations regarding the provision of legal aid to persons of limited means.

Article 19. (1) The promotion of sufficient employment is a subject of concern for the state authority.
(2) Statute provides for regulations regarding the legal position of those who are engaged in an employment and regarding their protection therein, as well as regarding co-determination.
(3) The right of every Dutch citizen to a free choice of his occupation is recognized, save for limitations provided by or pursuant to statute.

Article 20. (1) The securing of means of subsistence of the population and the promotion of welfare is a subject of concern for the state authority.
(2) Statute provides for regulations regarding entitlements to social security.
(3) Dutch citizens in this country who cannot provide for their own subsistence have a right to state assistance to be regulated by statute.

Article 21. Concern of the state authority is directed at the habitability of the land and the protection and improvement of the environment.

Article 22. (1) State authority takes measures to promote public health.
(2) The promotion of sufficient living space is a subject of concern for the state authority.
(3) It creates conditions for social and cultural development and for leisure activity.

Article 23. (1) Education is a subject of permanent concern for the government.
(2) Teaching is free, save for state supervision and, as regards forms of education designated by statute, the monitoring of the competence and morality of those who teach, all of which is to be regulated by statute.
(3) Public education is regulated by statute with due respect to the religion or belief of everyone.
(4) In each municipality, sufficient public primary education is offered by the state in a sufficient number of public schools. In accordance with regulations to be provided by statute, deviations from this provision may be permitted as long as an opportunity to receive such education is provided, whether or not in a public school.
(5) The requirements of the appropriateness to be applied to education to be financed wholly or partly from the public purse are regulated by statute with due respect for, as far as special education [bijzonder onderwijs] is concerned, the freedom of underlying direction.
(6) These requirements are regulated for primary education in such manner that the appropriateness of special education financed wholly from the public purse and of public education is

equally ensured. In the context of such regulation, in particular the freedom of special education regarding the choice of means of teaching and employment of teachers is respected.
(7) Special primary education which complies with the conditions to be provided by statute is financed from the public purse under the same criteria as public education. Statute provides the conditions under which contributions from the public purse are granted to special secondary and higher secondary education.
(8) The government reports annually to the States-General on the state of the education system.

Chapter 2. Government

§ 1. The King

Article 24. The crown is vested by hereditary succession in the lawful successors of King William I, Prince of Orange-Nassau.

Article 25. The crown passes, in the case of the death of the King, by virtue of hereditary succession to his lawful descendants, in which case the oldest child takes precedence, with further passage of the crown taking place according to the same rule. When there are no descendants of his own, the crown passes in an equal manner to the lawful descendants first of his parent, then of his grandparent, in the line of hereditary succession as long as they are blood relatives not more than thrice removed from the deceased King.

Article 26. The child which a woman carries at the moment of the death of the King is deemed already born for the purposes of hereditary succession. If it is stillborn, it is deemed never to have existed.

Article 27. Abdication leads to hereditary succession in accordance with the rules provided in the preceding Articles. Children born after the abdication, and their descendants, are excluded from hereditary succession.

Article 28. (1) The King who enters into a marriage without approval granted by statute thereby abdicates.
(2) If someone who can inherit the crown from the King enters into such marriage, then he is, together with the children born within that marriage, and their descendants, excluded from hereditary succession.
(3) The States-General deliberate and decide on a bill to grant approval in joint session.

Article 29. (1) If exceptional circumstances so require, one or more persons may be excluded from hereditary succession by statute.
(2) The bill for that purpose is submitted by or on behalf of the King. The States-General deliberate and decide on the matter in joint session. They may adopt the bill only with at least two-thirds of the number of votes cast.

Article 30. (1) If there is a prospect that there shall be no successor, he may be appointed by statute. The bill for that purpose is submitted by or on behalf of the King. After the submission of the bill, the Chambers are dissolved. The new Chambers deliberate and decide on the matter in joint session. They may adopt the bill only with at least two-thirds of the number of votes cast.
(2) If at the death of the King or at abdication there is no successor, the Chambers are dissolved. The new Chambers convene within four months after the death or abdication in joint session in order to decide on the appointment of a King. They may appoint a successor only with at least two-thirds of the number of votes cast.

Article 31. (1) An appointed King may be succeeded by hereditary succession only by his lawful descendants.
(2) The provisions regarding hereditary succession and the first paragraph of this Article apply mutatis mutandis to an appointed successor as long as he is not yet King.

Article 32. After the King has assumed the exercise of royal authority, he is as soon as possible sworn in and inaugurated in the capital city of Amsterdam in a public joint session of the States-General. He swears or promises allegiance to the Constitution and loyal exercise of his office. Statute provides further regulations.

Article 33. The King exercises royal authority only after he has attained the age of eighteen years.

Article 34. Statute regulates parental authority and guardianship over the King who is a minor and the supervision thereof. The States-General deliberate and decide on the matter in joint session.

Article 35. (1) If the council of ministers concludes that the King is incapable of exercising royal authority, it reports this, submitting the advice of the Council of State requested on the matter, to the States-General, which convene on the matter in a joint session.
(2) If the States-General share this conclusion, they declare that the King is incapable of exercising royal authority. Such declaration is published by order of the chairman of the session and enters into force immediately.
(3) As soon as the King is capable again of exercising royal authority, this is declared by statute. The States-General deliberate and decide on the matter in joint session. Immediately after the publication of this statute, the King resumes the exercise of royal authority.
(4) Statute regulates, where necessary, the supervision over the person of the King if he is declared incapable of exercising royal authority. The States-General deliberate and decide on the matter in joint session.

Article 36. The King may temporarily suspend the exercise of royal authority and resume such exercise by virtue of a statute, the bill for which is submitted by or on behalf of himself. The States-General deliberate and decide on the matter in joint session.

Article 37. (1) Royal authority is exercised by a regent:
a. as long as the King has not attained the age of eighteen years;
b. if a child not yet born can be called to take over the crown;
c. if the King has been declared incapable of exercising royal authority;
d. if the King has temporarily suspended the exercise of royal authority;
e. as long as after the death of the King or his abdication there is no successor.
(2) The regent is appointed by statute. The States-General deliberate and decide on the matter in joint session.
(3) In the cases stipulated in the first paragraph under c. and d., the descendant of the King who is his presumed successor is regent by operation of law, if he has attained the age of eighteen years.
(4) The regent swears or promises allegiance to the Constitution and loyal exercise of his office in a joint session of the States-General. Statute provides further regulations regarding regency and may provide for succession and replacement therein. The States-General deliberate and decide on the matter in joint session.
(5) Articles 35 and 36 apply to the regent mutatis mutandis.

Article 38. As long as the exercise of royal authority is not secured, it is exercised by the Council of State [Raad van State].

Article 39. Statute regulates who is a member of the royal house.

Article 40. (1) The King annually receives allowances charged to the Kingdom in accordance with rules to be provided by statute. That statute determines which other members of the royal house receive allowances charged to the Kingdom and regulates these allowances.
(2) The allowances charged to the Kingdom received by them, as well as assets which serve the exercise of their function, are exempt from personal taxation. Furthermore, what the King or his presumed successor receives from a member of the royal house by virtue of inheritance or gift, is exempt from inheritance, transfer and gift taxation. Further exemption from taxation may be granted by statute.
(3) The Chambers of the States-General may adopt bills for statutes stipulated in the preceding paragraphs only with at least two-thirds of the number of votes cast.

Article 41. The King organizes, with due respect for the public interest, his household.

§ 2. King and ministers

Article 42. (1) The government comprises the King and the ministers.
(2) The King is inviolable; the ministers are responsible.

Article 43. The Prime-Minister [minister-president] and the other ministers are appointed and dismissed by royal decree.

Article 44. (1) Ministries are established by royal decree. They are placed under the direction of a minister.
(2) Furthermore, ministers may be appointed who are not charged with directing a ministry.

Article 45. (1) The ministers together form the council of ministers [ministerraad].
(2) The Prime-Minister is chairman of the council of ministers.
(3) The council of ministers deliberates and decides on general government policy and promotes the unity of that policy.

Article 46. (1) Secretaries of state may be appointed by royal decree.
(2) A secretary of state [staatssecretaris] assumes, in the cases where the minister finds it necessary and with due regard to his instructions, his position as minister. The secretary of state is in that context responsible, notwithstanding the responsibility of the minister.

Article 47. All statutes and royal decrees are signed by the King and by one or more ministers or secretaries of state.

Article 48. The royal decree whereby a Prime-Minister is appointed, is signed also by him. The royal decrees whereby the other ministers and the secretaries of state are appointed or dismissed are signed also by the Prime-Minister.

Article 49. In a manner provided by statute, the ministers and secretaries of state, when assuming office, take an oath or make a declaration and promise before the King of their integrity, and swear or promise allegiance to the Constitution and loyal exercise of their office.

Chapter 3. States-General

§ 1. Organization and composition

Article 50. The States-General [Staten-Generaal] represent the entire Dutch people.

Article 51. (1) The States-General consist of the Second Chamber [Tweede Kamer] and the First Chamber [Eerste Kamer].
(2) The Second Chamber consists of one hundred and fifty members.
(3) The First Chamber consists of seventy-five members.
(4) In a joint session, the two Chambers are considered as one.

Article 52. (1) The term of session of both Chambers is four years.
(2) If for the provincial assemblies [provinciale staten] a term other than four years is established by statute, the term of session of the First Chamber is changed accordingly.

Article 53. (1) The members of both Chambers are elected on the basis of proportional representation within the limits to be provided by statute.
(2) Elections take place by secret ballot.

Article 54. (1) The members of the Second Chamber are elected directly by Dutch citizens who have attained the age of eighteen years, save for exceptions to be provided by statute with regard to Dutch citizens who are not residents.
(2) The following are excluded from the right to vote:
a. he who has been convicted to a prison sentence of at least one year for a criminal act so designated by statute in a final court judgment and who has at the same time been disqualified from the right to vote;
b. he who by virtue of a final court judgment has been declared incapable of carrying out legal acts because of a mental disorder.

Article 55. The members of the First Chamber are elected by the members of the provincial assemblies [provinciale staten]. The elections take place, save for the event of a dissolution of the Chamber, within three months following the elections of the members of the provincial assemblies.

Article 56. In order to be able to become a member of the States-General, it is required that one be a Dutch citizen, have attained the age of eighteen years, and not be disqualified from the right to vote.

Article 57. (1) No-one may be a member of both Chambers.
(2) A member of the Second Chamber may not at the same time be a minister, secretary of state, member of the Council of State, member of the General Chamber of Audit, National Ombudsman or substitute ombudsman, or a member of or procurator-general or advocate-general at the Supreme Court.
(3) Nevertheless a minister or secretary of state, who has tendered his resignation, may combine this office with a membership of the States-General, until a decision has been taken regarding that resignation.
(4) Statute may provide with regard to other public offices that they may not be exercised at the same time as the membership of the States-General or of one of the Chambers.

Article 57a. Statute regulates the temporary replacement of a member of the States-General because of pregnancy and delivery as well as because of illness.

Article 58. Each Chamber examines the letters patent of its newly appointed members and decides, with due regard to the regulations to be provided by statute, on disputes that arise with respect to the letters patent or the election itself.

Article 59. Everything else regarding the right to vote and the elections is regulated by statute.

Article 60. In a manner provided by statute, the members of the Chambers, when assuming their office, take an oath or make a declaration and promise in the assembly of their integrity, and swear or promise allegiance to the Constitution and loyal exercise of their office.

Article 61. (1) Each of the Chambers appoints a president from among the members.
(2) Each of the Chambers appoints a secretary. He and the other administrative staff of the Chambers may not at the same time be members of the States-General.

Article 62. The president of the First Chamber has the chairmanship over the joint session.

Article 63. Financial consideration for members and former members of the States-General and their surviving dependants are regulated by statute. The Chambers may adopt a bill on this matter only with at least two-thirds of the number of votes cast.

Article 64. (1) Each of the Chambers may be dissolved by royal decree.
(2) Each decree on such dissolution also contains an order for new elections to the dissolved Chamber and for the convention of the newly elected Chamber within three months.
(3) The dissolution takes effect on the day when the newly elected Chamber convenes.
(4) Statute determines the duration of the term of session of a Second Chamber operating after dissolution; the period may not be longer than five years. The term of session of a First Chamber operating after dissolution ends on the moment when the term of the dissolved Chamber would have ended.

§ 2. Procedures

Article 65. Annually, on the third Tuesday of September or at an earlier moment to be determined by statute, an explanation is given by or on behalf of the King in a joint session of the States-General regarding the policies to be pursued by the government.

Article 66. (1) The meetings of the States-General are public.
(2) The doors are closed when a tenth part of the number of members present so demand or when the president deems it necessary.
(3) The Chamber or the Chambers in joint session, respectively, then decide whether they should deliberate and decide with closed doors.

Article 67. (1) The Chambers may, each separately and in joint session, deliberate and decide only if more than half of the number of members in office is present at the meeting.
(2) Decisions are taken by a majority of votes.
(3) The members vote without any instructions.
(4) Matters are voted on orally and by individual calls when one member so demands.

Article 68. The ministers and the secretaries of state provide the Chambers, separately and in joint session, orally or in writing the information demanded by one or more members, where such provision is not in conflict with the interest of the state.

Article 69. (1) The ministers and the secretaries of state have access to the meetings and may participate in deliberations.
(2) They may be invited by the Chambers, separately and in joint session, to be present at the meeting.
(3) They may be assisted at the meeting by persons designated by them for that purpose.

Article 70. Both Chambers, both separately and in joint session, have the right of inquiry (enquête) to be regulated by statute.

Article 71. The members of the States-General, the ministers, the secretaries of state and other persons who participate in deliberations may not be prosecuted or held liable for what they have said in the meetings of the States-General or in committees thereof, of for what they have submitted to them in writing.

Article 72. The Chambers, both separately and in joint session, adopt rules of procedure.

Chapter 4. Council of State, General Chamber of Audit, National Ombudsman and permanent advisory bodies

Article 73. (1) The Council of State [Raad van State] or a division of the Council is heard on bills and drafts for ordinances [algemene maatregelen van bestuur] as well as proposals for

the ratification of treaties by the States-General. In cases to be provided by statute, such hearing may be omitted.
(2) The Council or a division of the Council is charged with the investigation in administrative disputes that are decided by royal decree, and proposes a decision.
(3) Statute may charge the Council or a division of the Council with deciding in administrative disputes.

Article 74. (1) The King is the president of the Council of State. The presumed successor of the King is a member of the Council by operation of law after having attained the age of eighteen years. By or pursuant to statute, other members of the royal house may be granted membership of the Council.
(2) The members of the Council are appointed for life by royal decree.
(3) They are dismissed upon their own request and because they have attained an age to be provided by statute.
(4) In cases provided by statute they may be suspended or dismissed by the Council.
(5) Statute regulates the further details of their legal position.

Article 75. (1) Statute regulates the organization, composition and competence of the Council of State.
(2) By statute, also other tasks may be assigned to the Council or a division of the Council.

Article 76. The General Chamber of Audit [Algemene Rekenkamer] is charged with investigating the revenue and expenditure of the Kingdom.

Article 77. (1) The members of the General Chamber of Audit are appointed by royal decree for life from a proposal of three persons drawn up by the Second Chamber of the States-General.
(2) They are dismissed upon their own request and because they have attained an age to be provided by statute.
(3) In cases provided by statute they may be suspended or dismissed by the Supreme Court [Hoge Raad].
(4) Statute regulates the further details of their legal position.

Article 78. (1) Statute regulates the organization, composition and competence of the General Chamber of Audit.
(2) By statute, also other tasks may be assigned to the General Chamber of Audit.

Article 78a. (1) The National Ombudsman, upon request or on his own motion, conducts investigations into the conduct of administrative authorities of the Kingdom and of other administrative authorities designated by or pursuant to statute.
(2) The National Ombudsman and a substitute ombudsman are appointed for a term to be provided by statute by the Second Chamber of the States-General. They are dismissed upon their own request and because they have attained an age to be provided by statute. In cases provided by statute they may be suspended or dismissed by the Second Chamber of the States-General. Statute regulates the further details of their legal position.
(3) Statutes regulates the competence and procedures of the National Ombudsman.
(4) By or pursuant to statute, also other tasks may be assigned to the National Ombudsman.

Article 79. (1) Permanent advisory bodies in matters of legislation and administration of the Kingdom are established by or pursuant to statute.
(2) Statute regulates the organization, composition and competence of such bodies.
(3) By or pursuant to statute, also tasks other than advisory ones may be assigned to such bodies.

Article 80. (1) The opinions of the bodies stipulated in this chapter are published in accordance with procedures to be provided by statute.
(2) Opinions given on the matter of bills which are introduced by or on behalf of the King are, save for exceptions to be provided by statute, transmitted to the States-General.

Chapter 5. Legislation and administration

§ 1. Statutes and other regulations

Article 81. Statutes [wetten] are adopted jointly by the government and the States-General.

Article 82. (1) Bills may be introduced by or on behalf of the King and by the Second Chamber of the States-General.
(2) Bills for which deliberation in the States-General in joint session is prescribed may be introduced by or on behalf of the King and, as far as the relevant Articles of Chapter 2 allow, by the joint session.
(3) Bills to be introduced by the Second Chamber or the joint session, respectively, are tabled by one or more of the members.

Article 83. Bills introduced by or on behalf of the King are transmitted to the Second Chamber or, if deliberation in the States-General in joint session is prescribed, to that assembly.

Article 84. (1) As long as a bill introduced by or on behalf of the King has not yet been adopted by the Second Chamber or the joint session, respectively, it may be amended by it, on the proposal of one or more members, and by the government.
(2) As long as the Second Chamber or the joint session, respectively, has not yet adopted a bill to be introduced by itself, it may be amended by it on the proposal of one or more members and by the member or members who have tabled the bill.

Article 85. As soon as the Second Chamber has adopted a bill or has decided to introduce a bill, it transmits it to the First Chamber, which considers it as transmitted to it by the Second Chamber. The Second Chamber may instruct one or more of its members to defend a bill introduced by it in the First Chamber.

Article 86. (1) As long as a bill has not yet been adopted by the States-General, it may be withdrawn by or on behalf of the initiator.
(2) As long as the Second Chamber or the joint session, respectively, has not yet adopted a bill to be introduced by it, it may be withdrawn by the member or members who have tabled it.

Article 87. (1) A bill becomes a statute as soon as it has been adopted by the States-General and confirmed by the King.
(2) The King and the States-General inform each other of their decision regarding any bill.

Article 88. Statute regulates the publication and entry into force of statutes. They do not enter into force before they have been published.

Article 89. (1) Ordinances [algemene maatregelen van bestuur] are adopted by royal decree.
(2) Regulations to be enforced by sanctions are provided there only pursuant to statute. Statute regulates the sanctions to be imposed.
(3) Statute regulates the publication and entry into force of ordinances. They do not enter into force before they have been published.
(4) The second and third paragraph apply mutatis mutandis to other generally binding regulations adopted by the Kingdom.

§ 2. Further provisions

Article 90. The government promotes the development of the international legal order.

Article 91. (1) The Kingdom is not bound by treaties and they are not terminated without prior approval of the States-General. Statute provides the cases where no such approval is required.
(2) Statute provides the manner in which approval is given and may provide for tacit approval.
(3) If a treaty contains provisions which deviate from the Constitution or necessitate such deviation, the Chambers may give approval only with at least two-thirds of the number of votes cast.

Article 92. Subject, where necessary, to the provisions of Article 91 (3), legislative, executive and judicial powers may be conferred upon international organizations by or pursuant to a treaty.

Article 93. Provisions of treaties and of decisions of international organizations, which by virtue of their content can be binding upon everyone, become binding after they have been published.

Article 94. Statutory regulations in force within the Kingdom are not applicable if such application is incompatible with provisions of treaties and decisions of international organizations that are binding on everyone.

Article 95. Statute provides regulations regarding the publication of treaties and decisions of international organizations.

Article 96. (1) The Kingdom is not declared to be in a state of war unless after prior consent of the States-General.
(2) Such consent is not required when consultation with the States-General has proven to be impossible as a result of a state of war existing in fact.
(3) The States-General deliberate and decide on the matter in a joint session.
(4) The provisions of the first and the third paragraph apply mutatis mutandis to a declaration that a war has ended.

Article 97. (1) For the purposes of defence and for the protection of the interests of the Kingdom, as well as for the upholding and promotion of the international legal order, there are armed forces.
(2) The government has the supreme command over the armed forces.

Article 98. (1) The armed forces consist of volunteers and may also comprise conscripts.
(2) Statute regulates compulsory military service and the power to defer drafting into actual service.

Article 99. Statute regulates exemption from military service because of serious conscientious objections.

Article 99a. In accordance with regulations to be provided by statute, obligations may be imposed for the purposes of civil defence.

Article 100. (1) The government provides the States-General with information in advance regarding the deployment or the making available of the armed forces for the upholding and promotion of the international legal order. That includes information in advance regarding the deployment or the making available of the armed forces for humanitarian assistance in case of an armed conflict.

(2) The first paragraph does not apply if pressing reasons prevent the provision of information in advance. In that case, information is provided as soon as possible.

Articles 101 and 102. (Repealed).

Article 103. (1) Statute regulates in which cases, for the maintenance of external and internal security, a state of emergency to be designated as such by statute may be declared by royal decree; statute regulates the consequences.
(2) In that context, deviations are permissible from the constitutional provisions regarding the competences of the governments of the provinces, municipalities and water boards, from the fundamental rights regulated in Article 6, in as far as the exercise of the right stipulated in that Article outside buildings and closed locations is concerned, 7, 8, 9, 12 (2) and (3) and 13, as well as from Article 113 (1) and (3).
(3) Immediately after the declaration of a state of emergency and then, as long as it has not been lifted by royal decree, each time they consider it necessary, the States-General decide on the continuation thereof; they deliberate and decide on the matter in joint session.

Article 104. Taxes of the Kingdom are raised by virtue of a statute. Other charges of the Kingdom are regulated by statute.

Article 105. (1) The budget of the revenue and expenditure of the Kingdom is established by statute.
(2) Annually, bills for general budget statutes are introduced by or on behalf of the King on the moment provided in Article 65.
(3) Account for the revenue and expenditure of the Kingdom is given to the States-General in accordance with the provisions of statute. The accounts approved by the General Chamber of Audit are submitted to the States-General.
(4) Statute provides regulations regarding the administration of the finances of the Kingdom.

Article 106. Statute regulates the monetary system.

Article 107. (1) Statute regulates private law, criminal law and civil and criminal procedure in general codes, save for the power to regulate certain subject-matters in separate statutes.
(2) Statute provides general rules of administrative law.

Article 108. (Repealed).

Article 109. Statute regulates the legal position of civil servants. It also provides regulations regarding their protection at work and regarding co-determination.

Article 110. The state respects openness in the exercise of its tasks in accordance with regulations to be provided by statute.

Article 111. Chivalric orders are established by statute.

Chapter 6. Judiciary

Article 112. (1) The judiciary is charged with adjudicating in disputes over rights and claims of private law.
(2) Statute may assign the adjudication in disputes which did not arise from private law relations either to the judiciary or to courts which do not form part of the judiciary. Statute regulates the procedures and the consequences of decisions.

Article 113. (1) The judiciary is furthermore charged with adjudicating on criminal acts.
(2) Disciplinary jurisdiction established by the state is regulated by statute.
(3) A sentence of deprivation of freedom may be imposed only by the judiciary.

(4) For adjudication outside the Netherlands and for military criminal law, statute may provide deviating regulations.

Article 114. The death penalty may not be imposed.

Article 115. With regard to disputes stipulated in Article 112 (2), administrative appeal may be allowed.

Article 116. (1) Statute designates the courts that form part of the judiciary.
(2) Statute regulates the organization, composition and competence of the judiciary.
(3) Statute may provide that persons not belonging to the judiciary participate in the jurisprudence thereof.
(4) Statute regulates the supervision by members of the judiciary charged with jurisprudence to be exercised over the exercise of the office of such members and of persons stipulated in the preceding paragraph.

Article 117. (1) The members of the judiciary charged with jurisprudence and the procurator-general at the Supreme Court are appointed by royal decree for life.
(2) They are dismissed upon their own request and because they have attained an age to be provided by statute.
(3) In cases provided by statute they may be suspended or dismissed by a court forming part of the judiciary designated by statute.
(4) Statute regulates the further details of their legal position.

Article 118. (1) The members of the Supreme Court [Hoge Raad] of the Netherlands are appointed from a proposal of three persons drawn up by the Second Chamber of the States-General.
(2) The Supreme Court is charged, in the cases and within the boundaries provided by statute, with cassation of judicial decisions because of a violation of the law.
(3) By statute, also other tasks may be assigned to the Supreme Court.

Article 119. The members of the States-General, the ministers and the secretaries of state are prosecuted for crimes committed in office, also after their leaving office, before the Supreme Court. The order to prosecute is given by royal decree or by a decision of the Second Chamber.

Article 120. The judge does not enter into a review of the constitutionality of statutes and treaties.

Article 121. Save for cases provided by statute, trials are conducted in public and judgments contain the reasons on which they are based. The judgment is handed down in public.

Article 122. (1) Pardon is granted by royal decree after the advice of a court designated by statute and with due regard to regulations to be provided by or pursuant to statute.
(2) Amnesty is granted by or pursuant to statute.

Chapter 7. Provinces, municipalities, water boards and other public entities

Article 123. (1) By statute, provinces [provincies] and municipalities [gemeenten] may be dissolved and new ones may be established.
(2) Statute regulates the change of provincial and municipal borders.

Article 124. (1) For provinces and municipalities, the power of regulation and administration regarding their local affairs [huishouding] is left to their governments.
(2) Regulation and administration may be demanded of the governments of provinces and municipalities by or pursuant to statute.

Article 125. (1) The head of the province and the municipality is the provincial assembly [provinciale staten] and the municipal council [gemeenteraad], respectively. Their meetings are public, save for exceptions to be regulated by statute.
(2) The government [bestuur] of the province also includes the provincial executive [gedeputeerde staten] and the King's Commissioner, the government of the municipality also includes the board of burgomaster and aldermen and the burgomaster.
(3) The King's Commissioner and the burgomaster are chairmen of the meetings of the provincial assembly and the municipal council, respectively.

Article 126. Statute may provide that the King's Commissioner is furthermore charged with the execution of an official instruction given by the government.

Article 127. The provincial assembly and the municipal council adopt, save for exceptions provided by statute or by them pursuant to statute, the provincial and the municipal ordinances [verordeningen], respectively.

Article 128. Save for the cases stipulated in Article 123, the conferral of powers within the meaning of Article 124 (1) to organs other than the ones stipulated in Article 125 may be effected only by the provincial assembly and the municipal council, respectively.

Article 129. (1) The members of the provincial assembly and of the municipal council are elected directly by Dutch citizens who are at the same time residents of the province or municipality, respectively, who fulfil the conditions that apply to elections of the Second Chamber of the States-General. For membership the same conditions apply.
(2) The members are elected on the basis of proportional representation within the limits to be provided by statute.
(3) Articles 53 (2) and 59 apply. Article 57a applies mutatis mutandis.
(4) The term of session of the provincial assembly and the municipal council is four years, save for exceptions to be provided by statute.
(5) Statute provides which offices may not be exercised simultaneously with membership. Statute may provide that disqualifications derive from family relation or marriage and that the commission of acts designated by statute may lead to a loss of membership.
(6) Members vote without instructions.

Article 130. Statute may confer the right to elect the members of the municipal council and the right to be a member of the municipal council to residents who are not Dutch citizens, as long as they at least fulfil the conditions that apply to residents who are also Dutch citizens.

Article 131. The King's Commissioner and the burgomaster are appointed by royal decree.

Article 132. (1) Statute regulates the organization of provinces and municipalities as well as the composition and competence of their governments.
(2) Statute regulates supervision of these governments.
(3) Decisions of these governments may be subjected to supervision in advance only in cases to be provided by or pursuant to statute.
(4) Annulment of decisions of these governments may only be effected by royal decree because of a violation of the law or the general interest.
(5) Statute regulates provisions in case of a non-performance with regard to regulation and administration demanded by virtue of Article 124 (2). By statute, provisions in deviation from Articles 125 and 127 may be effected in case the government of a province or a municipality grossly neglects its tasks.
(6) Statute provides which taxes may be raised by the governments of provinces and municipalities and regulates their financial relation with the Kingdom.

Article 133. (1) The dissolution and establishment of water boards [waterschappen], the regulation of their tasks and organization, as well as the composition of their governing bodies is effected, in accordance with regulations to be provided by statute, by provincial ordinance, in as far as nothing is provided otherwise by or pursuant to statute.
(2) Statute regulates the regulatory and other competences of the governing bodies of water boards, as well as the public character of their meetings.
(3) Statute regulates the provincial and further supervision of these governing bodies. Annulment of decisions of these governing bodies may be effected only because of a violation of the law or the general interest.

Article 134. (1) By or pursuant to statute, public entities for professions and enterprises and other public entities may be established and dissolved.
(2) Statute regulates the tasks and the organization of these public entities, the composition and competence of their governing bodies, as well as the public character of their meetings. By or pursuant to statute, regulatory competence may be conferred upon their governing bodies.
(3) Statute regulates the supervision of these governing bodies. Annulment of decisions of these governing bodies may be effected only because of a violation of the law or the general interest.

Article 135. Statute provides regulations for provisions in cases where two or more public entities are involved. In that context, the establishment of a new public entity may be provided for, in which case Article 134 (2) and (3) applies.

Article 136. Disputes between public entities are resolved by royal decree, unless they fall under the jurisdiction of the judiciary or such resolution is assigned by statute to others.

Chapter 8. Revision of the Constitution

Article 137. (1) A statute declares that an amendment of the Constitution as it proposes shall be considered.
(2) The Second Chamber may, whether or not upon such proposal introduced by or on behalf of the King, split a bill for such a statute.
(3) After the publication of the statute stipulated in the first paragraph, the Second Chamber is dissolved.
(4) After the new Second Chamber has convened, both Chambers consider in second reading the proposal for an amendment stipulated in the first paragraph. They may adopt it only with at least two-thirds of the number of votes cast.
(5) The Second Chamber may, whether or not upon such proposal introduced by or on behalf of the King, split a proposal for an amendment with at least two-thirds of the number of votes cast.

Article 138. (1) Before the proposals for an amendment of the Constitution adopted in second reading are confirmed by the King, by statute:
a. the adopted proposals and the provisions of the Constitution left unchanged may be adjusted to one another as far as necessary;
b. the division and position of chapters, sections and Articles as well as the titles may be modified.
(2) The Chambers may adopt a bill containing provisions stipulated in the first paragraph, sub a., only with at least two-thirds of the number of votes cast.

Article 139. The amendments of the Constitution, adopted by the States-General and confirmed by the King, enter into force immediately after they have been published.

Article 140. Existing statutes and other regulations and decisions which are incompatible with an amendment of the Constitution remain in force until a provision on that matter is effected in accordance with the Constitution.

Article 141. The text of the revised Constitution is published by royal decree, in which context chapters, sections and Articles may be renumbered and references be changed accordingly.

Article 142. The Constitution may by statute be brought into line with the Charter for the Kingdom of the Netherlands [Statuut voor het Koninkrijk der Nederlanden]. Articles 139, 140 and 141 apply mutatis mutandis.

[The supplementary provisions are omitted.]

Annex 11

SELECTED STATUTORY PROVISIONS FROM THE UNITED KINGDOM

Bill of Rights 1689 [An Act declareing the Rights and Liberties of the Subject and Setleing the Succession of the Crowne], as amended. Selected provisions: first part.[1]

Whereas the Lords Spirituall and Temporall and Comons assembled at Westminster lawfully fully and freely representing all the Estates of the People of this Realme did upon the thirteenth day of February in the yeare of our Lord one thousand six hundred eighty eight present unto their Majesties then called and known by the Names and Stile of William and Mary Prince and Princesse of Orange being present in their proper Persons a certaine Declaration in Writing made by the said Lords and Comons in the Words following viz

Whereas the late King James the Second by the Assistance of diverse evill Councellors Judges and Ministers imployed by him did endeavour to subvert and extirpate the Protestant Religion and the Lawes and Liberties of this Kingdome.

By Assumeing and Exerciseing a Power of Dispensing with and Suspending of Lawes and the Execution of Lawes without Consent of Parlyament.

By Committing and Prosecuting diverse Worthy Prelates for humbly Petitioning to be excused from Concurring to the said Assumed Power.

By issueing and causeing to be executed a Commission under the Great Seale for Erecting a Court called The Court of Commissioners for Ecclesiasticall Causes.

By Levying Money for and to the Use of the Crowne by pretence of Prerogative for other time and in other manner then the same was granted by Parlyament.

By raising and keeping a Standing Army within this Kingdome in time of Peace without Consent of Parlyament and Quartering Soldiers contrary to Law.

---

[1] This text has also been published separately in: Ph. Kiiver & N. Kornet, eds., *The Maastricht Collection: Selected National, European and International Provisions from Public and Private Law*, Second Edition (Groningen: Europa Law Publishing, 2010). It has also been published in a smaller compilation covering only the area of constitutional law: Ph. Kiiver, ed., *Sources of Constitutional Law: Constitutions and Fundamental Legal Provisions from the United States, France, Germany, the Netherlands, the United Kingdom, the ECHR and the EU*, Second Edition (Groningen: Europa Law Publishing, 2010).

By causing severall good Subjects being Protestants to be disarmed at the same time when Papists were both Armed and Imployed contrary to Law.

By Violating the Freedome of Election of Members to serve in Parlyament.

By Prosecutions in the Court of Kings Bench for Matters and Causes cognizable onely in Parlyament and by diverse other Arbitrary and Illegall Courses.

And whereas of late yeares Partiall Corrupt and Unqualifyed Persons have beene returned and served on Juryes in Tryalls and particularly diverse Jurors in Tryalls for High Treason which were not Freeholders,

And excessive Baile hath beene required of Persons committed in Criminall Cases to elude the Benefitt of the Lawes made for the Liberty of the Subjects.

And excessive Fines have beene imposed.

And illegall and cruell Punishments inflicted.

And severall Grants and Promises made of Fines and Forfeitures before any Conviction or Judgement against the Persons upon whome the same were to be levyed. All which are utterly directly contrary to the knowne Lawes and Statutes and Freedome of this Realme.

And whereas the said late King James the Second haveing Abdicated the Government and the Throne being thereby Vacant His Hignesse the Prince of Orange (whome it hath pleased Almighty God to make the glorious Instrument of Delivering this Kingdome from Popery and Arbitrary Power) did (by the Advice of the Lords Spirituall and Temporall and diverse principall Persons of the Commons) cause Letters to be written to the Lords Spirituall and Temporall being Protestants and other Letters to the severall Countyes Cityes Universities Burroughs and Cinque Ports for the Choosing of such Persons to represent them as were of right to be sent to Parlyament to meete and sitt at Westminster upon the two and twentyeth day of January in this Yeare one thousand six hundred eighty and eight in order to such an Establishment as that their Religion Lawes and Liberties might not againe be in danger of being Subverted, Upon which Letters Elections haveing beene accordingly made.

And thereupon the said Lords Spirituall and Temporall and Commons pursuant to their respective Letters and Elections being now assembled in a full and free Representative of this Nation taking into their most serious Consideration the best meanes for attaining the Ends aforesaid Doe in the first place (as their Aunctestors in like Case have usually done) for the Vindicating and Asserting their auntient Rights and Liberties, Declare

That the pretended Power of Suspending of Laws or the Execution of Laws by Regall Authority without Consent of Parlyament is illegall.

That the pretended Power of Dispensing with Laws or the Execution of Laws by Regall Authoritie as it hath beene assumed and exercised of late is illegall.

That the Commission for erecting the late Court of Commissioners for Ecclesiasticall Causes and all other Commissions and Courts of like nature are Illegall and Pernicious.

That levying Money for or to the Use of the Crowne by pretence of Prerogative without Grant of Parlyament for longer time or in other manner then the same is or shall be granted is Illegall.

That it is the Right of the Subjects to petition the King and all Commitments and Prosecutions for such Petitioning are Illegall.

That the raising or keeping a standing Army within the Kingdome in time of Peace unlesse it be with Consent of Parlyament is against Law.

That the Subjects which are Protestants may have Arms for their Defence suitable to their Conditions and as allowed by Law.

That Election of Members of Parlyament ought to be free.

That the Freedome of Speech and Debates or Proceedings in Parlyament ought not to be impeached or questioned in any Court or Place out of Parlyament.

That excessive Baile ought not to be required nor excessive Fines imposed nor cruell and unusuall Punishments inflicted.

That Jurors ought to be duely impannelled and returned.

That all Grants and Promises of Fines and Forfeitures of particular persons before Conviction are illegall and void.

And that for Redresse of all Grievances and for the amending strengthening and preserveing of the Lawes Parlyaments ought to be held frequently.

And they doe Claime Demand and Insist upon all and singular the Premises as their undoubted Rights and Liberties and that noe Declarations Judgements Doeings or Proceedings to the Prejudice of the People in any of the said Premisses ought in any wise to be drawne hereafter into Consequence or Example. To which Demand of their Rights they are particularly encouraged by the Declaration of this Highnesse the Prince of Orange as being the onely meanes for obtaining a full Redresse and Remedy therein. Haveing therefore an intire Confidence That his said Highnesse the Prince of Orange will perfect the Deliverance soe farr advanced by him and will still preserve them from the Violation of their Rights which they have here asserted and from all other Attempts upon their Religion Rights and Liberties. The said Lords Spirituall and Temporall and Commons assembled at Westminster doe Resolve That William and Mary Prince and Princesse of Orange be and be declared King and Queene of England France and Ireland and the Dominions thereunto belonging to hold the Crowne and Royall Dignity of the said Kingdomes and Dominions to them the said Prince and Princesse dureing their Lives and the Life of the Survivour of them And that the sole and full Exercise of the Regall Power be onely in and executed by the said Prince of Orange in the Names of the said Prince and Princesse dureing their joynt Lives And after their Deceases the said Crowne and Royall Dignitie of the said Kingdoms and Dominions to be to the Heires of the Body of the said Princesse And for default of such Issue to the Princesse Anne of Denmarke and the Heires of her Body And for default of such Issue to the Heires of the Body of the said Prince of Orange. And the Lords Spirituall and Temporall and Commons doe pray the said Prince and Princesse to accept the same accordingly.

And that the Oathes hereafter mentioned be taken by all Persons of whome the Oathes of Allegiance and Supremacy might be required by Law instead of them And that the said Oathes of Allegiance and Supremacy be abrogated.

I A B doe sincerely promise and sweare That I will be faithfull and beare true Allegiance to their Majestyes King William and Queene Mary Soe helpe me God.

I A B doe sweare That I doe from my Heart Abhorr, Detest and Abjure as Impious and Hereticall this damnable Doctrine and Position That Princes Excommunicated or Deprived by the Pope or any Authority of the See of Rome may be deposed or murdered by their Subjects or any other whatsoever. And I doe declare That noe Forreigne Prince Person Prelate, State or

Potentate hath or ought to have any Jurisdiction Power Superiority Preeminence or Authoritie Ecclesiasticall or Spirituall within this Realme Soe helpe me God.

Upon which their said Majestyes did accept the Crowne and Royall Dignitie of the Kingdoms of England France and Ireland and the Dominions thereunto belonging according to the Resolution and Desire of the said Lords and Commons contained in the said Declaration. And thereupon their Majestyes were pleased That the said Lords Spirituall and Temporall and Commons being the two Houses of Parlyament should continue to sitt and with their Majesties Royall Concurrence make effectuall Provision for the Setlement of the Religion Lawes and Liberties of this Kingdome soe that the same for the future might not be in danger againe of being subverted, To which the said Lords Spirituall and Temporall and Commons did agree and proceede to act accordingly.

[The remainder is omitted.]

Parliament Act 1911 [An Act to make provision with respect to the powers of the House of Lords in relation to those of the House of Commons, and to limit the duration of Parliament] as amended by, *inter alia*, the Parliament Act 1949 [An Act to amend the Parliament Act 1911].[2]

Whereas it is expedient that provision should be made for regulating the relations between the two Houses of Parliament:

And whereas it is intended to substitute for the House of Lords as it at present exists a Second Chamber constituted on a popular instead of hereditary basis, but such substitution cannot be immediately brought into operation:

And whereas provision will require hereafter to be made by Parliament in a measure effecting such substitution for limiting and defining the powers of the new Second Chamber, but it is expedient to make such provision as in this Act appears for restricting the existing powers of the House of Lords:

Section 1. (1) If a Money Bill, having been passed by the House of Commons, and sent up to the House of Lords at least one month before the end of the session, is not passed by the House of Lords without amendment within one month after it is so sent up to that House, the Bill shall, unless the House of Commons direct to the contrary, be presented to His Majesty and become an Act of Parliament on the Royal Assent being signified, notwithstanding that the House of Lords have not consented to the Bill.
(2) A Money Bill means a Public Bill which in the opinion of the Speaker of the House of Commons contains only provisions dealing with all or any of the following subjects, namely, the imposition, repeal, remission, alteration, or regulation of taxation; the imposition for the payment of debt or other financial purposes of charges on the Consolidated Fund, the National Loans Fund or on money provided by Parliament, or the variation or repeal of any such charges; supply; the appropriation, receipt, custody, issue or audit of accounts of public money; the raising or guarantee of any loan or the repayment thereof; or subordinate matters incidental to those subjects or any of them. In this subsection the expressions "taxation," "public money," and "loan" respectively do not include any taxation, money, or loan raised by local authorities or bodies for local purposes.
(3) There shall be endorsed on every Money Bill when it is sent up to the House of Lords and when it is presented to His Majesty for assent the certificate of the Speaker of the House of Commons signed by him that it is a Money Bill. Before giving his certificate the Speaker shall consult, if practicable, two members to be appointed from the Chairmen's Panel at the beginning of each Session by the Committee of Selection.

Section 2. (1) If any Public Bill (other than a Money Bill or a Bill containing any provision to extend the maximum duration of Parliament beyond five years) is passed by the House of Commons in two successive sessions (whether of the same Parliament or not), and, having been sent up to the House of Lords at least one month before the end of the session, is rejected by the House of Lords in each of those sessions, that Bill shall, on its rejection for the second

---

[2] This text has also been published separately in: Ph. Kiiver & N. Kornet, eds., *The Maastricht Collection: Selected National, European and International Provisions from Public and Private Law*, Second Edition (Groningen: Europa Law Publishing, 2010). It has also been published in a smaller compilation covering only the area of constitutional law: Ph. Kiiver, ed., *Sources of Constitutional Law: Constitutions and Fundamental Legal Provisions from the United States, France, Germany, the Netherlands, the United Kingdom, the ECHR and the EU*, Second Edition (Groningen: Europa Law Publishing, 2010).

time by the House of Lords, unless the House of Commons direct to the contrary, be presented to His Majesty and become an Act of Parliament on the Royal Assent being signified thereto, notwithstanding that the House of Lords have not consented to the Bill: Provided that this provision shall not take effect unless one year has elapsed between the date of the second reading in the first of those sessions of the Bill in the House of Commons and the date on which it passes the House of Commons in the second of these sessions.

(2) When a Bill is presented to His Majesty for assent in pursuance of the provisions of this section, there shall be endorsed on the Bill the certificate of the Speaker of the House of Commons signed by him that the provisions of this section have been duly complied with.

(3) A Bill shall be deemed to be rejected by the House of Lords if it is not passed by the House of Lords either without amendment or with such amendments only as may be agreed to by both Houses.

(4) A Bill shall be deemed to be the same Bill as a former Bill sent up to the House of Lords in the preceding session if, when it is sent up to the House of Lords, it is identical with the former Bill or contains only such alterations as are certified by the Speaker of the House of Commons to be necessary owing to the time which has elapsed since the date of the former Bill, or to represent any amendments which have been made by the House of Lords in the former Bill in the preceding session, and any amendments which are certified by the Speaker to have been made by the House of Lords in the second session and agreed to by the House of Commons shall be inserted in the Bill as presented for Royal Assent in pursuance of this section:

Provided that the House of Commons may, if they think fit, on the passage of such a Bill through the House in the second session, suggest any further amendments without inserting the amendments in the Bill, and any such suggested amendments shall be considered by the House of Lords, and, if agreed to by that House, shall be treated as amendments made by the House of Lords and agreed to by the House of Commons; but the exercise of this power by the House of Commons shall not affect the operation of this section in the event of the Bill being rejected by the House of Lords.

Section 3. Any certificate of the Speaker of the House of Commons given under this Act shall be conclusive for all purposes, and shall not be questioned in any court of law.

Section 4. (1) In every Bill presented to His Majesty under the preceding provisions of this Act, the words of enactment shall be as follows, that is to say:

"Be it enacted by the King's most Excellent Majesty, by and with the advice and consent of the Commons in this present Parliament assembled, in accordance with the provisions of the Parliament Acts 1911 and 1949 and by authority of the same, as follows."

(2) Any alteration of a Bill necessary to give effect to this section shall not be deemed to be an amendment of the Bill.

Section 5. In this Act the expression "Public Bill" does not include any Bill for confirming a Provisional Order.

Section 6. Nothing in this Act shall diminish or qualify the existing rights and privileges of the House of Commons.

Section 7. Five years shall be substituted for seven years as the time fixed for the maximum duration of Parliament under the Septennial Act 1715.

Section 8. This Act may be cited as the Parliament Act 1911.

Parliament Act 1949 [An Act to amend the Parliament Act 1911].

Section 1. The Parliament Act, 1911, shall have effect, and shall be deemed to have had effect from the beginning of the session in which the Bill for this Act originated (save as regards that Bill itself), as if –
(a) there had been substituted in subsections (1) and (4) of section two thereof, for the words "in three successive sessions", "for the third time", "in the third of those sessions", "in the third session", and "in the second or third session" respectively, the words " in two successive sessions", "for the second time", "in the second of those sessions", "in the second session", and "in the second session" respectively; and
(b) there had been substituted in subsection (1) of the said section two, for the words "two years have elapsed" the words "one year has elapsed":
Provided that, if a Bill has been rejected for the second time by the House of Lords before the signification of the Royal Assent to the Bill for this Act, whether such rejection was in the same session as that in which the Royal Assent to the Bill for this Act was signified or in an earlier session, the requirement of the said section two that a Bill is to be presented to His Majesty on its rejection for the second time by the House of Lords shall have effect in relation to the Bill rejected as a requirement that it is to be presented to His Majesty as soon as the Royal Assent to the Bill for this Act has been signified, and, notwithstanding that such rejection was in an earlier session, the Royal Assent to the Bill rejected may be signified in the session in which the Royal Assent to the Bill for this Act was signified.

Section 2. (1) This Act may be cited as the Parliament Act 1949.
(2) This Act and the Parliament Act 1911, shall be construed as one and may be cited together as the Parliament Acts 1911 and 1949.

Human Rights Act 1998 [An Act to give further effect to rights and freedoms guaranteed under the European Convention on Human Rights; to make provision with respect to holders of certain judicial offices who become judges of the European Court of Human Rights; and for connected purposes] as amended. Selected provisions: Sections 1 to 10 and Schedule 2.[3]

Section 1. (1) In this Act "the Convention rights" means the rights and fundamental freedoms set out in –
(a) Articles 2 to 12 and 14 of the Convention,
(b) Articles 1 to 3 of the First Protocol, and
(c) Article 1 of the Thirteenth Protocol,
as read with Articles 16 to 18 of the Convention.
(2) Those Articles are to have effect for the purposes of this Act subject to any designated derogation or reservation (as to which see sections 14 and 15).
(3) The Articles are set out in Schedule 1.
(4) The Secretary of State may by order make such amendments to this Act as he considers appropriate to reflect the effect, in relation to the United Kingdom, of a protocol.
(5) In subsection (4) "protocol" means a protocol to the Convention –
(a) which the United Kingdom has ratified; or
(b) which the United Kingdom has signed with a view to ratification.
(6) No amendment may be made by an order under subsection (4) so as to come into force before the protocol concerned is in force in relation to the United Kingdom.

Section 2. (1) A court or tribunal determining a question which has arisen in connection with a Convention right must take into account any –
(a) judgment, decision, declaration or advisory opinion of the European Court of Human Rights,
(b) opinion of the Commission given in a report adopted under Article 31 of the Convention,
(c) decision of the Commission in connection with Article 26 or 27 (2) of the Convention, or
(d) decision of the Committee of Ministers taken under Article 46 of the Convention,
whenever made or given, so far as, in the opinion of the court or tribunal, it is relevant to the proceedings in which that question has arisen.
(2) Evidence of any judgment, decision, declaration or opinion of which account may have to be taken under this section is to be given in proceedings before any court or tribunal in such manner as may be provided by rules.
(3) In this section "rules" means rules of court or, in the case of proceedings before a tribunal, rules made for the purposes of this section –
(a) by the Lord Chancellor or the Secretary of State, in relation to any proceedings outside Scotland;
(b) by the Secretary of State, in relation to proceedings in Scotland; or
(c) by a Northern Ireland department, in relation to proceedings before a tribunal in Northern Ireland –
(i) which deals with transferred matters; and

---

[3] This text has also been published separately in: Ph. Kiiver & N. Kornet, eds., *The Maastricht Collection: Selected National, European and International Provisions from Public and Private Law*, Second Edition (Groningen: Europa Law Publishing, 2010). It has also been published in a smaller compilation covering only the area of constitutional law: Ph. Kiiver, ed., *Sources of Constitutional Law: Constitutions and Fundamental Legal Provisions from the United States, France, Germany, the Netherlands, the United Kingdom, the ECHR and the EU*, Second Edition (Groningen: Europa Law Publishing, 2010).

(ii) for which no rules made under paragraph (a) are in force.

Section 3. (1) So far as it is possible to do so, primary legislation and subordinate legislation must be read and given effect in a way which is compatible with the Convention rights.
(2) This section –
(a) applies to primary legislation and subordinate legislation whenever enacted;
(b) does not affect the validity, continuing operation or enforcement of any incompatible primary legislation; and
(c) does not affect the validity, continuing operation or enforcement of any incompatible subordinate legislation if (disregarding any possibility of revocation) primary legislation prevents removal of the incompatibility.

Section 4. (1) Subsection (2) applies in any proceedings in which a court determines whether a provision of primary legislation is compatible with a Convention right.
(2) If the court is satisfied that the provision is incompatible with a Convention right, it may make a declaration of that incompatibility.
(3) Subsection (4) applies in any proceedings in which a court determines whether a provision of subordinate legislation, made in the exercise of a power conferred by primary legislation, is compatible with a Convention right.
(4) If the court is satisfied –
(a) that the provision is incompatible with a Convention right, and
(b) that (disregarding any possibility of revocation) the primary legislation concerned prevents removal of the incompatibility,
it may make a declaration of that incompatibility.
(5) In this section "court" means –
(a) the Supreme Court;
(b) the Judicial Committee of the Privy Council;
(c) the Court Martial Appeal Court;
(d) in Scotland, the High Court of Justiciary sitting otherwise than as a trial court or the Court of Session;
(e) in England and Wales or Northern Ireland, the High Court or the Court of Appeal.
(f) the Court of Protection, in any matter being dealt with by the President of the Family Division, the Vice-Chancellor or a puisne judge of the High Court.
(6) A declaration under this section ("a declaration of incompatibility") –
(a) does not affect the validity, continuing operation or enforcement of the provision in respect of which it is given; and
(b) is not binding on the parties to the proceedings in which it is made.

Section 5. (1) Where a court is considering whether to make a declaration of incompatibility, the Crown is entitled to notice in accordance with rules of court.
(2) In any case to which subsection (1) applies –
(a) a Minister of the Crown (or a person nominated by him),
(b) a member of the Scottish Executive,
(c) a Northern Ireland Minister,
(d) a Northern Ireland department,
is entitled, on giving notice in accordance with rules of court, to be joined as a party to the proceedings.
(3) Notice under subsection (2) may be given at any time during the proceedings.
(4) A person who has been made a party to criminal proceedings (other than in Scotland) as the result of a notice under subsection (2) may, with leave, appeal to the Supreme Court against any declaration of incompatibility made in the proceedings.
(5) In subsection (4) –

"criminal proceedings" includes all proceedings before the Court Martial Appeal Court; and "leave" means leave granted by the court making the declaration of incompatibility or by the Supreme Court.

Section 6. (1) It is unlawful for a public authority to act in a way which is incompatible with a Convention right.
(2) Subsection (1) does not apply to an act if –
(a) as the result of one or more provisions of primary legislation, the authority could not have acted differently; or
(b) in the case of one or more provisions of, or made under, primary legislation which cannot be read or given effect in a way which is compatible with the Convention rights, the authority was acting so as to give effect to or enforce those provisions.
(3) In this section "public authority" includes –
(a) a court or tribunal, and
(b) any person certain of whose functions are functions of a public nature,
but does not include either House of Parliament or a person exercising functions in connection with proceedings in Parliament.
(4) (Repealed).
(5) In relation to a particular act, a person is not a public authority by virtue only of subsection (3)(b) if the nature of the act is private.
(6) "An act" includes a failure to act but does not include a failure to –
(a) introduce in, or lay before, Parliament a proposal for legislation; or
(b) make any primary legislation or remedial order.

Section 7. (1) A person who claims that a public authority has acted (or proposes to act) in a way which is made unlawful by section 6 (1) may –
(a) bring proceedings against the authority under this Act in the appropriate court or tribunal, or
(b) rely on the Convention right or rights concerned in any legal proceedings,
but only if he is (or would be) a victim of the unlawful act.
(2) In subsection (1)(a) "appropriate court or tribunal" means such court or tribunal as may be determined in accordance with rules; and proceedings against an authority include a counterclaim or similar proceeding.
(3) If the proceedings are brought on an application for judicial review, the applicant is to be taken to have a sufficient interest in relation to the unlawful act only if he is, or would be, a victim of that act.
(4) If the proceedings are made by way of a petition for judicial review in Scotland, the applicant shall be taken to have title and interest to sue in relation to the unlawful act only if he is, or would be, a victim of that act.
(5) Proceedings under subsection (1)(a) must be brought before the end of –
(a) the period of one year beginning with the date on which the act complained of took place; or
(b) such longer period as the court or tribunal considers equitable having regard to all the circumstances,
but that is subject to any rule imposing a stricter time limit in relation to the procedure in question.
(6) In subsection (1)(b) "legal proceedings" includes –
(a) proceedings brought by or at the instigation of a public authority; and
(b) an appeal against the decision of a court or tribunal.
(7) For the purposes of this section, a person is a victim of an unlawful act only if he would be a victim for the purposes of Article 34 of the Convention if proceedings were brought in the European Court of Human Rights in respect of that act.

(8) Nothing in this Act creates a criminal offence.
(9) In this section "rules" means –
(a) in relation to proceedings before a court or tribunal outside Scotland, rules made by the Lord Chancellor or the Secretary of State for the purposes of this section or rules of court,
(b) in relation to proceedings before a court or tribunal in Scotland, rules made by the Secretary of State for those purposes,
(c) in relation to proceedings before a tribunal in Northern Ireland –
(i) which deals with transferred matters; and
(ii) for which no rules made under paragraph (a) are in force,
rules made by a Northern Ireland department for those purposes,
and includes provision made by order under section 1 of the Courts and Legal Services Act 1990.
(10) In making rules, regard must be had to section 9.
(11) The Minister who has power to make rules in relation to a particular tribunal may, to the extent he considers it necessary to ensure that the tribunal can provide an appropriate remedy in relation to an act (or proposed act) of a public authority which is (or would be) unlawful as a result of section 6 (1), by order add to –
(a) the relief or remedies which the tribunal may grant; or
(b) the grounds on which it may grant any of them.
(12) An order made under subsection (11) may contain such incidental, supplemental, consequential or transitional provision as the Minister making it considers appropriate.
(13) "The Minister" includes the Northern Ireland department concerned.

Section 8. (1) In relation to any act (or proposed act) of a public authority which the court finds is (or would be) unlawful, it may grant such relief or remedy, or make such order, within its powers as it considers just and appropriate.
(2) But damages may be awarded only by a court which has power to award damages, or to order the payment of compensation, in civil proceedings.
(3) No award of damages is to be made unless, taking account of all the circumstances of the case, including –
(a) any other relief or remedy granted, or order made, in relation to the act in question (by that or any other court), and
(b) the consequences of any decision (of that or any other court) in respect of that act,
the court is satisfied that the award is necessary to afford just satisfaction to the person in whose favour it is made.
(4) In determining –
(a) whether to award damages, or
(b) the amount of an award,
the court must take into account the principles applied by the European Court of Human Rights in relation to the award of compensation under Article 41 of the Convention.
(5) A public authority against which damages are awarded is to be treated –
(a) in Scotland, for the purposes of section 3 of the Law Reform (Miscellaneous Provisions) (Scotland) Act 1940 as if the award were made in an action of damages in which the authority has been found liable in respect of loss or damage to the person to whom the award is made;
(b) for the purposes of the Civil Liability (Contribution) Act 1978 as liable in respect of damage suffered by the person to whom the award is made.
(6) In this section –
"court" includes a tribunal;
"damages" means damages for an unlawful act of a public authority; and
"unlawful" means unlawful under section 6 (1).

Section 9. (1) Proceedings under section 7(1)(a) in respect of a judicial act may be brought only –
(a) by exercising a right of appeal;
(b) on an application (in Scotland a petition) for judicial review; or
(c) in such other forum as may be prescribed by rules.
(2) That does not affect any rule of law which prevents a court from being the subject of judicial review.
(3) In proceedings under this Act in respect of a judicial act done in good faith, damages may not be awarded otherwise than to compensate a person to the extent required by Article 5(5) of the Convention.
(4) An award of damages permitted by subsection (3) is to be made against the Crown; but no award may be made unless the appropriate person, if not a party to the proceedings, is joined.
(5) In this section –
"appropriate person" means the Minister responsible for the court concerned, or a person or government department nominated by him;
"court" includes a tribunal;
"judge" includes a member of a tribunal, a justice of the peace (or, in Northern Ireland, a lay magistrate) and a clerk or other officer entitled to exercise the jurisdiction of a court;
"judicial act" means a judicial act of a court and includes an act done on the instructions, or on behalf, of a judge; and
"rules" has the same meaning as in section 7 (9).

Section 10. (1) This section applies if –
(a) a provision of legislation has been declared under section 4 to be incompatible with a Convention right and, if an appeal lies –
(i) all persons who may appeal have stated in writing that they do not intend to do so;
(ii) the time for bringing an appeal has expired and no appeal has been brought within that time; or
(iii) an appeal brought within that time has been determined or abandoned; or
(b) it appears to a Minister of the Crown or Her Majesty in Council that, having regard to a finding of the European Court of Human Rights made after the coming into force of this section in proceedings against the United Kingdom, a provision of legislation is incompatible with an obligation of the United Kingdom arising from the Convention.
(2) If a Minister of the Crown considers that there are compelling reasons for proceeding under this section, he may by order make such amendments to the legislation as he considers necessary to remove the incompatibility.
(3) If, in the case of subordinate legislation, a Minister of the Crown considers –
(a) that it is necessary to amend the primary legislation under which the subordinate legislation in question was made, in order to enable the incompatibility to be removed, and
(b) that there are compelling reasons for proceeding under this section,
he may by order make such amendments to the primary legislation as he considers necessary.
(4) This section also applies where the provision in question is in subordinate legislation and has been quashed, or declared invalid, by reason of incompatibility with a Convention right and the Minister proposes to proceed under paragraph 2(b) of Schedule 2.
(5) If the legislation is an Order in Council, the power conferred by subsection (2) or (3) is exercisable by Her Majesty in Council.
(6) In this section "legislation" does not include a Measure of the Church Assembly or of the General Synod of the Church of England.
(7) Schedule 2 makes further provision about remedial orders.

[The remainder of the Act proper and Schedule 1 are omitted.]

Schedule 2 (Remedial Orders)

Paragraph 1. (1) A remedial order may –
(a) contain such incidental, supplemental, consequential or transitional provision as the person making it considers appropriate;
(b) be made so as to have effect from a date earlier than that on which it is made;
(c) make provision for the delegation of specific functions;
(d) make different provision for different cases.
(2) The power conferred by sub-paragraph (1) (a) includes –
(a) power to amend primary legislation (including primary legislation other than that which contains the incompatible provision); and
(b) power to amend or revoke subordinate legislation (including subordinate legislation other than that which contains the incompatible provision).
(3) A remedial order may be made so as to have the same extent as the legislation which it affects.
(4) No person is to be guilty of an offence solely as a result of the retrospective effect of a remedial order.

Paragraph 2. No remedial order may be made unless –
(a) a draft of the order has been approved by a resolution of each House of Parliament made after the end of the period of 60 days beginning with the day on which the draft was laid; or
(b) it is declared in the order that it appears to the person making it that, because of the urgency of the matter, it is necessary to make the order without a draft being so approved.

Paragraph 3. (1) No draft may be laid under paragraph 2(a) unless –
(a) the person proposing to make the order has laid before Parliament a document which contains a draft of the proposed order and the required information; and
(b) the period of 60 days, beginning with the day on which the document required by this sub-paragraph was laid, has ended.
(2) If representations have been made during that period, the draft laid under paragraph 2(a) must be accompanied by a statement containing –
(a) a summary of the representations; and
(b) if, as a result of the representations, the proposed order has been changed, details of the changes.

Paragraph 4. (1) If a remedial order ("the original order") is made without being approved in draft, the person making it must lay it before Parliament, accompanied by the required information, after it is made.
(2) If representations have been made during the period of 60 days beginning with the day on which the original order was made, the person making it must (after the end of that period) lay before Parliament a statement containing –
(a) a summary of the representations; and
(b) if, as a result of the representations, he considers it appropriate to make changes to the original order, details of the changes.
(3) If sub-paragraph (2) (b) applies, the person making the statement must –
(a) make a further remedial order replacing the original order; and
(b) lay the replacement order before Parliament.
(4) If, at the end of the period of 120 days beginning with the day on which the original order was made, a resolution has not been passed by each House approving the original or replacement order, the order ceases to have effect (but without that affecting anything previously done under either order or the power to make a fresh remedial order).

Paragraph 5. In this Schedule –
"representations" means representations about a remedial order (or proposed remedial order) made to the person making (or proposing to make) it and includes any relevant Parliamentary report or resolution; and
"required information" means –
(a) an explanation of the incompatibility which the order (or proposed order) seeks to remove, including particulars of the relevant declaration, finding or order; and
(b) a statement of the reasons for proceeding under section 10 and for making an order in those terms.

Paragraph 6. In calculating any period for the purposes of this Schedule, no account is to be taken of any time during which –
(a) Parliament is dissolved or prorogued; or
(b) both Houses are adjourned for more than four days.

Paragraph 7. (1) This paragraph applies in relation to –
(a) any remedial order made, and any draft of such an order proposed to be made, –
(i) by the Scottish Ministers; or
(ii) within devolved competence (within the meaning of the Scotland Act 1998) by Her Majesty in Council; and
(b) any document or statement to be laid in connection with such an order (or proposed order).
(2) This Schedule has effect in relation to any such order (or proposed order), document or statement subject to the following modifications.
(3) Any reference to Parliament, each House of Parliament or both Houses of Parliament shall be construed as a reference to the Scottish Parliament.
(4) Paragraph 6 does not apply and instead, in calculating any period for the purposes of this Schedule, no account is to be taken of any time during which the Scottish Parliament is dissolved or is in recess for more than four days.

[The remaining Schedules are omitted.]

Scotland Act 1998 [An Act to provide for the establishment of a Scottish Parliament and Administration and other changes in the government of Scotland; to provide for changes in the constitution and functions of certain public authorities; to provide for the variation of the basic rate of income tax in relation to income of Scottish taxpayers in accordance with a resolution of the Scottish Parliament; to amend the law about parliamentary constituencies in Scotland; and for connected purposes] as amended. Selected provisions: Sections 1, 28 and 29.[4]

Part I. The Scottish Parliament

Section 1. (1) There shall be a Scottish Parliament.
(2) One member of the Parliament shall be returned for each constituency (under the simple majority system) at an election held in the constituency.
(3) Members of the Parliament for each region shall be returned at a general election under the additional member system of proportional representation provided for in this Part and vacancies among such members shall be filled in accordance with this Part.
(4) The validity of any proceedings of the Parliament is not affected by any vacancy in its membership.
(5) Schedule 1 (which makes provision for the constituencies and regions for the purposes of this Act and the number of regional members) shall have effect.

[Sections 2 to 27 are omitted.]

Section 28. (1) Subject to section 29, the Parliament may make laws, to be known as Acts of the Scottish Parliament.
(2) Proposed Acts of the Scottish Parliament shall be known as Bills; and a Bill shall become an Act of the Scottish Parliament when it has been passed by the Parliament and has received Royal Assent.
(3) A Bill receives Royal Assent at the beginning of the day on which Letters Patent under the Scottish Seal signed with Her Majesty's own hand signifying Her Assent are recorded in the Register of the Great Seal.
(4) The date of Royal Assent shall be written on the Act of the Scottish Parliament by the Clerk, and shall form part of the Act.
(5) The validity of an Act of the Scottish Parliament is not affected by any invalidity in the proceedings of the Parliament leading to its enactment.
(6) Every Act of the Scottish Parliament shall be judicially noticed.
(7) This section does not affect the power of the Parliament of the United Kingdom to make laws for Scotland.

Section 29. (1) An Act of the Scottish Parliament is not law so far as any provision of the Act is outside the legislative competence of the Parliament.
(2) A provision is outside that competence so far as any of the following paragraphs apply –
(a) it would form part of the law of a country or territory other than Scotland, or confer or remove functions exercisable otherwise than in or as regards Scotland,
(b) it relates to reserved matters,

---

[4] This text has also been published separately in: Ph. Kiiver & N. Kornet, eds., *The Maastricht Collection: Selected National, European and International Provisions from Public and Private Law*, Second Edition (Groningen: Europa Law Publishing, 2010). It has also been published in a smaller compilation covering only the area of constitutional law: Ph. Kiiver, ed., *Sources of Constitutional Law: Constitutions and Fundamental Legal Provisions from the United States, France, Germany, the Netherlands, the United Kingdom, the ECHR and the EU*, Second Edition (Groningen: Europa Law Publishing, 2010).

(c) it is in breach of the restrictions in Schedule 4,
(d) it is incompatible with any of the Convention rights or with Community law,
(e) it would remove the Lord Advocate from his position as head of the systems of criminal prosecution and investigation of deaths in Scotland.
(3) For the purposes of this section, the question whether a provision of an Act of the Scottish Parliament relates to a reserved matter is to be determined, subject to subsection (4), by reference to the purpose of the provision, having regard (among other things) to its effect in all the circumstances.
(4) A provision which –
(a) would otherwise not relate to reserved matters, but
(b) makes modifications of Scots private law, or Scots criminal law, as it applies to reserved matters,
is to be treated as relating to reserved matters unless the purpose of the provision is to make the law in question apply consistently to reserved matters and otherwise.

[The remainder is omitted.]

Annex 12

THE ECHR

Convention for the Protection of Human Rights and Fundamental Freedoms signed at Rome on 4 November 1950 as last amended by Protocol 14 (1 June 2010), with Articles 1 to 3 of Protocol 1, Articles 1 to 4 of Protocol 4, Articles 1 and 2 of Protocol 6, Articles 1 to 5 of Protocol 7, Article 1 of Protocol 12 and Article 1 of Protocol 13.[1]

Preamble

The governments signatory hereto, being members of the Council of Europe, Considering the Universal Declaration of Human Rights proclaimed by the General Assembly of the United Nations on 10 December 1948;
Considering that this Declaration aims at securing the universal and effective recognition and observance of the Rights therein declared;
Considering that the aim of the Council of Europe is the achievement of greater unity between its members and that one of the methods by which that aim is to be pursued is the maintenance and further realisation of human rights and fundamental freedoms;
Reaffirming their profound belief in those fundamental freedoms which are the foundation of justice and peace in the world and are best maintained on the one hand by an effective political democracy and on the other by a common understanding and observance of the human rights upon which they depend;
Being resolved, as the governments of European countries which are likeminded and have a common heritage of political traditions, ideals, freedom and the rule of law, to take the first steps for the collective enforcement of certain of the rights stated in the Universal Declaration,
Have agreed as follows:

Article 1. The High Contracting Parties shall secure to everyone within their jurisdiction the rights and freedoms defined in Section I of this Convention.

---

[1] This text has also been published separately in: Ph. Kiiver & N. Kornet, eds., *The Maastricht Collection: Selected National, European and International Provisions from Public and Private Law*, Second Edition (Groningen: Europa Law Publishing, 2010). It has also been published in a smaller compilation covering only the area of constitutional law: Ph. Kiiver, ed., *Sources of Constitutional Law: Constitutions and Fundamental Legal Provisions from the United States, France, Germany, the Netherlands, the United Kingdom, the ECHR and the EU*, Second Edition (Groningen: Europa Law Publishing, 2010).

Section I. Rights and freedoms

Article 2. (1) Everyone's right to life shall be protected by law. No one shall be deprived of his life intentionally save in the execution of a sentence of a court following his conviction of a crime for which this penalty is provided by law.
(2) Deprivation of life shall not be regarded as inflicted in contravention of this Article when it results from the use of force which is no more than absolutely necessary:
(a) in defence of any person from unlawful violence;
(b) in order to effect a lawful arrest or to prevent the escape of a person lawfully detained;
(c) in action lawfully taken for the purpose of quelling a riot or insurrection.

Article 3. No one shall be subjected to torture or to inhuman or degrading treatment or punishment.

Article 4. (1) No one shall be held in slavery or servitude.
(2) No one shall be required to perform forced or compulsory labour.
(3) For the purpose of this Article the term "forced or compulsory labour" shall not include:
(a) any work required to be done in the ordinary course of detention imposed according to the provisions of Article 5 of this Convention or during conditional release from such detention;
(b) any service of a military character or, in case of conscientious objectors in countries where they are recognised, service exacted instead of compulsory military service;
(c) any service exacted in case of an emergency or calamity threatening the life or well-being of the community;
(d) any work or service which forms part of normal civic obligations.

Article 5. (1) Everyone has the right to liberty and security of person. No one shall be deprived of his liberty save in the following cases and in accordance with a procedure prescribed by law:
(a) the lawful detention of a person after conviction by a competent court;
(b) the lawful arrest or detention of a person for non-compliance with the lawful order of a court or in order to secure the fulfilment of any obligation prescribed by law;
(c) the lawful arrest or detention of a person effected for the purpose of bringing him before the competent legal authority on reasonable suspicion of having committed an offence or when it is reasonably considered necessary to prevent his committing an offence or fleeing after having done so;
(d) the detention of a minor by lawful order for the purpose of educational supervision or his lawful detention for the purpose of bringing him before the competent legal authority;
(e) the lawful detention of persons for the prevention of the spreading of infectious diseases, of persons of un-sound mind, alcoholics or drug addicts or vagrants;
(f) the lawful arrest or detention of a person to prevent his effecting an unauthorised entry into the country or of a person against whom action is being taken with a view to deportation or extradition.
(2) Everyone who is arrested shall be informed promptly, in a language which he understands, of the reasons for his arrest and of any charge against him.
(3) Everyone arrested or detained in accordance with the provisions of paragraph 1 (c) of this Article shall be brought promptly before a judge or other officer authorised by law to exercise judicial power and shall be entitled to trial within a reasonable time or to release pending trial. Release may be conditioned by guarantees to appear for trial.
(4) Everyone who is deprived of his liberty by arrest or detention shall be entitled to take proceedings by which the lawfulness of his detention shall be decided speedily by a court and his release ordered if the detention is not lawful.
(5) Everyone who has been the victim of arrest or detention in contravention of the provisions of this Article shall have an enforceable right to compensation.

Article 6. (1) In the determination of his civil rights and obligations or of any criminal charge against him, everyone is entitled to a fair and public hearing within a reasonable time by an independent and impartial tribunal established by law. Judgment shall be pronounced publicly but the press and public may be excluded from all or part of the trial in the interests of morals, public order or national security in a democratic society, where the interests of juveniles or the protection of the private life of the parties so require, or to the extent strictly necessary in the opinion of the court in special circumstances where publicity would prejudice the interests of justice.
(2) Everyone charged with a criminal offence shall be presumed innocent until proved guilty according to law.
(3) Everyone charged with a criminal offence has the following minimum rights:
(a) to be informed promptly, in a language which he understands and in detail, of the nature and cause of the accusation against him;
(b) to have adequate time and facilities for the preparation of his defence;
(c) to defend himself in person or through legal assistance of his own choosing or, if he has not sufficient means to pay for legal assistance, to be given it free when the interests of justice so require;
(d) to examine or have examined witnesses against him and to obtain the attendance and examination of witnesses on his behalf under the same conditions as witnesses against him;
(e) to have the free assistance of an interpreter if he cannot understand or speak the language used in court.

Article 7. (1) No one shall be held guilty of any criminal offence on account of any act or omission which did not constitute a criminal offence under national or international law at the time when it was committed. Nor shall a heavier penalty be imposed than the one that was applicable at the time the criminal offence was committed.
(2) This Article shall not prejudice the trial and punishment of any person for any act or omission which, at the time when it was committed, was criminal according to the general principles of law recognised by civilised nations.

Article 8. (1) Everyone has the right to respect for his private and family life, his home and his correspondence.
(2) There shall be no interference by a public authority with the exercise of this right except such as is in accordance with the law and is necessary in a democratic society in the interests of national security, public safety or the economic well-being of the country, for the prevention of disorder or crime, for the protection of health or morals, or for the protection of the rights and freedoms of others.

Article 9. (1) Everyone has the right to freedom of thought, conscience and religion; this right includes freedom to change his religion or belief and freedom, either alone or in community with others and in public or private, to manifest his religion or belief, in worship, teaching, practice and observance.
(2) Freedom to manifest one's religion or beliefs shall be subject only to such limitations as are prescribed by law and are necessary in a democratic society in the interests of public safety, for the protection of public order, health or morals, or for the protection of the rights and freedoms of others.

Article 10. (1) Everyone has the right to freedom of expression. This right shall include freedom to hold opinions and to receive and impart information and ideas without interference by public authority and regardless of frontiers. This Article shall not prevent States from requiring the licensing of broadcasting, television or cinema enterprises.
(2) The exercise of these freedoms, since it carries with it duties and responsibilities, may be subject to such formalities, conditions, restrictions or penalties as are prescribed by law and

are necessary in a democratic society, in the interests of national security, territorial integrity or public safety, for the prevention of disorder or crime, for the protection of health or morals, for the protection of the reputation or rights of others, for preventing the disclosure of information received in confidence, or for maintaining the authority and impartiality of the judiciary.

Article 11. (1) Everyone has the right to freedom of peaceful assembly and to freedom of association with others, including the right to form and to join trade unions for the protection of his interests.
(2) No restrictions shall be placed on the exercise of these rights other than such as are prescribed by law and are necessary in a democratic society in the interests of national security or public safety, for the prevention of disorder or crime, for the protection of health or morals or for the protection of the rights and freedoms of others. This Article shall not prevent the imposition of lawful restrictions on the exercise of these rights by members of the armed forces, of the police or of the administration of the State.

Article 12. Men and women of marriageable age have the right to marry and to found a family, according to the national laws governing the exercise of this right.

Article 13. Everyone whose rights and freedoms as set forth in this Convention are violated shall have an effective remedy before a national authority notwithstanding that the violation has been committed by persons acting in an official capacity.

Article 14. The enjoyment of the rights and freedoms set forth in this Convention shall be secured without discrimination on any ground such as sex, race, colour, language, religion, political or other opinion, national or social origin, association with a national minority, property, birth or other status.

Article 15. (1) In time of war or other public emergency threatening the life of the nation any High Contracting Party may take measures derogating from its obligations under this Convention to the extent strictly required by the exigencies of the situation, provided that such measures are not inconsistent with its other obligations under international law.
(2) No derogation from Article 2, except in respect of deaths resulting from lawful acts of war, or from Articles 3, 4 § 1 and 7 shall be made under this provision.
(3) Any High Contracting Party availing itself of this right of derogation shall keep the Secretary General of the Council of Europe fully informed of the measures which it has taken and the reasons therefore. It shall also inform the Secretary General of the Council of Europe when such measures have ceased to operate and the provisions of the Convention are again being fully executed.

Article 16. Nothing in Articles 10, 11 and 14 shall be regarded as preventing the High Contracting Parties from imposing restrictions on the political activity of aliens.

Article 17. Nothing in this Convention may be interpreted as implying for any State, group or person any right to engage in any activity or perform any act aimed at the destruction of any of the rights and freedoms set forth herein or at their limitation to a greater extent than is provided for in the Convention.

Article 18. The restrictions permitted under this Convention to the said rights and freedoms shall not be applied for any purpose other than those for which they have been prescribed.

Section II. European Court of Human Rights

Article 19. To ensure the observance of the engagements undertaken by the High Contracting Parties in the Convention and the Protocols thereto, there shall be set up a European Court of Human Rights, hereinafter referred to as "the Court". It shall function on a permanent basis.

Article 20. The Court shall consist of a number of judges equal to that of the High Contracting Parties.

Article 21. (1) The judges shall be of high moral character and must either possess the qualifications required for appointment to high judicial office or be jurisconsults of recognised competence.
(2) The judges shall sit on the Court in their individual capacity.
(3) During their term of office the judges shall not engage in any activity which is incompatible with their independence, impartiality or with the demands of a full-time office; all questions arising from the application of this paragraph shall be decided by the Court.

Article 22. The judges shall be elected by the Parliamentary Assembly with respect to each High Contracting Party by a majority of votes cast from a list of three candidates nominated by the High Contracting Party.

Article 23. (1) The judges shall be elected for a period of nine years. They may not be re-elected.
(2) The terms of office of judges shall expire when they reach the age of 70.
(3) The judges shall hold office until replaced. They shall, however, continue to deal with such cases as they already have under consideration.
(4) No judge may be dismissed from office unless the other judges decide by a majority of two-thirds that that judge has ceased to fulfil the required conditions.

Article 24. (1) The Court shall have a Registry, the functions and organisation of which shall be laid down in the rules of the Court.
(2) When sitting in a single-judge formation, the Court shall be assisted by rapporteurs who shall function under the authority of the President of the Court. They shall form part of the Court's Registry.

Article 25. The plenary Court shall
(a) elect its President and one or two Vice-Presidents for a period of three years; they may be re-elected;
(b) set up Chambers, constituted for a fixed period of time;
(c) elect the Presidents of the Chambers of the Court; they may be re-elected;
(d) adopt the rules of the Court;
(e) elect the Registrar and one or more Deputy Registrars;
(f) make any request under Article 26 § 2.

Article 26. (1) To consider cases brought before it, the Court shall sit in a single-judge formation, in Committees of three judges, in Chambers of seven judges and in a Grand Chamber of seventeen judges. The Court's Chambers shall set up Committees for a fixed period of time.
(2) At the request of the plenary Court, the Committee of Ministers may, by a unanimous decision and for a fixed period, reduce to five the number of judges of the Chambers.
(3) When sitting as a single judge, a judge shall not examine any application against the High Contracting Party in respect of which that judge has been elected.
(4) There shall sit as an ex officio member of the Chamber and the Grand Chamber the judge elected in respect of the High Contracting Party concerned. If there is none or if that judge is unable to sit, a person chosen by the President of the Court from a list submitted in advance by that Party shall sit in the capacity of judge.

(5) The Grand Chamber shall also include the President of the Court, the Vice-Presidents, the Presidents of the Chambers and other judges chosen in accordance with the rules of the Court. When a case is referred to the Grand Chamber under Article 43, no judge from the Chamber which rendered the judgment shall sit in the Grand Chamber, with the exception of the President of the Chamber and the judge who sat in respect of the High Contracting Party concerned.

Article 27. (1) A single judge may declare inadmissible or strike out of the Court's list of cases an application submitted under Article 34, where such a decision can be taken without further examination.
(2) The decision shall be final.
(3) If the single judge does not declare an application inadmissible or strike it out, that judge shall forward it to a Committee or to a Chamber for further examination.

Article 28. (1) In respect of an application sub-mitted under Article 34, a Committee may, by a unanimous vote,
(a) declare it inadmissible or strike it out of its list of cases, where such decision can be taken without further examination; or
(b) declare it admissible and render at the same time a judgment on the merits, if the underlying question in the case, concerning the interpretation or the application of the Convention or the Protocols thereto, is already the subject of well-established case-law of the Court.
(2) Decisions and judgments under paragraph 1 shall be final.
(3) If the judge elected in respect of the High Contracting Party concerned is not a member of the Committee, the Committee may at any stage of the proceedings invite that judge to take the place of one of the members of the Committee, having regard to all relevant factors, including whether that Party has contested the application of the procedure under paragraph 1 (b).

Article 29. (1) If no decision is taken under Article 27 or 28, or no judgment rendered under Article 28, a Chamber shall decide on the admissibility and merits of individual applications submitted under Article 34. The decision on admissibility may be taken separately.
(2) A Chamber shall decide on the admissibility and merits of inter-State applications submitted under Article 33. The decision on admissibility shall be taken separately unless the Court, in exceptional cases, decides otherwise.

Article 30. Where a case pending before a Chamber raises a serious question affecting the interpretation of the Convention or the Protocols thereto, or where the resolution of a question before the Chamber might have a result inconsistent with a judgment previously delivered by the Court, the Chamber may, at any time before it has rendered its judgment, relinquish jurisdiction in favour of the Grand Chamber, unless one of the parties to the case objects.

Article 31. The Grand Chamber shall
(a) determine applications submitted either under Article 33 or Article 34 when a Chamber has relinquished jurisdiction under Article 30 or when the case has been referred to it under Article 43;
(b) decide on issues referred to the Court by the Committee of Ministers in accordance with Article 46 § 4; and
(c) consider requests for advisory opinions submitted under Article 47.

Article 32. (1) The jurisdiction of the Court shall extend to all matters concerning the interpretation and application of the Convention and the Protocols thereto which are referred to it as provided in Articles 33, 34, 46 and 47.
(2) In the event of dispute as to whether the Court has jurisdiction, the Court shall decide.

Article 33. Any High Contracting Party may refer to the Court any alleged breach of the provisions of the Convention and the Protocols thereto by another High Contracting Party.

Article 34. The Court may receive applications from any person, non-governmental organisation or group of individuals claiming to be the victim of a violation by one of the High Contracting Parties of the rights set forth in the Convention or the Protocols thereto. The High Contracting Parties undertake not to hinder in any way the effective exercise of this right.

Article 35. (1) The Court may only deal with the matter after all domestic remedies have been exhausted, according to the generally recognised rules of inter-national law, and within a period of six months from the date on which the final decision was taken.
(2) The Court shall not deal with any application submitted under Article 34 that
(a) is anonymous; or
(b) is substantially the same as a matter that has already been examined by the Court or has already been submitted to another procedure of international investigation or settlement and contains no relevant new information.
(3) The Court shall declare inadmissible any individual application submitted under Article 34 if it considers that:
(a) the application is incompatible with the provisions of the Convention or the Protocols thereto, manifestly ill-founded, or an abuse of the right of individual application; or
(b) the applicant has not suffered a significant disadvantage, unless respect for human rights as defined in the Convention and the Protocols thereto requires an examination of the application on the merits and provided that no case may be rejected on this ground which has not been duly considered by a domestic tribunal.
(4) The Court shall reject any application which it considers inadmissible under this Article. It may do so at any stage of the proceedings.

Article 36. (1) In all cases before a Chamber or the Grand Chamber, a High Contracting Party one of whose nationals is an applicant shall have the right to submit written comments and to take part in hearings.
(2) The President of the Court may, in the interest of the proper administration of justice, invite any High Contracting Party which is not a party to the proceedings or any person concerned who is not the applicant to submit written comments or take part in hearings.
(3) In all cases before a Chamber or the Grand Chamber, the Council of Europe Commissioner for Human Rights may submit written comments and take part in hearings.

Article 37. (1) The Court may at any stage of the proceedings decide to strike an application out of its list of cases where the circumstances lead to the conclusion that
(a) the applicant does not intend to pursue his application; or
(b) the matter has been resolved; or
(c) for any other reason established by the Court, it is no longer justified to continue the examination of the application.
However, the Court shall continue the examination of the application if respect for human rights as defined in the Convention and the Protocols thereto so requires.
(2) The Court may decide to restore an application to its list of cases if it considers that the circumstances justify such a course.

Article 38. The Court shall examine the case together with the representatives of the parties and, if need be, undertake an investigation, for the effective conduct of which the High Contracting Parties concerned shall furnish all necessary facilities.

Article 39. (1) At any stage of the proceedings, the Court may place itself at the disposal of the parties concerned with a view to securing a friendly settlement of the matter on the basis of respect for human rights as defined in the Convention and the Protocols thereto.

(2) Proceedings conducted under paragraph 1 shall be confidential.
(3) If a friendly settlement is effected, the Court shall strike the case out of its list by means of a decision which shall be confined to a brief statement of the facts and of the solution reached.
(4) This decision shall be transmitted to the Committee of Ministers, which shall supervise the execution of the terms of the friendly settlement as set out in the decision.

Article 40. (1) Hearings shall be in public unless the Court in exceptional circumstances decides otherwise.
(2) Documents deposited with the Registrar shall be accessible to the public unless the President of the Court decides otherwise.

Article 41. If the Court finds that there has been a violation of the Convention or the Protocols thereto, and if the internal law of the High Contracting Party concerned allows only partial reparation to be made, the Court shall, if necessary, afford just satisfaction to the injured party.

Article 42. Judgments of Chambers shall become final in accordance with the provisions of Article 44 § 2.

Article 43. (1) Within a period of three months from the date of the judgment of the Chamber, any party to the case may, in exceptional cases, request that the case be referred to the Grand Chamber.
(2) A panel of five judges of the Grand Chamber shall accept the request if the case raises a serious question affecting the interpretation or application of the Convention or the Protocols thereto, or a serious issue of general importance.
(3) If the panel accepts the request, the Grand Chamber shall decide the case by means of a judgment.

Article 44. (1) The judgment of the Grand Chamber shall be final.
(2) The judgment of a Chamber shall become final
(a) when the parties declare that they will not request that the case be referred to the Grand Chamber; or
(b) three months after the date of the judgment, if reference of the case to the Grand Chamber has not been requested; or
(c) when the panel of the Grand Chamber rejects the request to refer under Article 43.
(3) The final judgment shall be published.

Article 45. (1) Reasons shall be given for judgments as well as for decisions declaring applications admissible or inadmissible.
(2) If a judgment does not represent, in whole or in part, the unanimous opinion of the judges, any judge shall be entitled to deliver a separate opinion.

Article 46. (1). The High Contracting Parties under-take to abide by the final judgment of the Court in any case to which they are parties.
(2) The final judgment of the Court shall be transmitted to the Committee of Ministers, which shall supervise its execution.
(3) If the Committee of Ministers considers that the supervision of the execution of a final judgment is hindered by a problem of interpretation of the judgment, it may refer the matter to the Court for a ruling on the question of
interpretation. A referral decision shall require a majority vote of two thirds of the representatives entitled to sit on the Committee.
(4) If the Committee of Ministers considers that a High Contracting Party refuses to abide by a final judgment in a case to which it is a party, it may, after serving formal notice on that Party and by decision adopted by a majority vote of two-thirds of the representatives entitled to sit

on the Committee, refer to the Court the question whether that Party has failed to fulfil its obligation under paragraph 1.

(5) If the Court finds a violation of paragraph 1, it shall refer the case to the Committee of Ministers for consideration of the measures to be taken. If the Court finds no violation of paragraph 1, it shall refer the case to the Committee of Ministers, which shall close its examination of the case.

Article 47. (1) The Court may, at the request of the Committee of Ministers, give advisory opinions on legal questions concerning the interpretation of the Convention and the Protocols thereto.
(2) Such opinions shall not deal with any question relating to the content or scope of the rights or freedoms defined in Section I of the Convention and the Protocols thereto, or with any other question which the Court or the Committee of Ministers might have to consider in consequence of any such proceedings as could be instituted in accordance with the Convention.
(3) Decisions of the Committee of Ministers to request an advisory opinion of the Court shall require a majority vote of the representatives entitled to sit on the Committee.

Article 48. The Court shall decide whether a request for an advisory opinion submitted by the Committee of Ministers is within its competence as defined in Article 47.

Article 49. (1) Reasons shall be given for advisory opinions of the Court.
(2) If the advisory opinion does not represent, in whole or in part, the unanimous opinion of the judges, any judge shall be entitled to deliver a separate opinion.
(3) Advisory opinions of the Court shall be communicated to the Committee of Ministers.

Article 50. The expenditure on the Court shall be borne by the Council of Europe.

Article 51. The judges shall be entitled, during the exercise of their functions, to the privileges and immunities provided for in Article 40 of the Statute of the Council of Europe and in the agreements made thereunder.

Article 52. On receipt of a request from the Secretary General of the Council of Europe any High Contracting Party shall furnish an explanation of the manner in which its internal law ensures the effective implementation of any of the provisions of the Convention.

Article 53. Nothing in this Convention shall be construed as limiting or derogating from any of the human rights and fundamental freedoms which may be ensured under the laws of any High Contracting Party or under any other agreement to which it is a party.

Article 54. Nothing in this Convention shall prejudice the powers conferred on the Committee of Ministers by the Statute of the Council of Europe.

Article 55. The High Contracting Parties agree that, except by special agreement, they will not avail themselves of treaties, conventions or declarations in force between them for the purpose of submitting, by way of petition, a dispute arising out of the interpretation or application of this Convention to a means of settlement other than those provided for in this Convention.

Article 56. (1) Any State may at the time of its ratification or at any time thereafter declare by notification addressed to the Secretary General of the Council of Europe that the present Convention shall, subject to paragraph 4 of this Article, extend to all or any of the territories for whose international relations it is responsible.
(2) The Convention shall extend to the territory or territories named in the notification as from the thirtieth day after the receipt of this notification by the Secretary General of the Council of Europe.

(3) The provisions of this Convention shall be applied in such territories with due regard, however, to local requirements.

(4) Any State which has made a declaration in accordance with paragraph 1 of this Article may at any time thereafter declare on behalf of one or more of the territories to which the declaration relates that it accepts the competence of the Court to receive applications from individuals, non-governmental organisations or groups of individuals as provided by Article 34 of the Convention.

Article 57. (1) Any State may, when signing this Convention or when depositing its instrument of ratification, make a reservation in respect of any particular provision of the Convention to the extent that any law then in force in its territory is not in conformity with the provision. Reservations of a general character shall not be permitted under this Article.

(2) Any reservation made under this Article shall contain a brief statement of the law concerned.

Article 58. (1) A High Contracting Party may denounce the present Convention only after the expiry of five years from the date on which it became a party to it and after six months' notice contained in a notification addressed to the Secretary General of the Council of Europe, who shall inform the other High Contracting Parties.

(2) Such a denunciation shall not have the effect of releasing the High

Contracting Party concerned from its obligations under this Convention in respect of any act which, being capable of constituting a violation of such obligations, may have been performed by it before the date at which the denunciation became effective.

(3) Any High Contracting Party which shall cease to be a member of the Council of Europe shall cease to be a party to this Convention under the same conditions.

(4) The Convention may be denounced in accordance with the provisions of the preceding paragraphs in respect of any territory to which it has been declared to extend under the terms of Article 56.

Article 59. (1) This Convention shall be open to the signature of the members of the Council of Europe. It shall be ratified. Ratifications shall be deposited with the Secretary General of the Council of Europe.

(2) The European Union may accede to this Convention.

(3) The present Convention shall come into force after the deposit of ten instruments of ratification.

(4) As regards any signatory ratifying subsequently, the Convention shall come into force at the date of the deposit of its instrument of ratification.

(5) The Secretary General of the Council of Europe shall notify all the members of the Council of Europe of the entry into force of the Convention, the names of the High Contracting Parties who have ratified it, and the deposit of all instruments of ratification which may be effected subsequently.

Protocol (No. 1) to the Convention for the Protection of Human Rights and Fundamental Freedoms. Paris, 20 March 1952.

The governments signatory hereto, being members of the Council of Europe,

Being resolved to take steps to ensure the collective enforcement of certain rights and freedoms other than those already included in Section I of the Convention for the Protection of Human Rights and Fundamental Freedoms signed at Rome on 4 November 1950 (hereinafter referred to as 'the Convention'),

Have agreed as follows:

Article 1. Every natural or legal person is entitled to the peaceful enjoyment of his possessions. No one shall be deprived of his possessions except in the public interest and subject to the conditions provided for by law and by the general principles of international law.
The preceding provisions shall not, however, in any way impair the right of a State to enforce such laws as it deems necessary to control the use of property in accordance with the general interest or to secure the payment of taxes or other contributions or penalties.

Article 2. No person shall be denied the right to education. In the exercise of any functions which it assumes in relation to education and to teaching, the State shall respect the right of parents to ensure such education and teaching in conformity with their own religious and philosophical convictions.

Article 3. The High Contracting Parties undertake to hold free elections at reasonable intervals by secret ballot, under conditions which will ensure the free expression of the opinion of the people in the choice of the legislature.

[Articles 4 to 6 are omitted.]

Protocol No. 4 to the Convention for the Protection of Human Rights and Fundamental Freedoms securing certain rights and freedoms other than those already included in the Convention and in the first Protocol thereto. Strasbourg, 16 September 1963.

[The Preamble is omitted.]

Article 1. No one shall be deprived of his liberty merely on the ground of inability to fulfil a contractual obligation.

Article 2. (1) Everyone lawfully within the territory of a State shall, within that territory, have the right to liberty of movement and freedom to choose his residence.
(2) Everyone shall be free to leave any country, including his own.
(3) No restrictions shall be placed on the exercise of these rights other than such as are in accordance with law and are necessary in a democratic society in the interests of national security or public safety, for the maintenance of ordre public, for the prevention of crime, for the protection of health or morals, or for the protection of the rights and freedoms of others.
(4) The rights set forth in paragraph 1 may also be subject, in particular areas, to restrictions imposed in accordance with law and justified by the public interest in a democratic society.

Article 3. (1) No one shall be expelled, by means either of an individual or of a collective measure, from the territory of the State of which he is a national.
(2) No one shall be deprived of the right to enter the territory of the state of which he is a national.

Article 4. Collective expulsion of aliens is prohibited.

[Articles 5 to 7 are omitted.]

Protocol No. 6 to the Convention for the Protection of Human Rights and Fundamental Freedoms concerning the abolition of the death penalty. Strasbourg, 28 April 1983.

[The Preamble is omitted.]

Article 1. The death penalty shall be abolished. No-one shall be condemned to such penalty or executed.

Article 2. A State may make provision in its law for the death penalty in respect of acts committed in time of war or of imminent threat of war; such penalty shall be applied only in the instances laid down in the law and in accordance with its provisions. The State shall communicate to the Secretary General of the Council of Europe the relevant provisions of that law.

[Articles 3 to 9 are omitted.]

Protocol No. 7 to the Convention for the Protection of Human Rights and Fundamental Freedoms. Strasbourg, 22 November 1984.

[The Preamble is omitted.]

Article 1. (1) An alien lawfully resident in the territory of a State shall not be expelled therefrom except in pursuance of a decision reached in accordance with law and shall be allowed:
a. to submit reasons against his expulsion,
b. to have his case reviewed, and
c. to be represented for these purposes before the competent authority or a person or persons designated by that authority.
(2) An alien may be expelled before the exercise of his rights under paragraph 1.a, b and c of this Article, when such expulsion is necessary in the interests of public order or is grounded on reasons of national security.

Article 2. (1) Everyone convicted of a criminal offence by a tribunal shall have the right to have his conviction or sentence reviewed by a higher tribunal. The exercise of this right, including the grounds on which it may be exercised, shall be governed by law.
(2) This right may be subject to exceptions in regard to offences of a minor character, as prescribed by law, or in cases in which the person concerned was tried in the first instance by the highest tribunal or was convicted following an appeal against acquittal.

Article 3. When a person has by a final decision been convicted of a criminal offence and when subsequently his conviction has been reversed, or he has been pardoned, on the ground that a new or newly discovered fact shows conclusively that there has been a miscarriage of justice, the person who has suffered punishment as a result of such conviction shall be compensated according to the law or the practice of the State concerned, unless it is proved that the non-disclosure of the unknown fact in time is wholly or partly attributable to him.

Article 4. (1) No one shall be liable to be tried or punished again in criminal proceedings under the jurisdiction of the same State for an offence for which he has already been finally acquitted or convicted in accordance with the law and penal procedure of that State.

(2) The provisions of the preceding paragraph shall not prevent the reopening of the case in accordance with the law and penal procedure of the State concerned, if there is evidence of new or newly discovered facts, or if there has been a fundamental defect in the previous proceedings, which could affect the outcome of the case.
(3) No derogation from this Article shall be made under Article 15 of the Convention.

Article 5. Spouses shall enjoy equality of rights and responsibilities of a private law character between them, and in their relations with their children, as to marriage, during marriage and in the event of its dissolution. This Article shall not prevent States from taking such measures as are necessary in the interests of the children.

[Articles 6-10 are omitted.]

Protocol No. 12 to the Convention for the Protection of Human Rights and Fundamental Freedoms. Rome, 4 November 2000.

[The Preamble is omitted.]

Article 1. (1) The enjoyment of any right set forth by law shall be secured without discrimination on any ground such as sex, race, colour, language, religion, political or other opinion, national or social origin, association with a national minority, property, birth or other status.
(2) No one shall be discriminated against by any public authority on any ground such as those mentioned in paragraph 1.

[Articles 2 to 6 are omitted.]

Protocol No. 13 to the Convention for the Protection of Human Rights and Fundamental Freedoms Concerning the abolition of the death penalty in all circumstances. Vilnius, 3 May 2002.

[The Preamble is omitted.]

Article 1. The death penalty shall be abolished. No one shall be condemned to such penalty or executed.

[Articles 2 to 8 are omitted.]

Annex 13

THE TREATY ON EUROPEAN UNION

Consolidated version of the Treaty on European Union incorporating the changes pursuant to the Treaty of Lisbon (2008/C 115/13)

PREAMBLE

HIS MAJESTY THE KING OF THE BELGIANS, HER MAJESTY THE QUEEN OF DENMARK, THE PRESIDENT OF THE FEDERAL REPUBLIC OF GERMANY, THE PRESIDENT OF IRELAND, THE PRESIDENT OF THE HELLENIC REPUBLIC, HIS MAJESTY THE KING OF SPAIN, THE PRESIDENT OF THE FRENCH REPUBLIC, THE PRESIDENT OF THE ITALIAN REPUBLIC, HIS ROYAL HIGHNESS THE GRAND DUKE OF LUXEMBOURG, HER MAJESTY THE QUEEN OF THE NETHERLANDS, THE PRESIDENT OF THE PORTUGUESE REPUBLIC, HER MAJESTY THE QUEEN OF THE UNITED KINGDOM OF GREAT BRITAIN AND NORTHERN IRELAND,

RESOLVED to mark a new stage in the process of European integration undertaken with the establishment of the European Communities,

DRAWING INSPIRATION from the cultural, religious and humanist inheritance of Europe, from which have developed the universal values of the inviolable and inalienable rights of the human person, freedom, democracy, equality and the rule of law,

RECALLING the historic importance of the ending of the division of the European continent and the need to create firm bases for the construction of the future Europe,

CONFIRMING their attachment to the principles of liberty, democracy and respect for human rights and fundamental freedoms and of the rule of law,

CONFIRMING their attachment to fundamental social rights as defined in the European Social Charter signed at Turin on 18 October 1961 and in the 1989 Community Charter of the Fundamental Social Rights of Workers,

DESIRING to deepen the solidarity between their peoples while respecting their history, their culture and their traditions,

DESIRING to enhance further the democratic and efficient functioning of the institutions so as to enable them better to carry out, within a single institutional framework, the tasks entrusted to them,

RESOLVED to achieve the strengthening and the convergence of their economies and to establish an economic and monetary union including, in accordance with the provisions of this Treaty and of the Treaty on the Functioning of the European Union, a single and stable currency,

DETERMINED to promote economic and social progress for their peoples, taking into account the principle of sustainable development and within the context of the accomplishment of the internal market and of reinforced cohesion and environmental protection, and to implement policies ensuring that advances in economic integration are accompanied by parallel progress in other fields,

RESOLVED to establish a citizenship common to nationals of their countries,

RESOLVED to implement a common foreign and security policy including the progressive framing of a common defence policy, which might lead to a common defence in accordance with the provisions of Article 42, thereby reinforcing the European identity and its independence in order to promote peace, security and progress in Europe and in the world,

RESOLVED to facilitate the free movement of persons, while ensuring the safety and security of their peoples, by establishing an area of freedom, security and justice, in accordance with the provisions of this Treaty and of the Treaty on the Functioning of the European Union,

RESOLVED to continue the process of creating an ever closer union among the peoples of Europe, in which decisions are taken as closely as possible to the citizen in accordance with the principle of subsidiarity,

IN VIEW of further steps to be taken in order to advance European integration,

HAVE DECIDED to establish a European Union and to this end have designated as their Plenipotentiaries:

(List of plenipotentiaries not reproduced)

WHO, having exchanged their full powers, found in good and due form, have agreed as follows:

TITLE I

COMMON PROVISIONS

Article 1
By this Treaty, the HIGH CONTRACTING PARTIES establish among themselves a EUROPEAN UNION, hereinafter called 'the Union', on which the Member States confer competences to attain objectives they have in common.
This Treaty marks a new stage in the process of creating an ever closer union among the peoples of Europe, in which decisions are taken as openly as possible and as closely as possible to the citizen.
The Union shall be founded on the present Treaty and on the Treaty on the Functioning of the European Union (hereinafter referred to as 'the Treaties'). Those two Treaties shall have the same legal value. The Union shall replace and succeed the European Community.

Article 2
The Union is founded on the values of respect for human dignity, freedom, democracy, equality, the rule of law and respect for human rights, including the rights of persons belonging to minorities. These values are common to the Member States in a society in which pluralism, non-discrimination, tolerance, justice, solidarity and equality between women and men prevail.

Article 3
1. The Union's aim is to promote peace, its values and the well-being of its peoples.
2. The Union shall offer its citizens an area of freedom, security and justice without internal frontiers, in which the free movement of persons is ensured in conjunction with appropriate measures with respect to external border controls, asylum, immigration and the prevention and combating of crime.
3. The Union shall establish an internal market. It shall work for the sustainable development of Europe based on balanced economic growth and price stability, a highly competitive social market economy, aiming at full employment and social progress, and a high level of protection and improvement of the quality of the environment. It shall promote scientific and technological advance.
It shall combat social exclusion and discrimination, and shall promote social justice and protection, equality between women and men, solidarity between generations and protection of the rights of the child.
It shall promote economic, social and territorial cohesion, and solidarity among Member States.
It shall respect its rich cultural and linguistic diversity, and shall ensure that Europe's cultural heritage is safeguarded and enhanced.
4. The Union shall establish an economic and monetary union whose currency is the euro.
5. In its relations with the wider world, the Union shall uphold and promote its values and interests and contribute to the protection of its citizens. It shall contribute to peace, security, the sustainable development of the Earth, solidarity and mutual respect among peoples, free and fair trade, eradication of poverty and the protection of human rights, in particular the rights of the child, as well as to the strict observance and the development of international law, including respect for the principles of the United Nations Charter.
6. The Union shall pursue its objectives by appropriate means commensurate with the competences which are conferred upon it in the Treaties.

Article 4
1. In accordance with Article 5, competences not conferred upon the Union in the Treaties remain with the Member States.
2. The Union shall respect the equality of Member States before the Treaties as well as their national identities, inherent in their fundamental structures, political and constitutional, inclusive of regional and local self-government. It shall respect their essential State functions, including ensuring the territorial integrity of the State, maintaining law and order and safeguarding national security. In particular, national security remains the sole responsibility of each Member State.
3. Pursuant to the principle of sincere cooperation, the Union and the Member States shall, in full mutual respect, assist each other in carrying out tasks which flow from the Treaties.
The Member States shall take any appropriate measure, general or particular, to ensure fulfilment of the obligations arising out of the Treaties or resulting from the acts of the institutions of the Union.
The Member States shall facilitate the achievement of the Union's tasks and refrain from any measure which could jeopardise the attainment of the Union's objectives.

Article 5
1. The limits of Union competences are governed by the principle of conferral. The use of Union competences is governed by the principles of subsidiarity and proportionality.
2. Under the principle of conferral, the Union shall act only within the limits of the competences conferred upon it by the Member States in the Treaties to attain the objectives set out therein. Competences not conferred upon the Union in the Treaties remain with the Member States.

3. Under the principle of subsidiarity, in areas which do not fall within its exclusive competence, the Union shall act only if and in so far as the objectives of the proposed action cannot be sufficiently achieved by the Member States, either at central level or at regional and local level, but can rather, by reason of the scale or effects of the proposed action, be better achieved at Union level.
The institutions of the Union shall apply the principle of subsidiarity as laid down in the Protocol on the application of the principles of subsidiarity and proportionality. National Parliaments ensure compliance with the principle of subsidiarity in accordance with the procedure set out in that Protocol.
4. Under the principle of proportionality, the content and form of Union action shall not exceed what is necessary to achieve the objectives of the Treaties.
The institutions of the Union shall apply the principle of proportionality as laid down in the Protocol on the application of the principles of subsidiarity and proportionality.

Article 6
1. The Union recognises the rights, freedoms and principles set out in the Charter of Fundamental Rights of the European Union of 7 December 2000, as adapted at Strasbourg, on 12 December 2007, which shall have the same legal value as the Treaties.
The provisions of the Charter shall not extend in any way the competences of the Union as defined in the Treaties.
The rights, freedoms and principles in the Charter shall be interpreted in accordance with the general provisions in Title VII of the Charter governing its interpretation and application and with due regard to the explanations referred to in the Charter, that set out the sources of those provisions.
2. The Union shall accede to the European Convention for the Protection of Human Rights and Fundamental Freedoms. Such accession shall not affect the Union's competences as defined in the Treaties.
3. Fundamental rights, as guaranteed by the European Convention for the Protection of Human Rights and Fundamental Freedoms and as they result from the constitutional traditions common to the Member States, shall constitute general principles of the Union's law.

Article 7
1. On a reasoned proposal by one third of the Member States, by the European Parliament or by the European Commission, the Council, acting by a majority of four fifths of its members after obtaining the consent of the European Parliament, may determine that there is a clear risk of a serious breach by a Member State of the values referred to in Article 2. Before making such a determination, the Council shall hear the Member State in question and may address recommendations to it, acting in accordance with the same procedure.
The Council shall regularly verify that the grounds on which such a determination was made continue to apply.
2. The European Council, acting by unanimity on a proposal by one third of the Member States or by the Commission and after obtaining the consent of the European Parliament, may determine the existence of a serious and persistent breach by a Member State of the values referred to in Article 2, after inviting the Member State in question to submit its observations.
3. Where a determination under paragraph 2 has been made, the Council, acting by a qualified majority, may decide to suspend certain of the rights deriving from the application of the Treaties to the Member State in question, including the voting rights of the representative of the government of that Member State in the Council. In doing so, the Council shall take into account the possible consequences of such a suspension on the rights and obligations of natural and legal persons.

The obligations of the Member State in question under this Treaty shall in any case continue to be binding on that State.

4. The Council, acting by a qualified majority, may decide subsequently to vary or revoke measures taken under paragraph 3 in response to changes in the situation which led to their being imposed.

5. The voting arrangements applying to the European Parliament, the European Council and the Council for the purposes of this Article are laid down in Article 354 of the Treaty on the Functioning of the European Union.

Article 8

1. The Union shall develop a special relationship with neighbouring countries, aiming to establish an area of prosperity and good neighbourliness, founded on the values of the Union and characterised by close and peaceful relations based on cooperation.

2. For the purposes of paragraph 1, the Union may conclude specific agreements with the countries concerned. These agreements may contain reciprocal rights and obligations as well as the possibility of undertaking activities jointly. Their implementation shall be the subject of periodic consultation.

TITLE II

PROVISIONS ON DEMOCRATIC PRINCIPLES

Article 9

In all its activities, the Union shall observe the principle of the equality of its citizens, who shall receive equal attention from its institutions, bodies, offices and agencies. Every national of a Member State shall be a citizen of the Union. Citizenship of the Union shall be additional to and not replace national citizenship.

Article 10

1. The functioning of the Union shall be founded on representative democracy.

2. Citizens are directly represented at Union level in the European Parliament.

Member States are represented in the European Council by their Heads of State or Government and in the Council by their governments, themselves democratically accountable either to their national Parliaments, or to their citizens.

3. Every citizen shall have the right to participate in the democratic life of the Union. Decisions shall be taken as openly and as closely as possible to the citizen.

4. Political parties at European level contribute to forming European political awareness and to expressing the will of citizens of the Union.

Article 11

1. The institutions shall, by appropriate means, give citizens and representative associations the opportunity to make known and publicly exchange their views in all areas of Union action.

2. The institutions shall maintain an open, transparent and regular dialogue with representative associations and civil society.

3. The European Commission shall carry out broad consultations with parties concerned in order to ensure that the Union's actions are coherent and transparent.

4. Not less than one million citizens who are nationals of a significant number of Member States may take the initiative of inviting the European Commission, within the framework of its powers, to submit any appropriate proposal on matters where citizens consider that a legal act of the Union is required for the purpose of implementing the Treaties.

The procedures and conditions required for such a citizens' initiative shall be determined in accordance with the first paragraph of Article 24 of the Treaty on the Functioning of the European Union.

Article 12
National Parliaments contribute actively to the good functioning of the Union:
(a) through being informed by the institutions of the Union and having draft legislative acts of the Union forwarded to them in accordance with the Protocol on the role of national Parliaments in the European Union;
(b) by seeing to it that the principle of subsidiarity is respected in accordance with the procedures provided for in the Protocol on the application of the principles of subsidiarity and proportionality;
(c) by taking part, within the framework of the area of freedom, security and justice, in the evaluation mechanisms for the implementation of the Union policies in that area, in accordance with Article 70 of the Treaty on the Functioning of the European Union, and through being involved in the political monitoring of Europol and the evaluation of Eurojust's activities in accordance with Articles 88 and 85 of that Treaty;
(d) by taking part in the revision procedures of the Treaties, in accordance with Article 48 of this Treaty;
(e) by being notified of applications for accession to the Union, in accordance with Article 49 of this Treaty;
(f) by taking part in the inter-parliamentary cooperation between national Parliaments and with the European Parliament, in accordance with the Protocol on the role of national Parliaments in the European Union.

TITLE III

PROVISIONS ON THE INSTITUTIONS

Article 13
1. The Union shall have an institutional framework which shall aim to promote its values, advance its objectives, serve its interests, those of its citizens and those of the Member States, and ensure the consistency, effectiveness and continuity of its policies and actions.
The Union's institutions shall be:
— the European Parliament,
— the European Council,
— the Council,
— the European Commission (hereinafter referred to as 'the Commission'),
— the Court of Justice of the European Union,
— the European Central Bank,
— the Court of Auditors.
2. Each institution shall act within the limits of the powers conferred on it in the Treaties, and in conformity with the procedures, conditions and objectives set out in them. The institutions shall practice mutual sincere cooperation.
3. The provisions relating to the European Central Bank and the Court of Auditors and detailed provisions on the other institutions are set out in the Treaty on the Functioning of the European Union.
4. The European Parliament, the Council and the Commission shall be assisted by an Economic and Social Committee and a Committee of the Regions acting in an advisory capacity.

Article 14
1. The European Parliament shall, jointly with the Council, exercise legislative and budgetary functions. It shall exercise functions of political control and consultation as laid down in the Treaties. It shall elect the President of the Commission.
2. The European Parliament shall be composed of representatives of the Union's citizens. They shall not exceed seven hundred and fifty in number, plus the President. Representation

of citizens shall be degressively proportional, with a minimum threshold of six members per Member State. No Member State shall be allocated more than ninety-six seats.

The European Council shall adopt by unanimity, on the initiative of the European Parliament and with its consent, a decision establishing the composition of the European Parliament, respecting the principles referred to in the first subparagraph.

3. The members of the European Parliament shall be elected for a term of five years by direct universal suffrage in a free and secret ballot.

4. The European Parliament shall elect its President and its officers from among its members.

Article 15

1. The European Council shall provide the Union with the necessary impetus for its development and shall define the general political directions and priorities thereof. It shall not exercise legislative functions.

2. The European Council shall consist of the Heads of State or Government of the Member States, together with its President and the President of the Commission. The High Representative of the Union for Foreign Affairs and Security Policy shall take part in its work.

3. The European Council shall meet twice every six months, convened by its President. When the agenda so requires, the members of the European Council may decide each to be assisted by a minister and, in the case of the President of the Commission, by a member of the Commission. When the situation so requires, the President shall convene a special meeting of the European Council.

4. Except where the Treaties provide otherwise, decisions of the European Council shall be taken by consensus.

5. The European Council shall elect its President, by a qualified majority, for a term of two and a half years, renewable once. In the event of an impediment or serious misconduct, the European Council can end the President's term of office in accordance with the same procedure.

6. The President of the European Council:
(a) shall chair it and drive forward its work;
(b) shall ensure the preparation and continuity of the work of the European Council in co-operation with the President of the Commission, and on the basis of the work of the General Affairs Council;
(c) shall endeavour to facilitate cohesion and consensus within the European Council;
(d) shall present a report to the European Parliament after each of the meetings of the European Council.

The President of the European Council shall, at his level and in that capacity, ensure the external representation of the Union on issues concerning its common foreign and security policy, without prejudice to the powers of the High Representative of the Union for Foreign Affairs and Security Policy.

The President of the European Council shall not hold a national office.

Article 16

1. The Council shall, jointly with the European Parliament, exercise legislative and budgetary functions. It shall carry out policy-making and coordinating functions as laid down in the Treaties.

2. The Council shall consist of a representative of each Member State at ministerial level, who may commit the government of the Member State in question and cast its vote.

3. The Council shall act by a qualified majority except where the Treaties provide otherwise.

4. As from 1 November 2014, a qualified majority shall be defined as at least 55% of the members of the Council, comprising at least fifteen of them and representing Member States comprising at least 65% of the population of the Union.

A blocking minority must include at least four Council members, failing which the qualified majority shall be deemed attained.
The other arrangements governing the qualified majority are laid down in Article 238(2) of the Treaty on the Functioning of the European Union.
5. The transitional provisions relating to the definition of the qualified majority which shall be applicable until 31 October 2014 and those which shall be applicable from 1 November 2014 to 31 March 2017 are laid down in the Protocol on transitional provisions.
6. The Council shall meet in different configurations, the list of which shall be adopted in accordance with Article 236 of the Treaty on the Functioning of the European Union.
The General Affairs Council shall ensure consistency in the work of the different Council configurations. It shall prepare and ensure the follow-up to meetings of the European Council, in liaison with the President of the European Council and the Commission.
The Foreign Affairs Council shall elaborate the Union's external action on the basis of strategic guidelines laid down by the European Council and ensure that the Union's action is consistent.
7. A Committee of Permanent Representatives of the Governments of the Member States shall be responsible for preparing the work of the Council.
8. The Council shall meet in public when it deliberates and votes on a draft legislative act. To this end, each Council meeting shall be divided into two parts, dealing respectively with deliberations on Union legislative acts and non-legislative activities.
9. The Presidency of Council configurations, other than that of Foreign Affairs, shall be held by Member State representatives in the Council on the basis of equal rotation, in accordance with the conditions established in accordance with Article 236 of the Treaty on the Functioning of the European Union.

Article 17
1. The Commission shall promote the general interest of the Union and take appropriate initiatives to that end. It shall ensure the application of the Treaties, and of measures adopted by the institutions pursuant to them. It shall oversee the application of Union law under the control of the Court of Justice of the European Union. It shall execute the budget and manage programmes. It shall exercise coordinating, executive and management functions, as laid down in the Treaties. With the exception of the common foreign and security policy, and other cases provided for in the Treaties, it shall ensure the Union's external representation. It shall initiate the Union's annual and multiannual programming with a view to achieving interinstitutional agreements.
2. Union legislative acts may only be adopted on the basis of a Commission proposal, except where the Treaties provide otherwise. Other acts shall be adopted on the basis of a Commission proposal where the Treaties so provide.
3. The Commission's term of office shall be five years.
The members of the Commission shall be chosen on the ground of their general competence and European commitment from persons whose independence is beyond doubt.
In carrying out its responsibilities, the Commission shall be completely independent. Without prejudice to Article 18(2), the members of the Commission shall neither seek nor take instructions from any Government or other institution, body, office or entity. They shall refrain from any action incompatible with their duties or the performance of their tasks.
4. The Commission appointed between the date of entry into force of the Treaty of Lisbon and 31 October 2014, shall consist of one national of each Member State, including its President and the High Representative of the Union for Foreign Affairs and Security Policy who shall be one of its Vice- Presidents.
5. As from 1 November 2014, the Commission shall consist of a number of members, including its President and the High Representative of the Union for Foreign Affairs and

Security Policy, corresponding to two thirds of the number of Member States, unless the European Council, acting unanimously, decides to alter this number.

The members of the Commission shall be chosen from among the nationals of the Member States on the basis of a system of strictly equal rotation between the Member States, reflecting the demographic and geographical range of all the Member States. This system shall be established unanimously by the European Council in accordance with Article 244 of the Treaty on the Functioning of the European Union.

6. The President of the Commission shall:
(a) lay down guidelines within which the Commission is to work;
(b) decide on the internal organisation of the Commission, ensuring that it acts consistently, efficiently and as a collegiate body;
(c) appoint Vice-Presidents, other than the High Representative of the Union for Foreign Affairs and Security Policy, from among the members of the Commission.

A member of the Commission shall resign if the President so requests. The High Representative of the Union for Foreign Affairs and Security Policy shall resign, in accordance with the procedure set out in Article 18(1), if the President so requests.

7. Taking into account the elections to the European Parliament and after having held the appropriate consultations, the European Council, acting by a qualified majority, shall propose to the European Parliament a candidate for President of the Commission. This candidate shall be elected by the European Parliament by a majority of its component members. If he does not obtain the required majority, the European Council, acting by a qualified majority, shall within one month propose a new candidate who shall be elected by the European Parliament following the same procedure.

The Council, by common accord with the President-elect, shall adopt the list of the other persons whom it proposes for appointment as members of the Commission. They shall be selected, on the basis of the suggestions made by Member States, in accordance with the criteria set out in paragraph 3, second subparagraph, and paragraph 5, second subparagraph.

The President, the High Representative of the Union for Foreign Affairs and Security Policy and the other members of the Commission shall be subject as a body to a vote of consent by the European Parliament. On the basis of this consent the Commission shall be appointed by the European Council, acting by a qualified majority.

8. The Commission, as a body, shall be responsible to the European Parliament. In accordance with Article 234 of the Treaty on the Functioning of the European Union, the European Parliament may vote on a motion of censure of the Commission. If such a motion is carried, the members of the Commission shall resign as a body and the High Representative of the Union for Foreign Affairs and Security Policy shall resign from the duties that he carries out in the Commission.

Article 18
1. The European Council, acting by a qualified majority, with the agreement of the President of the Commission, shall appoint the High Representative of the Union for Foreign Affairs and Security Policy. The European Council may end his term of office by the same procedure.
2. The High Representative shall conduct the Union's common foreign and security policy. He shall contribute by his proposals to the development of that policy, which he shall carry out as mandated by the Council. The same shall apply to the common security and defence policy.
3. The High Representative shall preside over the Foreign Affairs Council.
4. The High Representative shall be one of the Vice-Presidents of the Commission. He shall ensure the consistency of the Union's external action. He shall be responsible within the Commission for responsibilities incumbent on it in external relations and for coordinating other aspects of the Union's external action. In exercising these responsibilities within the Commission, and only for these responsibilities, the High Representative shall be bound by Commission procedures to the extent that this is consistent with paragraphs 2 and 3.

Article 19
1. The Court of Justice of the European Union shall include the Court of Justice, the General Court and specialised courts. It shall ensure that in the interpretation and application of the Treaties the law is observed.
Member States shall provide remedies sufficient to ensure effective legal protection in the fields covered by Union law.
2. The Court of Justice shall consist of one judge from each Member State. It shall be assisted by Advocates-General.
The General Court shall include at least one judge per Member State.
The Judges and the Advocates-General of the Court of Justice and the Judges of the General Court shall be chosen from persons whose independence is beyond doubt and who satisfy the conditions set out in Articles 253 and 254 of the Treaty on the Functioning of the European Union. They shall be appointed by common accord of the governments of the Member States for six years. Retiring Judges and Advocates-General may be reappointed.
3. The Court of Justice of the European Union shall, in accordance with the Treaties:
(a) rule on actions brought by a Member State, an institution or a natural or legal person;
(b) give preliminary rulings, at the request of courts or tribunals of the Member States, on the interpretation of Union law or the validity of acts adopted by the institutions;
(c) rule in other cases provided for in the Treaties.

[Titles IV and V are omitted.]

TITLE VI

FINAL PROVISIONS

Article 47
The Union shall have legal personality.

Article 48
1. The Treaties may be amended in accordance with an ordinary revision procedure. They may also be amended in accordance with simplified revision procedures.
Ordinary revision procedure
2. The Government of any Member State, the European Parliament or the Commission may submit to the Council proposals for the amendment of the Treaties. These proposals may, *inter alia*, serve either to increase or to reduce the competences conferred on the Union in the Treaties. These proposals shall be submitted to the European Council by the Council and the national Parliaments shall be notified.
3. If the European Council, after consulting the European Parliament and the Commission, adopts by a simple majority a decision in favour of examining the proposed amendments, the President of the European Council shall convene a Convention composed of representatives of the national Parliaments, of the Heads of State or Government of the Member States, of the European Parliament and of the Commission. The European Central Bank shall also be consulted in the case of institutional changes in the monetary area. The Convention shall examine the proposals for amendments and shall adopt by consensus a recommendation to a conference of representatives of the governments of the Member States as provided for in paragraph 4.
The European Council may decide by a simple majority, after obtaining the consent of the European Parliament, not to convene a Convention should this not be justified by the extent of the proposed amendments. In the latter case, the European Council shall define the terms of reference for a conference of representatives of the governments of the Member States.

4. A conference of representatives of the governments of the Member States shall be convened by the President of the Council for the purpose of determining by common accord the amendments to be made to the Treaties.

The amendments shall enter into force after being ratified by all the Member States in accordance with their respective constitutional requirements.

5. If, two years after the signature of a treaty amending the Treaties, four fifths of the Member States have ratified it and one or more Member States have encountered difficulties in proceeding with ratification, the matter shall be referred to the European Council.

Simplified revision procedures

6. The Government of any Member State, the European Parliament or the Commission may submit to the European Council proposals for revising all or part of the provisions of Part Three of the Treaty on the Functioning of the European Union relating to the internal policies and action of the Union.

The European Council may adopt a decision amending all or part of the provisions of Part Three of the Treaty on the Functioning of the European Union. The European Council shall act by unanimity after consulting the European Parliament and the Commission, and the European Central Bank in the case of institutional changes in the monetary area. That decision shall not enter into force until it is approved by the Member States in accordance with their respective constitutional requirements.

The decision referred to in the second subparagraph shall not increase the competences conferred on the Union in the Treaties.

7. Where the Treaty on the Functioning of the European Union or Title V of this Treaty provides for the Council to act by unanimity in a given area or case, the European Council may adopt a decision authorising the Council to act by a qualified majority in that area or in that case. This subparagraph shall not apply to decisions with military implications or those in the area of defence.

Where the Treaty on the Functioning of the European Union provides for legislative acts to be adopted by the Council in accordance with a special legislative procedure, the European Council may adopt a decision allowing for the adoption of such acts in accordance with the ordinary legislative procedure.

Any initiative taken by the European Council on the basis of the first or the second subparagraph shall be notified to the national Parliaments. If a national Parliament makes known its opposition within six months of the date of such notification, the decision referred to in the first or the second subparagraph shall not be adopted. In the absence of opposition, the European Council may adopt the decision.

For the adoption of the decisions referred to in the first and second subparagraphs, the European Council shall act by unanimity after obtaining the consent of the European Parliament, which shall be given by a majority of its component members.

Article 49

Any European State which respects the values referred to in Article 2 and is committed to promoting them may apply to become a member of the Union. The European Parliament and national Parliaments shall be notified of this application. The applicant State shall address its application to the Council, which shall act unanimously after consulting the Commission and after receiving the consent of the European Parliament, which shall act by a majority of its component members. The conditions of eligibility agreed upon by the European Council shall be taken into account.

The conditions of admission and the adjustments to the Treaties on which the Union is founded, which such admission entails, shall be the subject of an agreement between the Member States and the applicant State. This agreement shall be submitted for ratification by all the contracting States in accordance with their respective constitutional requirements.

Article 50
1. Any Member State may decide to withdraw from the Union in accordance with its own constitutional requirements.
2. A Member State which decides to withdraw shall notify the European Council of its intention. In the light of the guidelines provided by the European Council, the Union shall negotiate and conclude an agreement with that State, setting out the arrangements for its withdrawal, taking account of the framework for its future relationship with the Union. That agreement shall be negotiated in accordance with Article 218(3) of the Treaty on the Functioning of the European Union. It shall be concluded on behalf of the Union by the Council, acting by a qualified majority, after obtaining the consent of the European Parliament.
3. The Treaties shall cease to apply to the State in question from the date of entry into force of the withdrawal agreement or, failing that, two years after the notification referred to in paragraph 2, unless the European Council, in agreement with the Member State concerned, unanimously decides to extend this period.
4. For the purposes of paragraphs 2 and 3, the member of the European Council or of the Council representing the withdrawing Member State shall not participate in the discussions of the European Council or Council or in decisions concerning it.
A qualified majority shall be defined in accordance with Article 238(3)(b) of the Treaty on the Functioning of the European Union.
5. If a State which has withdrawn from the Union asks to rejoin, its request shall be subject to the procedure referred to in Article 49.

Article 51
The Protocols and Annexes to the Treaties shall form an integral part thereof.

Article 52
1. The Treaties shall apply to the Kingdom of Belgium, the Republic of Bulgaria, the Czech Republic, the Kingdom of Denmark, the Federal Republic of Germany, the Republic of Estonia, Ireland, the Hellenic Republic, the Kingdom of Spain, the French Republic, the Italian Republic, the Republic of Cyprus, the Republic of Latvia, the Republic of Lithuania, the Grand Duchy of Luxembourg, the Republic of Hungary, the Republic of Malta, the Kingdom of the Netherlands, the Republic of Austria, the Republic of Poland, the Portuguese Republic, Romania, the Republic of Slovenia, the Slovak Republic, the Republic of Finland, the Kingdom of Sweden and the United Kingdom of Great Britain and Northern Ireland.
2. The territorial scope of the Treaties is specified in Article 355 of the Treaty on the Functioning of the European Union.

Article 53
This Treaty is concluded for an unlimited period.

Article 54
1. This Treaty shall be ratified by the High Contracting Parties in accordance with their respective constitutional requirements. The instruments of ratification shall be deposited with the Government of the Italian Republic.
2. This Treaty shall enter into force on 1 January 1993, provided that all the Instruments of ratification have been deposited, or, failing that, on the first day of the month following the deposit of the Instrument of ratification by the last signatory State to take this step.

Article 55
1. This Treaty, drawn up in a single original in the Bulgarian, Czech, Danish, Dutch, English, Estonian, Finnish, French, German, Greek, Hungarian, Irish, Italian, Latvian, Lithuanian, Maltese, Polish, Portuguese, Romanian, Slovak, Slovenian, Spanish and Swedish languages, the texts in each of these languages being equally authentic, shall be deposited in the archives

of the Government of the Italian Republic, which will transmit a certified copy to each of the governments of the other signatory States.

2. This Treaty may also be translated into any other languages as determined by Member States among those which, in accordance with their constitutional order, enjoy official status in all or part of their territory. A certified copy of such translations shall be provided by the Member States concerned to be deposited in the archives of the Council.

PROTOCOL (No 1) ON THE ROLE OF NATIONAL PARLIAMENTS IN THE EUROPEAN UNION

THE HIGH CONTRACTING PARTIES,

RECALLING that the way in which national Parliaments scrutinise their governments in relation to the activities of the Union is a matter for the particular constitutional organisation and practice of each Member State,

DESIRING to encourage greater involvement of national Parliaments in the activities of the European Union and to enhance their ability to express their views on draft legislative acts of the Union as well as on other matters which may be of particular interest to them,

HAVE AGREED UPON the following provisions, which shall be annexed to the Treaty on European Union, to the Treaty on the Functioning of the European Union and to the Treaty establishing the European Atomic Energy Community:

TITLE I

INFORMATION FOR NATIONAL PARLIAMENTS

Article 1
Commission consultation documents (green and white papers and communications) shall be forwarded directly by the Commission to national Parliaments upon publication. The Commission shall also forward the annual legislative programme as well as any other instrument of legislative planning or policy to national Parliaments, at the same time as to the European Parliament and the Council.

Article 2
Draft legislative acts sent to the European Parliament and to the Council shall be forwarded to national Parliaments.
For the purposes of this Protocol, 'draft legislative acts' shall mean proposals from the Commission, initiatives from a group of Member States, initiatives from the European Parliament, requests from the Court of Justice, recommendations from the European Central Bank and requests from the European Investment Bank, for the adoption of a legislative act.
Draft legislative acts originating from the Commission shall be forwarded to national Parliaments directly by the Commission, at the same time as to the European Parliament and the Council.
Draft legislative acts originating from the European Parliament shall be forwarded to national Parliaments directly by the European Parliament.
Draft legislative acts originating from a group of Member States, the Court of Justice, the European Central Bank or the European Investment Bank shall be forwarded to national Parliaments by the Council.

Article 3
National Parliaments may send to the Presidents of the European Parliament, the Council and the Commission a reasoned opinion on whether a draft legislative act complies with the

principle of subsidiarity, in accordance with the procedure laid down in the Protocol on the application of the principles of subsidiarity and proportionality.

If the draft legislative act originates from a group of Member States, the President of the Council shall forward the reasoned opinion or opinions to the governments of those Member States.

If the draft legislative act originates from the Court of Justice, the European Central Bank or the European Investment Bank, the President of the Council shall forward the reasoned opinion or opinions to the institution or body concerned.

Article 4

An eight-week period shall elapse between a draft legislative act being made available to national Parliaments in the official languages of the Union and the date when it is placed on a provisional agenda for the Council for its adoption or for adoption of a position under a legislative procedure. Exceptions shall be possible in cases of urgency, the reasons for which shall be stated in the act or position of the Council. Save in urgent cases for which due reasons have been given, no agreement may be reached on a draft legislative act during those eight weeks. Save in urgent cases for which due reasons have been given, a ten-day period shall elapse between the placing of a draft legislative act on the provisional agenda for the Council and the adoption of a position.

Article 5

The agendas for and the outcome of meetings of the Council, including the minutes of meetings where the Council is deliberating on draft legislative acts, shall be forwarded directly to national Parliaments, at the same time as to Member States' governments.

Article 6

When the European Council intends to make use of the first or second subparagraphs of Article 48(7) of the Treaty on European Union, national Parliaments shall be informed of the initiative of the European Council at least six months before any decision is adopted.

Article 7

The Court of Auditors shall forward its annual report to national Parliaments, for information, at the same time as to the European Parliament and to the Council.

Article 8

Where the national Parliamentary system is not unicameral, Articles 1 to 7 shall apply to the component chambers.

TITLE II

INTERPARLIAMENTARY COOPERATION

Article 9

The European Parliament and national Parliaments shall together determine the organisation and promotion of effective and regular interparliamentary cooperation within the Union.

Article 10

A conference of Parliamentary Committees for Union Affairs may submit any contribution it deems appropriate for the attention of the European Parliament, the Council and the Commission. That conference shall in addition promote the exchange of information and best practice between national Parliaments and the European Parliament, including their special committees. It may also organise interparliamentary conferences on specific topics, in particular to debate matters of common foreign and security policy, including common security and defence policy. Contributions from the conference shall not bind national Parliaments and shall not prejudge their positions.

PROTOCOL (No 2) ON THE APPLICATION OF THE PRINCIPLES OF SUBSIDIARITY AND PROPORTIONALITY

THE HIGH CONTRACTING PARTIES,

WISHING to ensure that decisions are taken as closely as possible to the citizens of the Union,

RESOLVED to establish the conditions for the application of the principles of subsidiarity and proportionality, as laid down in Article 5 of the Treaty on European Union, and to establish a system for monitoring the application of those principles,

HAVE AGREED UPON the following provisions, which shall be annexed to the Treaty on European Union and to the Treaty on the Functioning of the European Union:

Article 1
Each institution shall ensure constant respect for the principles of subsidiarity and proportionality, as laid down in Article 5 of the Treaty on European Union.

Article 2
Before proposing legislative acts, the Commission shall consult widely. Such consultations shall, where appropriate, take into account the regional and local dimension of the action envisaged. In cases of exceptional urgency, the Commission shall not conduct such consultations. It shall give reasons for its decision in its proposal.

Article 3
For the purposes of this Protocol, 'draft legislative acts' shall mean proposals from the Commission, initiatives from a group of Member States, initiatives from the European Parliament, requests from the Court of Justice, recommendations from the European Central Bank and requests from the European Investment Bank, for the adoption of a legislative act.

Article 4
The Commission shall forward its draft legislative acts and its amended drafts to national Parliaments at the same time as to the Union legislator.
The European Parliament shall forward its draft legislative acts and its amended drafts to national Parliaments.
The Council shall forward draft legislative acts originating from a group of Member States, the Court of Justice, the European Central Bank or the European Investment Bank and amended drafts to national Parliaments.
Upon adoption, legislative resolutions of the European Parliament and positions of the Council shall be forwarded by them to national Parliaments.

Article 5
Draft legislative acts shall be justified with regard to the principles of subsidiarity and proportionality. Any draft legislative act should contain a detailed statement making it possible to appraise compliance with the principles of subsidiarity and proportionality. This statement should contain some assessment of the proposal's financial impact and, in the case of a directive, of its implications for the rules to be put in place by Member States, including, where necessary, the regional legislation. The reasons for concluding that a Union objective can be better achieved at Union level shall be substantiated by qualitative and, wherever possible, quantitative indicators. Draft legislative acts shall take account of the need for any burden, whether financial or administrative, falling upon the Union, national governments, regional or local authorities, economic operators and citizens, to be minimised and commensurate with the objective to be achieved.

Article 6
Any national Parliament or any chamber of a national Parliament may, within eight weeks from the date of transmission of a draft legislative act, in the official languages of the Union, send to the Presidents of the European Parliament, the Council and the Commission a reasoned opinion stating why it considers that the draft in question does not comply with the principle of subsidiarity. It will be for each national Parliament or each chamber of a national Parliament to consult, where appropriate, regional parliaments with legislative powers.
If the draft legislative act originates from a group of Member States, the President of the Council shall forward the opinion to the governments of those Member States.
If the draft legislative act originates from the Court of Justice, the European Central Bank or the European Investment Bank, the President of the Council shall forward the opinion to the institution or body concerned.

Article 7
1. The European Parliament, the Council and the Commission, and, where appropriate, the group of Member States, the Court of Justice, the European Central Bank or the European Investment Bank, if the draft legislative act originates from them, shall take account of the reasoned opinions issued by national Parliaments or by a chamber of a national Parliament.
Each national Parliament shall have two votes, shared out on the basis of the national Parliamentary system. In the case of a bicameral Parliamentary system, each of the two chambers shall have one vote.
2. Where reasoned opinions on a draft legislative act's non-compliance with the principle of subsidiarity represent at least one third of all the votes allocated to the national Parliaments in accordance with the second subparagraph of paragraph 1, the draft must be reviewed. This threshold shall be a quarter in the case of a draft legislative act submitted on the basis of Article 76 of the Treaty on the Functioning of the European Union on the area of freedom, security and justice.
After such review, the Commission or, where appropriate, the group of Member States, the European Parliament, the Court of Justice, the European Central Bank or the European Investment Bank, if the draft legislative act originates from them, may decide to maintain, amend or withdraw the draft. Reasons must be given for this decision.
3. Furthermore, under the ordinary legislative procedure, where reasoned opinions on the non- compliance of a proposal for a legislative act with the principle of subsidiarity represent at least a simple majority of the votes allocated to the national Parliaments in accordance with the second subparagraph of paragraph 1, the proposal must be reviewed. After such review, the Commission may decide to maintain, amend or withdraw the proposal.
If it chooses to maintain the proposal, the Commission will have, in a reasoned opinion, to justify why it considers that the proposal complies with the principle of subsidiarity. This reasoned opinion, as well as the reasoned opinions of the national Parliaments, will have to be submitted to the Union legislator, for consideration in the procedure:
(a) before concluding the first reading, the legislator (the European Parliament and the Council) shall consider whether the legislative proposal is compatible with the principle of subsidiarity, taking particular account of the reasons expressed and shared by the majority of national Parliaments as well as the reasoned opinion of the Commission;
(b) if, by a majority of 55% of the members of the Council or a majority of the votes cast in the European Parliament, the legislator is of the opinion that the proposal is not compatible with the principle of subsidiarity, the legislative proposal shall not be given further consideration.

Article 8
The Court of Justice of the European Union shall have jurisdiction in actions on grounds of infringement of the principle of subsidiarity by a legislative act, brought in accordance with the rules laid down in Article 263 of the Treaty on the Functioning of the European Union by

Member States, or notified by them in accordance with their legal order on behalf of their national Parliament or a chamber thereof.

In accordance with the rules laid down in the said Article, the Committee of the Regions may also bring such actions against legislative acts for the adoption of which the Treaty on the Functioning of the European Union provides that it be consulted.

Article 9

The Commission shall submit each year to the European Council, the European Parliament, the Council and national Parliaments a report on the application of Article 5 of the Treaty on European Union. This annual report shall also be forwarded to the Economic and Social Committee and the Committee of the Regions.

IUS COMMUNE EUROPAEUM

A peer-reviewed book series in which the common foundations of the legal systems of the Member States of the European Community are the central focus.

The *Ius Commune Europaeum* series includes horizontal comparative legal studies as well as studies on the effect of treaties within the national legal systems. All the classic fields of law are covered. The books are published in various European languages under the auspices of METRO, the Institute for Transnational Legal Research at Maastricht University.

Editorial Board: Prof.Dr. J. SMITS (chair), Prof.Dr. M. FAURE, Prof.Dr. CHR. JOERGES, Prof.Dr. J. DU PLESSIS and Prof.Dr. E. VOS.

Recently published:

Volume 90: *Evolutie van de basisbeginselen van het contractenrecht*, I. SAMOY (red.)
Volume 91: *Recidive in België en Nederland. Een analyse van 200 jaar rechtspraak en rechtsleer*, M. DAMS
Volume 92: *An EU-wide Letter of Rights. Towards Best Practice*, T. SPRONKEN (ed.)
Volume 93: *The Costanzo Obligation. The Obligations of National Administrative Authorities in the Case of Incompatibility between National Law and European Law*, M. VERHOEVEN
Volume 94: *The Effect of a Change of Circumstances on the Binding Force of Contracts. Comparative Perspectives*, R. MOMBERG URIBE
Volume 95: *The Landscape of the Legal Professions in Europe and the USA: Continuity and Change*, A. UZELAC and C.H. VAN RHEE (eds.)
Volume 96: *Constitutional Constraints on Ad Hoc Legislation. A Comparative Study of the United States, Germany and the Netherlands*, A. JASIAK
Volume 97: *The Social Security Position of Irregular Migrant Workers. New Insights from National Security Law and International Law*, K. KAPUY
Volume 98: *Educating European Lawyers*, A.W. HERINGA and B. AKKERMANS (eds.)
Volume 99: *The Draft Common Frame of Reference: A National and Comparative Perspective*, E. TERRYN, V. SAGAERT and M.E. STORME (eds.)
Volume 100: *Does Law Matter? On Law and Economic Growth*, M. FAURE and J. SMITS (eds.)
Volume 101: *The Power of Punitive Damages. Is Europe Missing Out?*, L. MEURKENS and E. NORDIN (eds.)
Volume 102: *The Changing Role of the European Council in the Institutional Framework of the European Union*, F. EGGERMONT
Volume 103: *Linked Contracts*, I. SAMOY and M.B.M. LOOS (eds.)